TE DUE

WOMEN

....

WOMEN

ROLES AND STATUS
IN EIGHT COUNTRIES

Edited by

JANET ZOLLINGER GIELE

AUDREY CHAPMAN SMOCK

A WILEY-INTERSCIENCE PUBLICATION

JOHN WILEY & SONS, New York • London • Sydney • Toronto

301.412
W 8725
1977

Library of Congress Cataloging in Publication Data:

Main entry under title:
Women.

"A Wiley-Interscience publication."
Includes bibliographies and index.
1. Women—Social conditions—Addresses, essays, lectures. 2. Women's rights—Addresses, essays, lectures. 3. Women in politics—Addresses, essays, lectures. I. Giele, Janet Zollinger. II. Smock, Audrey Chapman.

HQ1154.W884   301.41'2   76-39950
ISBN 0-471-01504-0

Printed in the United States of America

10 9 8 7 6 5 4 3 2 1

CONTENTS

....

FOREWORD

....

The women's movement of the 1960s and 1970s has shown itself to be neither a fad nor a passing phase. In the United States and around the world it is solidly based in the aspirations of millions of women and many men for equal treatment and fairness to all human beings, regardless of sex. It is set against the background of earlier and varied efforts in numerous lands to achieve political and economic rights for women. While it takes separate forms in different cultures, under different religious traditions, and at various stages of economic development, it carries throughout the world the common message that sex need not be a barrier to either freedom or opportunity.

The contributors to this book attempt to give some sense of the nature and diversity of the women's movement around the world. *Women: Roles and Status in Eight Countries* presents illustrative cases rather than attempting a comprehensive picture. The origins of the book are closely related to the work of the Ford Foundation in the area of equality of opportunity for women. To understand the role of its contributors, it is important to provide some background on that activity.

In 1972 the Foundation established an internal Task Force on Women to review what more it could do to advance their rights and opportunities through its grant-making program. Janet Giele, then at the Radcliffe Institute, was invited to become a consultant to that group. Early in her work with the Task Force it was decided to sponsor her preparation of a volume dealing with a fundamental analysis of the situation of women in the United States. Her successive draft chapters on subjects such as the family and women and

vii

work were presented to the Task Force for discussion and comment. In the course of this work, it appeared that wider perspectives might be added to her book if some analysis were done of the situation of women outside the United States. Janet Giele developed a framework for that analysis and with Foundation assistance commissioned several independent authors to prepare essays on other countries.

The Foundation staff saw in the papers that Dr. Giele commissioned the germ of another book that would provide an overview of the situation of women in selected countries around the world. Audrey Smock, who had done research in the field and who had had experience living in Africa and the Middle East, was asked by the Foundation to work with the authors of several papers to revise them. Some new papers were also commissioned and Dr. Smock herself wrote three chapters. Introductory and concluding chapters were written by the co-editors, and all the chapters have had the benefit of critiques by both. The Ford Foundation is grateful equally to Janet Giele and Audrey Smock for their contributions as both editors and authors. The book they have produced should add to the understanding of an insistent and important development in human affairs. Although the views expressed are those of the contributors and their collaborators, the Foundation is glad to be associated with them, and it looks forward to the publication of Dr. Giele's prior study on the status of women in the United States.

HAROLD HOWE II
Vice President for Education and Research
The Ford Foundation

September 1976

PREFACE

....

The primary purpose of this book is to increase our knowledge about women's roles and status in other countries. At the heart of the book are separate chapters for eight different countries, presenting a systematic and comprehensive description of women's position in particular societies. With the support of The Ford Foundation, a team of expert social scientists was commissioned to write chapters on the status of women in the countries in which they had expertise. Each of the authors employed the same framework for her analysis. Through the use of this comparative method, the book identifies some common standards by which women's status can be measured across societies despite vast differences in government, economy, and the family.

Each chapter begins with the historical and cultural background necessary to put contemporary conditions in that country into perspective. Then women's status and roles are examined in the context of the family, educational system, economic system, family planning facilities, and political system prevailing in that society. The Introduction by Janet Giele develops a new evolutionary framework for explaining differences in women's status across countries. The Conclusion by Audrey Smock assesses the cultural and structural factors shaping women's roles and seeks to identify practical policies that have improved women's position in different times and places.

The eight countries included in this book differ widely. Among Asian countries, highly developed Japan stands alongside poverty-stricken Bangladesh. In Africa, Ghana with its ethnic traditions of female autonomy and of women's important role in production and trade, stands in contrast to Egypt, straddling both Africa and the Middle East, with its strong patriarchal custom of secluding women. In Europe, socialist Poland differs from capitalist France. In America, the rich and developed United States contrasts sharply with Mexico, which is still growing rapidly and struggling to assimilate diverse elements of Indian and Spanish culture. The selection of countries was partly governed by the availability of qualified authors. We were primarily interested, however, in representing major cultural traditions and differing levels of development.

The value of the present volume stems from the zeal and expertise of its contributors. The author of each chapter presents a remarkably comprehensive picture of the country within a very brief space. The bibliographies will give students and scholars an excellent point of departure for further investigation of women's position in each country. We thank our contributors, who so faithfully drew on their general knowledge of a country while meeting our particular demands.

We are grateful to many people who read individual chapters or in other ways supplied helpful advice on the international study of women. Elinor Barber of The Ford Foundation is due special thanks for the personal interest she took in the project from the time of its conception through the final stages of writing and editing. Harold Howe II and Mariam Chamberlain also facilitated administrative coordination of our work within the Foundation. Rae Blumberg, Elise Boulding, Judith K. Brown, Hanna Papanek, Beatrice Whiting, Adrienne Germain, and Betty Skolnick deserve particular mention. We would also like to thank Christine Oppong, Soad Gadallah, James Bausch, Rounaq Jahan, Patricia Graham, Janet James, Hilda Kahne, Louise Lamphere, Laura Lein, Barbara Norwood, and Marjorie Shostak for their comments on drafts of chapters. At an early stage of the work, Elizabeth Dunn and Elzbieta Chodakowska supplied useful background papers. Arlene Mastandrea typed and proofread most of the manuscript. None of these persons, however, should be held responsible for our mistakes.

International Women's Year helped to create a climate of interest in women's position around the world. In its wake we launch this book knowing that it will soon be joined by other comparative efforts to describe and understand the role of women in society.

JANET ZOLLINGER GIELE

Brandeis University
Waltham, Massachusetts

AUDREY CHAPMAN SMOCK

The Ford Foundation
Nairobi, Kenya
November 1976

CONTRIBUTORS

....

MARY ELMENDORF, Ph.D., Union Graduate School, is presently Consultant to the World Bank, Office of Environment and Health Affairs. An anthropologist who has conducted research on women in Mexico and other Latin American countries, she is the author of *Nine Mayan Women: A Village Faces Change* (Wiley, forthcoming), *La Mujer Maya* (SEP/Setentas, 1974), "The Dilemma of Peasant Women," in *Women and World Development* (Overseas Development Council, 1976), and "The Mayan Woman and Change" in *Women Cross-Culturally: Change and Challenge* (Mouton, 1975). From 1952 to 1960 she was Chief of the CARE Mission in Mexico and since then has served on the faculties of Hampshire and Goddard College and the World Campus Afloat of Chapman College. She has been a Consultant to The Ford Foundation and the Overseas Development Fund on their Latin American Programs. Her present research deals with the impact of development on the roles and status of women, particularly in rural areas, and ways to integrate women into the development process.

JANET ZOLLINGER GIELE, Ph.D., Radcliffe College, Harvard University, is Lecturer with the rank of Associate Professor in the Heller School, Brandeis University. Her research presents a synthesis of findings on many aspects of women's roles. Examples include *Social Change in the Feminine Role* (dissertation, 1961), a comparison of the suffrage and temperance movements, "Centuries of Womanhood" (*Women's Studies*, 1972), and "New Developments in Research on Women" (Introduction to Viola Klein's

The Feminine Character, University of Illinois Press, 1972). Formerly a member of the faculty at Wellesley College, she joined the Radcliffe Institute in 1970. There as principal consultant to the Ford Foundation Task Force on Women she reviewed contemporary changes in American women's roles in a forthcoming book *Toward Equality for Women*. Her current research describes the emergence of national family policy in the United States.

SUSAN J. PHARR, Ph.D., Columbia, is Assistant Professor of Political Science at the University of Wisconsin, Madison. A comparative political scientist, she has conducted fieldwork in both West Africa and Japan and has explored a variety of issues relating to political behavior, political development, and gender roles. She has published a number of articles, the most recent of which is "The Japanese Woman: Evolving Views of Life and Role" in *Japan—The Paradox of Progress*, Yale University Press, 1976, edited by Lewis Austin. She currently is conducting research on American Occupation policies affecting the status of women in Japan, supported by a grant from the National Endowment for the Humanities, and is completing a book on women political activists in contemporary Japan. Before joining the faculty of the University of Wisconsin, she served as Staff Associate at the Social Science Research Council.

CATHERINE BODARD SILVER, Ph.D., Columbia University, is Associate Professor of Sociology, Brooklyn College. Her extensive knowledge of French society was applied to the status of women in an earlier article, "Salon, Foyer, Bureau: Women and the Professions in France," *American Journal of Sociology*, January 1973. She is also author of *Black Teachers and Urban Schools* (Praeger, 1973). At present she is comparing the roles of public bureaucracies and private enterprises in promoting women to leadership in the United States and France. She is also engaged in translating the works of Frédéric LePlay, a pioneer French sociologist of the nineteenth century.

AUDREY CHAPMAN SMOCK, Ph.D., Columbia University, is a social scientist who is Research Associate at the Institute for Development Studies, University of Nairobi, and Consultant to the Office of the Vice President, International Division, The Ford Foundation. A specialist in comparative international studies, she has lived in Ghana, Nigeria, Lebanon, and Kenya, and conducted research there as well. Her books include *Ibo Politics: The Role of Ethnic Unions in Eastern Nigeria* (Harvard University Press, 1971), *Comparative Politics: A Reader in Institutionalization and Mobilization* (Allyn and Bacon, 1973), and, with David R. Smock, *The Politics of Pluralism: A Comparison of Lebanon and Ghana* (Elsevier, 1975). Her present research deals with a comparative study of women's access to education and its impact on their roles in six countries: Ghana, Mexico, Kenya, Egypt, the Philippines, and Pakistan.

MAGDALENA SOKOŁOWSKA, M.D., Ph.D., University of Warsaw, and Master of Public Health, Columbia University, is Professor of Sociology and Chief, Department of Medical Sociology, Institute of Philosophy and Sociology, Polish Academy of Sciences, Warsaw. Her earlier study of women appeared in *Frauenemanzipation und Sozialismus: Das Beispiel der Volksrepublik Polen* (Hamburg: Rowohlt, 1973). Her most recent books are in the field of medical sociology: *Sociology of Disability and Rehabilitation* (Warsaw: Ossolineum, 1976) and, as editor, *Health, Medicine, Society* (Holland: Reidel, 1976). She is a member of the Executive Committee of the International Sociological Association and Chairperson of the Section on Medical Sociology, the Polish Sociological Association.

NADIA HAGGAG YOUSSEF, Ph.D., University of California, Berkeley, is an Egyptian social demographer who is Visiting Associate Professor in Sociology and Assistant Director for the NIMH Training Program in Demography at the University of Southern California. Her comparison of women's status in Latin America, the Middle East, and Soviet Islamic republics appears in *Women and Work in Developing Countries* (University of California Institute of International Studies, 1974) and in numerous articles. She has contributed chapters to *Women in the World: A Comparative Perspective* (ABC Clio Press, 1976) and *Women and World Development* (Overseas Development Council, 1976). She is now examining effects of migration in developing countries on family structure and women's roles. She is also interested in the impact of Marxist ideology on Muslim women in the Soviet Union.

WOMEN

....

Chapter One

INTRODUCTION:
THE STATUS OF WOMEN IN
COMPARATIVE PERSPECTIVE

Janet Zollinger Giele

The overwhelming evidence so far is that virtually no society in the world provides women equal status with men. Although anthropologists have found that women are given considerable social recognition and power in some societies, there exists no society in which their publicly recognized power exceeds that of men. After reviewing women's studies in a number of societies, Rosaldo and Lamphere (1974: 3) conclude:

> Everywhere we find that women are excluded from certain crucial economic or political activities, that their roles as wives and mothers are associated with fewer powers and prerogatives than are the roles of men. It seems fair to say then, that all contemporary societies are to some extent male-dominated, and although the degree and expression of female subordination vary greatly, sexual asymmetry is presently a universal fact of human social life.

Nevertheless there are women who have risen to important heights of achievement. Women novelists in feudal Japan of the eleventh century created works that are remembered today. Women in the salons of Renaissance France gave shape to the cultural life of the nation and stimulated important literary and philosophical works. Quaker women in nineteenth century America were leaders in fighting for women's rights and the abolition of slavery.

Juxtaposition of these facts poses a central empirical and theoretical question to any comparative study of the status of women: Why under some circumstances do women enjoy respect, higher status, and rewards that indicate equality or near-equality with men, and why is their position unquestionably inferior in others?

Two major steps must be taken to find an answer to these questions. First, we must define *status* and identify the signs that indicate whether it is high or low. Second, we must carry these measuring rods to several countries and time periods to measure the variations that occur under different social and cultural conditions.

Persons have high status when others look up to them, allow them latitude to come and go, and bestow on them rewards such as money, power, and love. Low status by contrast deprives a person of deference from others, freedom to make choices, material comfort, and emotional satisfaction. Frequently the low status person becomes an object of anger as well (Hochschild, 1975).

Because men and women frequently perform different *roles*, however, as husband or wife, doctor or nurse, field worker or home worker, the currency by which status is conferred on them is not always the same. A man may receive power, a woman love. As with apples and oranges, no one can say which is better. In order to use a common standard, one possibility is to compare opportunity for making decisions on the important matters that affect a person's life. Blumberg suggests seven types of "life options" that

3

affect the freedom and measure the relative status of women and men in all known societies. According to her,

> Life options include: deciding whether and whom to marry; deciding to termi-
> nate a union; controlling one's sexual freedom, pre- and extra-maritally; con-
> trolling one's freedom of movement; having access to educational oppor-
> tunities; de facto share of household power—and . . . controlling reproduction
> and completed family size to the extent that this is biologically possible [Blum-
> berg, 1975: 2].

To this list I would also add the importance of opportunity for political participation and cultural expression. Sanday (1974: 173) tells us that politi-
cal participation and membership in female solidarity groups noticeably improve women's status in the 12 non-Western and largely preagricultural societies that she compares. Tuchman (1975) shows that women in Western societies have also been the creators of culture by hosting salons or supporting societies that benefit cultural activities. From these suggestions I derive the following list of life options related to six major types of human activity performed in every known society:

1. *Political Expression.* Do women have rights (to join in community decisions, to vote, hold property, or public office) that are now enjoyed by men? Do important segments of the female population show clear signs of dissatisfaction or a sense of injustice compared with men? Is a social movement for women's rights in progress?

2. *Work and Mobility.* Are women's movements deliberately more restricted than men's? Are they active in the labor force? Do the jobs they hold enjoy equal rank with those held by men? Is their pay roughly equivalent and do they enjoy the same amount of leisure?

3. *Family Formation, Duration, and Size.* Are women subject to greater control and limitations in their choice of a marriage partner than men? Do they have the same right to divorce? What are the consequences if they are single or widowed? What are the restrictions on their movements beyond the family?

4. *Education.* Do females have the same access to educational oppor-
tunities as boys? Is their curriculum the same? Do they reach the same levels of educational attainment?

5. *Health and Sexual Control.* Are females subject to higher mortality or more serious physical or mental illness than males? Are they prevented from limiting conceptions and birth?

6. *Cutural Expression.* Do women make indentifiable contributions to

religious culture, the arts, or practical artifacts and inventions? Are they symbolically portrayed to be as valuable and worthy of respect as are men?

Several authors have already given comprehensive descriptions of the status of women in other countries. Raphael Patai compiled reports on the status of women in 24 countries. In all he found a shift toward greater equalization of opportunities for the two sexes since World War II. But the baseline of change for Europe was, he concluded, only a variant of that established several thousand years earlier in Egypt, Babylonia, Palestine, Greece, and Rome. In these societies six outstanding characteristics of the man-woman relationship were the following:

> 1. They were headed by a male ruler. 2. Men dominated women and considered them property. 3. Men were entitled to several wives as well as concubines, whereas women were restricted to premarital chastity and marital fidelity. 4. All or most occupations were male prerogatives, and women were confined to housework and to helping their menfolk in agricultural tasks. 5. Temple and secular prostitutes were available to men, but the average woman was supposed to have little or no contact with men except for members of her family. 6. The value of a woman was correlated with her ability to bear children (especially male children), yet women were regarded as ritually impure during their procreative period and, in particular, during and after their menses and delivery [Patai, 1967: 2–3].

In most cultures of Asia and Africa Patai found similar restrictions on women. Only in sub-Saharan Africa did he discover indigenous traditions that permitted greater latitude to women.

Westernization and modernization, according to Patai, are the primary forces loosening traditional restraints on women. Western women gained the vote in the first two decades of this century. Women in the non-Western world were granted it somewhat later. He predicted that restrictions in sexual modesty and marital fidelity will also eventually be relaxed in the East as they have been in the West.

In a more recent cross-cultural study of women in thirteen societies, Matthiasson proposed a different major factor to explain equality between the sexes—the role of women in economic production. She found that women in peasant groups in which women participate little in agriculture have low public status. Among peasants of China, North and Central India, Egypt, and Guatemala, men dominate village affairs. By contrast, in rice-growing regions of the Philippines and Cambodia, where women are heavily employed in planting, transplanting, weeding, and harvesting, the status of women is high, higher even than in comparable rice-growing regions of

China where women help on a less regular basis (Matthiasson, 1974: 433).

Both Patai's and Matthiason's findings bear similarities to Ester Boserup's theory of women's role in economic development. Using data on population levels, subsistence technology, and the economic roles of women, Boserup (1970: 15–35) shows recurring patterns in women's work, depending on the ecological context. We may infer from her theory that hunting-and-gathering societies were able to survive only in relatively rich surroundings where game and vegetable food were plentiful enough to support the sparse populations dependent on them. As population pressure grew, societies adopted hoe agriculture and a shifting form of cultivation. Particularly in black African societies where shifting cultivation was common, women did more agricultural work than men and appeared to enjoy considerable autonomy. Under still greater population pressure and certain natural conditions, dry plow agriculture emerged; there women typically have had a small part in production and their opportunity to engage in commerce and move about freely became more restricted. "The corollary of the relative decline in women's labour productivity is a decline in their relative status within agriculture . . ." (Boserup, 1970: 53). But in places where still more intensive cultivation demands irrigation, weeding, and transplanting, women as well as men contribute heavily to production: It was in regions with such intensive cultivation that Matthiasson found women's status relatively high.

The present volume contains eight essays on the status of women in developing and developed societies ranging from Bangladesh, Egypt, Mexico, and Ghana, to Japan, France, the United States, and Poland. Each chapter allows fairly precise comparison of women's life options across societies. In addition to a beginning section on tradition and image, each chapter carries a section on women's rights in law and politics, work, family, education, and health.

At the same time this selection of countries provides ample opportunity for the reader to experiment with major explanations of why women's status is high or low, their options enlarged or constricted. One who is interested in cultural variation and the effect of religious or political ideology can compare the two Muslim countries, Bangladesh and Egypt, with non-Western Japan, the mixed indigenous and colonial traditions of Ghana and Mexico, the Western examples of France and the United States, and the socialist case of Poland. If instead structural complexity is of primary interest, one can compare Bangladesh, which is only at the beginning of economic development, with Egypt, Mexico, and Ghana, which are in transition, and Poland, France, Japan, and the United States, which have reached fairly advanced levels of industrialization.

Life options for women appear to be related to modernization of *both* cultural tradition and structural features. The greatest constriction is apparent in Bangladesh and Egypt, both Muslim countries in early stages of development. Life options for women are widest in countries such as Poland, France, and the United States, which have experienced both modernization of ideology and economic development. Mexico and Ghana have traditions that contain interesting dualisms created by the combination of freedoms inherited from an indigenous culture and restrictions imposed by colonialism. Represented in a two-dimensional matrix, the eight countries may be classified approximately as in Table 1.

Table 1 Classification of Eight Countries by Ideological Tradition and Level of Structural Complexity

Ideological Tradition	Structural Complexity		
	Undeveloped	Transitional	Advanced
Socialist			Poland
Western			United States, France
Colonial and Non-Western		Mexico, Ghana	Japan
Muslim	Bangladesh	Egypt	

This Introduction presents a theoretical framework for relating modernization in each country to changes in the status of women. The Conclusion by Audrey Smock examines a number of thematic similarities such as cultural tradition, education, ideological change, and government intervention that in each society affect the status of women. These similarities can, however, also be comprehended within the larger modernization context.

THE IMPACT OF MODERNIZATION ON SEX ROLES

Different as they are, all the countries in this volume share a striking historical theme: women's status was high at some earlier time, then passed through a period of constriction, before showing improvement in recent times. Under the ancient Egyptian dynasties, hundreds of years before Christ, women's status was high, only to fall and remain low for a period of over a thousand years beginning with Greek and Roman influence, intensified by Muslim beliefs, and then especially degraded under Ottoman rule. Not until the Napoleonic invasion and subsequent reforms of the nineteenth century did Egyptian women's position begin to improve again. Ancient Bengal had women fertility goddesses and myths about women's high status and power. Today the status of women in Bangladesh is very low, and only in the last few decades have political and educational reforms begun. Native Mayan women of Mexico had a respected place before the Spanish Conquest. Precolonial Ghanaian women engaged in trade, agriculture, and control of property before the British taught them the middle-class ideal that a woman's place is in the home. The French family at the beginning of the Middle Ages allowed women independent control of property and equal status with men. But by the end of the Middle Ages family authority was vested in the male head, a situation that intensified throughout the nineteenth century. American women of the seventeenth and eighteenth centuries apparently participated more freely in the economic life of the nation than did those living just after 1800, when women were excluded from newly developing professions and institutions of higher education. Polish women obtained high rank through the convents during the Middle Ages. Queen Jadwiga and women writers of the sixteenth and seventeenth centuries were exemplars of women to whom wide opportunities were open. The repeated lowering of women's status in all eight countries calls for some explanation. One possibility is, of course, that every author has a universal romantic image of the past and has distorted the account. Another possibility, which we shall examine, is that the position of the sexes has changed with each stage of social evolution.

Scholars are now in considerable agreement that women's status is relatively high in simple societies based on hunting and gathering or cultivation of small shifting plots. They differ somewhat on the reasons, however. Johnson and Johnson (1975), from their study of South American Indian tribes in the Peruvian highlands, conclude that women's status is high where women work either with other women in cooperative work groups or where they share in complementary productive activities with their husbands. Sanday (1973) and Reiter (1975) report that women have high status where they have control over the fruits of their labor and opportunity to participate in communal decisions. Leacock (n. d., p. 4) concludes that the nature of foraging societies causes a direct relationship between production and consumption that is linked to the dispersal of authority and thus to women's likelihood of participating in community decisions.

With advanced agriculture, however, women's status appears to drop sharply. The most frequent explanation is that women lose their place in production. Plowing is heavy work; the furrows are long, the fields sometimes distant. Tending of draft animals and prolonged absence from the home under such conditions is thought by many scholars to be less compatible with childrearing and therefore leads to the withdrawal of women's labor from production (Buvinić, 1976: 12; Martin and Voorhies, 1975).

There is disagreement about what happens next. Some claim that modernization may actually narrow women's options by removing them from production to a purely domestic or ornamental role within the home, or by overburdening them with dual responsibilities as both paid workers and homemakers (Engels, 1884; Sacks, 1974; Boulding, 1974; Tinker, 1975). However others claim that the creation of factories, the move to the cities, and the broadening of educational opportunity gradually add options and remove the barriers faced by women in the previous agricultural era (Patai, 1967; Goode, 1963). One recent study of the Inuit Eskimo, who never went through an agricultural stage, shows women eagerly seeking education, jobs, and location in the city as a presumed improvement over the choices available in traditional life (McElroy, 1975).

It may be that both emancipation and constriction occur with modernization, depending on either the particular local conditions or the aspect of opportunity under observation. I shall present here one underlying theme that I have perceived in cross-cultural studies of women's status. The reader can then look for confirmation, refutation, or other alternatives in the chapters that follow.

In my view what emerges from various accounts of women's position in these eight societies and in a variety of other cultures and historical settings is a *curvilinear relationship between societal complexity and sex equality*. In other words, in the simplest societies men's and women's freedom of choice—their life options—are more nearly equal than in somewhat more complex societies. In fact it seems to be the *intermediate level of societal complexity that is most deleterious to the status of women*. When societies pass through this middle stage to become even more complex, the position of women seems to improve again.

The curvilinear idea found its first modern expression in the work of the sociologist, Gerhard Lenski (1966), who proposed it to explain why inequality between social classes is greater in agrarian societies than in simple hunting-and-gathering societies or advanced industrial nations. Lenski proposed a theoretical model in which inequality was highest in the agrarian societies, as shown in Figure 1. He reasoned that the hunter-gatherers and horticulturalists (who relied only on the hoe) had to rely on everyone's efforts in order to survive; they therefore had to reward everyone about equally. Although advanced industrial society was far more complex, it too had the same need to rely on efforts from a large variety of people. By contrast the intermediate technology of plow and draft animals used by agrarians made possible a food surplus by relying on the labors of male peasants. This surplus was amassed in the hands of a small, powerful elite

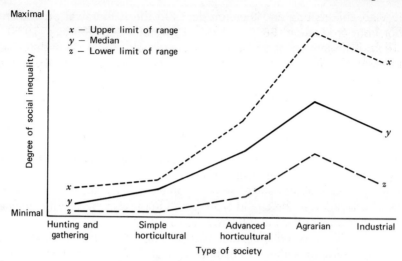

Figure 1 *Degree of social inequality by type of society.* Source. *Lenski, 1966: 437.*

who redistributed a portion just large enough to keep the producers alive. Many others became beggars, prostitutes, or expendables who drifted or died.

Blumberg and Winch (1972) were the first to extend the curvilinear hypothesis to power differences within families. They found simple nuclear families to be most common in hunting-and-gathering and industrial societies. Complex extended families that lodge power in a male head were most frequent in agrarian economics that relied on the plow. Furthermore the status of women in these complex extended families was low. Peasant women's mobility was restricted; they were subject to stringent demands for premarital virginity and subsequent chastity. In peasant agricultural societies throughout the world Blumberg, Carns, and Winch (1970) found "high gods" and "virgin brides."

A graph of sexual stratification, such as that shown in Figure 2, should thus also show a curvilinear relationship between societal complexity and the status of women. I have drawn the curve somewhat smoother than it would be if herding, fishing, and irrigation societies had been taken into account. The broken lines above and below the solid line indicate upper and lower limits that are dependent on local conditions. For instance, a hunting-and-gathering or horticultural society which gave women an important role in communal decision-making would be near the upper limit on the left-hand side of the graph, whereas a society that confined women to an isolated position would be near the lower limit. At the modern end of the continuum,

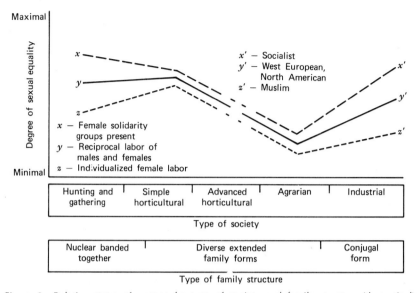

Figure 2   Relative status of women by type of society and family structure (theoretical). *Female solidarity groups (x) are described in Sanday, 1973, 1974. Reciprocal labor of males and females (y) and Individualized female labor (z) appear in Johnson and Johnson, 1975.*

women's status is nearer the upper limit in a society with a socialist tradition such as Poland, and nearer the lower limit in a society with a Muslim tradition, such as Bangladesh or Egypt. Countries with non-Western traditions, such as Japan, fall somewhere between these upper and lower limits on the right side of the graph. Countries with mixed horticultural, agrarian, or early modern elements, such as Mexico and Ghana, should be described by several points lying both to the left and to the right of the dip on the curve.

Both Lenski's graph and my graph are theoretical curves. That is, they describe what the picture would be if all the data were in. One aspect of testing the theory is to ask what dynamics underlie the curve. Why is it that a dip in women's status occurs at intermediate stages of societal complexity?

Earlier studies suggest that one of the central facts to examine in each society is women's role in production compared with men's and the effect that this division of labor has on the structure of the family. The family is a crucial factor in the relative life options of the sexes. For though it confers *similar status with respect to caste or social class,* it usually gives men and women quite *different status with respect to their sex roles.* To understand the effects of modernization on women's status it is then necessary to examine how sex roles in the division of labor and family type vary from one ideological tradition or one ecological niche to another. In the remainder of this Introduction I use examples from succeeding chapters to illuminate the relationship between sex roles and complexity of the society. Our sample of eight countries gives examples of women's status in preagricultural, agrarian, early modern, and advanced industrial societies.

Except for Ghana, where horticultural society has extended into modern times, a search for clues to women's preagricultural status has to reach back into myth and ancient history. Women in ancient Egypt at the height of its horticultural period were accorded high status. Female counterparts of Buddha had high status as "savioresses" in the tradition of Tantric Buddhism, as established in Bengal between the ninth and twelfth centuries A.D. Myth and prehistoric evidence suggest the presence of a matriarchy in Japan until the third century. Before the Spanish Conquest and establishment of the haciendas system in Mexico, Mayan women had an important role in cultivation and trade and enjoyed respect.

These examples are in accordance with our theoretical expectation that women's status is relatively high prior to the establishment of an agricultural system and patriarchal control. Perhaps the high status of women in Egypt, prehistoric Japan, and Mexico before the Conquest could be explained by better knowledge of their economies. All relied on some form of simple or advanced horticulture, which rested on an even earlier tradition of fishing, hunting, or gathering. We know from contemporary anthropological accounts that in both hunting-and-gathering and horticultural societies women's economic contribution is important. One study of hunting-and-gathering bands has shown that women provide 60 to 80% of the food supply by collecting nuts and roots (Lee and DeVore, 1968). Half of all simple horticultural societies in which roots and seeds are cultivated hold women and men equally responsible for production. In the rest men may clear the land by slash and burn techniques, but women are the primary cultivators. In advanced horticultural societies with larger plots and continuous cultivation, responsibility for production falls even more heavily on women (Lenski and Lenski, 1974: 191). Although women's heavy participation in production is not alone sufficient to assure high status, it is a necessary basic ingredient in the complex of female activity (control over produce, value placed on female produce, female political participation, and female solidarity groups) which Sanday (1973: 1694) finds associated with the development of female status. It may be in part because of these links that the myths and stories of prehistoric societies depict women in such prominent and highly valued roles.

Among our eight societies the family traditions of Ghana give the best example of women's relatively high status in preagrarian economies. In Ghana, where there has never been an agricultural tradition dependent on a field system, the plow, and large draft animals, women traditionally held land independently and participated in trade and cultivation. Their activity was not confined to the family system or directed by a male head. Thus relations between the sexes have been based on productive contributions by each. Even though women and men may specialize in different kinds of crops or trade, each has a stake in production. Such a foundation gives basis for greater equality than the agrarian systems of Europe, Japan, or the Middle East, where women are much more heavily dependent on male productive efforts.

It is the patriarchal tendencies of the peasant family that pose the greatest barriers to women's freedom. Patriarchal privilege is currently most evident in Bangladesh, Mexico, rural Japan, and parts of rural Egypt. The agrarian tradition dependent on the field system, the plow, and a peasant family was also present in feudal France and Poland, and this was carried to the United States in the memories of nineteenth century immigrants who had European peasant origins. Several common themes are present even in such different cultural traditions. Husbands have greater sexual latitude and opportunity, and women's virginity and chastity are guarded. Men control property and pass it on to sons. They have rights in religious authority and public office. By contrast women are regarded as unequipped for management or control of public and private affairs, though they may be loved and revered within the family and may be accorded a surprising degree of informal authority there (Collier, 1974).

The patriarchal theme in peasant society is related to major structural characteristics of agrarian production. First, the fields are primarily cultivated by men; this appears true wherever the plow has been introduced. Second, the family is the primary unit of production and consumption and assumes control over property. When this happens authority is generally lodged in a male head, as in the French family between the Middle Ages and the nineteenth century. In Japan similar patterns were introduced through the warring concerns of the *samurai*. The *purdah* system of Egypt and Bangladesh, though it originated through a combination of religious and tribal influences, nevertheless coincided with the widespread adoption of an agrarian system throughout the Mediterranean, Middle East, and Indian subcontinent.

It is hard for any book on women's status to give a sympathetic account of patriarchy, yet for the sake of understanding I propose the following interpretation. Because it must constantly attend to both production and consumption, the peasant family, whether it be Egyptian, Japanese, or French, rigidly assigns priority to production in order to prevent its seed or other capital from being eaten away. Because men are primarily responsible for production, their roles are more highly valued and control over resources is put in their hands. Women retain considerable power, but primarily in the emotional domain. Late medieval Europe celebrated the emotional virtues of women in the veneration of the Virgin Mary and the rise of courtly love. The Near Eastern invention of *purdah,* while repressive in many respects, nevertheless emphasized the value of women's moral purity as underpinning the honor of the whole family.

In both the agrarian and early modern society the middle level of structural complexity more than any other seems to hurt the status of women. It is as though the agricultural revolution brought an undifferentiated stream of human productive energy through a prism that separated it into a sphere of male production outside the home and a sphere of female consumption inside the home. Under conditions of scarcity the male productive elements were everywhere more highly valued; women's status therefore suffered a drop. In a country such as Ghana, which never passed through the agrarian period, the colonial experience had similar though less drastic effects. A woman's place was said to be in the home, and women were encouraged to withdraw from production. Their education taught them decorative skills and social graces. As in the Western societies which experienced the trend slightly earlier, there was concern with the *proper* role of women—with what was *suitable* education and *appropriate* work. It is hard to prove that these changes represented any improvement in the status of women, and many would argue that they showed a decline from women's status in the precolonial era. Indeed modernization often does seem to bring constriction in opportunity and therefore relative decline in status of women compared to men. This is especially evident in non-Western societies where native tradition gave women a larger role in production and a position of control and respect.

The same cannot be said, however, for the effects of modernization on agrarian societies. Although the earliest female workers in the factories were oppressed and exploited in Japan, the United States, and France, improvement of economic and educational opportunity gradually loosened the bonds of repressive patriarchy in the family and the state. In each of these countries women eventually gained the vote, the right to hold office and control conception, and greater access to family property and divorce. They were also more likely to get a higher education. Such rights had not been available in the same degree to ordinary peasant women although upperclass women had sometimes had a degree of access to education or property similar to men of their class.

Now modernization is proceeding somewhat further in countries such as Poland, France, the United States, and Japan. The dichotomy between home and work is being broken down into a still larger variety of options for both women and men. A new degree of structural complexity is in the process of being achieved both in the economic system and government.

On the economic side, more women are taking paid work as well as performing household duties. More men are doing household chores. Men have more leisure available for family activity, although they do not help so much as women would like and women are still overburdened. The dual-career family can be found in Poland, the United States, Great Britain, and Scandinavia (Fogarty et al., 1971). On the governmental side, public services in all modern societies have greatly expanded (Wilensky, 1975). Health care protection, pension plans, child care, and social security are to be found in France, Poland, the United States, and to some extent in Japan. All these services partly relieve the family of its functions. In the process women's primary role inside the family is diminished, as is men's major role of being the only breadwinner. At the same time women's options outside the home—in education, employment, and political and cultural expression—are widening even further (Olin, 1976).

In countries such as Poland communist beliefs about government responsibility and equality advanced these changes. In Japan adoption of Western democratic ideals along with economic development encouraged the shift. In France and the United States a combination of economic growth and an expansion of government services produced similar transformations. In every modern country the most advanced social thinking about sex roles is currently concerned not so much with women's *proper* roles as with the rejection of outmoded stereotypes and the promotion of personal liberation. The following section shows just how such an aim is realized by comparing specific life options in agrarian, early modern, and advanced industrial societies.

CHANGES IN LIFE OPTIONS

We now return to the question posed earlier: How can the status of women be compared across societies whose local conditions are so different? A first step is to specify indicators of women's status. We have already suggested six major areas in which women and men have varying control or "life options" in government, work, family, education, health and reproduction, and cultural expression. A second step is to suggest a hypothetical curve of opportunity that describes the typical range of choice in different societies. Then the conditions that lead to constriction or expansion of opportunity can be better understood.

Only a few attempts have been made to compare women's educational, political, and other types of opportunities across societies. Goode (1963) examined women's marital options in light of changing family patterns throughout the world. Boserup (1970) reviewed women's roles in the labor force. Chabaud (1970) compared educational opportunity for girls and women in various nations. Safilios-Rothschild (1971) showed the wide range of women's educational attainment and labor force participation in a number of European countries.

The present collection of studies on women's status in eight countries offers a unique opportunity to grasp both the interplay of life options within any one society and the availability of a particular type of opportunity in different societies. In the Conclusion Audrey Smock addresses the interplay of institutions and the dynamics by which one type of innovation such as education or governmental intervention affects other aspects of women's life in a given society. This Introduction, on the other hand, relates the degree of opportunity one is likely to encounter in a particular dimension, such as education or political expression, with the level of modernization of the society in question. In general the curvilinear hypothesis is borne out in every specific dimension of women's power to control choice or make decisions in the eight societies that are described in this volume.

Legal Status and Political Participation.   Women's highest participation in voting occurs in Japan, France, and the United States, where over 65 percent of women have voted in recent elections. By contrast perhaps only 10 percent of Bangali women and less than 20 percent of Egyptian women voted during the last decade. Voting may reflect most clearly the relation between women's family status and their role in public affairs. The *purdah* tradition of Muslim countries and women's low level of employment there militate against political participation outside the home. By contrast, in Japan and France, where women did not have suffrage until after World War II, women's voting rates are high by comparison. That roughly 49 percent of Japanese and 38 percent of French women are in the labor force reflects an economic and social structure which probably also encourages involvement in politics, at least to the extent of voting.

Records of women holding government office follow a somewhat more puzzling pattern. Women hold a few high offices in almost every government, but the pattern of special parliament seats for women is found only in Bangladesh and Egypt. In Canada, Great Britain, France, and the United States the proportion of parliament seats held by women ranges from 2 to 4 percent. The number of women in office rises at the local level, except in Japan. This pattern is particularly striking in France, where 85 percent of the *commune* offices are held by women.

It is not the economic development of modern societies that appears to give women access to high office so much as their political traditions. As can be seen in Table 2, countries with a socialist form of government, including the Scandinavian countries, have about twice as many women in their

Table 2 Percentage of Women in Parliaments, Local Assemblies, and the Total Labor Force, Nonagricultural and Agricultural, in Selected Countries since 1960[a]

	Parliament (% women)	Local Assemblies (% women)	Percentage of Total Labor Force	Percentage of Nonagricultural Workers	Percentage of Agricultural Workers
Developing Countries					
Egypt	0.0 (1970)		7.5 (1966)	11.5	3.9
Philippines	2.4 (1970)		31.9 (1970)	45.2	19.5
W. Pakistan	3.8[b] (1970)		8.8 (1961)	6.4	10.4
Mexico	4.8 (1968)		19.2 (1970)	28.8	5.2
Bangladesh	5.0[b] (1970)		15.1 (1961)	8.9	16.2
India	7.0 (1963)		17.4 (1971)	10.8	19.9
Ghana	13.6[b] (1966)		38.3 (1960)	40.7	36.5
Developed, with Work–Family Dichotomy					
Canada	1.6[c] (1968)		33.9 (1973)	35.3	13.5
France	1.6 (1969)	2.4 (1971)	34.5 (1968)	35.4	31.9
United States	2.3 (1974)	6.0 (1971)	37.4 (1972)	38.3	18.1
Japan	2.9 (1970)		39.1 (1970)	35.8	52.9
United Kingdom	4.1 (1970)	12.0 (1971)	35.7 (1966)	36.3	15.1
Austria	8.2 (1970)	8.0 (1970)	38.9 (1972)	36.8	50.3
West Germany	8.8 (1963)		36.0 (1971)	34.6	52.4
Scandinavian					
Norway	9.3 (1968)	9.5 (1972)	37.1 (1972)	37.8	32.0
Sweden	10.4 (1968)		37.1 (1972)	38.3	22.8
Denmark	11.2 (1970)	10.5 (1970)	40.1 (1972)	41.6	27.0
Finland	21.5 (1970)		42.1 (1970)	44.4	33.2
Eastern European, Socialist					
Poland	12.4 (1968)	15.4 (1968)	46.0[d] (1970)	40.5	54.8
Czechoslovakia	17.6 (1967)	19.9 (1967)	44.7 (1970)	38.2	49.5
USSR	28.0 (1968)	42.8 (1968)	50.4 (1970)	50.6	49.9

[a] Grateful acknowledgment is made to Elizabeth Dunn for help in the construction of this table and assistance with research on which it is based.
[b] Seats reserved for women.
[c] Five of six women were appointed.
[d] Includes unpaid family workers.

Sources. For information on women in parliaments, see United Nationa, 1967, E/CN.6/470; 1968, A/7197; 1969, A/7635; and 1970, A/8132. See also Women's Bureau, 1963; Gager, 1974; and Council on Foreign Relations, 1970, 1973. For women in local assemblies, see UN documents listed above; Heffermehl, 1972; and Sullerot, 1971. For labor force statistics, see International Labor Office, 1972, Table 2A; UN *Compendium of Social Statistics: 1967*, Table 42.

parliaments, 10 to 20 percent, as do the nonsocialist Western countries with 10 percent. The developing countries have about as many women in their national assemblies as do the Western nonsocialist countries.

The developed nonsocialist countries (the second group in Table 2) appear particularly ripe for change. Although women in these countries represent 35 percent or more of the labor force, they hold less than 10 percent of the seats in the national legislatures. As modern governments, even the nonsocialist variety, become more involved in social welfare, they move toward supplying needs formerly provided by the family. They spend more for health care, educational costs, and housing for the elderly. As social welfare programs expand and women's political involvement rises, a quantum leap may occur in the proportion of women holding national office. The pattern in the nonsocialist countries would then be more similar to that in the Scandinavian and Eastern ones.

Personal status laws that assure a woman the right of divorce, control of property, and custody over children (although remarkably late in being liberalized in Japan and France) are all clearly established in the modern countries. Such laws are still a subject of debate in Egypt, Bangladesh, and Ghana.

Women's groups in every country are typically social and apolitical, tied either to social welfare or religion. Small consciousness-raising experiments of the kind identified with women's liberation are found only in the more modern countries: Japan, France, and the United States.

In all dimensions of legal and political status Ghana and Mexico are most difficult to classify, perhaps because they have known both indigenous traditions in which women had high status and colonial or revolutionary governments that superimposed other ideas. Mexico, for example, has a high number of women elected officials who come from Yucatan, where an indigenous Mayan tradition of respect for women prevails. Revolutionary governments have feared women's conservative influence, however, and therefore have discouraged their participation.

Employment of Women. A number of indicators of women's employment options invite comparison across our eight societies. These include (1) women's rate of labor-force participation, (2) their work involvement at different points in life, (3) general attitudes toward the working woman, and (4) social policies governing work and benefits.

Perhaps the single most revealing statistic is women's labor-force participation. In Bangladesh and Egypt less than 10 percent of all women are gainfully employed. In Mexico the figure is 19 percent, in France 38 percent, in the United States 44 percent, in Japan 49 percent, and in Poland as high as 70 percent for some groups. These figures are, of course, for jobs in the modern sector. It is much harder to record the extent of women's work in the agricultural sector, which frequently consists of unpaid service within the family. In Egypt, for example, women's labor force participation in rural areas is a good deal higher than in the urban areas (over 40 percent as compared to men's 88 percent), and women constitute over half the total agricultural labor force in countries such as Japan, Austria, West Germany, and Poland (see Table 2). Nevertheless the data available on women's employment indicate that women are most likely to hold paid jobs in societies that have undergone either technical or ideological modernization.

At the same time all societies up to and including the early modern period consider some jobs more appropriate to women than others because they are either thought more suitable to the female nature or are subordinate to jobs held by males. Bangladesh and Egypt openly segregate women in certain occupations for reasons based on their *purdah* system. Yet Japan, the United States, France, and Poland, though they have official ideologies promoting sex equality, clearly extend ancient beliefs about women's duties inside the home to the related functions of teaching, nursing, and social work that now take place in jobs outside the home. Nevertheless the direction of the future seems clear: more occupations will open to women, as has already occurred in France, Poland, and the United States in the last decade.

Another indication of women's employment opportunities is the time during their lives that they are employed. In most agrarian societies such employment is continuous and hidden in the agricultural labor of women in the rural areas, or in the household chores of girls who are kept out of school (as in Egypt and Bangladesh). By contrast a new pattern develops in the industrializing society, in which women are more likely to work when they are young (from 20 to 25), and again when they are middle-aged and older (after 40), than when they are in their thirties and have young children at home. This pattern is particularly clear at present in Japan, Poland, and the United States. The employment of young women developed early in industrialization when, as in nineteenth century France, girls left rural areas to become domestics or factory workers (McBride, 1974; Scott and Tilly, 1975). Mill girls came from farms surrounding the New England industrial towns of Lowell and Manchester to live in dormitories and work in the textile factories of the 1830s and 1840s. Taeuber (1958) has documented a similar pattern for young unmarried Japanese women employed in the textile mills of the 1920s and 1930s; they came from farms, worked a few years, and then were married. The employment of older women appears to be a postwar phenomenon associated with the shorter childbearing period, longer life span, and expansion of job opportunities in the service sector.

For those countries still in early stages of modernization, such as Mexico or Ghana, where such job sequences have not yet been developed, it is much more likely that women will drift to the cities. They may enter trades or, without employment, fall into prostitution or rely on menial service occupations and employment as domestics.

In addition to actual behavioral patterns, norms and attitudes toward women's work also indicate life options. In Bangladesh and Egypt there is active disapproval of women's work, except in the highest educational groups who are somewhat liberated from strict ideas about *purdah*. In traditional societies such as Mexico, Ghana, and to some extent Japan, France, and the United States, there is strong to moderate feeling that women should not have to work, that they should be supported by their husbands and be able to devote themselves to home and cultural pursuits. However the modernization hypothesis suggests that the hold of these ideas will diminish rather than intensify. In Poland, the most liberated intellectual circles of every country, and especially in the United States, the employment of married women in business and industry is gaining increasing acceptance.

Government social policy toward women's working reflects the options available in different societies. In Egypt, for example, it is not clearly recognized that women have a right to their own earnings or the authority to enter into contracts whereas these points are much more firmly established in the industrial nations. During early industrialization in France, Japan, and the United States labor legislation governing women's work was largely protective in character. It barred them from working excessively long hours or in dangerous occupations. By contrast social policy in advanced industrial societies moves toward positive recognition of women's dual roles as wage earners and family members; some of the limits imposed by the protective labor laws are struck down. Maternity benefits are permitted or mandatory in countries such as France, Poland, and increasingly the United States. Legislation assuring equal pay and prohibiting discrimination in hiring and promotion of women is enacted, although some unfairness remains. In Japan women's pay is still only half of men's, and in France and the United States it is two-thirds of men's. These changing patterns suggest movement toward more flexible work structures where employment and family life of men and women have more in common.

Women's Status in the Family. Family systems vary in their impact on women's status by the degrees of hierarchy that they impose and the amount of choice that they allow. The internal division of labor between husband and wife and external policies of government and industry further affect the life options of women in the family.

Traditional societies like Egypt, Bangladesh, and prewar Japan were much more likely to look approvingly on arranged marriages at an early age. Under their systems the bride was under control of a wider kin group. In the

United States, France, and Poland, however, the conjugal pair make his and her own individual choice, and this is increasingly true in Japan. Couples in these countries are much more isolated from kin supports. Both Ghana and Mexico show characteristics of mixed systems. The high number of consensual unions and illegitimate births in Mexico testifies to the imperfect adoption of Western marriage forms. The three types of marriage in Ghana give official place to both the indigenous form and colonial influence.

In the Muslim systems women lack opportunity to seek divorce, control property, or inherit on an equal basis with men, but they do have the advantage of being dependent on the kin group for their support, with all the limitations this entails. Although the modern systems do not enforce such strict dependency, they still perpetuate the ideology that women's place is in the home. Yet they offer only precarious support in times of divorce, widowhood, or other difficulties. Girls in Eastern countries are frequently married before the age of 15. Girls in more modern countries marry at a later age, when they are more likely to have had independent educational or employment experience. The marriage systems in modern societies have also begun to shift toward an expectation that husband and wife are each other's equals in moral, spiritual, and family matters. The culmination of this trend can be seen in a change of French law, which in 1970 removed the designation of husband as *chef de la famille.*

While the modern countries accord women more independence and latitude in family matters, they nonetheless show strikingly similar concern with a woman's role as mother. Although women in Japan, France, and the United States enjoy considerable educational and occupational freedom, they are expected to take time out of their work lives to be at home with their young children. This pattern undoubtedly has interesting consequences for the children in modern society. The emotional bond between an educated mother and the child for whom she is sacrificing her own achievement probably differs from that between the Egyptian mother, who is primarily respected for her role as mother and homemaker, and her child. The bond is also probably qualitatively different from that experienced by the Latin American mother, who associates herself with *marianismo* and her husband with *machismo.* Women's care of their small children in modern society may also have a consistent effect on the job market and the mother's career. She not only lowers the demand for domestic service, but also lowers her investment in her own work and on-the-job experience. She probably thereby lowers her own pay for jobs that pay men better.

All the modern family systems, particularly those of the intelligentsia and those in the United States, Poland, and the Scandinavian countries, now show a trend toward role-sharing by husband and wife. Each earns some of the income and each helps with child care and domestic chores (Grønseth,

1971; Holmstrom, 1972; Fogarty, et al., 1971). Nevertheless the burden is still far from equal. Time studies continue to show that employed women have fewer hours of leisure than do men per day and per week (Szalai, 1973). The two-role problem for women observed by Myrdal and Klein (1956) is still far from solved.

Government supports to families in the form of old-age pensions are most fully developed in France, the United States, and Poland. France, Poland, and Egypt have the most liberal plans for maternity leave and return to work. The child-care system in France offers a wide variety of care although, as in the United States, there are still not enough places to meet the need. Generally these public supports appear to offer working women a set of options that liberate them somewhat from dependence on kin ties. The sharp rise of female-headed households in the United States, although alarming to some, may indicate that government assistance and employment opportunities have given women greater ability to survive without male support than was possible in the past, when they may have endured unhappy marriages rather than risk isolation and nonsupport (Rein and Heclo, 1973; Cutright, 1974).

Education.   Women's life options for education also vary across societies. Some indicators of different degrees of opportunity are (1) the levels of learning that women generally attain in a given country, whether it be mere literacy or a high school education; (2) the types of curriculum thought suitable to girls' and boys' education; (3) the uses that women make of their education once they have it; and (4) the ratio of males to females in the student body and faculties at each level.

One of the most powerful general indicators of women's educational opportunities is the percentage of the female population who are literate. The great majority of women in both Bangladesh and Egypt are still illiterate, yet progress is now being made to give girls at least a primary education. It is now thought that they will be better wives if they can read and write. However people in both of these countries and in Japan are still reluctant to give daughters too much education lest they hurt their marriage chances. At the other end of the scale of educational opportunity, illiteracy has virtually disappeared in France, Japan, Poland, and the United States, and the average woman has completed some level of secondary schooling.

The agrarian society that puts men in charge of family affairs and transactions with the outer world is slow to see the value of teaching a woman to read and write. Eradication of illiteracy among women apparently accompanies modernization. Estimates that only one-third of the male population were literate in fourteenth century England are comparable with estimates of literacy in today's developing countries like India. Studies of general educational levels in eighteenth century France and England show a correlation between literacy and industrialization. In the industrial north of England and the north of France, families sent their children to school, and literacy was higher in each of these regions. In 1790, just after the fall of the ancien régime, only 25 percent of French people were literate. By 1850 the proportion had risen to 60 percent, and by 1880 to 80 percent (Anderson, 1965a, 1965b). The Meiji period similarly brought modernization to Japan, and by the early 1900s literacy had been established.

Once primary education for females has been legitimized, the next step is acceptance of secondary education for girls. Some of the earliest girls' secondary schools were established in Florence during the Renaissance for daughters of elite families, in France during the seventeenth and eighteenth centuries, and in England during the seventeenth century. Educated men wanted to have alert, intelligent wives. The middle class wanted well-educated mothers to rear its children. Women's secondary schooling increased at a phenomenal rate during the nineteenth century in France, the United States, and other Western countries. In Russia, for example, there were 14 times as many girl students in secondary school in 1914 as there had been in 1873. Parents evidently wished to give a "cultural atmosphere" to their daughters (Kahan, 1965: 371–372). In the United States in 1890 more girls than boys graduated from high school (U.S. Bureau of Education, 1898–99).

Yet in all the eight societies described in this volume, girls' secondary school education is significantly different from boys' with respect to training for vocation and crafts. Boys get vocational and technical training that provides them with more salable skills for agriculture and industry. Girls are taught sewing, cooking, and other skills linked primarily with home economics, service industries, or two related branches of industry—food technology and textiles. Even in today's modern societies a high proportion of girls who are taking vocational training are in domestic science—as high as 66 percent in the United States, 47 percent in Argentina, and 29 percent in France (UNESCO, 1968. E/CN.6/498: 121–124).

A chief difference among countries is how they feel about these distinctions. Special educational tracks for girls are proudly accepted, even encouraged, in the traditional societies and in transitional societies such as Ghana. However modern countries such as France, the United States, and Poland greet sex-typed education with an increasingly critical eye. Socialist countries have proceeded farthest in preparing girls for industrial jobs. In Hungary 17 percent of girls enrolled in vocational courses, and in the USSR 33 percent, were preparing for industry in 1968 as compared with under 3 percent in France and under 1 percent in Argentina and the United States. Recently, however, there is a trend to require or encourage boys as well as girls to take domestic science, as in Norway and Poland (UNESCO, 1968. E/CN.6/498: 123, 145).

The way a country defines its curriculum for girls is closely related to the adult roles thought appropriate to women. In Japan, France, and the United States before 1970, a woman's education was defined as being of primary value for her role in the home as an educated wife and mother. In Poland, in the United States since the recent women's movement, and among the elite groups of Egypt, Bangladesh, and Mexico, women's education is increasingly defined in terms of a career of productive work outside the home.

Expectations about the uses of women's education inevitably affect the sex ratios in public education and institutions of higher learning. Generally speaking, societies in which the employment options are widest for women have sex ratios in educational institutions that most closely approach parity. The lowest ratio of female university students is found in the least modern country, Bangladesh, with 9.7 percent women. The highest ratios are found in countries such as United States and Poland, where more than 40 percent of post-secondary students are women.

Health and Fertility.   The precise way in which women's status is connected to demographic processes is not well understood. Our case studies, however, enable us to observe a strong association between the desire for a large family and the traditionalism of women's roles. In Bangladesh, Egypt, and Mexico most women have six or seven children; those in Ghana, four. In every country that gives women broader access to education and employment, as in Japan, the United States, France, and Poland, the birthrate has fallen markedly and two children is regarded as the ideal family size.

The correlation between lower birthrates and modernity in women's roles is related to a number of factors. Included here are only three, which are consequences of the change in family structure that accompanies modernization: (1) the decline of patriarchal attitudes; (2) the increase in women's independence; and (3) the institution of government programs that provide social security and other forms of family assistance.

In traditional societies such as Egypt and Bangladesh sons are clearly more highly valued than daughters. Furthermore, both in Catholic and Islamic countries, religious beliefs have impeded the spread of contraception. Large numbers of children, particularly sons, are highly valued because property passes to them and because a woman's status is dependent on the number of her surviving children. In Mexico her husband's status as well depends on having a large number of children. Such patriarchal attitudes are supported not only by the agrarian economic structure, which vests primary responsibility for support in the male, but also by an established religion that sanctions paternal authority in the peasant family. If such attitudes are to change, there probably must be a change in the economic structure such that the patriarchal peasant form is no longer viable. Reinterpretation of traditional religious beliefs has to occur as well. Once such change takes place a very rapid decline in fertility is possible, as in Japan between 1940, when the average number of children per woman was 5.14, and 1967, when it had fallen to 1.69.

A second, related change that causes decline in the birth rate is women's decreasing dependence on the family for status and support. There is now some evidence from the state of Kerala in India that women's increasing literacy is associated with greater opportunities for employment, later age at marriage, and a declining birth rate (Weinraub, 1974). Certainly our data on eight countries support this association. It seems quite logical that women who can read and write, hold a job, and earn money can see other ways of supporting themselves than by bearing more children. They may provide economic support for their families through their own work. Moreover, especially if they live in urban areas, they understand the economic cost to them of having more children. Modern societies that have slowed their population growth have about twice as many of their women in the paid labor force as societies just beginning to make this transition, and about three times as many as the traditional, high birthrate, high deathrate societies (Ridley, 1968: 17, 19; Tinker et al., 1974: 34).

Related to the decline of the patriarchal family and the growth of women's independence is yet a third factor in declining birth rates: the ability of government or the modern economy to provide security that the family cannot equal. Under such conditions children are increasingly seen as financial burdens who, unlike their peasant counterparts, are not expected to support parents in their old age. Certainly it is striking that in the modern countries described here the ideal number of children hovers at two or fewer (Frederiksen, 1969).

Changing Images of Women. Image connotes all the cultural associations—religious, artistic, intellectual, and normative—that define what a person is expected to be and against which a person may indeed rebel (Janeway, 1974: 167). In the past the state of being male or female closed off more opportunities than is the case in modern society. Generally speaking, the images of female and male come to hold more androgynous possibilities as modernization progresses.

In traditional societies such as Bangladesh, Egypt, or feudal France the patriarchy of the agrarian family structure is congruent with the order of the universe (Daly, 1973). God himself is male and so are Jesus, Buddha,

Confucius, and Mohammed. Just as disciples and apostles were male, so are the priests and holy leaders of the earthly religious communities established in these societies. Throughout the social structure male represents superior, female represents inferior. In the horizontal division of labor man stands for instrumental authority in the running of affairs, woman stands for affection and mediation as in the tradition of *marianismo*. The female deals with internal, parochial family affairs. A woman is expected to show modesty, covering her head in church or wearing a veil before strangers as in the *purdah* system. The male deals with external ties of family to universal institutions of church, state, and market. His is the "honor" that comes of well-managed family affairs.

In their treatment of women and men France and the United States during the nineteenth century are characteristic of early modern society. During the colonial period Ghana imported similar ideas. Under these systems each sex is perceived as having authority in a particular sphere. Women are given authority over household affairs, the care of young children, and the private needs of others. They are held to a higher standard of personal conduct and sexual morality, and seem more concerned with justice and peace than are men (Holter, 1970: 219). Men, on the other hand, are considered to be superior managers in the working world and in their handling of public, economic, political, and military affairs.

In no existing modern society has the androgynous ideal been fully realized. However a transformation of images is currently underway in the Scandinavian countries and among the intelligentsia of countries like Poland and the United States. Women are increasingly perceived as having greater capacity for authority—and men for affection—than was recognized in traditional society. Each sex is now more likely to be seen as capable of both serious employment and warm family relations. The division of dependency and responsibility between male and female is allowed to vary a bit more flexibly according to time and circumstance, not according to a fixed rule of who is dominant. Some believe, as Elizabeth Janeway, that the change has come largely from the introduction of feminine values ("Women find it much easier to imagine, to create and to work within relationships of shifting power and initiative . . . . ," p. 267). Others, like Mary Daly, suggest that because women have been living on the boundary, not at the center of society, their values are outsider values. As society is challenged to meet new crises, it must bring in these values. Flexibility is then reintroduced, not merely because women bring it, but because it can better meet new conditions than can rigid power relationships.

*   *   *

Summary

In this brief review I have attempted to show how women's status varies according to culture and historical circumstance. In societies where the agrarian mode of production dominates, as in Bangladesh, Egypt, and parts of Mexico, women are subject to heavy demands for childbearing; their movements are restricted; significant role choices are limited to family-related activity; and overt political activity and movements for self-expression are rare. By comparison the activity of women in societies with advanced horticulture and trade, such as Ghana, is freer and less circumscribed. When agrarian societies such as feudal France, Poland, and Japan modernized, they opened opportunities for women to control conception, move more freely, attain literacy and secondary education, engage in paid employment, and seek expression through women's voluntary associations. The most modern sectors of developed countries offer all these opportunities. The one great restriction they impose concerns freedom of movement. Mothers of young children may be more confined to home in modern society than are women who engage in advanced horticulture and trade.

In any society the structure of the family and its relation to the economy are the keys to understanding what opportunities are available to women. Women's opportunities are inextricably related to men's. Even if their economic roles are different, women and men in societies with preagrarian technology are employed in ways that promote equality.

Agrarian societies, however, make a fundamental differentiation between production and consumption, linking males to outside work and females to the home. Since in the agrarian society economic production takes place primarily within the peasant family, the family itself is the primary agent of sex inequality. The cultural legacy of peasant economies, which were historically associated with emergence of cities and "civilization," continues in the modern dichotomy between family work and paid work, with paid work receiving the greater public recognition and reward. For that reason it is perhaps not surprising that all the societies examined here contain certain universals in the inferior status accorded women.

Whether it be Bangladesh or Poland, women bear the children and teach the young. Their movements are thereby hampered, and their life options in education and employment are more restricted than are men's. Yet despite the secondary status accorded women in every society, there exists a difference in degree of inequality. The amounts of freedom and constriction vary across societies. Underlying women's different position in each country are the cultural and social factors explored in this book.

BIBLIOGRAPHY

Anderson, C. Arnold. 1965a. "Patterns and Variability in the Distribution and Diffusion of Schooling." In *Education and Economic Development*. Edited by C. A. Anderson and M. J. Bowman. Chicago: Aldine, pp. 314–344.

————. 1965b. "Literacy and Schooling on the Development Threshold: Some Historical Cases." In *Education and Economic Development*. Edited by C. A. Anderson and M. J. Bowman. Chicago: Aldine, pp. 347–362.

Barrett, Nancy Smith. 1974. "Women in Industrial Society: An International Perspective." Mimeo.

Blake, Judith. 1974. "The Changing Status of Women in Developed Countries." *Scientific American* **231** (September): 137–147.

Blumberg, Rae Lesser. 1975. "Economic Influences on Female Status and Fertility." Paper presented at the Annual Meeting of the American Association for the Advancement of Science. New York City, January 27.

————, Donald E. Carns, and Robert F. Winch. 1970. "High Gods, Virgin Brides and Societal Complexity." Paper delivered at the Annual Meeting of the American Sociological Association. Washington, D. C., August.

————, and Robert F. Winch. 1972. "Societal Complexity and Familial Complexity: Evidence for the Curvilinear Hypothesis." *American Journal of Sociology* **77** (March): 898–920.

Boserup, Ester. 1970. *Woman's Role in Economic Development*. London: George Allen and Unwin, Ltd.

Boulding, Elise. 1974. "Nomadism, Mobility and the Status of Women." Paper no. 1 of International Women's Year Studies on Women. Boulder, Colorado: Institute of Behavioral Science, University of Colorado.

Buvinić, Mayra. 1976. "A Critical Review of Some Research Concepts and Concerns." In *Women and World Development: An Annotated Bibliography*. Compiled by Mayra Buvinić. Washington, D.C.: Overseas Development Council, pp. 1–20.

Chabaud, Jacqueline. 1970. *The Education and Advancement of Women*. Paris: UNESCO.

Collier, Jane Fishburne. 1974. "Women in Politics." In *Woman, Culture and Society*. Edited by Michelle Z. Rosaldo and Louise Lamphere. Stanford, California: Stanford University Press.

Collins, Randall. 1971. "A Conflict Theory of Sexual Stratification." *Social Problems* **19** (Summer): 3–21.

Council on Foreign Relations, 1970, 1973. *Political Handbook and Atlas of the World 1970*, and *Supplement: The World This Year 1973*. New York: Simon and Schuster.

Cutright, Phillips. 1974. "Components of Change in the Number of Female Family Heads Aged 15–44: United States, 1940–1970." *Journal of Marriage and the Family* **36** (November): 714–727.

Daly, Mary. 1973. *Beyond God the Father: Toward a Philosophy of Women's Liberation*. Boston: Beacon Press.

Engels, Friedrich F. 1884. *Origin of the Family, Property, and the State*. Translated by E. Untermann. Chicago: Charles H. Kerr & Co., 1902.

Fogarty, Michael, Rhona Rapoport, and Robert N. Rapoport. 1971. *Sex, Career and Family*. London: George Allen and Unwin, Ltd.

Frederiksen, Harold. 1969. "Feedback in Economic and Demographic Transition." *Science* **166** (November 14): 837–841.

Gager, Nancy, Ed. 1974. *Women's Rights Almanac.* Bethesda, Maryland: Elizabeth Cady Stanton Publishing Co.

Giele, Janet Zollinger. 1971. "Changes in the Modern Family: Their Impact on Sex Roles." *American Journal of Orthopsychiatry* **41** (October): 757–766.

———. 1972. "Centuries of Womanhood: An Evolutionary Perspective on the Feminine Role." *Women's Studies: An Interdisciplinary Journal* **1:** 97–110.

Goode, William J. 1963. *World Revolution and Family Patterns.* New York: Free Press of Glencoe.

Grønseth, Erik. 1971. "The Husband Provider Role: A Critical Appraisal." In *Family Issues of Employed Women in Europe and America.* Edited by Andrée Michel. Leiden, The Netherlands: E. J. Brill, pp. 11–31.

Heffermehl, Karin B. 1972. "Status of Women in Norway." In "Symposium on Status of Women." Edited by Ruth B. Ginsburg. *American Journal of Comparative Law* **20:** 630–646.

Hochschild, Arlie. 1975. "The Sociology of Feeling and Expression." In *Another Voice.* Edited by Marcia Millman and Rosabeth Kanter. New York: Anchor Books.

Holmstrom, Lynda Lytle. 1972. *The Two-Career Family.* Cambridge, Massachusetts: Schenckman Publishing Co.

Holter, Harriet. 1970. *Sex Roles and Social Structure.* Oslo, Norway: Universitetsforlaget.

International Labor Office. 1972. *Yearbook of Labor Statistics.* Geneva: International Labor Office.

Janeway, Elizabeth. 1974. *Between Myth and Morning: Woman Awakening.* New York: Morrow.

Johnson, Orna R., and Allen Johnson. 1975. "Male/Female Relations and the Organization of Work in a Machiguenga Community." *American Ethnologist* **2** (November): 634–648.

Kahan, Arcadius. 1965. "Social Structure, Public Policy and the Development of Education and the Economy in Czarist Russia." In *Education and Economic Development.* Edited by C. A. Anderson and M. J. Bowman. Chicago: Aldine, pp. 363–375.

Leacock, Eleanor. 1972. "Introduction." In *The Origin of the Family, Private Property and the State,* by Frederick Engels. Edited by E. B. Leacock. New York: International Publishers.

———. n.d. "Women, Social Evolution, and Errors, Crude and Subtle." Mimeo.

Lee, Richard B., and Irven DeVore. 1968. *Symposium on Man the Hunter.* Chicago: Aldine.

Lenski, Gerhard. 1966. *Power and Privilege: A Theory of Social Stratification.* New York: McGraw-Hill Book Co.

———, and Jean Lenski. 1974. *Human Societies: An Introduction to Macrosociology.* New York: McGraw-Hill Book Co.

Martin, M. Kay, and Barbara Voorhies. 1975. *Female of the Species.* New York: Columbia University Press.

Matthiasson, Carolyn J., Ed. 1974. *Many Sisters: Women in Cross-Cultural Perspective.* New York: Free Press.

McBride, Theresa. 1974. "Traditional Socialization and the Process of Modernization for Women: Domestic Service in Nineteenth-Century France." Paper presented at the Berkshire Conference on the History of Women. Radcliffe College, October 25–27.

McElroy, Ann. 1975. "Canadian Arctic Modernization and Change in Female Inuit Role Identification." *American Ethnologist* **2** (November): 662–686.

Myrdal, Alva, and Viola Klein. 1956. *Women's Two Roles, Home and Work.* London: Routledge & Paul.

Olin, Ulla. 1976. "A Case for Women as Co-Managers: The Family as a General Model of Human Social Organization." In *Women and World Development.* Edited by Irene Tinker and Michèle Bo Bramsen. Washington, D.C.: Overseas Development Council, pp. 105–128.

Patai, Raphael. 1967. *Women in the Modern World.* New York: Free Press.

Rein, Martin, and Hugh Heclo. 1973. "What Welfare Crisis?: A Comparison among the United States, Britain, and Sweden." *The Public Interest* **33** (Fall): 61–83.

Reiter, Rayna, Ed. 1975. *Toward an Anthropology of Women.* New York: Monthly Review Press.

Ridley, Jeanne Claire. 1968. "Demographic Change and the Roles and Status of Women." *The Annals of the American Academy of Political and Social Science* **375** (January): 15–25.

Rosaldo, Michelle, and Louise Lamphere. 1974. *Women, Culture, and Society.* Stanford: Stanford University Press.

Sacks, Karen. 1974. "Engels Revisited: Women, the Organization of Production, and Private Property." In *Women, Culture, and Society.* Edited by Michelle Z. Rosaldo and Louise Lamphere. Stanford: Stanford University Press.

Safilios-Rothschild, Constantina. 1971. "A Cross-Cultural Examination of Women's Marital, Educational, and Occupational Options." *Acta Sociologica* **14:** 96–113.

Sanday, Peggy R. 1973. "Toward a Theory of the Status of Women." *American Anthropologist* **75** (October): 1682–1700.

———. 1974. "Female Status in the Public Domain." In *Women, Culture, and Society.* Edited by Michelle Z. Rosaldo and Louise Lamphere. Stanford: Stanford University Press, pp. 189–206.

Scott, Joan W., and Louise A. Tilly. 1975. "Women's Work and the Family in Nineteenth-Century Europe." *Comparative Studies in Society and History* **17** (January): 36–64.

Sullerot, Evelyne. 1971. *Women, Society and Change.* New York: McGraw-Hill.

Szalai, Alexander, Ed. 1973. *The Use of Time. Daily Activities of Urban and Suburban Populations in Twelve Countries.* The Hague: Mouton.

Taeuber, Irene. 1958. *The Population of Japan.* Princeton: Princeton University Press.

Tinker, Irene, et al. 1974. *Culture and Population Change.* Washington, D.C.: American Association for the Advancement of Science.

———. 1976. "The Adverse Impact of Development on Women." In *Women and World Development.* Edited by Irene Tinker and Michèle Bo Bramsen. Washington, D.C.: Overseas Development Council, pp. 22–34.

Tuchman, Gaye. 1975. "Women and the Creation of Culture." In *Another Voice.* Edited by Marcia Millman and Rosabeth Kanter. New York: Anchor Books, pp. 171–202.

United Nations. 1968. *Compendium of Social Statistics: 1967.* New York: United Nations.

United Nations. 1967-1970. "Political Rights of Women." E/CN.6/470 (1/9/67); A/7197 (12/12/68); A/7635 (12/15/69); A/8132 (12/15/70).

United Nations Economic and Social Council (UNESCO). 1968. E/CN.6/498. *Access of Girls and Women to Technical and Vocational Education.* Prepared by UNESCO. January 2.

U.S. Bureau of Education. 1898–99. *Report of the Commission, 1898–99.*

Weinraub, Bernard. 1974. "In Kerala, Smallest and Most Literate State in India, a Breakthrough in Birth Control is Taking Place." *The New York Times,* October 20, p. 13.

Women's Bureau. 1963. "Women in the World Today: Women in High Level Elective and Appointive Positions in National Governments." International Report no. 1, February. Washington, D. C.: U.S. Department of Labor.

Wilensky, Harold. 1975. *The Welfare State and Equality.* Berkeley: University of California Press.

Chapter Two

EGYPT: FROM SECLUSION TO LIMITED PARTICIPATION

Audrey Chapman Smock and Nadia Haggag Youssef

HISTORICAL AND CULTURAL BACKGROUND

Egypt has one of the longest continuous histories, reaching back more than 6000 years to the glories of the ancient pharonic empires. During this vast expanse of time the position of women within Egyptian society has varied considerably. The introduction of Islam following the Arab conquest of Egypt in 640 A.D. undoubtedly comprises the single most important determinant molding the character of Egyptian culture and as such had a profound effect on the status of women. However the role of women in pre-Islamic Egypt differed considerably from that in other parts of the Middle East and, at least initially, influenced the interpretation of Islamic precepts regarding the place of women. Moreover the Islamic social order, far from being static in Egypt, has undergone significant changes within the past fourteen centuries.

Unlike some of the other ancient cultures, such as the Greek, which relegated women to a subordinate status, ancient Egyptian civilization accorded women considerable prestige and rights. There are many indications that women commanded respect and were active participants in the life of the society. For instance, monuments depict wives on an equal level with their husbands. Although the homes of the wealthy did have separate quarters for men and women, women were not secluded. Records indicate that wives accompanied their husbands to all social functions. At meals men and women sat on mats together. Women also had the freedom to engage in business and commerce. Paintings from the IV through VI dynasties show women undertaking much of the farming, bringing the produce to market, trading at the market, and even steering large cargo boats. Those from the XII dynasty picture women spinning and weaving and playing musical instruments. Thus the scope of women's activities apparently went beyond child-rearing and caring for the house (Petrie, 1923: 27, 99).

The ancient Egyptian family was based on a matriarchal system in which descent was traced through the female line. All fixed property belonged to the women, and the house and land were inherited by the daughters through the mother. With this property went the responsibility for caring for other members of the family. As in other matrilineal descent systems, men often controlled the actual management of property. The pattern of inheritance and the absence of any barriers to affinity in marriage provided a strong inducement for brothers to marry sisters in order to keep the family's property. Even when the husband was not a brother or another close relative, he often was vested with legal rights over his wife's property usually associated with actual ownership. Nevertheless, if a woman could read and write, she could sell and make transactions without her husband's consent (Petrie, 1923: 109–110, 118–119).

An early marriage contract dating from 590 B.C. reveals that marriage in ancient Egypt resembled a business relationship more than a religious rite. Even after the widespread conversions to Christianity in the two centuries after the death of Jesus, marriages could be easily ended by either partner through divorce or annulment. Some marriage contracts mention a dowry from the women's family, whereas others state that the prospective husband agreed to make a bridal gift (Petrie, 1923: 114–117). These contracts and other documents suggest that women did have rights within the marriage and that the family did not consist of a superordinate husband and a subordinate wife. Within the family women were considered equal with men, and daughters were equal with sons (Paturet, 1886: 6).

The respect commanded by women derived in part from the nature of the Egyptian religion, which strongly emphasized fertility. As childbearers women were regarded as the major source and embodiment of all fertility and growth. Women took on religious functions and were even elected head priestesses. Some Egyptian goddesses achieved such widespread fame that they were worshipped outside Egypt (Langdon-Davies, 1928: 85–89).

The kingdom, like other forms of property, descended in the female line during most of the dynasties. Records indicate that at least under the first four dynasties women were allowed to rule. Later in Egyptian history the queen participated with the king in governing the kingdom. The system of female inheritance prompted some half brothers and full brothers to marry their sisters so as to bring about de facto male succession. These practices culminated in a system brought by the Ethiopians during the XXV and XXVI dynasties in which sister-queens also served as high priestesses (Petrie, 1923: 109–111).

There is some controversy as to how the conquest of Egypt by Alexander the Great in 323 B.C. and the later incorporation of Egypt into the Roman Empire in the first century A.D. affected the status of women. Greek society excluded women from business, scholarship, and public affairs, and even within the household most of the labor was performed by slaves; one writer described women in ancient Greek civilization as "isolated reproductive organs" (Langdon-Davies, 1928: 86). The adoption of Greek customs and laws, therefore, would have reduced the rights of Egyptian women and subordinated them to the male head of the family. However the Greek influence was limited primarily to a few upper-class urban families that had extensive contact with Greek culture and ideas. Similarly Roman law accorded women few of the legal rights that Egyptian women had traditionally held; under Roman law women did not have an independent legal status and merely passed from the *potestas* of the father into the household and rule of the husband. Women could not own property, and the husband alone possessed the right to initiate divorce. Consequently some sources assume that the status of women in Egypt during the Roman period was depressed by the imposition of Roman legal institutions and social values (Abdel Kader, 1973: 5). Other scholars assert that Egyptian practices and customs protected the status of women because, firstly, Roman law did not extend throughout the empire until the reign of Caracalla early in the third century and, secondly, contracts and agreements dating from the Roman period still granted women many of their traditional rights (Paturet, 1886: 63–64).

The influence of Islam on the status of women has been debated frequently, but invariably with reference to ninth century Arabian society rather than to Egypt. Islam, as an integral religion, formulates a total pattern of living rather than focusing primarily on theology. Hence Mohammed, unlike Jesus, was concerned with the role of women. The verses in the *Quran* and the *hadiths* (pronouncements of the Prophet) that deal with women do not, however, systematically define women's roles and status. Their ambiguity has provoked considerable controversy regarding the Prophet's views and intentions. The four major legal schools within Islam have differed in their interpretation of the sources of revelation, and legal scholars within the Hanafite school, the dominant tradition in Egypt, have changed some of their views with the passing of time.

The Arabian society that predated Mohammed's revelations apparently accorded women considerable freedom and did not maintain the seclusion of women. Pre-Islamic poetry depicts women as freely interacting with men and as actively participating in communal affairs (Smith, 1928). There seem to have been few restrictions on marriage and divorce, and women, at least under some circumstances, were able to choose their husbands (Shafiq, 1956: 21–27; Levy, 1965: 93). Nevertheless women did not enjoy secure legal rights. Moreover, despite evidence that women's status was not low, the society practiced female infanticide (Levy, 1965: 91).

Mohammed, it is thought by some, sought to transform the tribal basis of Arabian society by substituting a more family-oriented pattern based on a partnership between the sexes, albeit one in which the women was the junior partner. To accomplish his goal Mohammed attempted to invest women with secure legal rights, although not equal to those of men (Gibb, 1961). He also accepted them into the community of believers and offered them the same rewards of heaven enjoyed by men. Many general prescriptions in the *Quran* enjoin men to give their wife or wives a decent and respectable life. Mohammed also categorically banned the continued practice of female infanticide; he accorded to women the right to own property and to receive a share of inheritance. He somewhat reluctantly sanctioned the continuation of polygamy, but recommended that men limit themselves to one wife and did not allow them to marry more than four women at the same time. Similarly, despite his acceptance of divorce, Mohammed indicated that it was undesirable except under special circumstances. To prevent women from being forced into marriage, Mohammed specified that the free consent of the woman was a prerequisite (Charnay, 1971: 60).

Mohammed seems to have been somewhat ambivalent in his views about the character of women. In contrast with the prescriptions described above, which serve to protect and elevate the status of women, other Quranic injunctions emphasize the inferiority and unreliability of women and place them under considerable liabilities. One verse in the *Quran* states that "Men have authority over women because Allah has made the one superior to the other, and because they spend their wealth to maintain them. Good women are obedient. They veil their unseen parts as Allah has veiled them" (Dawood, 1959: 358). *Surah* (chapter) IV of the *Quran* implies that a woman is worth only half as much as a man by according women half as much inheritance as the male members of her family and by making her testimony in court worth half as much as a man's. This *surah* of the *Quran* also outlines many principles that work to the disadvantage of women: it allows a woman to be beaten for disobedience to her husband; it prevents a wife from interfering with her husband's rights to take three additional wives and to divorce her without cause; it compromises the principle of a woman's consent being a prerequisite for marriage by forcing a daughter to marry whomever her father or his representative designates. Other verses suggest that women are morally weak and generally unworthy spiritually. Mohammed is also alleged to have said that most of the inhabitants of hell, but few of those in paradise, are women (Gordon, 1968: 11–12).

It is difficult to evaluate the relative importance of these negative pronouncements. Many Muslims and Western scholars do not consider them conclusive evidence that the Prophet viewed women as definitely inferior to men rather than merely different. They cite the statement by Omar, the second caliph, that "In the time of paganism our women counted for nothing. This situation ceased when Allah made his revelation concerning them and defined their due" (quoted in Charnay, 1971: 60). Furthermore, they point out that Mohammed's invectives against women and their faults (fickleness, vanity, inconsistency, ingratitude) in the *hadiths* are balanced by the passages in which he censured men (for avariciousness, love of money, brutality, injustice, and impiety). Although the scholars and believers holding this perspective recognize that Mohammed accorded more rights to men than to women, they argue that the social system of Islam and its internal equilibrium ensure adequate compensations to protect women (Charnay, 1971: 59–60). On the opposing side, many Muslims and nonbelievers concur that "Quite clearly he adhered to the traditional estimation of the female as a lesser being" (Levy, 1965: 98).

Many scholars have claimed that the principles of patriarchal arbitrariness and sexual rigidity in the family expressed in the scripture do not fully reflect the Prophet's teachings. Islamic law, particularly those sections concerned with the family, were compiled and made final as part of the *Shari'a* two to three centuries after the death of the Prophet—at a time when the military success of the Islamic conquests in many parts of the world had led Muslims to regard women as interchangeable booty (Bellah, 1968: 16).

One major factor contributing to the conservative evolution of Islamic society with regard to the interpretation of the proper roles for women was the pressure of the ideal of tribal honor (Gibb, 1961). As Arab society became more family oriented through the impact of Islam, male honor came to depend on the virtue of the family's female members. At the same time men's image of women emphasized female sexuality and postulated that women were weak and irresponsible. Thus it was believed that free contact between men and women inexorably led to a sexual relationship. Seclusion and veiling of women served the purpose of protecting the family from possible humiliation by the transgressions of its women. Although the veil became a symbol of respectability, the very logic of seclusion reflected negatively on the character and value of women. Ultimately women were kept apart from men to shield men from the temptations that women, who were inherently untrustworthy, inevitably offered. The confinement of women to the home obviously limited the roles they could assume and their ability to enforce their rights.

The traditional roles and status of women in Egypt in pre-Islamic times differed considerably from those in Arabia, and therefore the impact of Islam on the status of women was not the same. Women in Egypt already held many of the rights that Islam introduced to other areas of the Middle East. Moreover for many centuries Egyptian society resisted the application of a more conservative interpretation of the prescriptions in Islam for women. Many classical Egyptian Arabic sources describe women as shopping, even buying clothes for their husbands. Ibn Al Hadj, a fourteenth century Egyptian jurist, inveighed against many of the practices of women which he perceived as contrary to Islamic laws, such as the use of henna, the tatooing of the body, the wearing of many jewels, and the removal of unwanted hair from the face; he would not have been aware of the manner in which women dressed if they had been veiled and secluded. A fifteenth century, three-volume biography of famous Egyptians lists more than 1000 women, some of whom played important roles in intellectual circles as scholars learned in Islamic law and as teachers in schools. The volume on women also mentions women who were members of Sufi orders, women who ran shops, and women who engaged in a variety of other activities that would have been incompatible with seclusion. At two points in Egyptian history, in the tenth and the thirteenth centuries, women briefly ruled until the caliphate objected. Studies of medieval Egyptian financial records indicate that men sometimes specified that the income from a *waqf* or religious endowment be given to daughters and their children so as to circumvent limitations on female inheritance (interview with Professor Hassanayn M. Rabie, May 14, 1974).

When Egypt came under the rule of the Turks in 1517, becoming part of the Ottoman Empire, Egyptian women suffered a loss in their rights and freedom. The Turks promulgated edicts based on a very conservative interpretation of the verses in the scripture relating to women, and these forced women into the pattern of seclusion in the home usually associated with Islam. Women were prohibited from entering shops, going to public places, accompanying their fathers or sons on the streets or in carriages, and walking on the streets at specified times. The oppressive impact of the Ottomans on Egyptian society and scholarly life has prompted many contemporary Egyptians to consider the three centuries from the inception of Turkish rule until the Napoleonic invasion a dark age in Egyptian history (interview with Professor Hassanayn M. Rabie, May 14, 1974).

Bonaparte's landing near Alexandria in 1798 initiated a new era of sustained contact with Europe that undermined considerably the authority of the Ottoman Empire over Egypt and stimulated the gradual modernization of Egypt. In 1882 a British expeditionary force landed in Egypt and installed a British proconsul who ruled the country from behind the scenes. Although the British never undertook any serious effort at stimulating social reform, their presence called attention to the treatment of women. Europeans resident in Egypt frequently were appalled by the seclusion, passivity, ignorance, and degraded status of Muslim women. This challenge provoked a variety of responses. Some Muslim traditionalists argued that the status of women in Islam was superior to that of women in the West and that the existing social order was based on divine revelation and therefore could not be changed. On the opposite side a few upper-class Egyptian families superficially emulated European customs. A third group of reformists sought to reinterpret Islam to show that before being corrupted Islam provided for greater equality for women [Ragai (Shafik), 1940: 136]. Among this group the works and writings of Mohammed Abdu and Kasem Amin had far-reaching effect. Kasem Amin's first book, *Les Egyptiens,* was written in 1894 to refute European criticisms of the Islamic social system of Egypt, particularly with regard to the status of women, polygamy, social classes, and divorce. His second book, *The Emancipation of Women,* published five years later, took a more liberal stand and demanded that women should be educated and accorded rights and opportunities equal to those enjoyed by men (Amin, 1899). A third book, *The New Women,* followed in 1900. Because Amin's second book raised fundamental issues with respect to men's misuse of the rights accorded to them by the Prophet and advocated a thorough revision of the social order, it caused an uproar throughout the Arab world (Gadalla, 1974: 60–61). However his first book, which argued more from a reformist perspective and employed direct references to the *Quran* and *hadith*, may have been more persuasive within his society.

As Kasem Amin pointed out in his writings, until that time women had few opportunities to be educated. During the Ottoman period all schools in Egypt were religion oriented and therefore catered primarily to boys and men. Women were admitted only to the *kuttabs*, which were attached to local mosques and taught the *Quran* by rote and sometimes the rudiments of reading, writing, and arithmetic. The *madrassah* and Al-Azhar, the mosque university, did not accept female students. Although girls from upper-class families frequently had private tutors at home, the prevailing cultural atmosphere dictated that their studies be confined to those subjects that prepared them to be wives and mothers.

During the nineteenth century some schools for girls were opened that did not follow the traditional Islamic pattern of education. Mohammed Ali, the ruler of Egypt generally credited with initiating the modernization of the country, founded a vocational school for training female midwives in 1832, but the school was able to attract only girls from orphanages and poor families. Beginning in the middle of the century, foreign missionary groups established a few schools for women that were considered suitable institutions for the daughters of elite families. In 1873 and 1875 the government instituted two public elementary schools fashioned on a European curriculum. It was not until 1900, though, that the girls attending these institutions were allowed to sit for their final examinations (Abdel Kader, 1973: 18–19).

The recognition of the right of women to receive an education came in the Constitution of 1923, which included an article (19) that made elementary education a minimum requirement for Egyptian children of both sexes from 6 through 12 years of age. Primary education became compulsory for both girls and boys in 1933. Although this law was never enforced and female education remained a very sporadic practice, it did prompt the construction of additional primary schools where girls were taught in the morning and boys in the afternoon (Abou Zeid, 1970). In 1927 only 2.3 percent of all women were literate, as compared to 11.4 percent of all males. Moreover 10 years later, after the enactment of supposedly compulsory primary education, the relative position of women had deteriorated further: 6.1 percent of all women were literate, while the male figure had risen to 23.5 percent. Of this small group of literate women, only 0.9 percent had an intermediate or high school certificate (census book of Egypt, 1960, Vol. 2, quoted in Abdel Kader, 1973: 28).

The first Egyptian women to pursue a higher education attended foreign universities, primarily in France and England. Soon after it was founded, Cairo University admitted women to the Faculty of Arts, with the first class of women graduating in 1933. Women were accepted to the Faculty of Medicine in 1928, Law in 1929, Commerce in 1936, and Engineering and Agronomy in 1945. By 1952, on the eve of the Nasserite revolution, 4033 Egyptian women had received university degrees (Shafie and Bassyouni, 1974).

Efforts to reform Egyptian society and improve the status of women originated with men. One motive inspiring some of these men was the association of nationalism with social reform. British colonization of Egypt in 1882 stimulated the rise of nationalism and calls for independence. One group of nationalists argued that the betterment of society and the education of all citizens was a prerequisite for political liberation of the country from British rule (Vatikiotis, 1969). This link between the status of women and the political state of the country became a theme that reappeared at several other points in Egyptian history. Surges of nationalism, particularly following perceived national failures, apparently have rekindled a critical national self-examination that focuses attention on social inequities. One important landmark in the masculine-led movement to ameliorate the condition of women came with the publication of the books of Kasem Amin at the end of the nineteenth century. Then Malak Hifny Nassef presented ten demands to improve women's rights to the first Egyptian Congress of 1911, all of which were unanimously rejected (Taha, 1964: 62). The Constitution of 1923 stated that all Egyptians were equal in front of the law and enjoyed equal rights without discrimination. Nevertheless the electoral law promulgated that same year restricted the right to vote to males (Shafie and Bassyouni, 1974).

Egyptian women slowly responded to the changed environment. Their first active participation in public life came during the 1919 uprisings in Egypt that sought to expel the British. Women went out into the streets in large numbers to demonstrate on March 16 and 19 in support of the male-armed rebellion and strikes, but to no avail (Shafie and Bassyouni, 1974). Active feminism in Egypt began in the same year, when Madame Huda Sha'rawi founded the Arab Feminist Union, which then became affiliated with the International Alliance for Women's Suffrage. Like the parent organization, the Arab Feminist Union sought the extension of suffrage to women. Egyptian women frequently date the origins of a woman's social reform movement in Egypt from 1923. In that year Huda Sha'rawi, on returning to Egypt from a conference on women in Rome, cast her veil into the Mediterranean as she stepped off the ship (Hussein, 1953: 440). Other elite Egyptian women slowly followed her example. The Egyptian branch of the Arab Feminist Union gradually enlarged its objectives and formulated an inclusive program aimed at raising the intellectual and social standards of Egyptian women to ready them for full participation in national life. Their goals included free access to all schools of higher education for women and reform of the marriage and divorce laws (Abdel Kader, 1973: 14). A magazine espousing the ideas of the feminists, *Fatat al-Sharq*, initiated publication during this period, and the Feminist Union of Egypt started a magazine, *El-Masria* (Gordon, 1968: 25).

Nevertheless the importance of this feminist activity should not be overestimated. At best the Egyptian Feminist Union appealed to the small group of well-educated women who had been exposed to Western culture. The vast majority of women remained secluded in their homes and behind their veils, and were not even aware of the Union's aims. Had they been informed of the objectives, it is doubtful that they would have supported them. For reasons that are discussed in greater detail in the next section, Egyptian women have tended to support the existing sexual division of roles, both because they have been socialized to accept it and because they receive social and psychological rewards for doing so.

WOMEN AND THE FAMILY

We now proceed to a more focused discussion on the religious system of Islam, and the pre-Islamic principles of social organization that Arab conquerors brought into Egypt, that affected the institutional position of Egyptian women within the kinship unit and within the larger society. Because a woman's status is expected to differ according to her marital status, the analysis separates the positions of unmarried and the married Egyptian women within the social structure.

Two interrelated considerations are of importance in understanding how kinship and family organization affect the place of women in Egyptian society. One is the stipulation that a woman always belongs to her own patrilineally defined kinship group. This originally tribal concept has several ramifications: explicit provisions are made within the kinship unit to ensure that a male relative from the patrilineal line will always be economically, legally, and morally responsible for a kinswoman regardless of her marital status. The second consideration pertains to the criterion of familial pride and ratification of male identity in the Muslim community, which depend largely, if not exclusively on conformity to behavioral norms that are conceived as having to do with male "honor." To a great extent this honor is realized through the chaste and discrete sexual behavior of womenfolk in a particular man's life. Premarital chastity of the daughter and sister, fidelity of the wife, continence of the widowed and divorced daughter or sister—these are basic principles on which a family's reputation and status in the community depend. Such principles of honor are at the highest level of cultural valuation. They reflect a solid body of cultural strictures that control behavior and act as effective checks on social relationships (Dodd, 1973; Hilal, 1970).

The interaction between the acknowledgment of economic and moral responsibility towards all kinswomen, which is prescribed by kinship institutions, and principles of familial honor, which depend on attributes of female sexual purity, has consolidated the position of exclusive control of women by male members of the kin group. Because male family members performing such a function receive the full institutional support of the religious and judicial systems, the sanctions invoked against women can be mighty, particularly when the principle of legitimacy is couched in terms of family honor. Honor alone, however, is not sufficient as a cultural ideal to implement control. For kinship sanctions to become fully effective, the kinship group must provide economic support for their women at all times. This is exactly what has happened in most Muslim societies to perpetuate the status of women as economic dependents. Only when family responsibility for the economic support of female relatives begins to be questioned will the present structure of control of women by male family members weaken.

The moral and economic commitments to their own kinswomen acknowledged by males are even stronger than those to their wives, who remain outsiders to the husband's kinship group. It is important to note that the responsibilities of male members of the kin group to their kinswomen persist irrespective of whether the woman is single, married, or divorced. Therefore adult males tend to hold two conflicting orientations toward women, one protective and the other exploitive. Whereas a man guards and protects the sexual purity of his daughters, sisters, and mother throughout his life so as to preserve the family's reputation, the code of male honor simultaneously specifies that a man can assert and verify his masculinity only through sexual prowess and domination of women. The common practice in Egypt, as elsewhere in the Islamic world, of marrying the daughter of one's uncle can be interpreted as an effort to maximize men's protective inclinations and minimize their exploitive tendencies (Hilal, 1970: 82–83).

We now consider the implications these principles have for women of different marital status. The position of the single woman in Egyptian society is the most precarious of all because any suspicion or mistrust of her moral conduct can stigmatize her and her family for life. It is self-evident that a social system in which men have to safeguard continually against a woman's actual or suspected sexual misconduct requires a strong machinery of social control geared to guarantee the insulation of the sexes and nonexposure to viable alternatives to marriage. Thus Muslim societies such as Egypt are characterized by numerous and highly effective institutional mechanisms that preclude contact with the opposite sex. These include, to mention only a few, sex segregation in most public and private schools, a rigid sex segregation in the labor market, and informal separation of the sexes in most recreational and many familial activities.

Tight control through an early, parentally supervised and controlled marriage, as well as strict seclusion before that event, instills the idea that only one life exists for women. Motivation is channeled in the direction of marriage by the creation of intense desires for familial roles, by extolling the rewards accruing from the wife-mother status, and by severe community censure of spinsterhood. Alternatives to marriage are viewed as compromising a girl's sexual ethics and seen as potential threats to her eventual chances of marriage. The mere fact that a girl is highly educated or employed often jeopardizes her chances of a good match. In the marriage market the working girl is still judged by many as loose, immoral, and in certain cases, promiscuous, in contrast to those girls who are secluded in their homes and thereby considered virtuous and chaste.

Societal mechanisms have succeeded well in channeling young girls into marriage by penalizing the "single" status. This is done in several ways. Whereas in other societies an unmarried girl who is educated or working enjoys emancipation from parental control, a more favorable bargaining position in the marriage market, and economic independence, in Muslim society she accrues none of these advantages. Her education, her employed status, even her professional standing will not liberate her from traditional family restraints. The freedom in decision-making enjoyed by employed Western women is practically unknown to employed unmarried women in Egypt. Working girls are expected to continue to live with their parents until marriage, contribute their earnings to the family budget, be restricted in their social life, and in many cases denied the right to choose whom and when to marry. Because activities involving the public are so easily linked with suspicions of promiscuous behavior, women who attend the university or go to work are likely to come under the continual scrutiny of their family in every move they make outside the home. It is precisely because of this strict control that marriage is seen to offer the single woman greater freedom.

Yet it is necessary to point out that Egyptian girls are not legally compelled to seclude themselves prior to marriage; neither can they be legally forced into an early marriage. Such decisions often involve self-choices that could not have endured for long without powerful mechanisms in Muslim society that motivate the woman's perception of a relationship between her social restrictions and her individual goals. That her individual goals tend to coalesce with a familial role stems from a firm realization that a woman's ultimate status within the social framework is derived exclusively from how well she meets societal and familial expectations. In this regard, one cannot but admire the effectiveness of institutional arrangements, not only in preventing women from seeking extrafamilial options, but more importantly in withholding all inducements that would make the typical Egyptian woman want to seek—even if only temporarily—an alternative life-style to marriage and motherhood.

Provision for the consequences of divorce is particularly important in Muslim society because of the high frequency of legal dissolution and because the right to initiate such proceedings is a prerogative vested primarily in men. The proportion of adult women reported in any census count as "currently divorced," which was 2 percent in 1960 and 1.7 percent of all adult Egyptian women in 1966 (Central Agency for Public Mobilization and Statistics, 1976: 10), does not accurately reflect the divorce rate because most divorced women are young and remarry quickly. Kinship institutions prescribe a distinct set of moral and financial obligations to provide the divorced female relative with status placement and economic support. The divorced woman invariably returns to her parents' home. The legal codes relieve her of a considerable portion of child-care responsibilities since religious family law statutes assign guardianship to either the maternal or paternal grandparents when the children are young. Because the social stigma attached to divorce is slight, the divorced woman is placed back in the marriage market to compete with the single girls. All these factors produce a situation in which the divorced woman is thought of as an "expectant wife" and as such is often subjected to the same family restrictions and controls imposed on the single girls so as to secure a remarriage that will reflect favorably on her own standing and that of her family.

The situation differs considerably for the widow who, together with her children, is expected to return to her family, where she is fully provided for financially but is not expected to remarry at the same rate as her divorced counterpart. Her older age, the presence of several children, and the cultural superstitions that label her as "bad omen," combine to represent a deficit in the marriage market. They also provide sufficient rationalization to seclude the widowed relative in her parental home, where a life of chastity, dedication to the memory of her late husband, and devotion to her children are the only activities deemed appropriate for her.

The status of the married woman in Egyptian social structure is the most difficult to define. Traditional Western literature has emphasized the inferiority of her status within the context of rigid systems of marital role allocations that uphold separate male and female worlds and exclude women from suprafamilial activities. This division of labor—with the man operating in the public sphere, and the woman in the private world of the home and children—is strongly sustained by the socialization process, the difference in age (typically 8 to 10 years), and the educational disparities between husband and wife. Many of the religiolegal prescriptions under which the Egyptian wife must function also provide justification for her subordinate position in the institutional structure.

To defend Islamic doctrine against the accusation that it discriminates against women, apologists continue to argue that Islamic law has always granted married women independent legal and property rights—a privilege only recently acquired by women in the Western world. However the gap between the options and rights that are legally available and those that are actually accessible to most women is very large. Moreover only a small minority of upper-class women ever hold property. Women often do not claim their inheritance because of their desire to appease the male kinsmen on whom they rely for support. Families rarely utilize the marriage contract as a vehicle for protecting the interests of the daughter. The bridal gift traditionally given by the husband to the wife may find its way into the hands of her family, and the woman may forego the portion of it payable on divorce to extricate herself from an unhappy marriage. Male family members appropriate their daughters' and sisters' property holdings on the grounds that these women will need their economic support in the event of divorce, separation, or widowhood.

But even when such rights are protected, they are hardly sufficient to outweigh the patriarchal arbitrariness contained in many of the legal codes regulating family behavior. By twentieth century standards, the religiolegal sanctioning of polygamy, the unilateral power of the husband in divorce, custody rights over his children, and enforcement of the return of a rebellious wife to the conjugal home, and the unequal female inheritance and weight of her legal testimony can hardly be viewed as congruent with an equitable position for married women. Obviously not all men take advantage of these privileges, but, their legal endorsement functions as a constant and concrete source of anxiety to many married women. To the extent that Egyptian women have no social and economic options outside of marriage, a factor that obviously constrains their behavior within marriage, do not always have the freedom to marry the man of their choice, and are explicitly discriminated against by existing family and marriage laws, it must be conceded that the Egyptian wife occupies a subordinate status in the sense that she is given few rights.

However the status of the Egyptian wife cannot be accurately defined by evaluating the rights accorded to her. Within the context of her domain—the women's world—the Egyptian wife has thus far elicited great respect and been given a considerable degree of real familial power. Although the wife is supposed to be submissive, devoted, and respectful to her husband, she is also an almost absolute manager of the house (Ammar, 1954: 50). The married woman occupies a central place within the family system. Her power within the family finds expression in the relationship she maintains with her husband, the strong influence she exerts over her children, even when they are adults, and the special position she occupies within her parental home by the mere virtue of having attained marriage and mother-hood. Thus it is important to distinguish between the rights women hold and the respect given to them. As the Egyptian case illustrates, within a particular social system these two discrete components of women's status may not be directly related; women's roles may be valued without women's receiving commensurate rights. In fact, it has been argued that respect for women is often inversely related to their rights (Goldberg, 1973: 68–70).

In Egypt the high status accorded to women has traditionally stemmed exclusively from marriage and maternal-related roles and is therefore grounded in the separation of familial and suprafamilial activities and power. Thus the respect and power commanded by women are made pos-sible by the male's suprafamilial orientation. Similarly women have very few options to become involved with the problems and activities of the larger world from which men derive their status and prestige. Women are able to draw on many sources of valuation for two important reasons: marriage and motherhood roles are greatly valued in the community and hence given very high status and respect, and such roles can be filled only by women because men are incapable of assuming them. This does not imply that the degree of patriarchy, male dominance, and male attainments of suprafamilial rewards is thereby reduced. It does, however, provide the basis for a mechanism of compensation whereby the limitation of options for women is translated into an asset as well as a liability.

Until now the Egyptian wife has found her world to be quite fulfilling. Except for a highly educated and politicized minority, few Egyptian wives conceive of their status and role within the home and in relationship to their husbands as "subordinate," "oppressed," "inferior," or "powerless." Such a perception (or misperception as the case may be) reflects the combined effects of a condition of "false consciousness" and a highly effective sociali-zation process. It may indicate, however, a volitional avoidance on the part of the average wife to enter into the mainstream of modern life because of the risk of threatening the security and the power she has accrued in her own world. Women's desire to attain status (i.e., rights) in areas from which men derive their authority and prestige can be achieved only at the expense of a reduction in the status (respect) given to roles only women can fulfill (Goldberg, 1973: 72). Even if this occurred only to a limited extent, it is understandable that the average Egyptian wife, who is so poorly prepared from the outset to engage in extrafamilial activities, would not desire to risk changing her situation from one in which she cannot lose to one in which she may not be able to win. The conspicuous absence of married women from the occupational world in Muslim countries (on the average only 1 percent of all married women work in nonagricultural sectors of the economy) and from participation in public life could very well be caused, in part, by their own assessment of the gains and losses involved.

It should not be assumed from the preceding analysis of women's roles within the kinship and family systems that Egypt is a homogeneous society in which all women receive comparable treatment. Within the framework of a shared culture there exist a variety of subgroups, each with its own code of behavior and life-style (El Hamamsy, 1958). The degree to which a woman is subjected to the pattern of seclusion and exclusion depends on many factors, among them the social class of her family, the place in which they live, and her education. Significantly, though the woman's religion, whether she is Muslim or Coptic Christian, does not in itself vitally affect her situation because the concern with maintaining the honor of the family is not religious in origin.

Because of their location in the stratification system, urban-educated women, particularly those from upper-class families, constitute an elite who are spared much of the moral censure imposed on other social groups. Many of these women continue their schooling beyond the age of 15, something few other Egyptian women do irrespective of the age at which they marry. Moreover, of the single women who work in Egypt, almost half of them hold either professional or white-collar jobs and by virtue of their education belong to this elite. It is important to realize, however, that the progressive attitudes of this minority and their families do not imply a rejection of the traditional role definitions for women. In Egypt, as in other Muslim societies, modernity brings with it a struggle to incorporate higher female education and occupational emancipation within the traditional boundaries of marriage and motherhood (Camilleri, 1967: 592–594). There has been no attempt to restructure relationships between the sexes in relation to society. Women from this elite group have somewhat increased options and greater freedom to pursue activities outside the home, but not at the cost of risking dishonor by violating fundamental conceptions of femininity. For this elite group the canons of seclusion and exclusion seem to have been reformulated and broadened to include within the women's sphere female institutions outside the home. Thus higher education and employment have become acceptable as long as they do not bring women into contact with men, thus compromising their reputations.

Contrary to what is generally assumed, the process of urbanization in and of itself has not engendered significant revisions in the role definitions or patterns of behavior considered acceptable for women. The 40 percent of the Egyptian population living in urban areas (Supreme Council for Family Planning, 1971: 4) do not have fundamentally different expectations for the women in their families than do the rural villagers. Urban living provides greater access to educational institutions, nonagricultural jobs, and foreign cultural influences that may broaden and enrich a woman's life. It also brings about more frequent contact with men on the street and in public places. However it does not insulate a woman and her family from the ever-present concern with family honor. Within an urban environment the family adjusts and perhaps slightly relaxes the canons of feminine modesty, but it does not stop its surveillance of a woman's behavior. Urbanization has had less of an impact on Egyptian society than might have been anticipated because Cairo and other Egyptian cities do not conform to the usual character of large urban centers. Cairo consists of many self-contained quarters in which the small-scale, personalized, and bounded qualities of the traditional community persist. Thus Cairo city life is not characterized by the anonymity and mobility that would enable the family to accord women greater freedom without an accompanying effect on their reputation. Moreover many of the families who migrate to urban centers maintain close contact with their home village (Dodd, 1973: 47–51).

Higher education constitutes the most potent force stimulating a reassessment of women's roles. As discussed in subsequent sections of this chapter, secondary and university education affects women in a variety of ways: it expands the horizons of the individual woman so that she seeks fulfillment through activities outside of the home as well as through the roles of wife and mother; it equips women with the skills needed to enter an occupation and the inclination to accept employment; it reduces women's childbearing and so lessens the burdens of childrearing (Dodd, 1973: 52–54). Education for women also seems to have an impact on male members of the family. A study of Egyptian youth shows that the attitudes of boys towards women's emancipation are strongly influenced by the degree of education that their mothers had attained; the sons of well-educated mothers tended to favor the principle of equal pay for women and to approve of the wife working after marriage, whereas the sons of illiterate mothers were the group most often opposing these aspects of women's liberation (Dodd, 1968: 168–169). Nevertheless it should be emphasized that the highly educated woman, despite her readiness to explore external sources of prestige and satisfactions, does so in addition to—and not instead of—fulfilling traditional role expectations.

EDUCATION

Today, more than 100 years after the establishment of the first public primary school for women and almost half a century after the enactment of compulsory primary education, the vast majority of women in Egypt remain illiterate. According to the 1968 census, the rate of illiteracy for Egyptian women 12 years and older is 67.5 percent. This figure rises to 90.7 percent in the rural areas, more than twice as high as the 43.9 percent illiteracy rate in urban areas (1968 census table quoted in Fahmy and Ramzi, 1974: 26). Over the years the female literacy rates have always lagged considerably behind the figures for males. For instance, for the population 10 years old and older, female illiteracy was reported as 93.9 percent in 1937, 84.3 percent in 1947, and 83.13 percent in 1960, as compared with 76.5 percent, 64.36 percent, and 56.19 percent for males in those years (census book of Egypt, 1960, quoted in Abdel Kader, 1973: 30). The statistics for women above the age of 15 show an even higher rate of female illiteracy and a greater discrepancy between men and women.

Egypt's present educational system dates from the rise to power of the Free Officers in 1952. In 1953 the military regime, then headed by Mohammed Neguib, issued a law beginning the unification of the first stage of the educational cycle. The government also expanded the educational budget to make education more generally available to all children between the ages of 6 and 12. The 1956 military campaign of England, France, and Israel to seize control of the Suez Canal brought about the nationalization of all foreign schools. Egypt gradually has consolidated all schools into four levels—primary, preparatory, secondary, and university—and placed them under the jurisdiction of the national Ministry of Education. The basic system of formal education consists of a primary stage lasting for six years, followed by three years of preparatory schooling and three years of secondary education.

According to the Egyptian government their educational policy is based on "the right of every citizen irrespective of sex to have access to free education at all stages according to the talents and abilities within the framework of equal opportunities" (Islahel-Sherbini, 1971: 2). Education is compulsory for all children of both sexes from six through 12 years of age.

The stated intention of the school curricula is to prepare women to improve living conditions within the family, to help increase incomes, and to enlighten women sufficiently for them to understand the outlines of the country's developing plans (Islahel-Sherbini, 1971: 2). Thus the Egyptian educational system theoretically provides equality of opportunity for Egyptian girls but does not attempt to prepare women for the same roles as men. The educational system therefore reinforces the underlying cultural division in sex roles. The emphasis on religion at all stages of the educational cycle also acts to promote a conservative attitude on issues relating to women.

Women's access to education has improved through time, but girls remain under a considerable disadvantage. Table 1 shows the proportional

Table 1   Proportional   Distribution   (%)   of   Egyptian   Students   according   to
Educational Stage in 1969/1970

	Female	Male
Primary	38	62
Preparatory	32	68
Secondary	37	69
Higher	25	75

Source.   Islahel-Sherbini, 1971: 2.

distribution of students at various stages of the educational cycle. The
enrollment of boys at all levels is considerably higher. Unlike the pattern in
many other countries, however, the percentage of female enrollment remains relatively constant at all levels.

Fewer girls begin school than boys and a slightly higher proportion drop
out of school. Of the female student body enrolled in Egyptian primary
schools in 1970, only one-fifth of them managed to reach the preparatory
cycle. The attrition rate for women in the first year of preparatory school was
also greater, 8 percent, as compared to 5.6 percent for the male students
(Badran, 1972: 54–55). Another significant decrease in the proportion of
female enrollment occurs between the secondary and university stages. It is,
however, more surprising that women comprise as much as 25 percent of
the student body at the university since higher education for Arab women
was until recently socially unacceptable.

Although the quantity and quality of education for women leave much to
be desired, female attendance has grown significantly in the last 20 years,
and in fact, more rapidly than male enrollment. This expansion of educational opportunities for women has occurred despite a high rate of population growth which has considerably increased the number of school-age
children. Between the 1953–1954 and 1970–1971 school years the number
of females registered in various stages of the education cycle more than
tripled, going from 630,000 to 1,931,000 (Central Agency for Public
Mobilization and Statistics, 1975:40). As Table 2 indicates, the proportional
distribution of women has improved at every level. The percentage of
eligible girls attending primary school went from 56 to 62 percent in the
short period from 1960–1961 to 1969–1970 (Khalifa and Khalifa, 1973:
85). One of the most dramatic increases has been at the college level; in
1952–1953 women comprised only 8.4 percent of all students, whereas in
1970–1971 their share had risen to 28.4 percent (Khalifa and Khalifa, 1973:
86).

Women's access to education lags behind men's for a variety of reasons.

Table 2 Educational Status of Females 10 Years and Over in the Last Three Egyptian Census Years

Educational Status	1947		1960		1966	
	Number	Percentage	Number	Percentage	Number	Percentage
Illiterate	59,646,224	88.2	7,539,024	83.9	8,335,290	78.9
Read and write	726,204	10.7	1,125,953	12.5	1,835,232	17.4
Less than Secondary Certificate	52,971	0.8	101,785	1.1		
Secondary Certificate	16,801	0.2	201,698	2.2	359,459	3.4
University Degree	4,033	0.1	23,635	0.3	33,277	0.3
Total	60,446,233	100.0	8,991,095	100.0	10,563,358	100.0

Source. The Central Agency for Public Mobilization and Statistics, 1975: 38.

First and foremost, the underlying cultural imperative for all girls to marry and have children limits the relevance of formal education; no society that restricts women's role options so completely will ever accord a high priority to education for women. Until recently education for girls was considered detrimental to the fulfillment of their future roles: families feared that it would be harder to find a husband for an educated daughter, and many men did not believe that educated women made good wives. Moreover the pursuit of education necessitated giving a girl far more freedom to leave the confines of the home than was traditionally acceptable and also brought increased exposure to nonfamilial influences. It also frequently involved delaying marriage beyond the age considered proper for assuring the sexual purity of women.

During the course of the twentieth century, particularly in the last 20 years, education for women has become more acceptable. Among middle- and upper-class families education for daughters is now perceived as a status symbol that enhances their marriage prospects. This evolution in respectability, however, has not changed the fundamental belief that other considerations should take precedence over education for women, namely, reputation, economics, and family needs. Because education for women is not socially valued, many families prefer to keep their daughters at home to assist with agricultural work and the care of younger children. Some 38 percent of eligible girls, most of them in rural areas, still forfeit the chance for schooling because their parents place personal convenience ahead of their daughter's intellectual development (Khalifa and Khalifa, 1973: 85). Thus girls remain far more vulnerable than boys to losing the opportunity to begin or continue their education.

The availability of sex-segregated schools with female teachers constitutes an important factor in determining the acceptability of education for wo- men. Although Egypt is predominantly Muslim, there has recently been a trend towards coeducation. Even when such educational institutions have separate facilities for men and women, as is the case with many of the universities, parents still fear that the proximity of members of the opposite sex will compromise the reputations of their daughters. At higher levels of the educational ladder girl students are also more likely to have male teachers. Women comprise almost half of the primary school teachers, somewhat less than one-fourth of the faculty members of preparatory and secondary schools, and one-fifth and one-tenth, respectively, of university lecturers and professors (figures supplied by Egyptian Ministry of Education; Badran, 1972: 60). Although young girls are allowed to attend coeduca- tional primary schools, most families insist that their daughters refrain from any contact with men after puberty, even in a school environment. This accounts in large part for the significant drop in female enrollment between the primary and preparatory stages of the education cycle and for the further erosion during the beginning years of preparatory school.

Families also favor the education of the sons ahead of daughters for economic reasons. Although tuition in government schools is free through all stages of education, parents of school children incur many additional expenses for books, educational materials, and proper clothing. Moreover during the years of school attendance the students are unproductive and do not contribute to their families' income. The large size of families and the absence of domestic help among lower-class families have placed on daughters much of the burden of housework and child-care. Sending a girl to school then entails both the direct expenses of financing her new needs and the indirect costs of replacing her household services. A family of modest means with many children usually accords the education of their sons a higher priority because it is a better investment. Irrespective of the level of education a daughter completes, her family expects her to remain in the home, whereas the education of a son brings with it direct economic benefits in the form of the salary commanded by the type of employment for which he becomes qualified. In the absence of a state system of social security this earning power of the sons comprises the parents' major source of financial protection for emergencies and support for old age.

Despite the government's policy to make education available to all groups in the society, most women who pursue their education through the secondary school and university levels probably come from middle- and upper-class backgrounds. This is much more the case among women than men. Firstly, members of the elite do not have to choose financially between educating their sons or their daughters. Secondly, such highly placed families can violate social codes calling for female seclusion without suffering the dire consequences to their reputation that other groups would incur. The social composition of the female student body in institutions of higher learning usually indicates that these women are being sent to school primarily to cultivate their desirability as wives and not to prepare them for careers. Nevertheless women are serious students and have a lower dropout rate at the university level than do their male peers (Badran, 1972: 67).

Enrollment figures for the 1969–1970 academic year indicate that the most popular university faculties for women students were, in decreasing order of preference, humanities, the medical sciences, and social sciences. Other fields attracting a sizable proportion of female students in that year included education, natural sciences, and law (UNESCO, 1973: 490–491). Women attending higher institutes, which are equivalent to the universities, comprised, as would be expected, 100 percent of the students studying home economics and more than half of the students in courses of social work, physiotherapy, tourism, and linguistics (Badran, 1972: 58, 59).

The Egyptian bias in favor of education for men may seem overwheming, but when evaluated in the context of the cultural definition of women's place in the society, Egypt's accomplishments in expanding women's access to education seem impressive. Perhaps emphasis should be placed on the gains made in the increase of females at every level of the educational system rather than on the high proportion of women who remain illiterate. This extension of education to women compares favorably with the record of many other Muslim countries. The fundamental dilemma confronting any advocate of a further sexual balancing of the structure of opportunity is how to justify a greater societal investment in women's education by a society that precludes the useful application of that education. As the next section demonstrates, acceptance of women having a career has lagged behind the acceptance of education for women. Whether Egypt can continue to maintain the present inequitable system of education and adherence to a pattern of female occupational exclusion remains to be seen. Education for women, the emancipation of their minds from the confines of household and children, seems inherently inconsistent with the limitations on women's economic and political participation characteristic of Egypt.

WOMEN AND WORK

Published statistics indicate that Egyptian women have an exceedingly low level of participation in economic activities outside the home. The total female activity rate, that is, the proportion of females in the labor force out of the total female population, reported in 1968 for all occupational sectors was 8.1 percent (Central Agency for Public Mobilization and Statistics, quoted in Fahmy and Ramzi, 1974: 42). This figure represents an increase of 5.8 percent within 21 years (Badran, 1972: 18). Egyptian statistics, it should be noted, very much underestimate the significant contributions of women to agriculture. In many ways women are the backbone of the rural economy. Nevertheless comparisons of Egyptian women's labor force participation rates in the modern sector with countries at comparable stages of economic development outside of the Islamic world indicate that the involvement of the Egyptian women in the work outside of the home is relatively low. Moreover Egypt's economic development has not been paralleled by an increase in the number of women who are employed in nonagricultural activities. Nor can the relative absence of women from the paid labor force be explained by an unfavorable structure of demand in the labor market. A detailed breakdown of the industrial and occupational structure of the work force in Egypt reveals that men hold jobs usually filled by women in other societies. For example, although Egypt specializes in "light" types of manufacturing, particularly textiles, which in other countries usually attract a high proportion of women workers, only 2 percent of all Egyptian factory workers are women.

The low level of economic participation of Egyptian women outside the home is characteristic of Islamic societies and reflects cultural definitions of the sexual division of labor. The women's sphere is seen as the household, and the external world of work and public affairs is reserved for men. Rural women can participate in agricultural cultivation only because this is considered to be part of their household duties. When quantitative data are compared, Muslim societies consistently show the lowest female activity rates in nonagricultural employment. The prohibition against women working finds expression in the resentment that both men and women alike express toward women's economic activities outside of the home. Muslim women are restricted by the suspicion, mistrust, and fear that paid employment outside the home represents for the family and the community at large. The issue at stake for the family head involves more than a challenge to his ability to provide economically for his relatives; more critically it is a challenge to his control over the whereabouts and consequent behavior of his women. This challenge affects the Muslim male equally in his role of father, brother, or husband, which explains why kinsmen feel compelled to assume economic responsibility for all their women whether these are single, divorced, or widowed.

Therefore, because of the sociocultural context, until now few Egyptian women have been motivated to seek employment unless compelled to do so by dire economic need or inspired to seek a career through higher education. In understanding the desires of the women themselves, it is important to remember that until now the acknowledgement of kinship support has eliminated from the Egyptian woman's existence the need to work for economic survival. At the same time the social and psychological penalties paid by the average Egyptian woman who opts to work far outweigh the social and economic advantages that women derive from the work situation, especially since female attainments in extrafamilial activities are not sources of social recognition. The implicit or explicit atmosphere of mistrust and suspicion, which surrounds all working women, is further compounded for the single girl into the fear of spinsterhood, and for the divorcee, into the likelihood of reduced chances for remarriage. For the married woman the penalities involved could lead to the disruption of her marital life, and possibly to its dissolution. Under a legal system in which polygamy is permitted and in which the rights to divorce and custody of children are the sole prerogative of the male, such threats and penalties assume a certain sense of reality.

Among the small group of women who opt for employment outside the home several striking trends can be seen. Well-educated middle- and upper-class Egyptian women have fewer inhibitions against working than women who come from social classes that have a greater need for a supplementary income. Related to this, women in the labor force are clustered in occupations that require an education. Sex segregation in the society also has its corollary in the types of jobs that women accept; at all levels of the occupational structure the suitability of jobs for women depends on the degree of contact with men they necessitate. Younger women and women from urban backgrounds have a greater tendency to seek employment than do older women and women residing in the rural areas.

Men from middle- and upper-class backgrounds seem to have more liberal attitudes toward their wives' and sisters' working. Men from these groups appear able to overcome the traditional scruples about women seeking employment as long as two conditions are met: their women must have sufficient education to obtain a position of prestige, and the jobs must involve contact only with other women. Consequently, as shown in Table 3,

Table 3   Distribution of the Labor Force According to Education

	1961			1969		
Level of Educational Attainment	Male (%)	Female (%)	Female Employment Rate (%)	Male (%)	Female (%)	Female Employment Rate (%)
Illiterate	66.2	82.2	7.8	62.9	58.9	6.1
Reads and writes	26.9	5.2	1.3	27.1	10.7	2.7
Less than University degree	5.3	9.9	11.3	7.0	24.0	19.2
University degree	1.5	2.5	10.1	2.3	6.2	13.9
Unknown	0.1	0.3	—	0.3	0.3	—
Total	100.0	100.0	6.4	100.0	100.0	6.5

Source.   The Central Agency for Mobilization and Statistics, 1969, quoted in Khalifa and Khalifa, 1973: 59.

educated women comprise a surprisingly high proportion of the Egyptian female labor force. Literate women, who are a small minority of the overall female population, constitute almost half of the female workers. The resultant distribution of employed females, shown in Table 4, does not conform to patterns found elsewhere. In Egypt most working women are employed in professional and technical occupations. Taken together, women professionals, managers, and white-collar workers comprise slightly more than two-

Table 4 Distribution (%) of Egyptian Workers in Occupational Categories by Sex in 1968

Occupational Categories	Ratio of Males (%)	Ratio of Females (%)	Total (%)
Scientific, professional, and technical occupations	75.4	24.6	100
Managers	94.8	5.2	100
Clerks (white-collar)	88.7	11.3	100
Salespersons	90.3	9.7	100
Agricultural occupations	93.9	6.1	100
Transports and communications	99.3	0.3	100
Laborers and workers	94.9	5.1	100
Employees in service sector	81.3	18.7	100
Average	91.9	8.1	100

Source. The Central Agency for Public Mobilization and Statistics, Review No. 66, seventh year, 1969, quoted in Fahmy and Ramzi, 1974: 42.

fifths of all employed women. This predominance of fields requiring an education is quite remarkable, particularly in light of Egypt's record in providing an education for women.

Most employed women are concentrated in the relatively few occupations that are considered respectable for women. Women in many countries complain of the rigidity in their occupational structure. However the obviously closed occupational opportunity structure that restricts women from employment involving contact with men makes the situation in Egypt, as in other Muslim countries, unique. The imperative of sex-segregated employment for women has accorded to men a virtual monopoly over many types of jobs commonly filled elsewhere by women. School teaching is the primary career to offer educated women social acceptance because of the conservative atmosphere the classroom provides. Sex separation at the postprimary levels has naturally served to feminize teaching in preparatory, secondary, and vocational schools for girls. Recently the medical profession has begun to become more acceptable, but only in the specialties of pediatrics and gynecology. Relatively few women seek jobs as saleswomen, factory workers, receptionists, typists, waitresses, or maids, careers that frequently attract high female participation in other cultures, because these careers involve interaction with men.

The greater labor force participation by women in urban areas, 10.6 percent as compared to 4 percent for rural families in 1969 (Fergany, 1972), may reflect the urban environment's somewhat more liberal attitude toward women working, more frequent opportunities for wage employment, and higher concentration of educated women. The disparity in activity rates for women may, however, also result from an underestimation of the economic contribution of women in rural settings. Contrary to what the 4 percent figure implies, rural women usually assist with farmwork. Rural housewives frequently undertake field work, food processing, seeding, animal husbandry, cutting, weeding, and carrying of fertilizer. Men cannot undertake some of these tasks without inviting public disapproval for engaging in what is regarded as a woman's job (Smith, 1970: 369; Hussein, n.d.: 2). A field survey done in Egypt indicated that 44 percent of adult rural females were involved in production, which was approximately half the proportion of rural males, but the women gave fewer days of work and hence gained less income from their land (Badran, 1972: 22). Little of the economic activities of women in rural areas finds its way into official statistics because this agricultural work is considered to be part of her duty as a wife (Fahmy and Ramzi, 1974: 35). Another reason is that few women receive wages for their labor or control the income from their productivity.

Statistics reveal that younger Egyptian women are far more likely to work than older ones. Female participation in the labor force reaches its maximum in the 10 through 14 age group and decreases proportionately with advancing age to a minimum in the 65 years and older group. Women under 35 constitute 70 percent of all women workers. In contrast male employment reaches a peak in the 35 through 39 age group and then declines gradually (Fahmy and Ramzi, 1974: 15). Two different lines of interpretation can be used to explain these trends. Because the seclusion of women, according to traditional mores, need not take place until puberty, preadolescent girls are allowed to engage in work. After the woman marries and has children it is increasingly less acceptable for her to undertake economic activities outside the home. Alternatively, it can be reasoned that younger women have a greater proclivity to disregard some traditional restrictions either because they are more likely to be educated or because standards are slowly changing. Nevertheless not too much should be made of this trend. Even among the 10 through 14 age group only 9.7 percent of the girls in 1960 were included in the labor force, as compared to 28.4 percent of the boys (Central Agency for Public Mobilization and Statistics, quoted in Fahmy and Ramzi, 1974: 41).

Other factors also contribute to women's low rates of participation. Many employers believe that women make poor workers. Problems with absenteeism are far more pronounced for women, particularly married women, than for men. Women tend to report late for work. Their lack of geographic mobility precludes the accepting of transfers even if such reassignments entail promotions (Badran, 1972: 25–26). Working women everywhere must cope with the problem of reconciling familial responsibilities with career obligations, but in Egyptian society the disapproval of women accepting employment outside the home exacerbates these difficulties. It should be noted, however, that women do not generally exhibit more problematic patterns of behavior or lower productivity than do their male co-workers (Badran, 1972: 26).

Provisions of the Egyptian labor code frequently make the hiring of women more expensive. Egypt's labor laws demand equality of pay while at the same time they require many special benefits for women. Many of the laws, some of which date back 40 years, also forbid the employment of women in types of work considered to be physically harmful or strenuous. Most of the regulations currently in force reflect the standards established by the I.L.O. conventions (Fahme and Taha, 1972). According to Egyptian law, women in the private sector are entitled to a pregnancy and confinement leave of up to 50 days with 70 percent of salary, in the government sectors this leave consists of one month with 100 percent of salary. Within regular working hours nursing mothers are granted two nursing breaks per day of 30 minutes each for a period of 18 months. Enterprises employing women are required to have seats to enable them to rest. Any employer of more than 100 women must provide—either independently or jointly—suitable nurseries for their employees' children under six. Furthermore a female worker who chooses to retire after marriage or childbirth may claim a leaving indemnity equal to one-half month's pay for each of the first five years of service plus one month's pay for each additional year. The social insurance act also includes some special benefits for women relating to medical care during confinement and premature pension at the age of 45 (Islahel-Sherbini, 1971: 5–6).

As in many other countries, many of the provisions regulating the employment of women are honored in the breach. For example, many enterprises fail to provide nursery facilities. According to 1970 statistics, there are only 978 nurseries catering to 46,998 children, some two-thirds of which are located in rural areas (Abdel Kader, 1973: 41). Despite the laws mandating that women receive equal pay for equal work, women are usually paid lower wages. The difference between the averages for women and men is more pronounced in agriculture than in industry and commerce, and smaller in the service sector (Badran, 1972: 17). Employers frequently contravene the 1959 law that forbids discrimination according to sex. Societal conventions defining the type of employment deemed appropriate for women discourage them from applying for many jobs, but women are also discriminated against by the government and private organizations, which reserve positions for men. Women therefore remain excluded from some occupations because the labor laws are not actively enforced. Each government agency, for instance, is accorded the freedom to set the criteria for the nomination, appointment, and promotion of personnel. Thus women are not seriously considered for many appointments primarily because they have not previously held such a rank.

Despite the cultural prohibitions and job restrictions, more women, particularly the younger and better educated ones, are seeking employment. The female work participation rate, while still very low, has risen continuously in the past twenty years. Furthermore, statistics on labor force distribution show that between 1960 and 1968 women increased their proportions within several categories: from 18.1 percent to 24.6 percent of employees in the scientific, professional, and technical occupations; from 4.8 to 11.3 percent of the white-collar workers; and from 14.6 to 18.7 percent of those in the service sector (based on figures given by the Central Agency for Public Mobilization and Statistics, quoted in Fahmy and Ramzi, 1974: 44).

Over the past few years, among urban educated circles in Egypt sentiment has been voiced informally concerning changes in the institutional position of the Egyptian woman in the social structure. Unfortunately the extent and degree to which this is reflected in women's overt behavior cannot be verified empirically, since no census material is available for this country since 1960.

Specifically, reference has been made to the position of the urban single and widowed woman with respect to the emergence of more positive attitudes toward her employability, in the context of overall changes experienced by Egypt as a whole. Some highly educated Egyptian women maintain that the modern woman in their country is beginning to find self-recognition and self-realization in work and in pursuing higher education. Apparently the motivation to achieve higher levels of education and seek employment is stronger than ever among the urban middle and upper classes. Older women whose previous social circumstances or early marriage had prevented them from completing their schooling are now beginning to return to school and work.

Economic pressures have undoubtedly induced changes in the attitudes of young Egyptian men. The implicit atmosphere of mistrust and suspicion that has traditionally surrounded the working woman in Islamic countries is lessening considerably in a country like Egypt, where young males may now find it more advantageous to marry girls who hold jobs. The economic advantages that a double salary can provide to the young married couple suddenly seem to appeal to couples desirous to improve their standard of living. Such economic motivations, if they are to continue over time, will soon translate themselves at the societal level into viewing and rewarding more favorably the status of the employed female. Cynthia Nelson notes, for example, that now that women's economic contribution is beginning to be valued in Egypt, female employment, which a decade ago may have been detrimental to the marriageability of a young Egyptian woman, now gives a woman an advantage in the marriage market (Nelson, 1968: 67–76). It is not yet clear though what kind of structural facilitators have been mobilized on a societal level to promote such positive attitudes toward female participation in the outside world.

One immediate effect that may be expected is a gradual desegregation in the labor market. If in fact we can document what is informally claimed, that is, that a greater opportunity structure for the employment of Egyptian women is appearing outside of the traditional sectors such as in trade, industry, tourism, hotel management, and scientific research, it is bound to have a significant effect on woman's self-image and identity in the country.

FERTILITY AND FAMILY PLANNING

A decline in mortality in the last 25 years with no concomitant change in the level of fertility has resulted in a rapid increase in population. The current rate of population growth, 2.54 percent, if unchecked, will bring about a doubling of the population within a 25 year period (Supreme Council for Family Planning, 1971: 3). This rate of annual population increase represents a substantial rise over the figures computed from previous censuses in this century, which varied from a low of 1.1 percent in 1927, to a high of 1.8 in 1947. The population of Egypt, which stood at 9,715,000 in 1897 (Meade, 1967: 21), was estimated to be 33,329,000 in 1970 (Supreme Council for Family Planning, 1971: 4). It is estimated that the population will reach 50,100,000 in 1985 (Badran, n.d.: 2). Such growth places a great strain on the country—from both the pace at which the population is growing and the total burden of its size. A considerable portion of Egypt's resources must be used to provide basic services for the growing population rather than being invested to accelerate economic development. Moreover Egypt as a whole is already densely populated and cannot sustain a doubling or tripling of its populace, particularly since most of its surface area is unsuitable for habitation or cultivation.

Official recognition of the population growth problem came in 1962. The National Charter issued in that year states that, "This increase [in population growth] constitutes the most dangerous obstacle that faces the Egyptian people in their drive towards raising the standard of production in their country in an effective and efficient way" ("The Charter", 1962: 61). The government established a national policy to reduce population growth in 1965, with the goal, set in 1969, to reduce the crude birth rate by one point per year for 10 years. The government provides free birth control service and subsidized contraceptives through both public and private medical facilities. As of 1970 the Supreme Council for Family Planning, the national body vested with responsibility for directing the program, reported that 619,000 people accepted family-planning services offered in the national program; 458,000 of these in the public sector and 161,000 in the private. This figure constituted 12.6 percent of the eligible couples—not a sufficiently high proportion to have a significant impact in reducing the rate of population growth (Supreme Council for Family Planning, 1971: 15).

Like many other countries, Egypt has cultural factors that greatly affect the willingness of couples to limit their fertility. One subject of some controversy has been the pronatal tendencies contained within Islam. Several writers have maintained that Islam's strong pronatal orientation stems less from direct injunctions to procreate than from the support of conditions that result in high fertility (Sklani, 1960: 831–836; Kirk, 1968: 231). The reputed famous statement of the Prophet, "Marry and reproduce so that I may be proud of you before God," is not borne out by any direct reference to it in the Quran. Children are viewed as among the richest blessings granted by Allah, but they do not constitute the primary values. Surrender and obedience surpass by far the importance of wealth and children. High fertility patterns may, however, have been encouraged by the fatalistic streak in Islam, which stems from the strong belief in the active providence of God. It is Allah who creates sexuality and determines procreation and barrenness.

By contrast the Quran contains no ambivalence with respect to the importance of marriage for the Muslim population at large. This importance is located in the following specific institutional and religious prescriptions: All Muslim males are enjoined to marry in order to "complete half their religion"; the early and universal remarriage of widowed and divorced women is highly encouraged and sanctioned; the purpose of marriage is explicitly stated to be not only procreation but the gratification of spiritual and physical needs. This means that sexual intercourse within marriage is given a positive valuation independent of reproduction itself.

On the other hand, fertility control is not prohibited in Islam. The Quran has historically justified coitus interruptus to protect the male's property, to preserve the wife's health, and to allay anxiety over numerous children. Modern legal opinions support measures to prevent conception, and religious leaders in several Muslim countries have endorsed family-planning programs by declaring them to be sanctioned by Islamic doctrine. Only abortion and permanent sterilization are still met with strong opposition from Islamic religious authorities.

The lack of doctrinal injunction against most methods of birth control may prove to be a double-edged sword. It is to be hoped that the very lack of prohibition will allow the introduction and acceptance of desired contraceptive techniques. Actually, however, the absence of an organized clergy in Islam has meant that every parochial leader can interpret his faith as he understands it. Individual definitions of the situation and consequent variations in interpretation could conceivably hinder the implementation of fertility control programs.

The status of women in Egyptian society has a very great impact on their reproductive behavior and at this time seems to encourage pronatal tendencies. Through socialization, limited access to educational facilities, and erosion of the incentive for working, women are systematically stripped of any options other than marital and motherhood-related roles. Prohibitions imposed informally by males act in combination with resistance to change by women and reinforce the system, despite initial breakthroughs in economic modernization. Women, fully aware of the importance of marital position and motherhood for commanding respect and status within their own kin group and the community at large, are not about to deemphasize their only bargaining position in the social structure. As an investment children represent much more than a form of social insurance against the threat of divorce or polygamy, for women derive status from their motherhood role even if they are divorced or rejected for a second wife. Offspring guarantee women status and respect that extend far beyond their position in the conjugal home; they raise her own family's valuation of her and that of the community at large. Hence women tend to continue childbearing activities throughout their reproductive years whether they are happily married or not.

The optimistic expectation of many demographers that increased participation of married women in the work force will reduce reproduction within marriage has to be approached with caution. Many working wives are able to escape the intrinsic contradiction between the economic and familial role, which is a necessary prerequisite for labor force participation to decrease fertility. The availability of inexpensive domestic help and babysitting services provided by family members enables most working wives to combine both activities without much strain or guilt. Hence it is questionable that a substantial entry of married women into the work force would result in a reduction in fertility. Women who do work have selected types of occupations that allow a certain amount of flexibility in work conditions: specifically, lower-class wives are often involved in cottage-type industrial production, whereas the upper-class wife often chooses a career in teaching, which offers her the opportunity to plan the birth of her child during the three-month fully paid summer vacation.

Education is the most significant variable affecting fecundity. An inverse relationship holds between education and reproductive behavior within marriage. For each 100 Egyptian wives, those with a university education had 394 children; with secondary schooling, 583; with primary education, 703; with no education whatsoever, 708 children. Or, stated another way, for every 100 children born to the illiterate Egyptian female, 87 were born to women who could only read and write, 63 to women with secondary schooling, and 53 to women with university degrees (El Badry and Rizk, 1967: 138). Thus the fertility level decreases monotonically as female educational status rises, with the standardized average parity of university degree holders equal to approximately one-half that of illiterate women.

Education operates to reduce fecundity in a variety of ways. By postponing marriage, higher education delays the start of childbearing. More importantly, education seems to expand a woman's horizons and alter her aspirations. Highly educated women show a far greater propensity to seek employment and become economically independent. Although the educated Egyptian woman is not ready to give up marriage for a career, her attempt to reconcile traditional roles with employment motivates her to have fewer children. For the educated woman the costs involved in having additional children frequently outweigh the perceived benefits. Survey findings demonstrate that more low-income and rural mothers see advantages in having a large family; they therefore are more likely to choose to have more children rather than utilize contraceptives. This decision partially reflects the significant potential contribution of children to agricultural productivity and the woman's role identity as a bearer of children. In contrast, working urban mothers and those from high-income families are aware of the expenditures of money, time, and effort required by additional children. This divergence involves fundamental differences in what the family will do for the child in terms of investments in education, medical care, food, clothing, and shelter, but it also results from the educated woman's lesser dependence on children as the sole source of security and status (Badran, n.d.). Education also makes women more aware of the types of contraception available and enables them to be more efficient users. Therefore highly educated women are more successful in achieving the desired number of children than are women with less education (Khalifa and Khalifa, 1973: 222). Consequently increasing women's access to education may be the most effective long-term means of reducing the rate of population growth.

WOMEN AND POLITICAL AND SOCIAL PARTICIPATION

Despite the entrance of women into many formerly male sectors of society, politics remains a male bastion in many countries. The separation in Muslim culture between the family-centered sphere of women and the male-dominated suprafamilial world traditionally made politics an exclusively male concern. Even after the 1952 revolution and the formal incorporation of women into the political system in 1956, many Egyptians, both men and women, still believe that women should refrain from involvement in politics. A few months before women were given the right to vote, the *ulema* (scholars of Islamic law) at Al Azhar, the mosque university, issued a *fatwah* (ruling based on their interpretation of religious law) stating that women's inherently unstable nature made them unfit to vote; they therefore forbade on religious grounds the implementation of the proposed law according suffrage to women. The Egyptian government, which has ultimate control over the appointment of the head of Al Azhar, conveniently found it necessary to send the incumbent rector to Yemen as the Egyptian ambassador. The passage of the law has not, however, completely transformed attitudes on the subject. A 1969 study of public opinion in Cairo, for example, revealed that one-third of the inhabitants, with a higher proportion of men than women, objected to women's involvement in political affairs for the following reasons: women are not equal to men; women belong exclusively in the home; and women's participation in political life is contrary to customs, traditions, and religion. More of the younger, educated, and middle-class respondents of both sexes favored women's participation more than the older, uneducated, and lower-class individuals (Diab, 1968: 281).

During the nearly 20 years since women were enfranchised, the majority of women have refrained from casting their ballot or engaging more actively in politics. Table 5 shows women's record of political participation between

Table 5   Women's Record of Political Participation in Elections to State Council

	Registered Voters		Candidates		Elected Members		Designated Members	
Year	*Male*	*Female*	*Male*	*Female*	*Male*	*Female*	*Male*	*Female*
1957	5,951,721	274,439	1207	6	348	2	2	—
1964	7,752,462	660,274	1727	25	342	8	10	—
1969	6,602,202	803,959	797	6	348	2	9	1
1971	7,171,785	907,382	1670	35	343	7	9	1

Source.   Shafie and Bassyouni, 1974.

1956 and 1971. It can be seen that the number of women who are registered voters or candidates is still very small in relation to the number of men. Most women who participate in government come from big cities. In the 1971 elections for the State Council, for instance, of the eight women elected, five were from Cairo, one from Alexandria, and one from Guiza (Shafie and

Bassyouni, 1974). In many rural communities women are virtually disen-
franchised because of male attitudes; membership in the Arab Socialist
Union, Egypt's only legal political party, is a prerequisite for voter registration, and in rural villages men frequently refuse to open the local branch of
the Arab Socialist Union to women (Harik, 1974: 235). Women's low rate of
political participation also results from a variety of other factors. Egyptian
law makes voting obligatory for men but not for women; women are
generally less interested in politics than are men and feel more constrained
by time because of their household responsibilities; as a consequence of
their upbringing many women do not feel capable of exercising their political rights; women fear public prejudice and familial objections (Badran,
1972: 45).

It has generally been more acceptable for women to participate in voluntary associations than in politics, particularly in organizations that have a
social-welfare orientation because the activities of such groups are seen as
compatible with women's traditional roles. According to a Ministry of Social
Affairs Survey, in 1960 there were 3195 voluntary associations with some
700,000 members, of whom 8 percent were women. Two-thirds of these
registered associations limited membership to men, about 20 percent were
mixed, and 4 percent were exclusively female. Reasons cited by the Ministry
for the low proportion of women included vestiges of traditional attitudes,
their lower degree of education, and traces of a capitalist system which
encouraged passivity in women. Shortly afterward the government embarked on a campaign to persuade voluntary organizations to refocus their
interests from religion to social welfare (Berger, 1970: 101), a move that
would increase the membership of women. It is difficult to assess the results
of this effort, but the next such official survey, 9 years later, show that the
participation of women had increased dramatically. Ministry of Social Affairs statistics for 1969 list 4992 voluntary organizations working in the
social welfare field, of which approximately one-fourth were located in
Cairo. A study of the organizations affiliated with the Cairo Regional Council
for Social Agencies indicates that three-fourths of the members were women
and that women comprised 83 percent of the board memberships (Badran,
1972: 47). This increase in membership of women between 1960 and 1969
may merely reflect differences in criteria for the inclusion of organizations
rather than a significant rise in women's involvement.

Studies show that education comprises an important factor in influencing
women to join voluntary associations. The vast majority of women members
have at least an intermediate level of education. Other considerations include the attitude of their husbands, the prior membership of friends, their
concurrence with the objectives of the organization, and, the burden of
household responsibilities (Badran, 1972: 47–48). It is possible, though, that

since most women members are housewives, younger, highly educated women may now prefer professional employment to membership in voluntary associations (Merriam, 1975), and thus may be leaving such groups to the less educated women.

Under both the Nasser and Sadat regimes the attitude of the Egyptian government toward the full political participation of women has been somewhat ambivalent. Many official statements have been made in favor of women assuming a greater part in the development of the country, and the principle of equality between the sexes has been written into the Constitution and the National Charter. However the government has been reluctant to assume the responsibilities of fulfilling these pledges. The acceptance of political women would, in many respects, signify approval for a drastic redefinition of roles for women, for it is doubtful that the active involvement of women in political life could come within the framework of the present cultural strictures. Changing the condition of women has never been viewed as sufficiently urgent a problem for the government to accord it a high priority. Moreover any serious effort to elevate the status of women would entail reform of the personal status law provisions on divorce, marriage, and inheritance; both administrations have been aware that many Egyptians would consider this a direct assault on the Islamic religion (Harik, 1974: 179). Of the two political leaders President Anwar El Sadat appears to be more sympathetic than was President Gamal Abdul Nasser. Nasser may have been more conservative or he may have decided on pragmatic grounds to postpone any radical measures designed to liberate women from the burden of traditional restrictions until they were supported by a broad section of the population. Consistent with this approach, his wife did not appear in public in Egypt until the 1964 visit of Mr. and Mrs. Krushchev (Mansfield, 1965: 115–116).

Government action thus far on issues relating to the status and roles of women has been primarily symbolic: statements supporting greater equality of women, the enfranchisement of women, and the appointment of two women to cabinet office. The National Charter, presented by Nasser in May of 1962 to establish the basic principles toward which the Egyptian political system would strive, states that, "Woman must be regarded as equal to man and must therefore, shed the remaining shackles that impede her free movement so that she might take a constructive and profound part in shaping life" ("The Charter", 1962: 74). The Constitution of 1971 reaffirms this commitment. According to Article 11, "The State shall guarantee the proper coordination between the duties of woman towards the family and her work in the society, considering her equal with man in the fields of political, social, cultural and economic life without violation of the rules of Islamic jurisprudence" (Constitution of the Arab Republic of Egypt, 1971: 11).

Similarly President Anwar El Sadat's Programme of National Action, endorsed by the national congress of the Arab Socialist Union in 1971, mentions the need for women to play a political role. On the subject of feminist organizations it exhorts that "The feminist movement is storing valuable capacities which should be given the opportunity to fully perform their mission in the field of national action" (Programme of National Action, 1971: 83).

Even on the level of abstract principles, official commitment has been less than wholehearted. The 1971 Constitution, for example, prefaces Article 11, which deals with the equality of women, with another that proclaims that the family is the basis of the society and commits the state to its preservation. Furthermore the wording of Article 11 itself emphasises the proper coordination between the duties of the women to the family and to society and makes the search for equality subject to the rules of Islamic jurisprudence. Other sections in this article on the social and moral constituents of the society pledge the state to abide by and promote the moral standards defined by Egyptian tradition (Constitution of the Arab Republic of Egypt, 1971: 10–11). However the maintenance of the existing social order, and particularly the Islamic conception of the family, is not compatible with any effort to redefine women's roles toward greater equality. Thus the Constitution seems to subordinate any improvement in the status of women to other goals that preclude any meaningful action on their behalf.

The manner in which women were accorded the right to vote is another illustration of the basic conservatism of the government. The Constitution of 1956 and subsequent legislation enfranchised women without providing the legal or institutional framework to facilitate their participation. By making voting for women optional and by failing to establish a women's wing of the Arab Socialist Union, the government virtually ensured that only a very small proportion of women would exercise their option to vote. Sadat's proposed reorganization of the Arab Socialist Union to strengthen the women's section, if carried out, may somewhat improve women's rates of political participation.

The reform of the personal status laws has been recognized by educated women and by the government as central to any effort to elevate the status of women and provide them with greater security. The religious underpinning of the personal status laws, however, makes their reform a particularly sensitive issue because opponents can easily raise the banner of Islam endangered. Nevertheless there do exist precedents for the modification of these laws. In 1920 women gained the right to go to court to seek divorce on grounds of desertion or impotence. These grounds were then expanded to include cruelty. The government also raised the legal age for marriage to 16 for girls and 18 for boys; the age at which the father could claim custody of minor children was raised to 9 for boys and 11 for girls (Hopkins, 1969: 243, 374). Unfortunately too few women are sufficiently educated to be aware of these rights.

A committee appointed in 1958 by the Egyptian government to review the personal status laws was composed primarily of Muslim sheiks but also included one woman lawyer. Among the proposals they considered were making polygamy illegal except in cases of "necessity" when the wife was sterile or had an incurable disease, raising the marriage age, abolishing the law whereby a husband can summon the police to force the return of his wife, and changing the divorce laws (Mansfield, 1965: 117–118). In August 1966, after several postponements, the committee published a new draft bill which was cautious and far weaker than the Tunisian reforms of 1956. Under the draft law polygamy was not eliminated, but the taking of a second wife was made grounds for divorce by the first wife. For both parties divorce could only be granted through the courts, which would first attempt to reconcile the couple. If the husband demanded the divorce and arbiters found that he was the party at fault, there were intimations that his petition for divorce might be denied. The father would still be awarded custody of the children. However the age at which he could claim the children was to be raised to 11 for boys and 13 for girls, and the mother's access to the children after that time was to be protected. Nevertheless the publication of the proposed revisions provoked strong complaints from the bastions of orthodoxy, which charged that the new law would violate the sanctity of the home. After a mass rally at Al Azhar University, the government withdrew the bill (Hopkins, 1969: 375–376).

Sadat's efforts to revise the personal status laws have similarly been frustrated by the unwillingness of the government to resist pressure from the conservative elements in the population. A new policy paper that originally included a proposed new law on the personal status of individual citizens, especially women, was presented to parliament by President Sadat in the spring of 1974 and was then endorsed in a national plebiscite (Tanner, 1974: 14). Again, when Al Azhar spearheaded protests that the law would contravene Islamic tradition, the government quietly eliminated these clauses.

Perhaps the most significant action of the government with regard to women has been the appointment of two Egyptian women to cabinet rank positions, both as Minister of Social Affairs. Dr. Hekmat Abu Zeid became the first woman minister in 1963; another woman, Dr. Aisha Rateb, followed her in 1971. The choice of this ministry obviously reflects the traditional feminine association with social affairs. It should be noted that men continue to hold the important administrative staff positions and determine most of the policy. Nevertheless the acceptance of women in the highest councils of the state sets a precedent that may inspire other women to greater participation in social and political activities.

Egypt, like other Muslim countries, does not provide fertile ground for the growth of a feminist movement. The lack of interest women exhibit in public affairs and their inclination to leave politics to men have stifled any strong stirrings of feminist activity. Moreover until now the respect and socio-psychological rewards derived by women from their traditional status have prevented women from expressing sentiments of protest and rebellion with respect to their secluded position. Seclusion of women within the home and its concomitant insulation from contemporary issues also make it difficult to organize women.

The very women who could provide the leadership for a feminist movement, those with education and high social standing, generally have little inclination to do so because they suffer the fewest disabilities under the present system. These women are freed from many of the restrictions that apply to less educated and lower-class women. Elite women dominate women's voluntary associations, most of which are exclusively social welfare in their orientation. Other women's organizations, like the Cairo Women's Club, resemble the sophisticated clubs of leisured society women found elsewhere in the world.

Two issues, feminine suffrage and the reform of the personal status laws, have inspired small groups of educated women to organize. The role of Huda Sha'rawi, the founder of the Egyptian Feminist Union, was mentioned earlier in this chapter. Two of the political parties dissolved by the 1953 law doing away with the then-existing groups were the National Feminist Party and the Daughters of the Nile (Abdel-Malik, 1968: 91). Upper-class women who do become active are tolerated because of their social background, but they are rarely taken seriously. One accusation leveled at them is that they seek to imitate the fashion of European ladies (Abdel Kader, 1973: 87), and the tone and scope of the activities of many of these associations frequently lend themselves to this charge. A few more strident women's organizations have been formed, but they have received little support from women or men. The position of the Arab Socialist Union as the only legal political party in Egypt means that any contemporary women's movement would have to be formed within its framework and would be limited by the need for prior endorsement by the male Egyptian political leaders.

Women have sporadically broken through the confines of seclusion into active political participation in times of great national fervor. As mentioned earlier, women spontaneously became involved in mass protests during the 1919 uprising against the British. Similarly the issue of the liberation of the Suez Canal aroused women in 1951 and 1952 (Berques, 1960: 165). Defeat in the 1967 war also engendered considerable soul-searching on the part of all Egyptians and a willingness to reconsider the role of women in society. The following statement by an Egyptian, Muslim man illustrates this trend:

> In the months following our military defeat, an awareness has been growing of our own internal shortcomings and errors, and an insistence upon the need for more radical, internal reform . . . . On this particular subject of the emancipation of women, I have more than once heard with my own ears quite ordinary men-in-the-street declare that one of the reasons why the Israelis defeated us was that their women took part, not only in the preparation, but even in the execution of that war—flying airplanes, driving armoured vehicles, carrying guns [quoted in Nelson, n.d.: 34].

Since that war, efforts by Egyptian women to take a more active part in the "struggle for liberation" throughout the Arab world, although not very frequent or significant, have generally been endorsed (Nelson, n.d.: 33). It remains to be seen whether the new mood of national self-confidence resulting from the Arab world's sudden central role in world affairs will be an impetus for change or for reaction.

CONCLUSION

We now come to the critical issue of predicting future influences on the status of the Egyptian woman. It has been shown that the position of the Egyptian woman is not exactly a favorable one. Cultural strictures requiring the seclusion of women continue to limit a woman's role options primarily to being a wife and a mother. Adult Egyptian women have very low rates of participation in school attendance, employment, and political activism. Even when compared with the figures for other Arab states, the percentage of adult Egyptian females who are literate and the female proportion of the total nonagricultural, economically active population are not encouraging (Commission on the Status of Women, 1973: 14, 19).

The question that now should be asked is what realistic prospects exist in Egyptian society to undermine the persistence of such a condition. Some discernable forces already at work in Egyptian society may have significance for the modernization of Egyptian females. Recently women's access to education has improved considerably. More than half of eligible Egyptian girls now begin primary school. The proportion of female enrollment at the secondary school and university levels has also increased dramatically. As the Egyptian economy has been progressively nationalized and Arabic has replaced foreign languages as the medium through which business is conducted, Egyptian women have had new work opportunities in jobs formerly held by foreign women. Labor force statistics indicate that Egyptian women are gradually moving into some nontraditional occupational fields. The marriage age for women in Egypt is also somewhat higher now than it was formerly; figures indicate that 19 is the median age of marriage for women (Statistical Office, 1973: 473). The progressive decline in women's fertility during the last 10 years, though still not of sufficient magnitude to lower dramatically the rate of population growth, provides another indication that forces are currently restructuring women's role options (UNESCO, 1973: 473).

Perhaps the most important considerations in predicting the demise of the traditionally subordinate social position of the Egyptian woman are the currently emerging economic constraints. The effect of these on the eventual "liberation" of the Egyptian woman can be predicted along several lines. First, it may become increasingly difficult for male members of the kinship group to meet their obligations to provide economically for all their women-folk in need. This could mean the beginning of the end of the Egyptian woman's economic dependency upon the male. Fragmented evidence of the incipient disintegration of traditional family responsibilities has already been suggested by the higher work participation rate of divorced women in Egypt. This indicates that divorced females are not receiving the same kind of economic support that is granted to women in other marital statuses, although such support has traditionally been prescribed. The divorced woman may have become the first to be rendered self-responsible in the conflict between the continued extension of family support and increasing economic demands. Single women may soon follow. With the advent of higher levels of economic development, rising expectations and aspirations may well create a situation in which Egyptian families will need to depend on additional sources of income that a well-trained and employable unmarried daughter could provide.

One other important way in which economic constraints may operate to affect the position of the woman is by way of lowering the economic valuation of children in Egyptian society and thereby devaluing somewhat maternal related roles. The sweeping change of economic and political modernization experienced by Egypt may bring about an incipient decline in infant mortality rates. Under current economic conditions in Egypt children are still perceived as economic assets—cheap labor and a form of social security for aged parents. Successive increases in national productivity levels, new systems of economic production that reduce drastically the opportunities for unskilled workers and child labor, coupled with rising levels of individual family expectations and aspirations, are expected to effect a reevaluation of values and attitudes related to childbearing. As children become more difficult and more expensive to raise, a reduction in their high valuation is expected to occur. This is of course the very cornerstone of the demographic transition that, when set in motion, will increasingly guarantee the survival of most births. The literature abounds in references to the immediate effect of this phase on the fertility levels. Not much systematic research has been carried out on the effects of a decline in the economic value of children on the role-related behavior and concepts of self-identity among women.

For the Egyptian woman the structural ramification of a reduction in the value attached to children, and consequent lower appreciation of the one and only role and function from which she derived high status for so long, could be severe. The danger lies in the particular mechanisms of adjustment that will be made available to women during the transition to a restructured and redefined situation that supports and honors women's status in terms of their accomplishments in areas from which men derive their authority and prestige.

Theoretically we conceptualize a smooth progression from the time when men begin to place less value on having large families to the development of conditions in which (a) the male's valuation of woman's traditional role declines and (b) women themselves begin to manifest significant interests in suprafamilial activities and functions. Realistically, however, neither the Egyptian man nor woman is even halfway prepared for such a restructuring of the sex roles. This means that there will be considerable gaps of time during which Egyptian women will be granted neither respect nor rights, and during which they will have to struggle hard to establish sources from which to draw status placement and self-identity. In the industrialization of the Western world, women were "culturally" prepared to cope with the structural ramifications of the demographic and economic transition that resulted in a lower economic value attached to children. The institutional arrangements in Muslim Egypt have, unfortunately, not provided sufficient mechanisms for allowing women to gradually prepare themselves for such a drastic transformation. We foresee considerable difficulty within Egypt as well as within other Muslim societies as they attempt to redefine what specific types of extrafamilial activities are appropriate or acceptable for women to pursue, even when women are granted the right to work and the right to be educated.

BIBLIOGRAPHY

Abdel Kader, Soha. 1971. "Conservative and Modern Egyptian Families." M.A. Thesis. Cairo: The American University in Cairo.

———, Compiler. 1973. "A Report on the Status of Egyptian Women, 1900–1973." Cairo: The American University in Cairo Social Research Center.

Abdel-Malik, Anouar. 1968. *Egypt: Military Society.* Translated by Charles Lam Markmann. New York: Vintage Books.

Abou Zeid, Hekmat, et. al., 1970. *The Education of Women in the U.A.R. During the 19th and 20th Centuries.* Paris: UNESCO.

Ammar, Hamed. 1954. *Growing Up in an Egyptian Village: Silva, Province of Aswan.* New York: Octagon Books.

Amin, Kassem. 1899. *The Emancipation of Women.* Cairo.

Badran, Hoda. 1972. "Arab Women in National Development: A Study of Three Arab Countries: Egypt, Lebanon and Sudan." Prepared for the Seminar on Arab Women in National Development, Cairo, sponsored by UNICEF in cooperation with the League of Arab States Functional Literacy Centre.

————. n.d. "Population and Development: Egyptian Women's Perception." Unpublished paper.

Badry, M. A. El, and Hanna Rizk. 1967. "Regional Fertility Differences among Socio-Economic Groups in the United Arab Republic." *Proceedings of the World Population Conference 1965,* Vol. II. New York: United Nations.

Bellah, Robert. 1968. "Islamic Tradition and the Problem of Modernization." Mimeo.

Berger, Morroe. 1964. *The Arab World Today.* New York: Doubleday.

————. 1970. *Islam in Egypt Today: Social and Political Aspects of Popular Religion.* London: Cambridge University Press.

Berques, Jacques. 1960. *Les Arabes D'Hier à Demain.* Paris: Édition du Seuil.

Camilleri, Carmel. 1967. "Modernity and the Family in Tunisia." *Journal of Marriage and the Family* **29**: 592–598.

Census of Population. 1963. Cairo: Department of Statistics and Census.

Central Agency for Mobilisation and Statistics. 1969. Review No. 66, seventh year.

Charnay, Jean-Paul. 1971. *Islamic Culture and Socio–Economic Change.* Leiden: E. J. Brill.

"Charter, The." 1962. Cairo: Information Department.

"Children and Youth in National Planning and Development in the Arab States." 1970. Report of a UNICEF Seminar, Beirut, Lebanon, February.

Central Agency for Mobilization and Statistics, 1975. *The Egyptian Woman in Two Decades (1952—1972).* Cairo: Population Studies and Research Centre.

Churchill, Charles W. 1967. "The Arab World." In *Women in the Modern World.* Edited by Raphael Patai. New York: Free Press, pp. 106–128.

Commission on the Status of Women. 1973. *Study On the Interrelationship of the Status of Women and Family Planning.* New York: United Nations Economic and Social Council.

"Constitution of the Arab Republic of Egypt, The." 1971. Cairo: Ministry of Information.

Dawood, J. J., Translator. 1959. *The Koran.* Rev. Ed. Middlesex, England: Penguin Classic.

Deonna, Lawrence. 1970. *Moyen-Orient: Femme du combat, de la terre et du sable.* Geneva: Labor et Fides.

Diab, Fuad. 1968. "Measuring Public Opinion in Cairo Toward Granting Political Rights to the Egyptian Woman." In *Readings in Social Psychology in Arab Countries.* Edited by Loweis Melika. Cairo: Dar El Kawmia.

Dodd, Peter C. 1968. "Youth and Women's Emancipation in the United Arab Republic." *The Middle East Journal* **22** (Spring): 159–172.

————. "Family Honor and the Forces of Change in Arab Society." *International Journal of Middle East Studies* **4** (January): 40–54.

El-Hennawy, Nemat. 1973. "Population and Development in Egypt." Prepared for the Symposium on Population and Development of the United Nations Economic and Social Council, Cairo. E/CONF.60/SYM.I/33.

Fahme, Aish Ahmad, and Hamdi Muhammed Taha. 1972. "Arab Women in Labor Legislations." Prepared for the Conference on Arab Women in National Development, Cairo. Sponsored by UNICEF, League of Arab States, and Arab States Adult Functional Literacy Centre.

Fahmy, Noha, and Nahed Ramzi. 1974. "Women's Role in Social Development." Presented at the Afro-Arab Parliamentary Congress, Cairo, May.

Family Planning Programme of the Arab Republic of Egypt. 1971. Cairo: Supreme Council for Family Planning.

Fergany, Nader. 1972. "Egyptian Women and National Development." Paper prepared for the Conference on Arab Women in National Development. Sponsored by UNICEF, League of Arab States, and Arab States Adult Functional Literacy Centre.

Gadalla, Saad. 1974. "Country Report: Egypt." Prepared for Conference on "The State of the Social Sciences in the Middle East," Alexandria, May.

Gibb, H. A. R. 1961. "Women and the Law." In "Colloque sur la sociologie musulmane." *Correspondence d'Orient, Actes.* Brussels, September, pp. 233–248.

Goldberg, Steven, 1973. *The Inevitability of Patriarchy.* New York: William Morrow and Company.

Gordon, David. 1968. *Women of Algeria: An Essay on Change.* Cambridge, Massachusetts: Harvard University Middle East Monograph No. XIX.

Hamamsy El, Laila. 1958. "The Role of Women in the Development of Egypt." *The Middle East Forum* **33** (June): 592–601.

Harik, Ilya F. 1974. *The Political Mobilization of Peasants: A Study of an Egyptian Community.* Bloomington, Indiana, and London: Indiana University Press.

Hilal, Jamil M. 1970. "Father's Brother's Daughter, Marriage in Arab Communities: A Problem for Sociological Explanation." *Middle East Forum* **XLVI**(4): 73–84.

Hopkins, Harry. 1969. *Egypt The Crucible: The Unfinished Revolution in the Arab World.* Boston: Houghton Mifflin Company.

Hussein, Aziza. 1953. "The Role of Women in Social Reform in Egypt." *The Middle East Journal* **7**: 440–450.

———, et. al. n.d. "Country Report on the Arab Republic of Egypt." Cairo: Mimeo. Prepared for the United Nations Commission on the Status of Women.

Islahel-Sherbini. 1971. "Working Paper on Egypt." Prepared for the United Nations Seminar on the Participation of Women in Economic Life, Libreville, Gabon, July–August. SO245/3 (9) Gabon.

Khalifa, Ahmed M., and Atef F. Khalifa. 1973. *Status of Women in Relation to Fertility and Family Planning in Egypt.* Cairo: National Center for Sociological and Criminological Research.

Kirk, Dudley. 1968. "Factors Affecting Moslem Natality." In *Population and Society.* Edited by Charles Nam. Boston: Houghton Mifflin.

Langdon-Davies, John. 1928. *A Short History of Women.* London: Watts and Company.

Levy, Reuben. 1965. *The Social Structure of Islam.* Cambridge: Cambridge University Press.

Mansfield, Peter. 1965. *Nasser's Egypt.* London: Penguin African Library.

Mazhar, Ismail. 1949. *Women in the Age of Democracy.* Cairo: El Haditha Press.

Meade, Donald C. 1967. *Growth and Structural Change in the Egyptian Economy.* Homewood, Illinois: Richard D. Irwin, Inc.

Merriam, Kathleen Howard. 1975. "The Emergence of Egyptian Women into Public Life of Contemporary Egypt." *Newsletter* (American Research Center in Egypt) **94:** 3–8.

Muhyi, Ibrahim Abdulla. 1959. "Women in the Arab Middle East." *Journal of Social Issues* **XV**(3): 45–57.

Nelson, Cynthia. 1968. "Changing Roles of Men and Women: Illustrations from Egypt." *Anthropological Quarterly* **41**(2): 57–77.

———. 1972. "Selection and Emancipation: Changing Roles of Man and Woman in the Middle East." Unpublished paper.

———. 1973. "Women and Power in Nomadic Societies of the Middle East." In *The Desert and the Sown: Nomads in the Wider Society.* Edited by C. Nelson, Berkeley: University of California Institute of International Studies, pp. 43–59.

———. n.d. "The Politics of Segregation: Women and Power within Pastoral and Sedentary Societies of the Middle East." Mimeo.

Nortman, Dorothy. 1973. *Population and Family Planning Programs: A Factbook.* New York: Population Council.

Omran, Abdel R., Ed., 1973. *Egypt: Population Problems and Prospects.* Chapel Hill.: University of North Carolina.

Paturet, G. 1886. *La Condition Juridique de la Femme Dans L'Ancienne Egypte.* Paris: Ernest Leroux.

Petrie, W. M. Flinders. 1923. *Social Life in Ancient Egypt.* London: Constable and Company, Ltd.

"Programme of National Action." 1971. Presented by President Anwar El Sadat to the Second General National Congress of the Arab Socialist Union. Cairo: Ministry of Culture and Information.

Prothro, Edwin Terry and Lutfy Najib Diab. 1974. *Changing Family Patterns in the Arab East.* Beirut: American University of Bierut.

Rabie, Hassanayn M. Interview. May 14, 1974.

Ragai (Shafik), Doris. 1940. *La Femme et le Droit Religieux de l'Egypte Comtemporaine.* Paris: Librairie Orientaliste Paul Geuthner.

"Role of Arab Women in National Development." 1972. Report of a Conference sponsored by UNICEF, League of Arab States, and Arab States Adult Functional Literacy Centre. Cairo.

Salem, Elie. 1965. "Arab Reformers and the Reinterpretation of Islam." *The Muslim World* **LV**(4): 311–320.

Shafie, Erfan, and Amvra El Bassyouni, 1974. "The Role of Women in Economic and Political Development." In *Proceedings of the Afro-Arab Inter-Parliamentary Women's Conference.* Cairo, May.

Shafiq, Doria. 1956. *The Egyptian Woman.* Cairo: Dar El Gamaheer.

Sklani, Mahmud. 1960. "La Fécondité dans les pays arabes." *Population* **15** (October–December): 831–836.

Smith, Harvey, et. al. 1970. *Area Handbook for the United Arab Republic (Egypt).* Washington, D.C.: U.S. Government Printing office.

Smith, Margaret. 1928. *Rābia' the Mystic and Her Fellow-Saints in Islam.* Cambridge: Cambridge University Press.

Statistical Office, Department of Economic and Social Affairs. 1968. *Demographic Yearbook 1967.* New York: United Nations.

———.1973. *Demographic Yearbook 1972.* New York: United Nations.

Supreme Council for Family Planning. 1971. "Family Planning Programs in the Arab Republic of Egypt." Cairo: Ahram Press.

Taha, Ahmed. 1964. *Woman: Her Struggle and Work.* Cairo: Dar El Gamaheer.

Tanner, Henry. 1974. "Sadat Says War Made Egypt Truly Free." *The New York Times,* April 14.

UNESCO. 1973. *Statistical Yearbook 1972.* Paris: United Nations.

Vatikiotis, P. 1960. *The Modern History of Egypt.* London: Weidenfeld and Nicolson.

Wilbur, Donald N. 1969. *United Arab Republic–Egypt: Its People, Its Society, Its Culture.* New Haven: Human Relation Area Files.

Youssef, Nadia H. 1971. "Social Structure and the Female Labor Force: The Case of Women Workers in Muslim Middle Eastern Countries." *Demography* **8** (November): 427–449.

———. 1974. *Women and Work in Developing Countries.* Berkeley: University of California, Population Monograph Series, No. 15.

Zanati, M. S. 1959. *The Relationship Between Men and Women Among the Arabs.* Cairo: Dar El Gameat El Masria.

Chapter Three

BANGLADESH: A STRUGGLE WITH TRADITION AND POVERTY

Audrey Chapman Smock

HISTORICAL AND CULTURAL BACKGROUND

Bangladesh, formerly East Bengal and then East Pakistan, although one of the newly independent states on the world scene, shares in two of the oldest and richest traditions. Its roots reach back in two directions, both to ancient Indic civilizations and to Islamic culture. This northeast corner of the Indian subcontinent has been influenced by successive Indian civilizations but its people have retained a certain autonomy and cultural distinctiveness. Although the lack of extensive archaeological excavation and research in the area has made it difficult to detail its cultural history during the formative and classic ages of Indian civilization, from what is known it seems that the northeast stood outside of the mainstream, at the periphery of the major cultural changes that slowly diffused through the northern half of the subcontinent (Wilbur, 1964: 191). The crystallization of the Bengali language from the classical Sanskrit during the Indian medieval period provided the region with a linguistic underpinning for its separate cultural identity (Spear, 1958: 197). Following the conquest by Muslim invaders from Central Asia, a substantial portion of the people gradually converted to Islam. This reinforced the sense of distinctiveness and eventually found expression in the demand to create an independent state.

Many of the major Indian empires, such as the Mauryan of the third and second centuries B.C., the Gupta of the fourth and fifth centuries A.D., and the Mughal of the sixteenth through eighteenth centuries, conquered the territory and brought it at least temporarily under their political dominion, but until the imposition of British colonial rule, the hold of central India over this outlying region was always tenuous. Agents of an emperor who remained in his faraway capital could rarely do much beyond collecting some taxes. Thus, since this province did not necessarily adopt the religion or mores of its conquerers, the nominal incorporation of the northeast in a far-flung Indian empire does not necessarily tell us anything about its culture or society at a particular stage of Indian history. Conversions to Islam during the era of Islamic empires, for example, came more as a spontaneous response to the preachings of itinerant Sufi mystics and Muslim teachers than as a result of state policies encouraging such religious change. The greater effectiveness of British rule derived largely from the advantages conferred by their technology and the proximity of their administration.

Unlike India's other invaders, Britain did not enter India from the northwest or locate their capital at Delhi. The British East India Company, the agent of the British crown, established its base in the northeast, and extended Britain's control from there throughout the subcontinent. Therefore from the end of the eighteenth through the middle of the nineteenth centuries, Bengal province stood at the center rather than at the periphery. Even

83

under the British Raj, however, Britain's impact was limited by its conservative social policies; for reasons that are discussed later in this chapter, British
influence permeated the Hindu-dominated portions of Bengal far more than
the eastern, predominantly Muslim half of the province.

Because of the absence of extensive archaeological excavation and research in the Bengal region, little is known about the details of the lives of
women in the ancient cultures. There exists almost nothing specifically
relevant to Bengal prior to the ninth century Buddhist Pala dynasty. The
culture of the indigenous peoples living in the northeast prior to the Aryan
migrations of the second millennium B.C. doubtlessly differed considerably
from that of the Aryan invaders. Because no sites comparable to those of
Harappa and Mohenjo Daro in the northwest have been discovered, it is
only possible to speculate about the indigenous culture. Similarly, merely
the briefest hints of women's place in the Aryan Vedic society can be found
in the religious texts that constitute the primary legacy of this era. By
examining the nature of India's civilizations and by analyzing the extant
literature and law books written elsewhere in India, some inferences can be
made about women's place in pre-Buddhist Bengali societies. Three dimensions of Indian civilization figure prominently in an attempt to reconstruct
the role of women: the central role of religion, the tendency for religion to
express itself through the intricate regulation of society, and the intermingl-
ing of cultural layers.

As practiced in India, the Vedic religion of the Aryan invaders, Buddhism,
Hinduism, and Islam have all—implicitly or explicitly—considered women
to be spiritually inferior to men. In civilizations frequently dominated by the
search for religious truths and spiritual salvation, women rarely have had
access to the philosophic and religious literature or the freedom to pursue
their liberation by leaving home to undertake a life of meditation and
penance. Textual references imply that in Vedic times some young girls did
study under teachers to learn sacred scripture, but by the beginning of the
Christian era, even exceptional women were not expected to master philosophy and religious literature. In the classic division of Indian society into
four orders—the Brahman priests, the warrior-kings, the mercantile class,
and the workers—members of the three highest orders were considered
eligible for full religious initiation. However initiation ceremonies vested
only young men of these classes with the sacred thread that endowed them
with ritual purity and high status. Women born into the priestly order were
excluded from officiating for religious ceremonies. Therefore only sons
could perform the funeral rites essential for the passage of the soul into the
next world. The inability of women to perform these essential rituals accounts in large part for the greater value always placed on male children
(Basham, 1954: 158–178).

In theory Buddhism and Islam accorded to women a fuller role in the religious community, but the practice of both of these religions in India, with the exception of Tantric Buddhism, tended to be socially conservative. Although Buddhists did establish separate orders for women, in the Buddhist spiritual hierarchy a nun, no matter how pious and experienced, was always subordinate to the youngest and most junior male novice. Moreover Buddhist Indian society still considered marriage and the care of children the true function of women and discouraged them from devoting their lives to learning, asceticism, and meditation. Regardless of the intentions of the early Islamic leaders in Arabia toward women and the provisions in Islamic law that could be construed as conferring rights on women, the form in which Islam reached India, more than five centuries after the life of Mohammed and through the aegis of Afghans and Mongols, clearly accorded women a subordinate religious and social status. Indian Muslims have excluded women from full membership in the religious community and have not observed many of the Muslim practices that benefit women.

The major exception to this Indic pattern of women's spiritual inferiority is found in the Tantric Buddhism prevalent in Bengal under the Pala dynasty of the ninth through twelfth centuries A.D. On a philosophical level Tantric Buddhism emphasized the duality of the universe as represented by the male and female principles and postulated the existence of female counterparts or wives of Buddha and the bodhisattvas, saints who remained on the brink of time and eternity to help humans attain salvation. On a popular level Tantric Buddhism devoted considerable attention to these "savioresses" and often assumed character of fertility goddess worship. Women could join active female religious orders and become fully initiated into the secret rites of the sect (Wilbur, 1964: 191–192; de Bary et al., 1958: 191–194). Tantric Buddhism disappeared from Bengal either just before or during the period of the Muslim invasions.

Religions in India, most particularly Hinduism and Islam, have defined an extensive pattern of intricate regulations organizing society and establishing behavioral patterns. Perpetuation of these religions has depended on the observance of these codes of conduct rather than on the maintenance of strong church hierarchies, as in Christianity. Typically this all-inclusive law has failed to distinguish between what would be classified as religious, ethical, and legal considerations. The juxtaposition in India of a highly complex, hierarchically structured society with detailed and specific social codes has established pressures for each person to follow his or her proper *dharma*, or ordained role, and fulfill the duties established for his or her group and sex. This has meant that customs relating to the role of women in society have had the binding force of religion.

Hindu law evolved from several sources: the Vedas of the Aryans, some of which date back to the middle of the second millennium B.C.; law codes, the most influential being the Code of Manu, which was written early in the Christian era; and custom. Muslim law is derived from four sources: divine revelation as written down in the *Quran; hadith,* the teachings of the prophet Mohammed preserved by tradition; *ijma,* the consensus of the community; and after the first centuries, deduction by analogy from the first three sources by men learned in the schools of Islamic law. Moreover as Islam spread beyond the Arabian peninsula, many of the customary laws of the converted populations found expression in the body of Muslim law as practiced in that area (Smith, 1963: 39, 53). Hence the inclusiveness and specificity of Hindu law, and its relegation of women to an inferior status, influenced the evolution and interpretation of Islamic law.

Indians have typically adjusted to new philosophies of life by tolerating them and eventually absorbing many of their central concepts. On the subcontinent syncretism has been the major dynamic of change. Each new religion has merely added another cultural veneer and set of practices. Various cultural layers have been imposed, one over the other, without giving rise to sharp discontinuities. Thus it is not possible to understand the character of Islam in Bangladesh without reference to the context of the Indian civilization in which it developed.

From the very beginning of its history in India, Islam has absorbed beliefs and practices characteristic of Hinduism (Titus, 1959: 156). The vast majority of the population of Bangladesh, irrespective of what they may claim to census takers, descend from lower-caste Hindus who became Muslims through group conversions inspired by Sufi saints and Muslim teachers or by fear of the military power of Muslim conquerors. Most of these original converts were given little instruction in the new faith, and therefore they and their descendents never gave up many of the indigenous rituals and customs. Villagers within Muslim communities continued to worship spirits, observe Hindu festivals, venerate Hindu holy men, maintian aspects of the caste system, and use Brahman priests (Titus, 1959: 170). Therefore, as one Bangali* woman has acknowledged, "Bangali Muslim women live in a cultural environment which is a combination of Islamic traditions and pre-existing Hindu customs" (Abdullah, 1974: 2).

Moreover, despite a strong sense of communal identity emphasizing differences between Muslims and Hindus, Bengalis also have historically acknowledged a common attachment to the Bengali language and culture, and this culture owes more in its development to Hinduism than to Islam. Even the form of Islam spread by members of Sufi orders and Muslim preachers, which brought many of the conversions, resembled the mys-

*Citizens of Bangladesh are referred to as Bangalis to distinguish them from the Indian Bengalis.

tical and devotional Vaishnava form of Hinduism prevalent in the area (Ellickson, 1972: 72). Furthermore, because of their greater access to education, economic power, and high administrative positions, the resurgence of Hinduism under British rule enabled Bengali Hindus to assume leadership over many areas of life in that province. Muslims, who resented their displacement from political power, long avoided involvement in colonial institutions. Most of the modern intellectual, literary, and political figures in Bengal during the colonial period were Hindus. Muslim analysts themselves have acknowledged that the eclectic character of Hinduism has had perhaps as much impact as the austere and uncompromising tone of Arabic Islam on the culture of what is now Bangladesh (Sayeed, 1967: 18). Furthermore even after the 1947 partition of the subcontinent into two independent states on the basis of religion, East Pakistan retained a significant Hindu minority, 16 percent of the population.

A consideration of the ancient Indian concept of femininity, therefore, illuminates both the past and contemporary roles women have played in Bangladesh. Lawbooks, political and social treatises, and literature all stress women's subordination and inferiority. Families preferred sons because only males could perpetuate the line, perform requisite rites, and assist the parents in their old age. Furthermore girls needed dowries and were therefore costly. Regardless of the class into which a woman was born, early law books assigned her a status equivalent to that of the lowest order of society, a worker. Moreover women were always treated as minors under the law. Women passed from the tutelage of their parents to that of their husbands at marriage, and their sons on widowhood. The first duty of the good woman was to serve and obey her husband. The archetype of Indian womanhood, Sita, the heroine of the epic poem *Ramayana*, epitomized the virtuous and faithful wife by accompanying her husband Rama into exile and thereby enduring great hardship on his behalf (Basham, 1954: 177, 181). An influential lawbook ascribed to the sage Manu prescribed that a woman, "should do nothing independently even in her own house. In childhood subject to her father, in youth to her husband, and when her husband is dead to her sons, she should never enjoy independence" (quoted in Basham, 1954: 180). It goes on to say that "though he be uncouth and prone to pleasure, though he have no good points at all, the virtuous wife should ever worship her lord as a god" (quoted in Basham, 1954: 181).

But there was another side to women's place in the society. As one Indian specialist summarized it, the woman "was at once a goddess and a slave, a saint and a strumpet" (Basham, 1954: 182). In addition to the passages emphasizing women's subordination and subservience, others in the lawbooks accorded them honor and esteem. Although women were limited to serving as wives and mothers, these roles evidently commanded a certain degree of respect. Lawbooks entreat husbands to care for their wives, to cherish them, and even to provide them with jewelry and luxuries. Men were reminded by the lawbooks that when making love they should attempt to satisfy their wives as well as themselves (Altekar, 1962). Although most authorities rejected the right of women to inherit property, a woman could retain the individual gifts given to her by her family and husband. One treatise, the *Arthasastra,* even allowed women to keep considerable sums of money (Basham, 1954: 158, 178). Surviving fragments of literature indicate that at least a few exceptional Indian women, none of whom are known to be from the area presently constituting Bangladesh, wrote Sanskrit poetry and drama. This means that during at least some stages of Indian history, upper-class women must have been given a secular education. Higher-class prostitutes too were frequently well educated and accomplished in the arts, much in the same manner as the Greek *hetaira* (Basham, 1954: 183).

Once Islam became a significant religious and political force on the subcontinent, from the eleventh century onward, Islamic and Hindu cultural images of women interplayed and mutually influenced each other. What is striking, though, is the number of similarities between them in the consideration and treatment of women. In both cultures women had a subordinate status and were subservient to men, with functions relating exclusively to roles as wives and mothers. Hence the central virtues for women involved patience, humility, and self-sacrifice. Muslim and Hindu culture also shared a preoccupation with the chastity of women because the reputation of the entire family depended on the purity of its women. Women became the repositories of the family's honor, but they were precarious repositories, since both cultures portrayed women as possessing unlimited lust and an obsession with sex. Thus both cultures were predisposed to separate the sexes so as to prevent women from consorting with men other than their husbands and staining the family honor. Islam probably arrived in India with *purdah,* systematic sex segregation, already the common practice for the upper classes; this in turn promoted such tendencies already present in Indian society. Although Indians frequently trace the origin of *purdah* to the attempts of Indian families to protect their women from the Islamic invaders, textual evidence portrays the seclusion of royal women and restrictions on the movement of upper-class women as far back as the Mauryan period of the third century B.C. Though these efforts to reduce contact between women and men did not amount to the systematic removal of women to separate quarters, hidden from the world, as in *purdah,* they do show a similar direction of intent (Altekar, 1962: 167–172; Thomas, 1964: 198–208; Basham, 1954: 179–180; Berques, 1960: 155–172; Dodd, 1973). The adoption of *purdah* by elite Hindu families probably came initially in imitation of the new ruling class and then spread because it was commensurate with other Hindu cultural attitudes toward women.

Despite these similarities in the consideration of women, Hinduism and Islam differed in many fundamental respects. Although Indic society limited women to serving as wives and mothers, it traditionally accorded greater value to the fulfillment of these roles than did Islam. In Indian society women could not aspire beyond their specific assigned roles in the scheme of things, but neither could any other person or group deviate from his *dharma* or duty; like the other members of the society, women could enhance their prospects for spiritual liberation and social commendation by carrying out the obligations relevant to their *dharma*. According to the weltanschauung of Indian society, what mattered most was not one's position but the manner in which he or she fulfilled the *dharma* associated with it. Thus the virtuous wife and mother had just as good a chance as a man for rebirth into a higher social order in the next life.

Islam on the one hand confers many more legal rights on women than does Hinduism while, on the other, it often treats women as having less inherent worth. This contradiction has its roots in the character of pre-Islamic Arabic society and the attempts of Mohammed to reform it. During the five centuries between the life of the Prophet and the appearance of Islam as a significant force in Bengal, the character of Islam changed considerably, particularly with regard to its treatment of women. As discussed in greater detail in Chapter 2, there was some ambiguity in the Prophet's own attitude toward and teachings about women as well as considerable tension between the ideals he preached and the realities inherent in the society he sought to revise. Some scholars trace the more conservative orientation of women to the resurgence of underlying tribal conceptions (Gibb, 1961). Others point out that the Islamic family laws that became part of the *Shari'a* date from two or three centuries after the death of the Prophet and claim that they reflect the tendency of the Muslim conquerors to treat women as war booty (Bellah, 1968: 16). Whatever the reason, Islam, by the time of its entry into the subcontinent, incorporated principles of patriarchal arbitrariness and sexual rigidity not compatible with many of Mohammed's teachings. Of the two dimensions present in the Islamic view of women, the Afghans and Mongols brought to India the heritage of women's presumed inferiority more than the acceptance of her legal rights. Although Islam accords many rights to women, few Muslim Bengali women have been able to exercise them. The rights accorded women in the *Shari'a* include the following: the right to refuse an arranged marriage, the right to *mehr*, or dower, which is part of the husband's property gifted to the wife at the time of marriage; the right to initiate divorce proceedings under limited circumstances; the right to inherit and own property in her own right; and the right to retain custody of young children after divorce (Lateef, 1973: 30).

Over the centuries the interplay between Muslim and Hindu attitudes toward women seems to have reinforced the most conservative tendencies in each. Hindu women lost some of their dignity and freedom without gaining additional legal rights. The lack of comparable inheritance, property, and divorce provisions in Hinduism seems to have made it more difficult for Muslim women to exercise the rights accorded them. Moreover, as another manifestation of their incomplete conversion, some Muslim communities maintained Hindu marriage practices; these included parts of the religious ceremony, the dowry system whereby the bride's family makes the bridal gift, and the immolation of widows (Titus, 1959: 171). Even among those Muslims who sought to follow universal Muslim law, Hindu customs at least indirectly weakened the provisions for sexual equality within Islam. Through the interaction of the two cultures, women came in many ways to be considered more as symbols of status and as emblems of family prestige than as human beings to be valued in their own right (Lindenbaum, 1973).

Throughout its history as East Bengal, a British province, and as East Pakistan, one of the two areas constituting the country of Pakistan, Bangladesh has been a deprived and exploited area. This obviously has limited its opportunities for development, and in a part of the world in which women have a low priority, it has further reduced their potential for advancement. The imposition of British colonial control over Bengal provided the base from which the British Raj was extended over India. Bengali Hindus, freed from their subservience to Muslim overlords, generally welcomed the colonial system. In contrast Muslims resented their displacement from power and sought to remain aloof from the colonial administration, Western schools, and new economic enterprises. Over time the Bengali Hindus experienced a kind of cultural renaissance while the Muslims increasingly lagged behind. British efforts to introduce a more efficient land revenue system by vesting the former tax collectors of the Mughal empire with ownership of the land over which they had formerly had jurisdiction, while at the same time raising the tax rates, brought about an economic revolution. The Muslim tax collectors could not meet the payments and were forced to sell the land to men who could, the Hindus who had prospered under the British. This brought about a new pattern of Hindu absentee landlords controlling large tracts of land farmed by Muslim peasants, who were thus turned into tenants with an insecure hold over their own economic destinies (Spear, 1958: 535–537). Some Indian nationalists, like Jawaharlal Nehru, have even claimed that the plunder of the province of Bengal supported the British industrial revolution (Nehru, 1959: 207–210). One does not have to support such an extreme contention to recognize that during the colonial period neglected, predominantly Muslim East Bengal continuously fell behind the more prosperous, predominantly Hindu western part of the province.

Independence in 1947 and the partition of Bengal between India and Pakistan brought severe dislocations in the economy. East Pakistan, whose economy was oriented toward Calcutta, the capital of West Bengal, was deprived of its markets. Exchanges of population between the two halves of Bengal, amounting to millions of people, wreaked further havoc. Furthermore East Pakistani society lost its upper class: Hindu landlords fled to West Bengal, Hindu entrepreneurs attempted to remove their investments, and the educated Bengalis in government service left for India.

During the 24 years that Bangladesh was part of Pakistan, it was often governed more like a colony than like an integral part of an independent state. Although the eastern part supplied the bulk of Pakistan's foreign exchange through the sale of jute, the Pakistani government invested most of these earnings in the development of the western half. Concentration of political power in the bureaucratic and military elites, in which Bengalis were grossly underrepresented, deprived East Pakistan of the political clout it would have had under a freely elected parliamentary regime by virtue of its larger population. The economy of East Pakistan, which was severely dislocated by the partition of Bengal, remained relatively stagnant during the first decade of independence. Under the regime of Mohammed Ayud Khan, from 1958 to 1971, a somewhat more equitable division of resources between the two parts of the country took place, but the economic gap between East and West Pakistan continued to grow. Moreover Bengali alienation increased as it became clear that West Pakistanis intended to monopolize political power indefinitely (Jahan, 1972).

Events finally culminated in a bloodbath in the spring of 1971 now referred to as the Bangali War of Liberation. When free elections based on universal suffrage were finally held in Pakistan in 1970, a Bengali political party, the Awami League, won the largest number of seats in the federal parliament, and the expected occurred. The West Pakistani civil and military elites would not countenance a Bengali-dominated regime, especially one that had campaigned on a platform of economic autonomy for East Pakistan. The failure of negotiations led to a call by the Awami League for complete independence which provoked brutal military suppression and wanton victimization of the civilian population by the Pakistani army. Very few women joined the Mukti Bahini (freedom fighters) but they suffered disproportionately as victims in the struggle. In the course of the struggle many Pakistani soldiers engaged in the ultimate violation of Muslim society, the widespread rape of its women. Thus when the plight of East Pakistan and particularly the fate of its women finally received worldwide publicity, it came too late; irreparable damage had been done. Many of the thousands of women raped by the Pakistani soldiers have become social outcasts.

With one of the highest population densities and lowest per capita incomes in the world, the grinding poverty of Bangladesh severely limits the

options of all of its inhabitants, particularly its women, whose life-styles have always been accorded a low priority. Unlike other parts of the world with such consistently high population densities, Bangladesh combines pressure on the land with a level of urbanization that is very low even among Third World countries; at the time of the 1961 census the level of urbanization was 5 percent, and it is perhaps 6 percent today. By 1961 high rates of population growth in a limited land area had produced a density of 1300 people per square mile, and the average holding had been reduced to an unviable 1.5 acres per family. The land reform acts of the early fifties redistributed the property of Hindu landlords who had fled to India at the time of partition and introduced strict ceilings on the amount of land a family could retain, but an estimated 44 percent of the population remains landless or ekes out an existence on less than an acre (Bertocci, 1974: 100–101). Moreover the primitive state of the technology does not allow the maximum utilization of the small acreage. Bangladesh's poverty has precluded large-scale investments in fertilizer, irrigation, research, and equipment. Crop yields are very dependent on the unreliable monsoon rains. The area thus experiences periodic famines when monsoons fail to bring sufficient rains for a number of years, as well as catastrophic flooding from heavy monsoons and typhoons.

WOMEN IN THE FAMILY

The life of a Bangali woman, from birth to death, reflects two basic principles of Bangali social organization: the segregation of the sexes and the dependence of women. As in many societies, the minority of women residing in urban centers, particularly those from upper-class families, have a somewhat wider range of opportunities and are freed from some of the restrictions imposed on their rural sisters. However because of the very low level of urbanization in Bangladesh and the tendency of some men to leave their families behind in the village when they move to towns and cities, only a very small group of women experience this greater freedom; not more than 5 percent of the women of Bangladesh are urban. Moreover of these urban women a mere one-third are literate, and only 1.27 percent are employed in a modern occupation (Jahan, 1973: 3). Thus the vast majority of women live bound by traditional cultural prescriptions with little chance to leave the confines of their homes for contact with the outside world. The kinship boundaries of the family and the physical limits of the household very much define the world of the average Bangali woman. Poverty and illiteracy have further locked women into traditional roles by reducing the challenges deriving from development and by eliminating incentives for change.

One fundamental norm governing Bangali social organization, the segregation of the sexes, follows the tradition prevalent throughout most of the Islamic world. In Bangladesh, as in the Middle Eastern Muslim societies, the conjunction of a high valuation of feminine chastity with the presumption that women are driven by ungovernable impulses and are therefore unreliable has resulted in a form of social organization based on a strict separation of men from women. The principle of sex segregation finds expression both in physical seclusion of women and in the distinction between the social roles assigned to women and men. This sharp dichotomy virtually eliminates any opportunity for women to assume roles other than those of wife and mother. These are the only roles deemed compatible with women's nature and with the required avoidance of contact with members of the opposite sex who are not members of the family. Social respectability depends entirely on women's fulfilling the traditionally prescribed social roles.

The word *purdah,* which literally means curtain, refers to the system for secluding women and enforcing standards of feminine modesty in Bangladesh and other countries throughout southern Asia. *Purdah* in its most complete and extreme form has two dimensions: physical segregation of living space and concealment of the female face and body. To fulfill the principles of *purdah,* segregation of living space is achieved by setting aside for women areas of the home compound and by reserving enclosed portions of public meeting places and facilities. Concealment of the face and body, when it is necessary for a woman to leave the home, can be provided by the portable seclusion of the *burqa,* or concealing cloak, a garment that totally covers the woman from the top of her head to the bottom of her feet, with slits through which she can see. Although the *burqa* may seem cumbersome, by wearing it a woman can gain mobility without violating *purdah* restrictions (Papanek, 1973: 289, 294–296).

The vast majority of women in Bangladesh observe *purdah* in varying degrees from puberty or sometimes earlier. The rigidity of the *purdah* observation depends on the economic situation of the family, the age of the women, and the place in which the family lives. Strictness in adopting *purdah* restrictions is usually related to the financial standing of a family because, in a country in which most of the people live below or just at the poverty line, only the more affluent can provide the conditions enabling their women to withdraw into complete seclusion. Only the well-to-do can afford to employ servants to relieve women of household tasks requiring them to leave the house, and likewise, to construct sufficiently large living quarters to be able to isolate female members from guests so that even the sound of their voices will not be heard. Many affluent families in rural areas are now building latrines in their homes to facilitate the complete confinement of their women in *purdah.*

Traditionally a family that improved its financial position would attempt to enhance its social standing by placing its women in a stricter compliance with the rules of female seclusion. Therefore upward mobility was generally associated with the degree to which women within a particular family remained in *purdah*. This may still be the practice among upwardly mobile families moving into middle-class status. However exposure to Western education and life-styles has led many of the urban upper-class families to permit their women to discard the outer symbols of *purdah*. Upper-class women residing in cities do not usually wear a *burqa* or a veil, and they seem to have fewer, rather than more, restrictions placed on their mobility than do other women in Bengali society. However these elite families continue to subscribe to the underlying principles of *purdah*.

The prevailing poverty of Bangladesh and the resultant living conditions do not make it possible for most women to adopt a strict *purdah*. Nevertheless virtually all Bangalis, whether rural or urban, continue to associate *purdah* with respectability and to endorse its concomitant principles of the separation of the sexes and feminine modesty. Little systematic research has been conducted on the precise extent to which poorer women are secluded, but the literature on prewar (of independence) East Pakistan suggests that rural women in the lower economic groups attempted to emulate the practices of the middle class as much as they could. It was reported that most women remained within their own compounds as much as possible and only ventured outside very discreetly. Because it was considered particularly important for the younger women to be sequestered, the mother or mother-in-law often performed any work, such as searching for firewood and drawing water, that brought women into contact with other villagers. By so doing, the older woman was able to protect the reputation of her daughter or daughter-in-law (Abdullah, 1974: 24–26).

Prewar village studies document the prevalence of *purdah* observation. Two women researchers in the Comilla district of Bangladesh, for example, both reported that seclusion of women and *burqa*-wearing were very widespread (Adbullah, 1974: 24–26; McCarthy, 1967: 35–36). The significance of this finding is underscored by the location of the headquarters for the Pakistan Academy of Rural Development in this district, because this institution made a concerted effort to diffuse a wide variety of innovations affecting women, as well as new agricultural practices. The apparent success of their program with their male targets was shown by the results of an intensive attitude survey; a sample of males from surrounding villages evinced greater modernity than a comparable sample of Bangali industrial workers with many years of factory experience (Inkeles and Smith, 1974: 194–204). Exposure to programs of the Academy apparently did little to change women's inclinations to practice *purdah*. In fact, at least one woman organizer for the Academy used her income to keep other female relatives in stricter seclusion (Abdullah, 1974: 25–26).

Historically the physical seclusion of women behind the veil in the Middle East has been more of an urban than a rural phenomenon. Women in rural villages, who frequently worked in the fields, could not afford the luxury of withdrawing into the confines of the home. It is very likely as well that the urban middle class in Bangladesh is the group most prone to adopt *purdah* in its stricter forms. The physical isolation of females is a luxury that few rural families can afford and apparently is too traditional for highly educated, upper-class, urban families. In the last census available for the area of Bangladesh, women had considerably higher ecomomic activity rates in the rural areas, almost 3 times as high as in the urban sector (Government of Pakistan, 1961: Vol. 4, 96–100), even though women's contributions to farming were almost certainly greatly underreported. In most cases such employment in rural villages would not be compatible with the maintenance of strict *purdah*.

In considering the prevalence of strict *purdah* it should be remembered that urban women comprise only a small fraction of the overall female population and that most urban women are members of working-class families. Moreover living conditions in urban areas, particularly the housing patterns, do not make it possible for women to withdraw as completely from the outside world as in the rural villages. From the female participation in the nonagricultural labor force reported in the 1961 census (Government of Pakistan, 1961: Vol. 4, 96–97), it appears that many urban women from working-class families do work, and some of them almost certainly are continuously exposed to men outside their families. Nevertheless even these women attempt to adhere to accepted standards of feminine modesty. The results of one recent survey indicate that women of this class frequently entertain the hope that an improvement in the family's financial situation will enable their daughters to observe *purdah* more completely (Jahan, 1973: 11).

Many, perhaps most, middle-class women continue to be restricted to a separate world of women with continual surveillance by male members of the family to enforce proper standards of behavior. The seclusion of urban middle-class women, however, involves the separation of the sexes into distinct institutional spheres and limitations on contact and communication between the sexes, not the same traditional isolation of women found in rural Bengal. Many middle-class families still hold fairly conservative attitudes, and even permission for younger female members to work temporarily does not necessarily mean that the practice of *purdah* has been discarded. Female employment among the middle class is still very much the exception rather than the rule, and women who are allowed to accept jobs outside the home generally work in a predominantly female environment. Twenty years ago a study of the employment of middle-class Muslim women in Dacca, the capital of Bangladesh and its largest urban center, indicated that 11 percent of the women in the sample who were working still wore a *burqa* and that one-third of the nonemployed women in these same families observed strict *purdah* (Husain, 1958: 14). In the changed economic circumstances in which many middle-class families now find themselves, they may look more favorably on the employment of their women to secure the income necessary to support their middle-class style of life. Some of these same families may decide, however, that the observance of *purdah* is even more integral to the maintenance of a middle-class status.

The question of whether the principle of female inferiority is inherent in the widely practiced segregation of the sexes and the sharp distinction in the social roles assigned to men and women in Bangali society is difficult to answer and obviously subjective in nature. It can be argued that within the Islamic social order the fact that women operate within the family and that men dominate activities in the suprafamilial world does not necessarily mean that women's roles are assigned less value. In many Islamic countries, such as Egypt, women are compensated for the restriction in their role options by the honor the society accords them as wives and mothers. Women who conform to familial and societal expectations receive considerable rewards. In Bangladesh, as well, women who subscribe to *purdah* norms enhance the social standing of their families. It may also be assumed that many Bangali women are treated with respect and sometimes even deference by their families.

It is interesting and perhaps significant to note, though, that the social science literature on Bangali society tends to dwell on signs of women's presumed inferior status rather than on the importance of traditionally female social roles. This seems to be the case irrespective of whether the analyst is male or female, Bangali or foreigner. According to one Bangali woman social scientist, "Bangali women, both rural and urban, traditional and modern live in a social system which sanctifies an unequal and inferior status for women" (Jahan, 1973: 33). Some male Bangali scholars have said that men dominate all societal spheres, domestic and nondomestic, and that women suffer from thorough discrimination underpinned by social and religious mores (Hossain and Waliullah, 1975: 27). The very process of comparison and ranking of female and male social status is, of course, very untraditional and in itself may imply the acceptance of a more modern perspective on society.

Although it is only possible to speculate at this point, it may be that the emphasis in the literature reflects a change in the societal valuation of female roles. Women's primary source of prestige has traditionally derived from the ability to bear children, particularly male heirs, and this attitude may be affected by the population pressure on the land and by the inability of many families to feed additional mouths. The transition presently underway in the system of marriage payments comprises one possible indication of this reduced valuation of female roles. Muslim tradition provides that the family of the groom should incur most of the expenses related to the marriage and should give a dower, or bride price, payable on demand to the bride. This dower system implied that the prestige brought by a chaste woman and by the children she would bear was worth a considerable investment. At some point within this century, however, many Bangali communities began adopting the Hindu practice whereby the bride's family presents the groom with a dowry and assumes most of the costs of the wedding ritual. To secure educated husbands for their daughters, many families now also agree to reimburse the costs of the man's education (Abdullah, 1974: 19; Lindenbaum, 1973: 11; Ellickson, 1972: 132). The movement toward a dowry system appears to elevate the worth of men relative to women and of male roles over female roles.

By modern standards signs of women's inferior status abound in Bangali society. For instance, in the corpus of accepted Islamic law, one man is often equated with two women, such as in the inheritance laws or in the weighing of testimony of legal witnesses. Childrearing practices and the treatment of female adults within the family also dispute the notion that women are kept separate but considered equal. According to one anthropologist's interpretation, whereas the birth of a son is heralded with the cry of "God is Great," the arrival of a daughter brings only the "whisper of Quranic prayer" in her ear. "This difference in response to the sex of a newborn baby is but a foreshadowing of the sharp differences in roles and behavior patterns that the child will learn and act out later in life" (Bertocci, 1974: 114–115). Realizing that their status within the family and future security, if widowed or divorced, depend upon their sons, mothers frequently exhibit a strong preference for infant sons. Because male children are considered more desirable, their mothers nurse them longer, and families favor their boys in the food they are given to eat, in the medical attention they receive, and in the willingness to invest in their upbringing. As a consequence of this differential treatment, the mortality rate for girls under 5 ranges from 35 to 50 percent higher than that for boys in the same age group (Mosley, Chowdury, and Aziz, 1970: 5). This differential treatment also reinforces the socialization patterns in which little girls are taught to act with the deference and retiring demeanor synonymous with the Bangali conception of femininity, thus preparing them for the roles of wife and mother.

Between the ages of 12 and 15 a girl's family arranges a marriage for her, and she is suddenly thrust into strange surroundings with people whom she does not know. The young bride often becomes little more than a servant to her in-laws, subservient to the demands of her husband and to the adult women in the family. This transition to the roles of wife and mother, for which the girl has been prepared since birth, is in itself a reminder of the value the society attaches to these roles. During these early years of marriage the young man is pressured to produce male children for her new family as a means of improving her position, but her low status means that she is not accorded adequate care in her initial childbearing period. Again, just as in infancy, this differential treatment between male and female young adults leads to a far higher mortality rate for women in the age groups 15 to 19 through 35 to 39 (Khan and Khan, 1975: 15). High maternal mortality results from poor diet, repeated pregnancies, unhygienic environments, and physical abuse (Lindenbaum, 1973: 6–8).

It should be noted that women's social status improves with age and with the bearing of male children. Bangali women, particularly the senior female in a two- or three-generation household, are reputed to have considerable influence over family affairs. However even with regard to family matters, such important subjects as the final arrangement of marriages and the disposition of property remain an almost exclusively male enterprise.

Moreover studies of family decision-making, while on very limited and atypical samples, have failed to verify that women actually assume a powerful role in family affairs. In one survey, for example, of couples in a government low-income housing colony in Dacca, three-fourths of the respondents had husband-dominated relationships in which the husband assumed as his prerogative the right to make decisions on most matters without consulting his wife (Carlow, Reynolds, Green, and Khan, 1971: 571–583). Another study of slum women in Dacca found that less than 3 percent of the wives independently made household decisions on any subject, but more of the husbands conferred with their wives than did those in the other survey (Choudhury, 1975). Hence it does not seem that women's confinement to the home and its designation as a female sphere mean that women exercise control over domestic affairs. Men, at least in an urban lower-income environment, seem to dominate within the home as well as outside of it.

Even more important than this question of female social status are the psychological implications for women of the restrictive role allocations. The Bangali social order requires a rigid division of labor in which women are confined to activities that can be performed within and related to the home while men are left to pursue economic and political interests in the suprafamilial sphere. Under this system women who wish to be socially acceptable are not allowed to choose any other role but that of wife and mother. Even under a more relaxed observation of *purdah* that does not require female seclusion, most women still remain limited to traditionally female roles in a predominantly female environment. Over the centuries such strictures have convinced women that they are mentally and morally incapable of dealing with the male world. They have also fostered intense feelings of dependency that are incompatible with any kind of assertive behavior, even the claiming of rights accorded through religious tradition. Women have willingly adopted *purdah* both because they have been socialized to accept its practice as the only proper way for respectable women to behave and because it affords them a shelter from the outside world. This symbolic shelter, however, exacts a high price, the acceptance of male domination (Papanek, 1973: 289, 294–296).

Thus by fostering an extreme dependency, the prevailing social system has discouraged women from asserting their rights. Women remain under the guardianship of men throughout their lives, first under their fathers, then their husbands or brothers, and finally their sons. Thus, although the *Shari'a*, or existing national legislation, assigns not inconsiderable rights and prerogatives to Muslim Bangali women, this is not reflected in the social order. The failure to provide women with religious or secular education leaves many women unaware of their rights. Even women who know of their rights find it difficult to claim them because of their dependent positions.

The very young age at which families marry their daughters, which in itself contravenes the minimum age established by national law, places women under a fundamental disability. Until recently it was quite common for girls to marry between 7 and 11 years of age, despite the fact that a 1929 law of the colonial government established 14 as the minimum age. Even now few families wait until a girl reaches 16, the minimum age set by the 1961 Muslim Family Laws Ordinance, which was passed by the military regime then governing Pakistan and which is still applicable in Bangladesh. The average age of marriage in 1961 was 13.8 for rural girls and 15.9 years for urban females (Dunn, 1973: 28); the 1961 legislation has had little effect on the marriage age (Ellickson, 1972: 44). A girl of less than 16, who has been socialized to defer to the wishes of her elders, is not likely to demand that her father protect her interests when setting the marriage contract. Nor is she in a position to challenge her family's choice of a husband. Although the principal motive in marrying girls at such a young age is to protect their chastity, the groom's family also realizes that a young bride tends to be more submissive. The timid, compliant bride, who is treated more like a surbordinate than an equal by her husband's relatives, rarely evolves into a demanding, assertive woman in such an environment.

Since the prevailing social system forces women to rely on their male relatives for protection and support, under such circumstances women often forego exercising specific rights to gain long-term social placement and security. More specifically the fundamental insecurity inherent in the marital relationship makes the woman's own kinship group her fundamental source of security and protection. In a society in which at least one out of every six marriages ends in divorce (Ellickson, 1972: 45; Bertocci, 1974: 113) and in which the initiative for the divorce action invariably comes from the husband, women realize that at some poimt in their lives they may have to turn to their own kinship group for assistance. The provisions of the Muslim Family Laws Ordinance (1961), which make it possible for the woman to divorce her husband, which regulate a man's taking a second wife, and which require a husband petitioning for divorce to first submit to outside efforts to reconcile the couple, have not changed this fundamental relationship. The Dissolution of Muslim Marriage Act of 1939, which was enacted by the colonial government, also listed conditions under which a woman might sue for divorce, including desertion, imprisonment, impotency, insanity, cruelty, and marriage prior to puberty, but few women learned about the law or were able to use it to redress their wrongs (Lateef, 1973: 31). It seems unlikely that the 1961 law, although more comprehensive, will have a greater impact, especially when neither the Pakistani nor Bangali governments have, at least up to the present, attempted to vigorously enforce its provisions. Even in communities where people are aware of the terms of this 1961 statute, few women have dared to contravene local customs to take advantage of it (Ellickson, 1972: 62).

This dependence on their own kinship group makes most women reluctant to claim their share of inheritance from their family's estate. In one village survey of the Comilla district, for example, only 2 percent of the women interviewed said that they had demanded the portion of their father's property due them. The vast majority of women preferred to defer to their brothers in the hope that their brothers in return would then look after them and show concern for them (Abdullah, 1974: 27). These women believed that their long-term interests were better secured by reinforcing their brothers' traditional obligation to support and protect them than by receiving a fixed inheritance.

One of the primary sources of compensation for women's vulnerability to divorce within the Islamic social order is the *mehr*, the financial settlement agreed on in the marriage contract; the groom sets this aside for the bride before marriage, and it is subject to full payment at the time of divorce. In many instances, however, the woman's family prevails on her to forego the *mehr* in order to enhance her prospects for remarriage. The family fears that other men may be reluctant to marry a divorced woman who is known to have demanded the *mehr*, thus prolonging the period during which they will have to support the woman. Many families also consider it more prestigious not to claim this payment because it implies that the woman does not need the money (Jahan, 1973: 17; Abdullah, 1974: 19).

Thus there exists a considerable gap between women's legal rights and the actual practices inhering in Bangali society. Women commonly take full advantage of only one right, the widow's right to a share of her husband's property, which amounts to one-fourth of his estate if a man dies childless or one-eighth if he has children. In exercising this right the woman is often motivated by a desire to claim her share of the estate on behalf of her son. If necessary, women often will even engage in a legal battle for the property (Abdullah, 1974: 32).

Women's greater inclination to assert their rights to a share of the property of their husbands is related to the treatment of widows in Bangali society. The typical 10 to 15 year difference in the ages of wives and husbands at marriage means that most woman face the prospect of a relatively early widowhood in a system that precludes an independent social status for the unattached woman (Lindenbaum, 1973: 6). The young widow is usually remarried, often to a brother-in-law so that the property of the family is kept intact. An older widow, and by the age of 30 many women are grandmothers and regarded as old women, does not have as many opportunities for another marriage. Statistics indicate a sharp increase in the number of widowed females after the age of 34 without a corresponding increase in the availability of widowed males (Jahan, 1973: 12). Therefore a widow who has children usually remains with them and does not marry again (Ellickson, 1972: 45). Under this arrangement the mother becomes dependent on her sons, competing directly with their wives for attention and support. This competition between two generations of women is a major theme in Bangali proverbs and literature (Lindenbaum, 1973: 6–7). It is quite understandable that a widow would seek to strengthen her position within her son's household by bringing into it an inheritance.

Much of this section's analysis and the literature on which it was based refer primarily to prewar East Pakistan. The traumas since undergone by that society—the widespread rape of women by Pakistani soldiers during the war of independence, the severe economic dislocation attendant on the destructiveness of that war and the slow reorganization following the war, the continual threat of major famine, and the chaos and lack of authority after the overthrow of the Rahman regime—have called the principles of Bangali social organization into question. It is not so much that the ideals of feminine modesty, separation of the sexes, and female dependence have been reformulated as that they have become somewhat irrelevant. In a society that highly values feminine modesty, many families cannot even afford a sari to cover their women's breasts. In a system that encourages female seclusion or retirement into the home, many women no longer have male relatives who will assume the burden of their economic support (communication with Adrienne Germaine, November 1975). In a social order that fosters female dependence, women are now forced to fend for themselves and are unable to cope with the need to compete in the male world into which they have suddenly been thrust (Ellickson, 1975).

At this point in time it is very difficult to predict the course that Bangali society will follow regarding the redefinition of and revaluation of female roles. In a system that can no longer assure female protection, will women be penalized for moving beyond the confines of the traditional roles of the wife and mother toward greater economic independence? Are the present conditions merely temporary aberrations or are they the beginning of a new social order? These are some of the questions for which only time can provide answers.

EDUCATION

The *purdah* system, by encapsulating most women within the structural confines of family-related roles and the spatial limits of the household, has not been conducive to the development of education for women. In a society of scarcity in which the private world of the family marks the boundaries of awareness and concern for most women, education for females has been seen to have little utility. Until recently it was considered unnecessary, even undesirable, to educate girls because such book learning, whether religious or secular, might render them unsuitable for their traditional duties. Families believed that they could best prepare girls for their future roles as wives and mothers by vesting them with responsibilities in the home that would give them practical experience in cleaning, cooking, and child-care. The early age at which girls were married left little time for both this training and formal learning. Furthermore many feared that education for their daughters would create problems by making the girls less compliant and obedient to their elders; it was assumed that educated women might refuse to do housework, might be difficult to control, and might attempt to arrange their own marriages (Husain, 1956: 93–95).

Maintenance of *purdah* itself has constituted another major consideration precluding education for most women. The limited development of educational facilities in the region has meant that most children must travel some distance to a neighboring village to attend school, and few families have been willing to allow their daughters to do so for fear that both their security and their observation of *purdah* would be hampered (Abdullah, 1974: 20–21). This has particularly been true with regard to postprimary education, but the early imposition of *purdah,* often well in advance of the onset of puberty, has limited even primary school attendance. The correlation between the strictness in the practice of *purdah* and the social standing of the family has meant that the rural families which could most easily afford to educate their daughters have been the most reluctant to allow them to attend school.

In the past a small minority of women were taught at home by private tutors or by educated fathers and brothers. These women were usually the daughters of wealthy men or belonged to families with a particular respect for education. Men whose work brought them into contact with the towns were also more likely to try to educate their daughters. Even these women, however, received an education that was usually fairly elementary with an emphasis on learning the scriptures and/or preparing them to be wives (Husain, 1956: 94; Abdullah, 1974: 21).

The contemporary educational system in Bangladesh originated in the 1835 decision by the British Indian Government to support Western education taught in the English language. Until the middle of the nineteenth century, though, the only schools for women were a few institutions established by Christian missionaries. Few Muslim girls attended these schools because their link with the colonial order, the Christian religious instruction in the curriculum, and the association of Western education with employment, made them unacceptable to Muslims. However when secular schools for women opened and government grants-in-aid became available to support private schools for girls in the second part of the nineteenth century, Muslims remained disinclined to take advantage of the opportunities. In 1881, 0.86 percent of school-age females in Bengal were attending school; in 1891 the percentage was 1.61; in 1901, 1.8; and by 1910, 4.32 (Forbes, 1973: 1, 13). Most of those attending school were doubtlessly Hindus since Hindus generally had a much more favorable attitude toward Western education and were encouraged to educate their daughters by the *Brahmo Samaj* and other modernist Hindu organizations. No comparable groups urging greater freedom and more education for women developed in the Bengali Muslim community.

Throughout the colonial period educational opportunities for women lagged considerably behind the development of educational facilities for men. For the British administration the need for clerks to assume middle and lower level positions in the government and in private enterprises provided the principal motivation for investments in education, and it was taken for granted that these jobs would be filled by men, not by women. Education for the sake of enlightenment or for the purpose of preparing Bengalis for self-government concerned few colonial administrators. The reliance on grants-in-aid to private schools as the major source of support for educational expansion and the rather conservative social policy of the British government also meant that little was done directly to encourage the opening of schools for females. It is therefore not surprising that in 1947, at the time of independence for Pakistan, women comprised only 10.3 percent of the primary school students, 8.7 percent of the secondary school enrollees, and a scant 1.6 percent of the university student body (Government of Pakistan, 1969: 170).

After independence the government of Pakistan also did not consider education for women to be a high priority. The conservative nature of the governing elites, many of whom were drawn from the military, precluded any major effort to improve women's access to education. Furthermore the focus during Pakistan's first decade on establishing a viable state and defining its Islamic character and the concern during the second decade with maintaining the integration of Pakistan were not conducive to promoting social reform.

The economic disparity between West and East Pakistan, and the discriminatory revenue allocation by the West Pakistani–dominated central government in favor of the West, resulted in the more rapid development of infrastructure in the West. During the first decade of independence enrollment in primary schools increased 4.5 times more in the West than in the East. Whereas enrollment in secondary schools declined by 6.6 percent in East Pakistan, it increased by 64 percent in the western part of the country. Similarly, university attendance went up 11.2 percent in the East versus 38 percent in the West (Jahan, 1972: 30–31). During the next decade the growth of educational facilities in the western half of the country continued to outstrip that in the East. Unlike the earlier period, however, this decade brought to East Pakistan also a continuous increase in enrollments at all levels of the educational system (Jahan, 1972: 81–82). As might be expected, the cumulative impact of such limitations on the expansion of the East Pakistani educational system was significant, particularly at the secondary and university level. By 1965–1966 West Pakistan, with a lower population base than East Pakistan, had 50 percent more secondary school students and more than twice the university enrollment (Government of Pakistan, 1969: 185–186).

During the past 25 years attitudes toward education for women have changed somewhat. A survey undertaken in villages of the Comilla district in 1966 reveals something of this evolution: among the families included in the sample there were only 11 educated women over 25, but 72 percent of the girls between the ages of 7 and 12 were then attending school (Abdullah, 1974: 20–21). By 1970, as shown in Table 1, women constituted 35.3 percent of the primary school students, 15.7 percent of those attending secondary school, and 9.7 percent of those enrolled at the university level. Though these figures represent a considerable improvement on the abysmal situation prevailing at the time of Pakistan's independence, the access of women to education in Bangladesh today even compares unfavorably with

Table 1   Enrollment of Female Students in Bangladesh, 1949–1970

Academic Year	Percentage Primary School Students	Percentage Secondary School Students	Percentage University School Students
1949–1950	23.9	9.1	.2
1954–1955	25.6	10.2	4.9
1959–1960	26.4	12.3	7.9
1964–1965	31.7	15.2	9.0
1969–1970	35.3	15.7	9.7

Source.   Computed from Pakistan Central Statistical Office, 1969: 170–173, 186; United Nations Statistical Office of Economic and Social Affairs, 1974: 761.

that in many other Muslim countries (Commission on the Status of Women, 1973: 14).

Some families are now more inclined to educate their daughters through the primary level because it is considered prestigious to do so. A girl with some education often has better marriage prospects, particularly in urban areas, because educated men prefer educated wives. In the more liberal communities the fears that primary-level education would radically transform girls and make them reluctant to assume their traditional roles seem to have evaporated.

Nevertheless Bangali society still does not place a high value on female education. Almost two-thirds of the school-age girls do not begin primary school. In most rural communities families intent on educating their daughters remain very much the exception, not the rule. In a milieu of scarcity the low priority accorded to female education inevitably means that scarce resources will be employed for purposes other than educating women. Although tuition for the initial years of primary school is free, many families cannot afford even the small costs involved for books and clothing. If they can scrape together enough money to support only some of their children, they always prefer to finance the education of their sons. When it is considered that few women work and thus few are able to contribute to the support of their parents in their old age, the decision to invest in educating sons is a rational one. Another major consideration depressing female enrollment is the obligation of girls to help their mothers with the housework and to care for younger children in the family. These duties continue to take precedence over schooling both because it is convenient for the family and because this experience is seen to relate more directly than school attendance to the future roles these girls will assume (Abdullah, 1974: 21–22).

The relative absence of sex-segregated school facilities that would enable young girls to remain within a female environment also discourages their school attendance. The government, which has not been able to provide each village with a primary school, cannot afford to establish many girls' schools. In 1966 the government provided only 197 primary schools and 19 high schools for women out of a total of 24,510 primary and 59 high schools run by the government. In the same year in East Pakistan there were 1399 female private primary and 176 female private high schools (Zaki and Khan, 1970: 33, 41). The fees in private schools for girls are far beyond the means of all but the small number of middle- and upper-class families. Furthermore, as shown in Table 2, virtually all girls in primary school and many at the

Table 2   Female Primary and Secondary School Teachers in Bangladesh, 1947–1966

Academic Year	Percentage Female Primary School Teachers	Percentage Female Secondary School Teachers
1947–1948	3.8	3.8
1950–1951	4.4	5.3
1955–1956	2.5	4.0
1960–1961	2.1	5.5
1965–1966	2.3	7.0

Source.   Computed from Pakistan Central Statistical Office, 1969: 174–175.

secondary school level are taught by male teachers. Women constitute less than 3 percent of the primary school teachers and only 7 percent of the secondary school instructors.

Those girls fortunate enough to begin school usually drop out after the fifth or sixth grade. As Table 1 shows, women comprise only 15.7 percent of the students in secondary school. Moreover as few as 1.7 percent of rural women, as contrasted with 20.8 percent of rural males, continue their schooling after the age of 15 (Jahan, 1973: 7). Two major considerations dictate the short length of most girls' school careers. First, a primary education confers the basic skills in reading, writing, and arithmetic deemed appropriate for women. Any further education, it is believed, would not be useful and might even be counterproductive by predisposing women against fulfilling their traditional role obligations. Second, the onset of puberty necessitates the observation of purdah and therefore precludes attendance in a coeducational environment (Jahan, 1973: 7). Urban women, who have more access to private girls' schools and who have fewer purdah restrictions imposed on them, have greater opportunities for schooling after puberty.

At the apex of the educational system women comprise 9.7 percent of university enrollment. Although the universities are coeducational, female students are somewhat insulated from contact with male students through the provision of separate reading rooms, lounges, and classroom seats (usually the first two or three rows) for women. Thus women who are so inclined can spend 4 years in a coeducational institution without ever engaging in a single conversation with a male classmate (Jahan, 1973: 16). It is difficult to ascertain the proportion of women who pursue a higher education and maintain a *purdah* mentality. Although there are not many female university professors, the presence of some women on the faculty provides nontraditional role models for female university students. Many girls do interact with male classmates, and even if it is only to discuss mutual academic interests it is still something that few of them have ever done before. Girls also participate in student political activities, although probably to a lesser extent than do boys (communication with Adrienne Germain, 1975).

Of the 5000 women enrolled at the bachelor degree stage in the 1969–1970 academic year and the 500 female students pursuing postgraduate education in that year, the majority were pursuing liberal arts programs that did not prepare them for any particular careers (Zaki and Khan, 1970: 90–91). Of the 1970 female university graduates, 1100 were in the arts and 200 in science; no females were reported to have received a bachelor of commerce degree (Zaki and Khan, 1970: 111–112). At the postgraduate level in 1970, 400 women received a master of arts degree and 150 a master of science degree (Zaki and Khan, 1970: 115–116). It seems likely that most women choose studies considered suitable for women that will enable them to be highly cultivated wives whose advanced degree will enhance their husbands' social status (Dunn, 1973: 43). What is perhaps more significant is that a sizable number of female university students now opt for fields, like economics, statistics, mathematics, and the pure sciences, that are not traditionally feminine and offer the possibility of career application.

WOMEN AND THE ECONOMY

The economic activity of women in Bangladesh strongly reflects the limitations imposed by its poverty and by the strictures of *purdah*. The low level of economic development, the high rate of male unemployment, and the cultural norms relating to the seclusion of women have combined to discourage women from seeking employment outside the home. The role of women in the labor force has several outstanding characteristics. First, Bangali women have one of the lowest levels of reported economic participation in the world. Second, most of the women classified as economically active are unpaid. Third, Bangladesh has an extremely high dependency ratio (Bean, 1968: 391–410). Fourth, educated women who do work outside of the home almost invariably pursue careers in occupational fields that do not bring them into contact with men.

In the 1961 prewar census, which unfortunately is the last one available for Bangladesh, only 10.8 percent of all females were classified as economically active, and women comprised a mere 5.2 percent of the civilian labor force. Of the women in the civilian labor force 11.1 were in the rural and 4.8 percent in the urban sector (Government of Pakistan, 1961: Vol. 4, 96–100). The proportion of Bangali women reported to be in the labor force is low, even relative to many other Muslim countries. Several other Muslim countries—such as Syria, Jordan, Iraq, Egypt, Morocco, Iran, and Pakistan—have a similarly low female standardized activity rate, but virtually all of these states have better female sex ratios in nonagricultural employment (Bean, 1968; Durand, 1971: 19).

Moreover two-thirds of the women classified as economically active fell into the category of "unpaid family labor" and did not receive any wages (Government of Pakistan, 1961: Vol. 4, Table 5). These women remained in the home, observing purdah, and assisted another member of the family with farming or with a craft. If the census definition of economic participation had been stricter, as was the case in the 1951 census, these women would not have been considered members of the labor force. The proportion of the Bangali female labor force that is unpaid is almost twice as high as the average for Asia (Bean, 1968).

Despite the figures quoted above, it should not be surmised that women do not make an important economic contribution to the welfare of their families. Particularly in the rural areas, women's roles go far beyond cooking, cleaning, and childrearing. Women probably grow most of the vegetables and much of the fruit. They undertake almost all of the processing of rice, the major food crop, including the postharvest work, husking, winnowing, and parboiling. They are responsible for the storage of rice as well. Women also care for livestock and prepare fuel from dung. In some rural communities it is common for poorer women to work in the homesteads of others during the harvesting period to earn extra money (Bertocci, 1974: 94–96).

The extent of women's economic contribution does not find its way into the census figures for a variety of reasons. Many of the activities women undertake are done within the confines of the household and are not remunerated. Therefore much of this work is considered to be an extension of their role as housewives and is not reported. The fact that the census takers are male and probably consult only the male heads of households may also bias the census enumeration of women's labor force participation. Even when women cultivate crops independently or hire themselves out as paid laborers, their families may be reluctant to admit this to a stranger since it involves a loss of status. In any case one should hesitate to accept the census records as valid indicators of women's economic roles in 1961 and even less so today, when many more women are being forced to work for the survival of their families.

Although women do not remain economically inactive, their work prior to the war of independence was usually limited to tasks that did not interfere with the observation of *purdah*. In prewar East Pakistan, and at least to some extent today, women who went beyond the accepted division of labor to visibly farm on the family's plots usually risked the contempt of their villages (Dumont, 1973: 54). These restrictions on the type of activities considered acceptable for women obviously do not lend themselves to a rational use of woman power and resources. Moreover no matter how hard women work, they still remain economically dependent.

The high dependency ratio in Bangladesh results from a variety of factors: the low rate of female participation in the labor force, the high incidence of male unemployment, and the large number of children who are too young to make a productive contribution. Male unemployment has been estimated to be at least 18 percent of the male labor force (Masihur Rahman Khan, 1972: 45). In spite of the high infant mortality rates nearly half of the population is under 15 years of age (Government of Bangladesh, 1973: 5, 37). In 1961 the civilian labor force comprised only 34.3 percent of the total population; thus each person who was productively employed had to support two other persons who were not. The severe economic dislocations following the struggle for independence, cyclones, floods, droughts, and postindependence mismanagement have probably raised the dependency ratio even further.

The sexual role allocation in the nonagricultural sector of the economy reflects the division of labor inherent in the concept of *purdah*. For women the appropriateness of a particular occupational category is often determined principally by how much contact it necessitates with members of the opposite sex and only secondarily by whether it is commensurate with traditional female role images. As Table 3 shows, the 1.27 percent of Bangali women engaged in a modern occupation stand at both extremes of the status hierarchy. At one end of the spectrum are the educated, middle-class women who are pursuing professional careers in such fields as teaching and medicine that enable them to deal exclusively with female clienteles. At the other, women work alongside men in such low-status jobs as domestic service, road construction, and factory labor. The greatest opportunity for female employment in urban areas appears to be in the manufacturing and mechanical sector, which in the 1961 census accounted for over half of the female nonagricultural labor force. In some cases factory owners have

Table 3   Female Participation in the Nonagricultural Labor Force by Occupation, 1961

Occupation	Number of Females	Percentage of Female Sector
Professional, technical, and related	8,224	4.34
Managerial, administrative, clerical	944	0.46
Sales and related	18,513	3.53
Forestry and fishing	3,163	2.68
Mine, quarry, and related	134	14.39
Transport and communication	179	0.12
Manufacturing and mechanical	118,516	17.10
Construction and general labor	3,806	1.56
Service, sports, entertainment, and related	58,004	20.55
Workers not classified	2,306	3.83
Unemployed	726	1.38
Total female nonagricultural labor force	214,515	

Source.   Computed from Government of Pakistan, 1961, Vol. 4: 96–97.

organized sex-segregated assembly lines. In others, however, women risked their reputations by subjecting themselves to contact with male supervisors and male co-workers.

The application of the concept of *purdah* to occupation selection has resulted in several trends atypical of women's employment patterns elsewhere. The division of labor between the sexes has made trade and retail sales work an almost exclusively male field in Bangladesh, in contrast with the patterns inhering in the non-Muslim countries of Asia and Africa. Most Bangali secretaries, typists, and receptionists as well are men because office work necessitates frequent dealings with male associates. Although teaching is considered an appropriate career for women, primary school teaching, which in Western society is invariably typed as "women's work," in Bangladesh is done primarily by men. Women are discouraged from pursuing this occupation because of the difficulties an unattached woman could encounter living in a village and teaching the coeducational student bodies typical of most primary schools. Nursing, another profession frequently associated with women's traditional nurturing role, also attracts few women. By requiring personal service to nonfamily members who are not related by bonds of interdependence and by its association with sickness, nursing violates fundamental restrictions on women (Papanek, 1971: 525–526).

Purdah, which acts to exclude women from many occupational fields, also in theory could create occupational opportunities for women in the "contact services" by providing them with a female clientele reluctant to seek the services of male professionals. Women in strict *purdah* will not expose themselves to a male professional, even if this means that they must forego medical care, legal services, or educational opportunities (Papanek, 1971: 522). Logically then *purdah* should lead to the creation of a parallel female occupational sector catering exclusively to women. This, however, has not occurred in Bangladesh. The limited access of women to education has severely constrained the training of female professionals. Unlike the situation in some other Muslim societies, such as Egypt, where the majority of women enumerated in the labor force are educated and employed in a professional, technical, or white-collar capacity, in Bangladesh most women workers have little education. Professional, technical, and related work accounted for less than 4 percent of the female labor force in 1961. In 1961 there were only 620 women doctors, 267 women registered nurses, 47 registered midwives, and 18 women health visitors in all of Bangladesh to provide for a female population of approximately 35,000,000 (Bangladesh Bureau of Statistics, 1972: 267–268).

As part of the population program it is planned to train 13,500 women as field workers. Attainment of this goal would improve considerably the care of rural females and provide a major source of employment for women. It may also present rural women with a nontraditional role model.

As might be expected, few Bangali women have attained top managerial or administrative positions placing them in a hierarchical position over men. This partially reflects the exclusion of women from the Civil Service of Pakistan, the East Pakistan Civil Service, and the Foreign Service, the three premier governmental agencies that controlled much of the decision-making, during the time that Bangladesh was part of Pakistan. Despite reforms by the Bangali government qualifying women for appointment to the high levels of the administrative and foreign services, virtually no women have been admitted. Similar conditions prevail in the private sector.

Nevertheless few women professionals or executives complain of job discrimination in recruitment, salary, or promotion (Jahan, 1973: 24–25). This may tell something about their lack of sensitivity on these issues, but it may also reflect real opportunities for advancement. Undoubtedly in a situation where male supremacy is so taken for granted, men do not feel threatened by the presence of one or two exceptional women, especially women who are so little inclined to challenge the principle of male superordinance. The general absence of social and economic competition from women may alleviate the inclination shown by male elites in other societies to retaliate against women by imposing discriminatory conditions of service. The few women in such high positions may be integrated on the basis of their class background, with their gender ignored.

The exceptional economic circumstances now faced by Bangladesh, where thousands have died of starvation and where large portions of the population remain on the brink of succumbing to hunger and malnutrition, raise some important questions regarding the economic future of women. The plight of women in such a deteriorating economy is particularly severe because women traditionally have received the leftovers of men, and during a period of extreme scarcity there are less and less of such leavings. Moreover a significant proportion of the unknown number of girls and women raped by Pakistani soldiers during the 9 months of army terror and 3 weeks of war have not been accepted back by their families because of the shame their presence would bring. From suffering and despair sometimes come the seeds of reform, and this does seem to be happening to a limited extent in Bangladesh.

The programs catering to women established by the government and private agencies since the war reach only a small portion of the female population, but this is characteristic of virtually all endeavors in Bangladesh, irrespective of their target populations. Therefore in evaluating the impact of these programs one should keep in mind that all programs in Bangladesh are constrained by the lack of trained people, the scarcity of resources, the confusion, and the lack of information that inhibits the efforts to improve the condition of women. Moreover the mere existence of the new awareness that women have needs deserving of attention and assistance constitutes a big step forward.

The most important agency involved in these programs to improve women's conditions is the Bangladesh Women's Rehabilitation and Welfare Foundation. This foundation, originally established in 1972 as the National Board of Bangladesh Women's Rehabilitation, has as its major goals the introduction of measures on an emergency basis to provide care and facilities to the most desperate section of the war-affected women, and the economic emancipation of women through the provision of more opportunity to participate in economically fruitful labor (National Board of Bangladesh Women's Rehabilitation Programme, 1974: 1–2). Although it has had official approval and was for a time a government organ, most of its funding has come from international and voluntary agencies. It has launched a number of pilot projects for both rural and urban women and has established several day-care centers, but most of its programs are still in the planning stage. The Christian Organization for Relief and Rehabilitation coordinates 52 women's centers which attempt to assist needy women, through cooperative or partially cooperative organizations, to help themselves. Several voluntary agencies offer adult literacy courses in the belief that such skills constitute the first step toward improving productivity (Zeidenstein and Zeidenstein, 1973: 23–28).

The plight of the country and of individual families has not stimulated a systematic rethinking about the differential use of male and female labor. This probably was to be expected, since conditions in Bangladesh have tended to produce reactions to cope with imminent disasters rather than long-term planning and fundamental reevaluations of societal principles. However the failure to employ more productively the resources and energy of the female half of the Bangali population has thus far limited the potential for agricultural development and will continue to do so unless major reforms are enacted (Dumont, 1973: 19).

A critical question for the future is whether more women will be provided with opportunities to make a greater productive contribution to the welfare of their families. Observers report that women are demonstrating a much greater inclination to work. Large numbers of Bangali women have participated in "food for work" and rural relief projects (communication with Adrienne Germain, November 1975). In the depressed labor market, however, most employers prefer to give jobs to men, and it is doubtful that many married women will find paid employment. In the rural areas women may gradually move into working the fields. At the same time, though, rural women may be displaced from their traditional role in the processing of harvested rice. The change from hand labor to rice mills appears to accompany the introduction of new, high-yielding rice varieties because of the larger crops (Martius and Hardor, 1975), and small, privately owned rice mills operated by men have already been opened in several communities. Consequently women's economic prospects, at least in the short term, do not seem bright.

FERTILITY AND FAMILY PLANNING

Most Bangali women spend their lives locked into an endless cycle of childbearing that undermines their health and severely circumscribes their ability to undertake any activities outside the home. The reported ideal family size, 6.47 children for rural and 5.64 for urban families (Masihur Rahman Khan, 1973: 47), combined with a high rate of child mortality, requires that women spend a considerable portion of their adult lives pregnant or nursing. Repeated pregnancies in physically weakened and frequently malnourished women give rise to a variety of medical problems, including a deficiency disorder called *shutika* that has symptoms of diarrhea, headache, dizziness, and weakness and also results in a high mortality rate for women during their childbearing years (Lindenbaum, 1973: 8–9).

Women as individuals and the society as a whole suffer the consequences of the high level of fertility. Nationally it translates into a rate of population growth of 3 percent a year, which brings 2 million additional children annually to a small country that already cannot sustain its 76 million people. According to Abdul Malik Ukil, former Minister for Health and Family Planning, "Bangladesh is confronted with the greatest menace of the century—the Population Explosion." If the rate of population increase is not limited, the population will double within two decades, to equal that of contemporary China within the next 50 years (Ukil, 1972: 1). Since Bangladesh is approximately the size of the state of Wisconsin and its present density of 1340 people per square mile already is one of the highest in the world for an agricultural economy, little room remains for these future generations to eke out an existence. Obviously such a high rate of population growth also exacts a price in terms of limiting the possibilities for economic growth. Some 9 percent of the annual national income must be invested merely to maintain the prevailing, dismally low standard of living (Azizur Rahman Khan, 1972: 48–49). Moreover the Malthusian race is being lost: food crop production is not keeping pace with the rate of population increase. One recent study has concluded that, "There has been a perceptible decline of per capita food availability over the past 15 years" (Chen and Chowdhury, 1975: 3).

Research on the impact of the Bangladesh civil war on fertility in a rural area indicates that the conflict brought about a decline in fertility. However this reduction appears to have been only temporary. Preliminary data point to a return to the prewar level and possibly even to a rise over prevailing prewar rates (Curlin, Chen, and Hussain, 1975).

Most women apparently do not make an effort to limit the size of their families. Prewar surveys indicate that despite the high incidence of illiteracy and the prevailing conservatism the national family planning program initiated by the Pakistani Government had been able to bring an awareness of the existence of modern contraception to some 85 percent of the target population. However in 1968–1969 only 3.7 percent of eligible Bangali women were actual users of such contraceptive devices (Khan and Khan, 1975: 31). It is possible that many more women resorted to traditional methods of contraception and abortion and tried to space their pregnancies through prolonged breast-feeding. Nevertheless the vast majority of the population continue to be nonusers of contraceptives.

The high level of fertility reflects several basic considerations. As in other poor, predominantly agricultural societies, people believe that the benefits of having many children, particularly male children, outweigh the costs. Although daughters are often considered a financial burden, families regard sons as economic assets who in childhood will provide a source of cheap labor and in adulthood will support their aged parents. In this equation families ignore the consequences of continual childbearing for the health and well-being of their women and tend to underestimate the actual expenses involved in childrearing. The high rate of infant mortality also leads people to have many children so that at least some sons will survive to adulthood. In the absence of any national system of social security, children comprise the best form of old-age insurance.

Prevailing societal norms do not offer women incentives to limit the size of their families. By circumscribing women's role options and by providing only one channel, marriage and motherhood, through which women can gain social acceptance, Bangali culture encourages women to bear many children. Women realize that their status and security depend directly on their producing male heirs for their husbands' families and conform to these expectations rather than risk their futures. Moreover the low level of education prevailing among Bangali women means that few of them probably comprehend how the various forms of contraception operate and that many would be unable to use a birth control device effectively.

Although the *Quran* does not explicitly preclude the practice of birth control and, as discussed in the chapter on Egypt, even contains several passages that seem to encourage it, the practice of Islam in Bangladesh has not been conducive to the introduction of family planning. Many, and perhaps most, Bangalis assume that the use of contraceptives is contrary to Islamic precepts. Conservative political leaders and religious figures reinforced this idea when they inveighed against earlier efforts by the government of Pakistan to provide family planning services on the grounds that contraception was contrary to Islamic teachings. In addition, Islam as commonly practiced in Bangladesh has fostered a fatalistic attitude toward life that is inconsistent with planning and taking precautions to control fertility. There is evidence that women with large families have less inclination to practice birth control than women who have fewer than their ideal number of children (Mosena and Stoeckel, 1971: 567–570).

Some analysts have suggested that the practice of *purdah,* rather than Islamic doctrine itself, encourages the high level of fertility prevalent among Muslim Bangali women. Although Hindu and Islamic precepts regarding the use of contraceptives do not differ significantly, Hindu Bangali women have a lower average number of live births and demonstrate greater awareness of and approval for family planning than do Muslim Bangali women. In contrast with the Muslim women, Bangali Hindu women are not secluded and can move about freely. Furthermore the two groups of Bangali women at the ends of the status spectrum who observe *purdah* less rigidly, those of upper-class and those of lower-class backgrounds, are usually more aware of the availability of contraceptive devices, and in the case of the upper-class women more inclined to use them, than the majority of Bangali women (Aitken and Stoeckel, 1971: 75–87).

Although it is possible to blame cultural and economic considerations for the inclination of Bangalis to have large families, the failure of more people to accept population control may just as well be caused by the ineffectiveness of all family planning programs to date. The low rate of contraceptive users may be partially a result of the lack of access to information, supplies, and services for those who are interested. The Pakistani national family planning program mentioned earlier was in full operation for only 1.5 years in the area of Bangladesh. In that relatively brief period it managed to create awareness in 85 percent of the target population. The fact that this awareness was not then translated into greater application may have reflected the lag in the development of service facilities and the limitations of the local workers, most of whom were illiterate, low-status village women, in moving beyond a simple information role. Several small-scale model programs developed in the private sector and introduced since the war have made a significant impact in the adoption of family planning practices (Khan and Khan, 1975: 31–32).

The government has recognized, at least on paper, that any effort to improve economic conditions depends on stabilizing the size of the population. Bangladesh's first five-year plan, covering the years 1973 to 1978, adopts population limitation as one of its fundamental objectives. Planners state that "No civilized measure would be too drastic to keep the population of Bangladesh on the smaller size of 15 *crore* [approximately double its present population] for sheer ecological viability of the nation" (Government of Bangladesh, 1973: 538). In keeping with this outlook and its goal of eventual zero population growth, the plan contemplates the introduction of laws raising the legal age of marriage, legalizing abortion, and making sterilization compulsory for either the husband or the wife after the birth of the second child. Planners also recognize that social measures designed to bring about women's emancipation are an essential part of any serious effort to reduce the birth rate (Government of Bangladesh, 1973: 539).

Although the Bangali Government has endorsed these objectives, it has been slow in actually putting into operation a national family planning program. The confusion, inefficiency, and political considerations affecting the implementation of virtually all government projects have combined to delay the initiation of a large-scale family planning effort. Nevertheless the introduction of a major campaign with 13,500 women as trained fieldworkers seems to be only a matter of time. A World Bank consortium has allocated $47 million to support the national program, elaborate plans have been drawn up, and a directorate has been established. Whether this program will be able to surmount the many administrative, cultural, and environmental obstacles to reduce the rate of population growth remains to be seen. Its chances for success will be greater if the family planning campaign is merely a prelude to the introduction of broader policy measures designed to widen women's role options.

Population control is an imperative for Bangladesh and, if achieved, would reduce the burdens on the individual woman. However the initiation of a major family planning program, particularly under the present circumstances, carries with it potentially negative repercussions for women. Although in principle planners advocate fundamental reforms freeing women from the sexual stereotypes which dictate that women should be solely wives and mothers, it seems very doubtful that this will become a major policy objective of any Bangali regime in the near future. The extremely sensitive nature of these proposed reforms, the difficulties inherent in developing and implementing relevant programs, and the absence of a strong commitment on the part of the existing or past regimes all make such measures unlikely. Therefore, despite the recognition that traditional constraints on women's roles and women's subordinate position in society encourage large families (Fazhur Rashid Khan, 1973: 201), it seems quite probable that a national family planning program will not attempt to grapple with the issue of women's place in society. Campaigns to reduce births, if not accompanied by reforms to increase the scope of women's roles, may further devalue women's familial roles without offering them an alternative source of fulfillment and prestige.

WOMEN AND POLITICS

Women have formally been members of the political community since 1935, when the British administration enacted the Government of India Act. This law enfranchised all adults, women and men, who met the specified standards of education and income. Nevertheless the participation of women in any form of political activity during the last 40 years has been minimal. Politics involves the competition for and the exercise of power, and women in Bangladesh have been effectively blocked from access to power in any arena, domestic or public. The sexual division of labor underlying the practice of *purdah* clearly assigns to men management and leadership in the public sphere. The extension of the franchise to women during the British Raj came more through the application of abstract political principles held by British officials than as a consequence of demands made by the women themselves. Few Muslim women participated in the independence movement, and the handful of Muslim women who did address women's meetings or collect money included virtually no Bangali (Minault, 1974).

After the partition of India into two countries in 1947, women in Pakistan continued to be formally recognized as having legitimate, if limited, political rights, but they also were denied any meaningful political role. The first Pakistani constitution, which was finally adopted in 1962, 15 years after independence, reserved 6 seats for women, 3 from each of the two wings, out of a total body of 156 members. A 1967 constitutional amendment increased the number of women to 8 but reduced their relative representation within the larger National Assembly of 218 (Nyrop et. al., 1971). In light of their lack of political consciousness, the provision of reserved seats for women might have better protected their interests than would their inclusion in the general electorate. Even so, the proposed number of seats was very inadequate. Moreover the reservation of seats in the 1967 constitution amounted to little because so little power was accorded to the parliament.

Prior to the establishment of Bangladesh, under the British and the Pakistanis the nature of the political system and the dynamics of political activity excluded women, and for that matter most men, from any meaningful form of involvement. The British never pretended that their administration was anything other than an imperial autocracy. Despite the brief adoption of a parliamentary system, political leadership under the Pakistanis remained predominantly in the hands of a small bureaucratic and military elite that did not admit women into its inner sanctum, just as under the British. Neither the Pakistan Civil Service nor the army recruited women into its ranks. During Pakistan's early years civil servants governed by virtue of the vacuum created by the inability of politicians to reach a consensus about the institutional and ideological forms the new country should adopt. Intervention by the military confirmed this balance. The Pakistanis held only two elections based on universal suffrage, in 1954 and in 1970, and in neither case were the results fully respected. During the struggle for independence, first from the British and then from the Pakistanis, mass movements based on street demonstrations constituted the major instrument of influencing policies and changing governors. Although casting a ballot in a sex-segregated polling booth may be construed as compatible with the practice of *purdah,* attending open meetings and engaging in large-scale protests certainly cannot be. Thus the failure to institutionalize a parliamentary political system denied women even the limited participation granted by the various voting laws and constitutions.

The initial Constitution of the Republic of Bangladesh, enacted shortly after independence, set aside 15 seats for women in a 300-member parliament. It stipulated that during the first 10 years these women would be chosen by the other members of parliament; subsequently they would be directly elected from single-member constituencies. In the section dealing with fundamental rights, the Constitution pledged that the State should not discriminate against any citizen on the grounds of sex and accorded women equal rights with men in all spheres of public life. The equality of opportunity that it promised, however, was qualified by another article which enabled the State to reserve for members of one sex any class of employment or office considered by its nature to be unsuitable for members of the opposite sex (Government of Bangladesh, 1972).

At least initially the Bangali government fostered some political participation on the part of women. In its first national election, which was held in 1973, one year after independence, 56 percent of the electorate voted (Jahan, 1974: 14); of this 56 percent perhaps as many as 10 percent were women. Women from middle- and upper-class families and women who were educated had higher rates of participation. Shortly after the 1973 election a survey conducted in two urban constituencies on a sample of 262 women, most them from this type of background, found that 79 percent had voted (Jahan, 1974: 10). Two women candidates also unsuccessfully contested general seats. More significantly, after ridiculing the suggestion that the Awami League appoint a woman cabinet minister, Sheik Rahman reversed his position and selected two women to assume, for a brief time, junior minister of state positions, one in the ministry of social welfare and the other in the Ministry of Education. In so doing he may have been responding to the demands of the women's section of the Awami League, which hitherto had been primarily a forum for the wives of politicians and which had had little grass-roots organization. However the extent of women's political involvement should not be exaggerated. Women's participation in the 1973 election was at best nominal, and women remained at the periphery of the political system.

Moreover, just as under the British and the Pakistanis, parliamentary government survived for only a brief time. By February of 1975, less than 2 years after the installation of the first elected Bangali parliament and cabinet, constitutional provisions were suspended and all power was vested in Sheik Mujib Rahman. Six months later a group of military officers overthrew the regime in a bloody coup, and Sheik Rahman and several other leading members of his administration were killed. The military group's hold on power proved to be tenuous, and the elimination of the Rahman government initiated a series of countercoups that has left something of a power vacuum in a country that can ill-afford the absence of a decisive administration. Whether a civilian or military group eventually emerges victorious, it seems very unlikely that a viable parliamentary system will return in the near future. Again, the centralization of authority, in addition to its other repercussions, will serve to exclude women. The opportunity for women to become true members of the political community and to share power can come only through the institutionalization of a participant political process.

Moreover only a stable government will have the inclination and ability to redress social and economic imbalances.

With everything that has been said in the preceding pages, it should come as no surprise that there are no active women's organizations in Bangladesh actively questioning traditional constraints imposed on women or seeking to uplift women from their depressed economic and social conditions. The most visible agency engaged in efforts to improve women's opportunities is a nonpolitical, formerly semigovernmental foundation already mentioned, the Bangladesh Women's Rehabilitation and Welfare Foundation, whose founder, chairman, and executive director are men. The only Bangali woman described as a true feminist, Rokeya Sakhawat Hussain, died more than a half century ago. She devoted her life to the cause of women's education in the belief that education would provide the means through which women could achieve economic independence and renounce strict *purdah*. In pursuit of her goal she established the first Muslim girls' school in Calcutta and wrote short stories, articles, and a novel (Jahan, 1973: 25–26).

Few Muslim women's organizations existed prior to the 1947 partition of India. In the aftermath of the creation of Pakistan some elite women established small associations, most of which catered to urban women and were either elite social clubs or neighborhood women's clubs that brought together educated women for social purposes. Some women's associations also engaged in voluntary work, such as running a school or a handicraft center, to improve the socioeconomic conditions of poorer and less-educated women. The most important of these organizations, the All Pakistan Women's Association, was founded by the wife of Pakistan's first prime minister and eventually had 20 branches in East Pakistan (Ahmed, 1967: 45–46). Later better-educated women set up a few more goal-oriented organizations. One of these, the Business and Career Women's Club, sought to promote the interests of career women. The leadership of this group, as well as that of the All Pakistan Women's Association, the paramount elitist organization, came from non-Bangali, upper-middle-class women in Bangladesh (Jahan, 1973: 27–30).

After the war of independence Bangali women replaced the West Pakistani women officers of the established women's associations, but otherwise it is business as usual for these associations. The one more-radical organization that existed for a time, the Mahila Parishad, concerned itself with leftist political causes rather than with women's problems. Thus the latent disquiet about women's current situation has not given rise to any organized political demands. This silence provides further testimony to the psychological and social implications of *purdah*. Women in the privacy of their own homes may question the ability of men to uphold their obligations within the *purdah* order. Voicing these doubts publicly and visibly is another matter. It is also instructive that current female discontent stems from the breakdown of *purdah* and the need for women to emerge from its shelter and fend for themselves. Women have not rejected the rigidity of *purdah* and its restrictions, but instead implicitly continue to endorse them.

CONCLUSION

Whether one is assessing the rights women exercise, the role options available to them, or the influence they hold, the status of Muslim women within Bangali society is very low. Women exercise less control over their lives and have fewer channels for elevating their status and increasing their security than in any of the other societies considered in this volume. Rounaq Jahan, a leading Bangali female social scientist, has described the women of her country as among the most oppressed in the world (Jahan, 1973: 1). The term *oppression* has the kind of ideological overtone that this book has attempted to avoid, but it seems to be an accurate description of the status of Bangali women.

The treatment of women under the Bangali social system is riddled with cruel paradoxes. Cultural prescriptions embodied in socialization practices prepare women for only one role in life, that of the wife and mother, but the society seems to accord less value to the traditionally feminine roles. Respectability and social acceptability for women depend on adhering to strict standards of feminine modesty and sexual segregation that render women dependent on men for support and security. However the male-dominated society has recently not been able to provide its women with physical protection or with the basic necessities of life. The division of labor between the sexes underlying the *purdah* social order severely limits women's economic productivity in Bangladesh, one of the poorest countries of the world, which can ill-afford the luxury of losing the full potential of half of its adult labor force. By vesting women with only one way of improving their status and security, the bearing of children, the society encourages a high level of fertility in a region that cannot sustain its present population.

Despite this evidence of their disadvantaged position, Bangali women do not feel oppressed. The universal acceptance of the structural and cultural attributes of *purdah* continues to render acceptable the limitations on women's freedom of choice and opportunity. Women, no less than men, endorse the precepts that sanctify an inferior and dependent status for them. Both men and women consider women's subordinate position natural, inevitable, and proper. A small number of women, most of whom belong to middle- and upper-class families, have been able to circumvent the cultural and economic barriers to women's access to education and employment, but even these women have not challenged the basic rules of the *purdah* system. Furthermore, by accommodating these women on its own terms, the male-dominated social system has been able to drain off the potential leadership of any movement to transform the social conditions under which most women live.

Many elements in the present situation offer little hope that women's condition will improve in the near future. The movement away from the traditional Muslim practice, in which the groom's family provided a bride price, to one in which the bride's family offers a dowry is one indication that the society accords less value to feminine roles than it formerly did. The treatment of the so-called "war heroines," the women violated by Pakistani soldiers, constitutes another ominous sign. The deteriorating economic situation means that women, who traditionally are the last to be fed, clothed, and educated, will receive even less. In a region of extreme want women and young children will be the most vulnerable to diseases related to malnutrition. This may raise the infant mortality rate even higher and, by doing so, depress even more the worth of childbearing. Moreover in the struggle for survival women's inability to make a greater economic contribution may be resented; but when and if women do shed *purdah* in the face of economic adversity, they will risk offending their families and thus suffer a further loss of prestige and status.

Bangladesh is presently at a major crossroad. Many of its most fundamental norms, including the segregation of the sexes and female dependence, cannot be sustained. Most people still endorse these values, but fewer and fewer families can afford to adhere to them. Women have been caught in the middle of a conflict between economic survival and social prestige. It is very difficult to predict the manner in which this inconsistency between ideals and reality will be resolved.

Nevertheless some limited grounds exist for optimism. For the first time there has been public recognition that women disproportionately suffer the burdens of war, poverty, illness, and hunger. The social conscience of at least a small segment of the male elite has been aroused by the traumas Bangali women have undergone in the last few years. Moreover this commitment to accord women greater social and economic opportunities has come at a time when Bangladesh has had to grapple with the very survival of its people and when it could easily have ignored or deferred the consideration of social reforms. Hence the fact that only limited measures have been initiated to accomplish these goals may presently be less significant than the existence of some programs designed to better women's lives.

BIBLIOGRAPHY

Abdullah, Tahrunnesa Ahmed. 1974. "Village Women as I Saw Them." Mimeo. Originally published in Bengali in 1966 by the Pakistan Academy for Rural Development.

Afsaruddin, Mohammed. 1964. "Rural Life in East Pakistan." Dacca: Social Science Research Project, University of Dacca.

Ahmed, Shereen Aziz. 1967. "Pakistan." In *Women in the Modern World*. Edited by Raphael Patai. New York: Free Press, pp. 42–58.

Aitken, Annie, and John Stoeckel. 1971. "Muslim-Hindu Differentials in Family Planning Knowledge and Attitudes in Rural East Pakistan." *Journal of Comparative Family Studies* **VI** (Spring): 75–87.

Altekar, A. S. 1962. *The Position of Women in Hindu Civilization*. Delhi: Motilal Banarsidass.

Badruddin, Umar. 1974. *Politics and Society in East Pakistan and Bangladesh*. Dacca: Mowla Brothers.

Bangladesh Bureau of Statistics. 1972. *Statistical Digest of Bangladesh, 1970–1971*. Dacca: Government Printer.

Basham, A. L. 1954. *The Wonder That Was India*. New York: Grove Press.

Bean, Lee L. 1968. "Utilisation of Human Resources: The Case of Women in Pakistan." *International Labour Review* **97** (April): 391–410.

Bellah, Robert. 1968. "Islamic Tradition and the Problem of Modernization." Mimeo.

Berques, Jacques. 1960. *Les Arabes D'Hier à Demain*. Paris: Édition du Seuil.

Bertocci, Peter J. 1974. "Rural Communities in Bangladesh: Hajipur and Tinpara." In *South Asia: Seven Community Profiles*. Edited by Clarence Mahoney. New York: Holt, Rinehart, and Winston.

Callard, Keith. 1957. *Pakistan: A Political Study*. London: Allen and Unwin.

Campbell, Robert D. 1963. *Pakistan: Emerging Democracy*. Princeton: Van Nostrand.

Carlow, Raymond W., Richard Reynolds, Lawrence W. Green, and N. I. Khan. 1971. "Underlying Sources of Agreement and Communication between Husbands and Wives in Dacca, East Pakistan." *Journal of Marriage and the Family*. **33** (August): 571–583.

Chen, Lincoln, and Rafigul Huda Chowdhury. 1975. "Demographic Change and Trends of Food Production and Availabilities in Bangladesh (1960–1974)." Dacca: The Ford Foundation, mimeo.

Choudhry, M. T., and M. A. Khan. 1964. *Pakistan Society*. Lahore: Noorsons.

Choudhury, R. H. 1975. *A Socio Economic Survey of Slum Women*. Dacca: BIDS.

Commission on the Status of Women. 1973. *Study on the Interrelationship of the Status of Women and Family Planning, Addendum*. New York: United Nations Economic and Social Council.

Curlin, George T., Lincoln C. Chen, and Sayed Babur Hussain. 1975. "Demographic Crisis: The Impact of the Bangladesh Civil War (1971) on Births and Deaths in a Rural Area of Bangladesh." Dacca: The Ford Foundation, mimeo.

de Bary, William Theodore, et. al., compilers. 1958. *Sources of Indian Tradition*. New York: Columbia University Press.

Dodd, Peter C. 1973. "Family Honor and the Forces of Change in Arab Society." *International Journal of Middle East Studies* **4** (January): 40–54.

Dumont, Rene. 1973. "Short Notes on Some Villages and Some Problems." Mimeo.

Dunn, Elizabeth M. 1973. "The Women of the People's Republic of Bangladesh." Unpublished paper.

Durand, John D. 1971. "Regional Patterns in International Variations of Women's Participation in the Labor Force." Mimeo.

East Pakistan, Bureau of Statistics. 1970. *Statistical Digest of East Pakistan, 1964–1969.* Dacca: East Pakistan Government Press.

Ellickson, Jean. 1972. "A Believer among Believers: The Religious Beliefs, Practices, and Meanings in a Village in Bangladesh." Unpublished, Ph.D. dissertation, Michigan State University.

———. 1975. "Observations from the Field on the Condition of Rural Women in Bangladesh." Paper prepared for International Seminar on Socio-Economic Implications of Introducing HYV's (High Yielding Varieties) in Bangladesh. Kotbari, Comilla, April 9–11.

Farooq, G. M. 1970. "Dimensions and Structure of Labor Force Participation and Their Changes in the Process of Economic Development: A Case Study of Pakistan." Unpublished Ph. D. dissertation, University of Pennsylvania.

Forbes, Geraldine. 1973. "Social Service and Politics: Bengali Women in the Independence Movement." Paper presented at the 9th Annual Conference on Bengali Studies, Columbia University, New York.

Germaine, Adrienne. 1975. Personal communication, November.

Gibb, H. A. R. 1961. "Women and the Law." In "Colloque sur la sociologie musulmane." *Correspondence d'Orient, Actes.* September. Brussels: pp. 233–248.

Government of Bangladesh. 1972. "The Constitution of the People's Republic of Bangladesh." Dacca: Government Printer.

———. 1973. *The First Five Year Plan, 1973–1978.* Dacca: Government Printer.

Government of East Pakistan. 1969. *Manpower Planning in East Pakistan.* Dacca: Department of Planning and Economic Development.

Government of Pakistan, Central Statistical Office. 1969. *Twenty Years of Pakistan in Statistics, 1947–1967.* Karachi: Government of Pakistan Press.

Government of Pakistan, Ministry of Home and Kashmir Affairs. 1961. *Population Census of Pakistan 1961.* Vol. 4. Karachi: Government of Pakistan Press.

Hossain, Monowar, and Syed Waliullah. 1975. "Some Aspects of Socio-Economic Environment in Bangladesh." Paper prepared for Seminar on Population Policy of Bangladesh. Dacca, May 15–25.

Hossain, T., et. al., Editors. 1972. *Proceedings of the Seminar in Family Planning.* Dacca: Ministry of Health and Family Planning.

Husain, A. F. A. 1956. *Human and Social Impact of Technological Change in Pakistan.* Dacca: Oxford University Press.

———. 1958. *Employment of Middle Class Women in Dacca.* Dacca: Dacca University Socio-Economic Research Board.

Inkeles, Alex, and David H. Smith. 1974. *Becoming Modern: Individual Change in Six Developing Countries.* Cambridge, Massachusetts: Harvard University Press.

Jacobsen, Doranne. 1970. "Hidden Faces: Hindu and Muslim Purdah in a Central Indian Village." Unpublished Ph. D. dissertation, Columbia University.

Jahan, Rounaq. 1972. *Pakistan: Failure in National Integration.* New York: Columbia University Press.

———. 1973. "Women in Bangladesh." Paper presented to the Ninth International Congress of Anthropological and Ethnological Sciences. Chicago, August.

———. 1974. "Political Participation of Women in the 1973 Election in Bangladesh." Paper presented at the annual meeting of the Association for Asian Studies. Boston.

Karim, Nazmul. 1956. *Changing Society in India and Pakistan: A Study in Social Change and Stratification*. Dacca: Oxford University Press.

Khan, Azizur Rahman. 1972. "The Cost of Population Growth." In *Proceedings of the Seminar in Family Planning*. Dacca: Ministry of Health and Family Planning, pp. 48–49.

Khan, Fazhur Rashid. 1972. "Socio-Cultural Determinants of High Fertility in Bangladesh." In *Proceedings of the Seminar in Family Planning*. Edited by T. Hossain et. al. Dacca: Ministry of Health and Family Planning, pp. 197–202.

Khan, Masihur Rahman. 1972. "Demographic Profile of Bangladesh." In *Proceedings of the Seminar in Family Planning*. Edited by T. Hossain et al., Dacca: Ministry of Health and Family Planning, pp. 48–49.

———, and Aminur Rohman Khan. 1975. "Demographic Processes in Bangladesh." Paper prepared for Seminar on Population Policy, Bangladesh. Dacca, May 15–21.

Lateef, Shahida. 1973. "In a Community." *Seminar: The Status of Women* **165** (May): 29–34.

Lindenbaum, Shirley. 1968. "Women and the Left Hand: Social Status and Symbolism in Pakistan." *Mankind* **6**: 530–544.

———. 1973. "The Value of Women." Paper presented to the Ninth Annual Conference on Bengali Studies, Columbia University, New York.

———. 1974. "The Social and Economic Status of Women in Bangladesh." New York and Dacca, The Ford Foundation, mimeo.

Mahmood, Shaukat. 1964. *Muslim Family Law Ordinance, 1961*. Lahore: Pakistan Law Times Publication.

Mahoney, Clarence, Ed. 1974. "Editor's Introduction." In *South Asia: Seven Community Profiles*. New York: Holt, Rinehart, and Winston, pp. 81–84.

Maron, Stanley, Ed. 1957. *Pakistan: Society and Culture*. New Haven, Connecticut: Human Relation Area Files.

Martius, Gudrun, and V. Hardor. 1975. "Women's Participation in Various Activities of Rice Processing—with Special Reference to HYV." Paper prepared for International Seminar on Socio-Economic Implications of Introducing HYV's in Bangladesh. Kotbari, Comilla, April 9–11.

McCarthy, Florence E. 1967. "Bengali Village Women: Mediators between Tradition and Development." Unpublished M.A. thesis, Michigan State University.

Minault, Gail. 1974. "Parda Politics: The Role of Muslim Women in Indian Nationalism 1911–1924." Paper presented at the Annual Meeting of the Association for Asian Studies, Boston.

Mirza, Sarfaraz Hussain. 1969. *Muslim Women's Role in the Pakistan Movement*. Lahore: Research Society of Pakistan, University of the Punjab.

Mosena, Patricia, and Stoeckel, John. 1971. "The Impact of Desired Family Planning Practices in Rural East Pakistan." *Journal of Marriage and the Family* **33** (August): 567–570.

Mosley, Wiley H., A. K. M. Alauddin Chowdury, and K. M. A. Aziz. 1970. *Demographic Characteristics of a Population Laboratory in Rural East Pakistan*. Dacca: Center for Population Research.

National Board of Bangladesh Women's Rehabilitation Programme. 1974. *Women's Work*. Dacca: Bangladesh Cooperative Book Society Ltd.

Nehru, Jawaharlal. 1959. *The Discovery of India*. Garden City, New York: Doubleday and Company.

Nyrop, Richard F., et. al. 1971. *Area Handbook for Pakistan*. Washington, D.C.: U.S. Government Printing Office.

Papanek, Hanna. 1971. "Purdah in Pakistan: Seclusion and Modern Occupations for Women." *Journal of Marriage and the Family* **33** (August): 517–530.

———. 1973. "Purdah: Separate Worlds and Symbolic Shelter." *Comparative Studies in Society and History* **15** (June): 289–325.

Qureshi, Ishtiaq H. 1962. *The Muslim Community of the Indo-Pakistan Subcontinent.* The Hague: Mouton.

Rahim, Muhammad A. 1963. *Social and Cultural History of Bengal.* Karachi: Pakistan Historical Society.

Roy, Manisha. "Bengali Women as Respect Objects: An Analysis of Male–Female Relationships in Contemporary Urban West Bengal." Paper presented at the Ninth Annual Conference on Bengali Studies, Columbia University, New York.

Sayeed, Khalid B. 1967. *The Political System of Pakistan.* Boston: Houghton Mifflin Co.

Schuman, Howard. 1967. "Economic Development and Individual Change: A Social Psychological Study of the Comilla Experiment in Pakistan." Occasional Papers in International Affairs. Cambridge, Massachusetts: Center for International Affairs, Harvard University.

Smith, Donald Eugene. 1963. *India as a Secular State.* Princeton: Princeton University Press.

Spear, Percival. 1958. *The Oxford History of India,* 3rd ed. Oxford: Oxford University Press.

Statistical Office, Department of Economic and Social Affairs. 1974. *Statistical Yearbook, 1973.* New York: United Nations.

Stoeckel, John, and Moqbul A. Chawdhurry. 1973. *Fertility, Infant Mortality and Family Planning in Rural Bangladesh.* Dacca: Oxford University Press.

Thomas, Paul. 1964. *Indian Women Through the Ages.* Bombay: Asia Publishing House.

Titus, Murray T. 1959. *Islam in India and Pakistan: A Religious History of Islam in India and Pakistan.* Calcutta: Y.M.C.A. Publishing House.

Ukil, Abdul Malik. 1972. "Foreword." In *Proceedings of the Seminar in Family Planning.* Edited by T. Hossain et al. Dacca: Ministry of Health and Family Planning, p. 1.

Von Vorys, Karl. 1965. *Political Development in Pakistan.* Princeton: Princeton University Press.

Ward, Barbara, Editor. 1963. *Women in the New Asia.* Paris: UNESCO.

Weinraub, Bernard. 1974. "Bangladesh at Age 3 Is Still a Disaster Area." *The New York Times,* December 20, p. 4.

Wilbur, Donald N. 1964. *Pakistan: Its People, Its Society, Its Culture.* New Haven, Connecticut: Human Relations Area Files Press.

Youssef, Nadia H. 1971. "Social Structure and the Female Labor Force: The Case of Women Workers in Muslim Middle Eastern Countries." *Demography* **8** (November): 427–449.

———. 1974. "Women and Work in Developing Countries." Berkeley: University of California, Population Monograph Series, No. 15.

Zaki, W. M., and M. Sarwar Khan. 1970. *Pakistan Education Index.* Islamabad: Central Bureau of Education.

Zeidenstein, Sondra, and Laura Zeidenstein. 1973. "Observations on the Status of Women in Bangladesh." Unpublished paper.

Chapter Four

MEXICO: THE MANY WORLDS OF WOMEN

Mary Elmendorf

HISTORICAL AND SOCIOLOGICAL BACKGROUND

Mexico is now the largest Spanish-speaking country in the world, both in area and population, and, as such, strives for more independence, especially from its neighbor to the north, the United States, and for international prominence, particularly among Latin American countries. Within Mexico today there exist many Mexicos, just as there have always been, ranging from the modern, urban, metropolitan area of Mexico City, rapidly approaching a population of 10 million, to another 10 million living in isolated Indian communities and still speaking their native languages. In many ways the problems of women are concentrated at the two ends of this spectrum, since their status is generally a function of whatever socioeconomic group to which they belong.

Rapid economic development in Mexico has not brought with it more equal distribution of income or wealth. According to Ifigenia Navarrete's acute analysis of what happened to Mexico's economy between 1950 and 1957, the national product increased by 148 percent, from 38.8 million pesos to 94.4 million, but the relative position of low-income groups worsened considerably. Rapid economic development took place, but income distribution became more unequal (Hanke, 1967: 111).

In fact, 1 percent of Mexico's population monopolizes 66 percent of the national income, while the other 99 percent, among whom many are women, share the remaining 34 percent of the wealth, giving them an annual per capita income of $530, which is relatively high for Latin America (Gonzalez Casanova, 1968: 469).

Many people, both men and women, are questioning whether industrialization and increased modernization contain the answer to Mexico's problems of socioeconomic development or of raising the status of women.

As Mexico moves away from its historic bilateral and dependent relationship with the United States toward a closer identification with the problems of the developing nations, there are signs of a new revival of its "continuing Revolution" (Pellicer, 1973). Perhaps, as there is new concern for Third World people and oppressed groups, there will arise an awareness of the problem and potentials of women with Mexico.

Pre-Columbian Society: 21,000 B.C. to 1519 A.D. Despite prevailing opinions the number of people who think of themselves as Mexicans is very small. As Octavio Paz says:

Our territory is inhabited today by a number of races speaking different languages and living on different historical levels. A few groups still live in prehistoric times. Others, like the Otomis who were displaced by successive invasions, exist on the outer margins of history [Paz, 1961: 11].

Because so few specifics— yet so many vestiges—of earliest Mexican culture remain, we must depend on the theoretical reconstruction of what has
been from well-known archaeological remains and more recent findings
such as the Bonampak murals, figurines from Jaina and Tlaltilco, the various
codices, and some of the Indian chronicles, which themselves have never
been interpreted by historians from the woman's perspective. We must also
look for information in materials to be found in isolated Indian groups of
Mexico today, many of which have preserved with amazing purity their
ancient language, culture, and customs. Certain anthropological studies, on
the other hand, may give us a new view of pre-Columbian societies and help
clarify the role and status of women within them, both in the past and in
relation to contemporary Mexico (Arizpe, 1972; Chiñas, 1973; Collier,
1973; Elmendorf, 1972, 1973; Friedlander, 1974; Hellbom, 1967; Lewis,
1959; Pozas and Pozas, 1971; Otero, 1944; and Villa Rojas, 1969).

In any case, to understand Mexico today one must be aware of the
richness and variety, both ethnic and cultural, of the pre-Columbian Mexicans and the still-prevailing influences of those cultures.

There are few real data with which to assess the role of women in
pre-Columbian societies. Chroniclers such as the Spanish Conquistadors
and, later, the friars, Bishop Diego de Landa and Bartolomeo de las Casas
and others, gave detailed views of the indigenous cultures, but with a
religious, cultural, and sexual bias that makes their findings open to question. Historians and anthropologists disagree radically, even about specific
Indian groups such as the Aztecs. For instance, the Mexican anthropologists
Gamio (1916) and Leon-Portilla (1958) have written that women enjoyed
high prestige and played vital cultural roles. Some historians, however, have
argued that women had an inferior place, both in Aztec and Mayan
societies, based on their circumscribed duties. One historian concluded that
among the Aztecs, "The most degrading epithet that could be applied to any
Mexican, aside from calling him a dog, was that of 'woman' " (Macias,
1971: 1).

A pioneering study by a Swedish woman anthropologist, Anna Hellbom,
used material from the Aztec codices, which indicated that in Aztec society
women were esteemed in their roles as wives and mothers (Hellbom, 1967).
Although few historians and analysts have noted this, women receive considerable attention in the codices. While the father was educating his sons,
the mother was educating her daughters to perform their special roles.
Although these roles were confined to the home in most cases and were
sexually defined, they were not necessarily considered of less significance.
From the very earliest childhood females were taught to be skilled and
diligent housekeepers. According to the codices, a woman's husband was
selected by the gods, so she had to accept the choice. She was to remain a

virgin until she married, for if she lost her virginity before marriage, her husband would never forgive or trust her. Once married she was urged to be a submissive and self-abnegating wife. A "good" woman was reserved and patiently bore the reproaches of her husband and in-laws. She treated her husband tenderly and calmed and pacified him, even when he no longer wanted to live with her. "You are to stay inside the house," says one Aztec source, "as the heart remains inside the body" (Hellbom, 1967: 90–91). Both men and women were killed for committing adultery, women by hanging, men by stoning (Peterson, 1959: 123).

Women sometimes played very important societal roles outside the home as well, from the usual production of foodstuffs and clothing to many professional occupations, such as midwifery, serving in religious orders, being medicine women, and even running businesses (Hellbom, 1967: 229). Women priests ran special schools for these professional women, but little is really known about them (Petersen, 1962). Aztec women could also enter into contractual relations, inherit and possess property from either parent, and claim justice in the courts. Archaeological remains and new findings such as the Bonampak murals, some codices, and figurines from Jaina show that there were at least some women priests and military leaders.

The hierarchy of gods and goddesses, as well as the relationships of their positions with the men and women of the time, also suggests a respected place for women in society. The importance of one of the principal female deities of the Mayans, Ix Chel, the Earth Goddess, is indicated by the many representations of her that have been found. More vital to the understanding of Mexico today, however, is the Aztec goddess Tonantzin, also known as Coatlicue or Cihuacoatl—serpent mother, mother of the gods, weeping woman—whose ancient hillside shrine is now the site of the Basilica of the Virgin of Guadalupe. This ubiquitous mother goddess provided the early Christian fathers with an ideal transfer figure for the Virgin Mary, many of whose characteristics she already possessed, thereby facilitating the establishment of the cult of *marianismo* in Mexico (Brenner, 1929, 1970: 150–154; Stevens, 1973: 94; Sundel, 1967: 7).

Among the elite of pre-Columbian society were well-educated and influential women such as Malintzin, better known as Malinche, the Indian maiden who became the mistress of Cortez and who, in her role as his interpreter, betrayed her own people and helped bring about their massacre by the Spanish cannon and cavalry (Gruening, 1928: 79). In the original drawings of the scenes of the Conquest, she is depicted as the same size as Cortez, and therefore apparently as important (Brenner, 1929, 1970: 62). A recent study shows that Malinche, the daughter of a chief, had been sold as a child and later resold to the Spaniards. But the more important point is why history has given Malinche the blame for the fall of Tenochtitlan. Was it because her power was really greater than Montezuma's, or was it because she was a woman that to this day her name has been a synonym for traitor (Alegria, 1975: 73–76)?

Colonial Period (1525–1810). To understand the Spanish conquest of Mexico, and the later implications for womens' roles, it is vital to remember the high level of civilization prevailing in the Aztec empire. When the Spaniards arrived in 1519, Montezuma's capital city was a carefully organized metropolis with a nobility, an incipient middle class, and of course a servant or possibly slave class. The level of material well-being was high, and the population was more than twice as large as that of Seville, the largest city in Spain. The invaders numbered a mere few hundred. They had come to get rich, and they had come from a country that very probably demonstrated the worst aspects of the feudal oligarchies of Europe. Finally, they were far from the control of the Spanish crown and, at least during the first 30 years, had an almost completely free hand in exploiting the people, the land, and the resources that they found in Mexico. When Cortez finally conquered Tenochtitlan, with the help of Malinche and numerous rebellious tribes unfriendly to the Aztecs, he and his men acted only to satisfy their own personal ambitions. The result of this rapaciousness was devastating for the native population, and above all for the women, who were not only slaves like everybody else, but also the objects of sexual exploitation. After all, no women had accompanied the discoverers; not until much later were European women brought over to help form the new aristocracy.

Indian women under the Aztec Empire had been accorded personal dignity and specific rights that had been scrupulously recognized in their own culture. When they lost their social position and became servants to the Spanish conquerors, their general situation deteriorated. Not only were they expected—whatever their previous social class—to perform activities formerly undertaken by a servant group, but they were also expected to bear the children and satisfy the sexual needs of the conquerors. In time the Spaniards came to define them as "bad women" and thus "fair game" for illicit sexual relations (Macias, 1971: 3).

After the initial period of gross and untrammeled plundering, the Spanish crown began to exercise more authority. Little by little this resulted in some elementary legal protection for the Indian. Slavery did not disappear, but specific rules and regulations regarding its exercise were put into effect by the viceroys and their administrators. It was during this later period that the *hacienda* system began to evolve, a curious blend of European feudalism and extractive exploitation of human and natural resources for the benefit of Spain and the dominant classes in New Spain.

In a sense there were two conquests of Mexico, one by the Conquistadores and another by the Church. Much of what we know of the colonial period has come from the writings of the early friars and missionaries, Franciscans and Dominicans for the most part, who wrote detailed chronicles of the era. Some, such as de las Casas, were truly interested in the local population, often learning the indigenous languages and carrying to the people what little learning of Catholicism and the Spanish language they were to receive. Great efforts were made to convert the few remaining Indian nobles and to bring through them their families and tributaries into the Church; mass baptisms of as many as 14,000 Indians were not uncommon.

It must be remembered that a mere 10 years passed between the original conquest and the miraculous appearance of a Virgin on a hill near the shrine and dwelling of the Aztec goddess, Tonantzin, ancient mother of deities, to Juan Diego, a poor and humble Indian convert. This apparition left proof of her faith-arousing visitation through roses and, even more dramatically, through her own image, which appeared on Juan Diego's carrying net. That image (in whose eyes, if one looks carefully, can be seen the reflection of an Indian man) is now called Our Lady the Mother of God—in the Aztec language still Tonantzin—and hangs on display above the main altar of the great basilica on the outskirts of Mexico City.

That the Catholic Church was able to transform this image into a powerful Christian symbol of Mary is testimony to the skill of the early fathers. Yet this is only one of many, many other cases of "Idols behind Altars" that have been documented (Brenner, 1929, 1970: 159). The Lady of Guadalupe has become the patron of Latin America, and as such she symbolizes not only continuity between the precolonial religion and Catholicism, but also the close association of women with the Church. To this day it is the women of Mexico who are the strength of the Church. Both the upper-class women of Mexico City and other cities and the simple village peasant women who often see their priest no more than once a year support the Church and derive what little solace and status they can from their identification with religious activity, even though they are often oppressed by the authoritarianism and paternalism of the Church (Inda, 1975).

At the end of the colonial period there were only 2400 nuns in all of New Spain, but they were objects of veneration and held very high social status. Standards for admission to the novitiate were so high that this "spiritually privileged class also constituted a socially privileged minority" (Lavrin, 1972: 367). Not only did they have to satisfy rigorous religious requirements, they also had to meet the usual Spanish class and racial qualifications—clean blood from Christian ancestors—a restriction that eliminated all non-Spaniards and, later on, those with even remote Jewish ancestry. The "endowed" nuns, with their elegant and exclusive black veils, reflected the class system of colonial society and made their final professions to the accompaniment of opulent and worldly celebrations paid for by their families or by patrons from high society. Nuns could own their own cell, even have one specially built for them, keep servants, have slaves, and invite young female relatives or friends to share quarters with them. The worldly character of most of the nunneries in New Spain in the seventeenth and eighteenth centuries came under criticism, but the nuns, in 1660, refused to limit the number of their personal servants, live in dormitories, and eat in refectories, and even held strikes to keep their personal incomes and privileges (Lavrin, 1972: 375).

Meanwhile those Spanish women who lacked dowries or patrons, then as now, had to settle for the life of the lay sister, usually one of menial labor. A few women with special talents in music might join their more fortunate sisters, their talents being accepted in lieu of dowry, but Indians, except for a few royal Indians, mestizos, and free Negroes remained at the bottom of the ladder, doing the menial work and lacking even a vote in the life of the community.

Among the nuns was an extraordinarily gifted woman, Sor Juana Inés de la Cruz, who left the court and entered the monastery because, as she tells us, "of her aversion to matrimony, and to dedicate herself to studies with more devotion" (Torres-Rioseco, 1947: 24). The following quotation throws some light on the somewhat ambiguous status of women of her time and class:

> As a young nun, and patronized by two successive viceroys and their wives until 1686, Sor Juana was able to write poetry and continue her studies in literature, science, and theology. But despite her privileged position as a favorite of the viceroys, she eventually had to face the hostility of a society that held all women to be inferior to all men. Writing poetry was one thing, but Sor Juana's interest in scientific and theological questions raised a storm that is reflected in her poetry and other writings. "I have prayed God to subdue the light of my intelligence," she confessed, "leaving me only enough to keep his law, for anything more (according to some persons) is superflous in a woman" [Macias, 1971: 4].

As elsewhere in the Western world, seventeenth century Mexican society could not accommodate a woman with Sor Juana's intellectual interests. Throughout the colonial period in Mexico, an intellectual woman remained an anomaly. Though certainly not typical, the life of Sor Juana exposed the prejudices and values, both social and religious, of the colonial society of New Spain (Lavrin, 1972: 384).

The colonial period lasted three centuries. There were steady improvements in civil government, but ecclesiastical authority and control remained of major importance. As the Indians lost their old priests, temples, idols and customs, many of them turned to Tonantzin, now the Virgin of Guadalupe. On the other extreme of the social scale were the privileged nuns, carrying on their struggle as women as they sought fulfillment in the religious life. These two extremes vividly illustrate the religiosity of Mexican women, and help to explain the emergence of the cult of *marianismo,* which appears to result in part from the submissiveness that women have always shown toward the Church (Stevens, 1973: 95).

Independence (1810–1910). Because the struggle for independence of 1810 to 1821 was primarily a political phenomenon, there was very little change in the condition and way of life of most Mexican women. A small number of exceptional women were educated in the few secular schools established before 1855, but one could say of most women, as was reported in the 1916 Feminist Congress in Yucatan, that, "They lived, they made tortillas, and they died."

In sharp contrast with this pattern of life in the villages, was the style lived by the upper classes, really the "afterglow" of the old viceregal society, which was vividly portrayed by Frances Calderon de la Barca, Scottish wife of Spain's first minister to Mexico from 1838 to 1840. Her descriptions in *Life of Mexico* of political, economic, and social situations add insight to the situation of the early forties. The old feudal life still held sway, and in society at large the old family names and titles had not lost their prestige. Servants still abounded even though slavery had been abolished, and the extremes of privilege and poverty were great (Calderon, 1843, 1970: 365–371).

After a long series of internal disruptions, rebellions, and administrative changes, Benito Juarez, a Zapotec Indian, became president and put into effect laws of reform. Some of these had a profound effect on Mexican women. On the one hand, with the Church nationalized the nunneries were suppressed and women who, like Sor Juana, were disinclined to marry, no longer had this alternative. On the other hand, with the coming of the Reform movement women who wanted an education and a chance to work outside the home had opportunities on a scale that had previously not existed. Margarita Maza de Juarez, who was not only wife but "colaborador" of Juarez, was a key figure in stimulating efforts for liberal reforms for women. In her personal life and actions she was a symbol of the "austerity and vigor of democracy" (Mendieta, 1972). In 1860 Juarez announced that the government would actively support primary education, and that "education of women will also be attended to, giving it the importance it deserves because of the influence women exercise over society" (Macias, 1971: 16).

Many of Juarez's plans, however, particularly the expansion of the system of primary schools for the benefit of girls as well as boys, were thwarted by the French intervention that occurred during the United States Civil War. With Emperor Maximilian and Empress Carlotta came a return to the elegant court life for a few women, and for Mexico strong European influences in trade, education, and politics during 7 years. After the nationalist rebellion, which ended in Maximilian's death, the country remained in a state of chaos and internal factionalism until the Porfiriato, the period dominated by Porfirio-Diaz, which lasted from 1874 until 1910. The number of women attending primary school increased slowly but steadily, and several female normal schools were established in the Federal District and leading cities. By the end of the nineteenth century some states reported almost as many literate females as males, which certainly had important implications for womens' roles. Between 1888 and 1904 professional schools of medicine, law, and commerce in Mexico City admitted (sometimes reluctantly) their first women students. On the eve of the revolution several thousand middle-class women were working at white-collar jobs.

By the end of the Porfiriato, attitudes toward women, the sex mores, and the roles "good" or "bad" women were expected to play in society had changed somewhat, but the situation of women in Mexico in 1910 was not substantially improved. The increased opportunities for middle-class women to study and work were not paralleled by similar developments for poorer women. In fact the conditions of poorer women often worsened as large numbers of them, lacking other means of support, became domestic servants or prostitutes. The Civil Code of 1864, which accorded to adult single women almost the same rights as men, left married women *imbecilitas sexas* under the absolute power of their husbands, with the same rights as children. Until 1910 womens' emancipation had made little headway in Mexico, and only a small number of female schoolteachers and professional women had become advocates of the movement (Macias, 1971: 4–17).

Mexican Revolution to the Present (1910–1976). It has been said that "the greatest revolution a country can know, is the one which changes the condition and way of life of its women" (Quoted in Elu de Leñero, 1969: 162). Certainly in Mexico during the Revolutionary years, 1910 to 1918, many womens' lives were altered as some took up complete management of homes, farms, businesses, and families. Others, particularly the peasant women with their children and *metates,* joined the troops, serving as needed quartermaster corps, spies, and active soldiers, often forming the rear guard and on some occasions taken as hostages. Several women held the ranks of sergeant and lieutenant, and some were colonels (Encuentro de Mujeres, 1972 b: 26). One of these women soldiers, Margarita Neri, commanded a unit of 400 Indians (Turner, 1967: 604).

Even though women had proved themselves equal to men both in the ranks and as officers during the years of conflict, they were not recognized or given political power afterward. The victorious Carranzista group held that, "The fact that some exceptional women possess the necessary qual-ifications to exercise satisfactorily their political rights, does not demand the conclusion that these (rights) should be conceded to women as a class" (Encuentro de Mujeres, 1972a: 26). Although both Francisco I. Madero and Venustiano Carranza received support from a number of educated women and several feminist societies, in the period from 1911 to 1915 the only reform they enacted directly affecting women was a divorce law that pro-vided for absolute divorce for the first time in Mexican history. Carranza argued that the new law, by making legal marriage dissoluble, would counter the tendency of the poorer class to remain in the *amasiato,* or free union, state and would thereby reduce the number of illegitimate children. He also maintained that the law would benefit middle- and upper-class women, because they would no longer have to tolerate their husbands' adultery. However most moderate feminists opposed the law because its provisions clearly favored men in the grounds for divorce and failed to provide women and dependent children with adequate alimony and child-support arrangements. Carranza did not make any effort to improve educa-tional opportunities for women, hire more women in government posts, or initiate other measures to assist women to become more self-sufficient (Macias, 1971: 8–9).

The Constitution of 1917, adopted at the end of the Revolution, included several articles and provisions legally supporting the rights and privileges of women. The *Ley de Trabajo,* or Labor Law, together with the Family Rela-tions Law, included such requirements as equal pay for equal work regard-less of sex or nationality, shorter hours for night work, paid leaves and job security for pregnancies, and obligatory day-care arrangements at places employing more than 49 women. However the Federal Election Law, which was passed the following year, specifically excluded women from voting in federal elections. In 1922 women were given the right to vote in Yucatan, the first state to do so, and in late 1923 four women were elected deputies to the state legislature there. One of these women, Elvira Carrillo Puerto, then established residence in San Louis Potosí, where women had just been granted the vote, and ran for the seat from that district to the Chamber of Deputies. She was elected, but the Chamber of Deputies refused to recog-nize her credentials and did not admit her (Gruening, 1928: 629). Legisla-tion enacted in 1932 for the Federal District and territories accorded women equal legal rights with men, the right to enter into contracts, the right to hold office or jobs outside the home, and even the right to sell joint properties with the husband's consent. Five years later President Cardenas proposed a constitutional amendment that would specifically recognize the citizenship of women in Mexico. Although it was approved unanimously in both houses of Congress and by every state legislature, the law was never put into effect because of political maneuvering. Subsequent legislation in 1953, 16 years later, sponsored by President Ruiz Cortines cleared the way for complete participation by women in the political life of the country, explicitly stating that women had the right to vote in any and all elections in the country, as well as hold any office, elective or appointive (Navarrete, 1969, 1973: 123).

Entrance into World War II on the side of the Allies reinforced Mexico's close economic relationship with the United States. Rapid, extensive industrialization also characterized this period. For women this meant an acceleration of migration from the villages, entrance into the factories, and the rise of a middle class that had an increasing demand for servants. Some women found new economic freedom. Others, who derived their status from their husbands' positions, benefitted by the upgrading of many men.

Much was accomplished by and for women during this time. A few individual women had reached the tops of their professions, but as late as the middle 1950s they thought of themselves as "a generation of rebels" who had successfully rebelled against "the shackles which kept them tied to their homes and dependent on men . . ." (Gutierrez, 1955). A number of women were "firsts" in their professions. The first woman to become a member of the Supreme Court was Maria Lavalle Urbina, now a permanent member of the Mexican Commission to the United Nations and a member of the OAS Inter-American Commission for Women. The first woman mayor of a Mexican village, Maria Elena Ramirez, was so popular that after her death the townspeople of Xochimilco drafted her sister as her replacement. Amalia de Castillo Ledon, who was Ambassador to Sweden and Switzerland, founded the Mexican Alliance of Women and became Undersecretary in the Ministry of Education, President of the Inter-American Commission of Women, and the first woman to address the Senate. Another woman highly active in politics, leader of the women's section of the Institutional Revolutionary Party (PRI), principal Mexican political party, was Margarita Garcia Flores, a well-known economist. Adela Formoso de Obregon Santacilia, writer and orator, founded the Womens' University. Rosario Castellanos, outstanding both as a writer and as a diplomat, was Mexico's Ambasssador to Israel at the time of her death in 1974. Earlier, with a friend from high school, Dolores Castro, she formed part of a group called "La Generación de 1950." Rosario Castellanos' paper "On Feminine Culture," which denied the existence of a feminine culture, was thought by some of her contemporaries to mark the intellectual beginnings of the liberation of women in Mexico. Dr. Maria de la Luz Grovas, founding president of the Mexican Association of University Women, was one of the first women professors at the National University of Mexico (UNAM). She set up a hostel in her home for young women from the provinces who came to attend the University. The first woman from an upper-class Mexican family to become a film actress, Dolores del Rio, continues to be a model for many young women. Many of these women are still very active in their professions, and some are participating today with younger women in the Mexican feminist movement.

The improvement in opportunities for women in the 1950s resulted primarily from the efforts of pioneering women, most of whom were from the upper class. But the success of these exceptional women did not, of course, end the systematic discrimination against their sisters. Some of their success depended on the help of other women from the villages, who could be hired at incredibly low wages as domestics. Live-in servants were the rule, not the exception, for the middle and often the upper-lower classes. The achievements of the 1950s were nonetheless great. Mexico has had and still has proportionately more congresswomen, more women as high government officials, more women doctors, dentists, lawyers, and other professionals, than the United States. Although womens' suffrage in Mexico was not completely effected until 1953, Mexico was a pioneer in much other legislation affording equal rights for women (Navarrete, 1969, 1973: 123).

WOMEN IN CONTEMPORARY INSTITUTIONS

Within Latin American cultures Mexico falls into the Indo-Mestizo grouping along with the Andean countries. A cultural pattern similar to that of countries having strong Indian heritages with European overlays persists in Mexico, although with more vertical and horizontal mobility than in most other Latin American countries. Mexico still has areas in which Indians and non-Indians interact in what have been termed *caste* systems (Stavenhagen, 1970: 266–270).

In Mexico, "The Indian is defined ethnically not racially" (Beals, 1965: 35). The domestic servant, when she changes her uniform for her day off, can become *mestiza* or Indian, depending on her plans. Among the large lower class—rural and urban—that is defined as mestizo/a there are many cultural patterns that remain Indian. Mexico does not seem to have welded together her two dominant cultural heritages—the Indian and the Spanish.

In Mexico we have "centuries of womanhood" as we look at the many Mexicos: the primitive, the archaic, the historic, and the modern. As the woman relates to her family, culture, religion, and to her own feeling of self-freedom and pride she forms part of an evolutionary process, which in some ways is giving her more freedom in having a larger part of her behavior not determined by her sex. (Giele, 1972: 99). But in Mexico the evolutionary process is not a single continuum. Families and even individuals find themselves living in different historical periods.

In understanding Mexico today, with its rapid modernization and economic development, we must be aware of the growing middle class and of pressures for change in the roles of both men and women.

Family.   Mexico is in a period of great change. As Mexico looks for its own reality, it is faced with the loss of values of the old cultures and a rejection of many of the values of the modern. Mexico is not a homogeneous country, and family patterns vary greatly (Leñero, 1968a: 194). The crucial factor is that *situational circumstances* have created a wider range of alternative patterns of behavior for women to supersede the single traditional role circumscribed by culture and sustained by family ideals (Youssef, 1972: 346–347).

Despite the many drastic changes brought about in the last 50 years, the Mexican woman is still expected to fulfill herself—to receive honor and pride—through the accomplishments of her family, really those of the males. "What greater ambition does the Mexican woman have than to assure that her sons, her husbands, her brothers realize themselves as 'persons'?" (Augustin Yañez quoted by Encuentro de Mujeres, 1972a: 27). The stereotype of "the woman in the home" remains even among many intellectuals and professionals. Women may add new roles, but shedding their childbearing or childrearing roles, or sharing them with Mexican males, is only gradually being explored (Elu de Leñero, 1971: 34).

In Mexico, as in most of Latin America, the family is the basic structure, which in spite of pressures toward the nuclear family, still retains many of the traditional forms of the extended family. Among the privileged social group the family still operates as a unit to control political and financial power, with control still exercised over the status of female members. Women in both urban and rural areas often wield great power and influence within the kinship networks, the marital alliances, and home territories. In this world of home and family the woman often holds decision-making prerogatives. New research is revealing many hitherto unexplored areas in which women often exercise great power (Chiñas, 1973). Great diversity is found in the family structure. A team of social scientists* conducted a national investigation of the Mexican family in 1966–67 in the Federal District and 14 states, involving 2457 men and 2953 women. The results pointed out the dichotomies between old and young, rich and poor, rural and urban, between various regions under differing foreign influences (for example, the states bordering the United States as compared with the more isolated), very religious and less religious families, traditional and progres-

*From Instituto Mexicano de Estudios Sociales (IMES).

sive, ignorant and educated, those integrated and those marginal to the social organization (Leñero Otero, 1968a: 32–33).

The same research showed that the average size of the Mexican family has increased in recent years. During 1966–67 the number of children born to a Mexican couple during 20 years of marriage averaged 6.9, with the possibility that by the end of fertility 7 or more would be the average (Elu de Leñero, 1971: 17). The large size of the Mexican family relegates most Mexican women to a life dominated by childbearing and childrearing, with the absence of the father in the home considered normal (Elu de Leñero, 1971: 34). Because of absence of labor-saving devices or services, as well as cooperative attitudes on the part of the husband, the poorer women in both rural and urban areas spend most of their time in arduous, repetitive work, while the urban upper-class women continue in absolute economic dependence on the man (Elu de Leñero, 1969: 33). The classic, but still controversial study *Five Mexican Families* by Oscar Lewis points out the malaise and the lack of "love" or demonstration of affection found both among the rural and urban poor caught in "the culture of poverty" and, most shockingly, among the *nouveaux riches* who aspire to the North American material culture (Lewis, 1959: 294–350).

The Latin American family organization in general and the Mexican family structure in particular have been described as patriarchal institutions emphasizing male supremacy and female subordination (Youssef, 1974: 83). Two types of explanation have been employed to account for the Mexican family pattern: one basically historical, the other cultural. One approach traces the origin of family relationships to the conquest of Mexico and the concomitant sexual exploitation of Indian women by Spanish men. According to this theory, the woman became the symbol of the conquered, subdued Indian, and the man the symbol of the conquering, demanding Spaniard. The mestizo child born of this union looked down on both his mother as a devalued person and his father as an exploiter. Nevertheless when he became an adult, the mestizo male emulated his father's treatment of his mother, and a distinctive family pattern was then passed from generation to generation (Peñalosa, 1968: 682).

The second and more common approach analyzes the Mexican family pattern in the framework of deeply embedded cultural factors, perhaps best summarized in the concept of *machismo*. *Machismo* refers to a sense of exaggerated masculinity or a cult of virility whose chief characteristics are extreme "aggressiveness and intransigence in male-to-male interpersonal relationships and arrogance and sexual aggression in male-to-female relationship" (Stevens, 1972b: 315). It is generally agreed that *machismo* is a Latin American phenomenon, with roots in Old World culture, perhaps

Ibero-American, perhaps Mediterranean, including Mozarabic influences. Many of the constituents of this attitude can be found even today in Italy and Spain, but the most complete expression occurs in Latin America (Stevens, 1973a: 91). Moreover of the Latin American nations Mexico has been described by Latin Americans as the nation most afflicted with the *machismo* syndrome, with Peru and Colombia, also important seats of Spanish control, vying for second place.

According to Nora Kinzer, some social scientists believe that *machismo* is primarily a lower-class phenomenon although she says it doesn't exist. (Kinzer, 1973: 302–303). Others say that it cuts across class lines, thriving where two cultures mix, whether Indian and Spanish or African and European (Stevens, 1973c: 5).

The male pattern of behavior has its corollary in reciprocal female traits formerly referred to as *hembrismo* (Bermúdez, 1955: 93–94), now called *marianismo* (Stevens, 1973a). While the traditional stereotype of the man envisions him as a strong individual, conquering, dominant, and argumentative, the woman is pictured as dependent, conformist, unimaginative, and timid (Elu de Leñero, 1969: 25). At the same time, perhaps as a special veneration to the figure of the Virgin Mary, women are considered to be morally superior to men and spiritually stronger (Stevens, 1973a: 315). With regard to the institutionalization of the *marianismo* syndrome, it is important to note that the worship of Mary has developed further in Mexico than elsewhere in Latin America. Thus although the cultural definition of masculinity demands the subordination of women and their conformity to behavioral norms that protect and enhance male honor, the societal norms also reward women by conferring prestige and high esteem to qualities such as purity, patience, humility, sacrifice—the same qualities cultivated by nuns. Men put women on a pedestal and simultaneously relegate them to a life of suffering by being inattentive and unfaithful.

To comprehend the implications of *marianismo* it should be understood that far from being a standard imposed only by men, *marianismo* has received considerable support from women themselves. Some scholars have even claimed that Latin American women have consciously contributed to the perpetuation of the myth of male dominance and the concomitant sexually defined division of roles because it offers them many advantages. *Machismo* is born of male insecurity rather than strength, and this affords many possibilities for feminine control behind the scenes. These analysts also have disagreed strongly with the usual portrayal of Mexican women as passive and have argued that these women manipulate and maximize the existing values to achieve their own ends (Stevens, 1973a: 316).

One key to understanding *machismo* is the role of children. A man's masculinity is demonstrated largely by his ability to make sexual conquests;

since boasting is easy, the only real proof of virility is the repeated pregnancies of a wife and/or mistress. To have children, especially sons, is to affirm one's understood role as a male. The woman is compensated by her children for the lifelong burden of multiple pregnancies and a husband who must be unfaithful to her in order to assert his masculinity. Machismo carried to its logical conclusion excludes a woman from the sphere of public affairs, but it also enables her to reign supreme in her own household.

For the great majority who bear children, the status they enjoy as mothers is very high. To become a mother is in many ways a rite of passage to adulthood. "A wife's status increases as her family grows, reaching its highest when she herself becomes a mother-in-law to her sons' wives" (Chiñas, 1973: 59). To a large extent the love and even reverence accorded to mothers in Mexico results from the negative impact on the children of the fathers' machismo role. The man may succeed on one front only to lose on another, for after seeing how he treats their mother, his children's sympathies can lie only with her. Sons, rather than endorsing the patriarchal pretensions of the father, retain a primary attachment to the mother and view her as the only person who loves unconditionally (Fromm and Maccoby, 1970: 116). As a consequence Mexican society may be viewed as a patriarchy interwoven with a matriarchy, with the main figure of attachment for individuals—regardless of age—as the mother (Fromm and Maccoby, 1970: 114). Men, it appears, have the "outward and visible" signs of power, while women rule through the acknowledged superiority of their "inward and spiritual grace."

Some social scientists have found in the remnants of traditional Indian cultures a striking lack of machismo (Chiñas, 1973; Elmendorf, 1972, 1973; Wolf, 1959, 1964). Although, of course, there is great variation among Indian groups, in general it appears that the rural Indian woman enjoys far more equality than her white or mestiza sisters (Wolf, 1959, 1964: 220). A study of the Isthmus Zapotecs indicates that the everyday roles of the sexes tend to be mutually dependent and complementary in both the economic division of labor and other aspects of the social system (Chiñas, 1973: 1). Similar themes also appear in two other microstudies of mestizo villages (Arnold, 1973; Schwartz, 1962). Among the Mexican non-Indian peasants more signs are found of the machismo characteristics and related alcoholism among the day laborers than among the ejiditarios, or small landowners (Fromm and Maccoby, 1970: 55).

In the barrios, or shanty-towns, surrounding the metropolitan areas the male–female relationship reflects the machismo–marianismo dichotomy. The prescribed masculine role is one of irresponsibility, and the woman "feels the necessity of ennobling herself by suffering even if she by temperament may be happy and capable" (Lomnitz, 1973a: 6). The man looks to his male friends for affection and pleasure, and the woman to her children and brothers. The woman often depends more on her brother than on her husband, because the role of the brother is the only one in which the culture permits the man to be responsible without appearing weak. Social organization is based on units of four or five nuclear families—*family* used in the broadest sense—which form extended and compound units to make up a supportive network that serves as the basic security for women and children. Male and female really have "segregated conjugal roles," which other members of the extended family can assume if necessary. Interestingly in the Mexican *barrio* the "family" appears to remain relatively stable though partners change. When a man deserts the family, the woman frequently turns without much difficulty to a free union with another man. This marginal woman of the *barrio* may differ from her middle-class counterpart in that her suffering is joined with residual strength (Lomnitz, 1963b: 7). This is part of the coping pattern that she has developed.

When we speak of family in Mexico, we must make it clear that we are referring to both legal and nonlegal unions.

> A large number of women are forced to substitute for marriage non-legal living arrangements in the form of transient relationships of short or ephemeral duration, consensual unions of some durability, and polygamous concubinal unions with married men [Davis, 1964: 37, as quoted in Youssef, 1974: 104].

The prevalence of consensual unions and illegitimate births makes clear that many women are completely dependent on their own resources for themselves and their children, without recourse to the rights and reciprocities of legal unions. Family controls are inadequate to enforce chastity or to protect young women, who are often forced to work away from home.

In a recent IMES study of 5413 parents, a large number did fit into the traditionally delineated patterns of role-playing, but they were not as sharply defined as the *machismo* sterotype would demand, with the husband refusing all responsibility for household tasks and excluding the woman from important family decisions. "From 25% to 60% showed egalitarian tendencies with shared functions and decisions. One fourth could be considered highly egalitarian" (Leñero Otero, 1968a, 1971: 196). According to women informants, decisions on where to live, what furniture to buy, where the children should go to school, and whether to have more children were frequently made together (Leñero Otero, 1968a, 1971: 328–329). Male and female informants in another survey related that the decision on whether to have more children was reached jointly, although female informants more often described the decision as a mutual one than did their husbands (Elu de Leñero, 1969: 136).

The Mexican man typically distinguishes between his wife, whom he sees as meant for procreation, and his mistress, with whom he expects to have a physically pleasurable relationship. A "good" woman is not expected to enjoy sex, nor is she instructed in it; it should not be unexpected that a full 50 percent of the women interviewed regarded sex as a "painful duty." Another 50 percent of the informants believed marriage to be an obstacle to their personal development (Elu de Leñero, 1969: 150–151).

It might be expected that this "perceived" dissatisfaction among women would eventually give rise to demands for changed patterns of relationships. One study of responses to a questionnaire by similar samples of girls in coeducational and all-girls schools shows a definite change in attitudes between 1959 and 1970. Among the girls interviewed in 1970, for example, significantly fewer agreed that "men are superior to women." In both types of schools the female respondents also believed that parents should be fairer in their relationships with their children, thus implying that parents were abusing their sociocultural power (Diaz-Guerrero, 1967, 1973). Because the socialization of the Mexican woman has been shown to take place primarily with regard to relationships with her immediate family, a breakdown in the present close, even formalized system of family relationships would probably produce a profound alteration in the beliefs and behavior of Mexican women (Diaz-Guerrero, 1967: 139–141).

Critics have begun to raise questions about the Mexican family and the restraints it imposes on its women. Maria del Carmen Elu de Leñero has warned that unless the nuclear family can be supportive of all its members, allowing the wife as well as the husband and children to find self-fulfillment, it must be replaced (Elu de Leñero, statement at the American Association for the Advancement of the Sciences conference, AAAS–CONACYT, Mexico City, 1973). Her statement may have reflected the sentiments of some of Mexico's elite group of professional women, but the vast majority of Mexico's women remain too bound by traditional patterns of socialization to voice objections.

Work. When assessing the economic opportunities available to contemporary women, it is important to keep in mind Mexico's rapid economic development from a predominantly agricultural country to a semiindustrialized nation. Figures from the last national census in 1970 show that slightly less than 40 percent of the labor force presently work in the agricultural sector (Tienda, 1974: 39). Census data indicate that 10.8 percent of the female labor force work in agriculture and related fields. Information on the participation of women in the rural areas is not sufficient to provide a full picture of the agricultural labor force or the female contribution to it (Gonzalez, 1974: 6). Development of the economy and increasing urbanization have opened new opportunities for women workers in the production forces, but they have not resolved the many problems associated with women's working.

In the last 40 years the number of economically active women in the paid work force has more than quadrupled. In 1930 women made up only 4.6 percent of the paid labor force; this increased to 7.4 percent in 1940, to 13.6 percent in 1950, and to 18 percent in 1960. The increase from that date to 1969 brought the figure to only 19.0 percent (Gonzalez, 1974: 4).

Although women's economic activity rates have increased during the intense development process of the last 40 years, the magnitude of internal inequalities within the nation has widened, and related variations are found in women's work patterns. For instance Tienda used a socioeconomic scale to divide the Mexican states into three groups. A positive but not absolute relationship was found between degree of development and female partici- pation, ranging from 9.1 percent in Zacatecas to 20.1 percent in Nuevo Leon and 29.7 percent in the Federal District. The participation of married female and male workers showed minimal influence by the degree of development. Within the three states of modernization the level and pattern of the female labor force varied with the family life-cycle phases. All three groups showed a well-defined primary peak among female workers during their early twen- ties, and the magnitude of the inflection varied positively with the level of development.

Women's share of employment varies considerably in two ways, geo- graphically and sectorally. Although women's work rates correlate positively with the degree of development of the Mexican states, development does not seem to alter drastically the industrial employment structure, and the sex stratification characteristic of the less-developed Mexican states persists in the more developed ones (Tienda, 1974: 132). Women predominate in only one sphere of the economy, personal services, and supply more than one- third of the personnel in one other, social services. At first glance the presence of 89.2% of the women workers in nonagricultural activities makes them seem more "modern" than the men. However 60.1% of these women are employed in service occupations, many of them very low-paying jobs. Nearly one-fifth (19.8%) of the working women are domestics in private homes, and another 6.6% clean buildings, prepare and sell vegetables, and work in similarly low-status, low-paying jobs. Many of these women, along with the ambulatory vendors, are underemployed and underpaid (Gonzalez, 1974: 6–7).

On the other hand, Mexican women hold one-half of the professional positions in the public and administrative sector, one-fourth in the com- merce sector, and one-fifth in the industrial branches of manufacturing (Youssef, 1974: 36). Some women are now directors of automobile factories, and others head auto transport, electrical, export, hotel, and other industries. And many are lawyers, journalists, economists, and so forth, not to mention executives and administrators in many branches of government and educational institutions (Gonzalez, 1974: 12). These are exceptional cases. More typical of the economic development in Mexico is the reinforcement or enhancement of the division of labor by sex (Tienda, 1974: 133). The continued practice of sex labeling of occupations has meant that although women's job opportunities have expanded, their actual range of employment options has not increased significantly. Many believe that the concept of "the woman's place is in the home" has not died, but has merely been transmuted into the concept of "women's work" (Chaney, 1973: 104). Women fill jobs that are extensions of the functions that women perform in the home: domestic work; restaurant work, in which 50 percent of the personnel are women; teaching in lower schools, nursing; and secretarial employment. Factory work constitutes another area considered "women's work," because the dull, repetitive jobs found in industry are thought to be especially suited to their unimaginative temperaments. Such a premium is put on being able to work at all that women take whatever jobs they can find; usually these are the lowest, most boring jobs society has to offer. Nevertheless even these jobs often constitute a step toward liberation, since the woman employed in the factory has the opportunity to become economically independent of men and has contact with a wider group (Encuentro de Mujeres, 1972b: 36).

By 1968 Mexican women comprised 19.2 percent of the labor force (Navarrete 1969, 1973: 32). Not included in this figure is the work done in the home—cooking, childrearing, and family supporting—except by women who are paid servants. In Mexico, as in most countries, "Domestic work is considered a secondary sexual characteristic instead of an economic category" (Larguia and Dumoulin, 1971: 38). Mexican husbands are reluctant to share domestic roles and depreciate the contribution of the woman by saying, "And you, what are you complaining about? You don't do anything" (Encuentro de Mujeres, 1972a: 36). The dual roles for the upper-class woman are lightened by the paid domestic, but she is not freed from household responsibility, only made overseer of the household, and in so acting sometimes oppresses other women. Many working women such as factory workers spend their "free time" in doing housework (Piho, 1973: 45).

Women have not yet fully been accepted into the working force, particularly among the upper classes. Many Mexican families, especially middle-class and upwardly mobile families, exert pressure on the woman not to seek employment. It is estimated that 60 percent of all Mexican men still have the final decision on whether their wives may seek outside work (Elu de Leñero, 1969: 126). Written permission of the husband was formerly required by law as a precondition to a woman's being accepted for a job. Often the prospective husband of a woman who has a job makes it a precondition for marriage that she leave her job, and the woman usually accepts this. For women from the privileged social groups, the idleness of the wife comprises an essential part of the life-style. "The middle class in general, sees feminine parasitism as a virtue: the most beautiful adornment of the home, of her husband, is the wife, a living testimony to his manhood, wealth and power" (Hernandez, 1971: 102). Thus in middle- and upper-class families in which the wife's education is most likely to qualify her for white-collar employment, the husband is most inclined to object to the wife's independent employment because he interprets this employment as reflecting negatively on his role as the protector and head of the household.

Men who head lower-class families cannot afford the luxury of preventing women from working because women's salaries often help support the entire family (Youssef, 1974: 11). Today in many rural and urban Mexican families, where economic pressures are great, the adolescent girl is expected to work and contribute all or most of her earnings to supplement family income. Divorced, widowed, or separated Mexican women have the highest economic activity rate, 28.6 percent; married women the lowest, 8.5 percent (Tienda, 1974: 49). Employment rates among divorced and separated women in Mexico are higher than those in any other Latin American country except Ecuador (Youssef, 1974: 111); Ecuador includes rural housewives among the economically active.

Although the Catholic Church has opposed wage earning by married women as inimical to the family and contrary to woman's femininity, Catholic clergyman have contributed to legitimizing some women's educational and occupational emancipation "by providing opportunities for higher education in racially and socially segregated climates and by recruiting upper class women for semi-occupational functions" (Youssef, 1974: 103). An identity other than that prescribed by the family roles is thus made possible for middle- and upper-class women under the aegis of the Church. This results in work participation without economic need and delayed marriage or nonmarriage "with little residue of imposed penalty or shame" (Youssef, 1974: 103).

For the rural woman there is enormous disparity between their statistical representation and their actual amount of labor performed in the agricultural sector. In 1972 only 10.8% of the female labor force was listed as economically active in agriculture and related fields, even though in many parts of rural Mexico the unit of production is the family, with each member performing a necessary role (Gonzalez, 1974: Table I). In those parts of Mexico in which families still engage in subsistence agriculture, the woman serves a fundamental and indispensable role because the division of labor gives her

Table 1   Female Labor Force Participation Rates by Marital Status in Mexico

Single	Married	Consensual Union	Divorced, Widowed, or Separated	Average
24.0	8.5	12.0	28.6	16.4

Source.   IV Censo de Poblacion, Resumen General: Cuadro 31, quoted in Tienda 1974, Table 4.

integral economic and social functions, but at the same time she is tied irrevocably to the family and to family enterprises, to numerous arduous and demanding tasks, to years of immobilization through many pregnancies and childrearing. Often if asked whether she works, the rural woman answers negatively, partly because she receives no money, but also because she considers her labor as part of her duty, even though she may help, along with her children, in planting or harvesting and in the care of animals and gardens. Often the woman carries the complete responsibility of the farm for long or short periods while her husband is working in the city (Encuentro de Mujeres, 1972b: 26).

In some traditional communities with Indian or related peasant values, the woman often has a feeling of autonomy and dignity, and does not consider her work onerous or debasing. In fact, the work of women is considered not only a skill and technique, but of equal importance with that of men in certain traditional Indian communities (Chiñas, 1973; Elmendorf, 1973; Kaberry, 1939, 1973: 36; Paul, 1974; Wolf, 1959, 1964: 221).

Modernization and the integration of the peasant into the economy as a paid worker frequently have made women marginal in the productive process by reducing their roles to working in the home and caring for children. In the rural areas women with children can generally find paid work only on a part-time basis and without a contract, doing such things as the picking of cotton, tobacco, coffee, and cocoa (Encuentro de Mujeres, 1972a: 28). Since the 1960s the poverty of some of the rural areas has driven Indian women to the streets of Mexico City, where they sell fruits, nuts, and so forth. Many prefer being street vendors to being live-in domestic servants (Arizpe, 1972). Many young women come from the provinces to a city and still find only three choices of work: domestic, factory, and prostitution.

For the women of the nineteenth and early twentieth centuries, the textile industry provided opportunities to work, but at substandard wages. Since the 1930s the ratio of women to men has decreased as the jobs have become relatively better paying, with women no longer in the majority in the textile factories (Keremitsis, 1974). In many cases the female textile workers—even the unmarried, childless ones—assume responsibility for their family group. Thus the woman factory worker suffers two forms of exploitation: first, as a worker in her conditions of service and, second, as a woman in her family obligations (Piho, 1973: 14, 77–78).

One of the prime expressions of discrimination against women lies in their arbitrary assignment to domestic work. In fact, 49 out of every 100 women working in the service sector are domestic servants, according to 1970 census data (Bowen, 1975: 138). Domestic work in Mexico often comes close to slavery. The protective laws are weak, and there is still no minimum wage. Legislators have repeatedly avoided passing regulations that would establish hourly wages, vacations, and other fringe benefits for domestics. Social security coverage is now available but optional. The most domestic servants can legally expect is given in the Federal Work Law, Article 123: "Domestic workers have the right to rest sufficiently, to eat their food and sleep during the night."

It should be pointed out, however, that domestic service does have positive aspects as an occupation. In Mexico City, as in some other Latin American cities, the majority of young women migrating from the villages find work first as domestics. Many of these work their way upward through the social classes, often gaining prestige and new skills as they work for wealthier patrons, while receiving housing and a kind of autonomy. It can be a positive learning experience, and it enables a young migrant to survive in the urban setting and to use it as a channel for upward mobility within the broad spectrum of the lower class. But for many others, including the monolingual Indians, in Mexico as in other Latin American countries it can be exploitation of the worst sort (Smith, 1973: 193; Myers, 1973: 164).

For women fortunate enough to find work of any kind, it is a truism that they will receive less pay than a man would for filling the same job. According to the Department of Economic Statistics, women's salaries are sometimes only 40 percent of men's, with women often earning little more than half as much as men (Encuentro de Mujeres, 1972a: 30). The 1969 census tables which divided nonagricultural laborers by sex and by income level showed that 45 percent of working women fell into the lowest income group as compared with 18.9 percent of the men; 72.2 percent of women workers were listed in the two lowest income categories whereas only 53.9 percent of the men were so classified (Gonzalez, 1974: 14). In the neediest classes the practice of paying women less than men for equal work often takes on dramatic proportions. Throughout Mexico the lowest-salaried jobs in the textile and electronic industries are held by women (Encuentro de Mujeres, 1972b: 37). It should also be noted that the number of maquiladoras (women who take precut sewing from factories in their homes) has increased tremendously in past years. Because these women work at home, the factory owners are exempted from paying them the minimum wage, social security, and other benefits (Encuentro de Mujeres, 1972b: 38).

In the case of the *maquiladoras* laws are being evaded; there are other cases, however, in which laws passed for the protection or benefit of women act to militate against their employment. The Constitution of 1917, enacted before other countries exhibited comparable concerns, sought to change some of the existing inequalities in employment for men and women, while still retaining some protective legislation. Women were to be legal equals with men, and according to Article 123 would receive equal pay for equal work. Most of the protective legislation dealt with women's functions as mothers: women during the last three months of pregnancy must not be required to perform jobs requiring great physical effort; during the month after birth they must be given time off with pay; during lactation they must be given time to nurse their children; nurseries must be established at any company having greater than a certain number of women; and so on (Navarrete, 1969, 1973: 117–118). However many of the laws guaranteeing protection and equal rights for women have never been enforced because of differences in local interpretation.

Even a woman who has attained a relatively high position in the working or professional force faces many problems that do not beset a man in the same situation. To quote from a statement made by one of Mexico's leading women economists:

If you're a woman who has arrived professionally, if you have made your mark in the academic world, people look at you critically. If you are married, they wonder how you've done it, if you are unmarried, they think you must be a lesbian; if you are a mother, you have not taken care of your children. There is no way to win, but that doesn't keep us from trying [made at the AAAS–CONACYT conference, June–July, 1973 "Science and Man in the Americas"].*

The legal framework of women's employment is being changed, but it is difficult to know whether these reforms will improve substantially the conditions under which women work and promote equality as intended, without structural changes. Under one new law both employers and employees, whether or not they have women employees, will contribute to a fund for the establishment of day-care centers; 506 centers catering to 165,000 children are projected by the end of 1976 (Gonzalez, 1974: 18–19). Because child-care presents a major problem for most working women, a network of

---

*During these meetings, on very short notice Mexican women set up an excellent two-day conference, "Women in the Americas," in which for the first time top professionals from universities and research institutes were brought together with representatives from the newer activist organizations.

adequate day-care centers could facilitate the entrance of more women into the labor force. However even if all of the 506 centers are functioning by the end of 1976, they will not fulfill the existing needs of working mothers.

Significantly, the problems that working women confront have now achieved national recognition. In an article on the front page of "Excelsior," August 22, 1974, the Presidential Task Force on the "Study of Women's Participation in Labor" reported that women then made up 20 percent of the total labor force in Mexico and that adequate figures were still not available for the agricultural sector. The commission also found that women who are employed suffer considerable discrimination and are subjected to other unnecessary problems deriving in part from the obsolete labor laws. According to the report, these laws restrict women rather than protect them, bringing about greater underemployment and an unemployment rate nearly three times as great for women as for men. To improve women's economic opportunities the commission recommends various reforms, including repeal of the laws prohibiting women's employment in certain occupations and a change in the federal Labor Law (Uzeta, 1974). In his annual State of the Nation address, in September 1974, President Echeverria approved the recommendations of the Committee which had been passed by Congress, and on December 31, 1974, the *Diario Oficial* announced the changes in the Mexican constitution relating to legal rights for women along with requested reforms and additions to the federal Labor Law and related constitutional amendments. Now we must see whether these reforms will be fully implemented and what this will mean for women.

Education. Education for women has not been easily achieved. In large part this has been caused by the belief by many Mexican men that education defeminizes women. Some, like Felix Palavicini, Minister of Education under Carranza, have even claimed that "An intellectual woman would produce weak or degenerate children" (Palavicini, 1910: 56). Educated women, more so in the past, have also found their marital prosepcts decreased because of the traditional male prejudice against marrying an intellectually equal or superior woman (Macias, 1971: 15).

Contemporary statistics clearly demonstrate that prejudice against women in education has not yet disappeared. Girls constitute 50 percent of all primary students, but only 25 percent of those in secondary school and 18.4 percent of the university enrollment (Ruddle and Odermann, 1972: 134).

At all levels of the educational system there exists a high attrition rate: only 7 out of 100 children who start primary school finish. Of the elementary school graduates, 75 percent go on to secondary schools; 50 percent of those entering secondary school complete it, with 79 percent of their number going on to the preparatory level. Of the preparatory graduates 97 percent matriculate at a university, with 38 percent receiving a degree. Girls constitute 50 percent of the students in the first year of primary school, 35 percent of the initial secondary school class, 18 percent of the preparatory school entrants, and 21 percent of the beginning university students. However for girls the percentage of students finishing each of these levels is higher than that for boys. The female drop out rate is highest between school cycles, not during them, suggesting that motivational factors are more important in women since they must overcome additional sociocultural obstacles to achieve higher education (Heredia, 1973: 8–9, 15, 16). Data drawn from a nationwide study of over 5000 men and women confirm these trends (see Table 2). Official national census data for 1970 show the male/female ratio

Table 2   Comparison of Male and Female Educational Levels

Years of Study	Men	Women
Don't know	0.1%	0.1%
None	8.3%	10.3%
1–3 years of study	19.7%	22.7%
4–6 years of study	28.7%	27.0%
7–9 years of study	13.2%	19.6%
11–12 years of study	9.2%	14.0%
13–15 years of study	6.5%	4.9%
16 years of study or more	14.3%	1.4%
Totals	100.0%	100.0%

Source.   Elu de Leñero, 1969: 54.

fairly equal in primary school. However, the gap widens in secondary school, where approximately 60 percent of the students are male, and at the university level where the male ratio jumps to over 80 percent.

All public primary schools in Mexico are coeducational with official textbooks* and the same curriculum for both sexes. Most public secondary schools are also coeducational, but there has been a continuing increase in the number of private secondary schools for girls. Boys and girls preparing for normal school begin a preteacher training program in public secondary schools. Larger numbers of girls than boys elect teacher-training programs and fewer girls take technical courses. As a result 40 percent of all advanced students in normal schools are women, whereas women comprise only 8 percent of the university students and 12.5 percent of those enrolled in an

*New, controversial textbooks reflect the rural–urban dichotomy and cultural pluralism and show some efforts to destereotype male–female images (Vasquez de Knauth, 1973).

institute of higher education in a technical field (Ruddle and Odermann, 1972: 171). In 1967 women comprised 16.7 percent of the student body at the higher university level. Women constituted 58.6 percent of those in the School of Education and 40.8 percent of the students in the School of Dentistry. Other departments preferred by women include the social sciences, in which they formed 28 percent of the students; chemistry, 25.5 percent; and medicine, 18 percent (Navarrete, 1969, 1973: 27). On a national level only 1.5 percent of the men and 0.5 percent of the women go on to professional schools at the university level. For instance in 1971 at the National University 20 percent of the students in the School of Humanities were women; women comprise a little more than 17 percent in medicine, 9.2 percent in dentistry, 13 percent in commerce, and 12 percent in law. Women made up only 0.4 percent of students in the school of engineering and a little more than 2 percent in the school of architecture, with very few in agriculture (Gonzalez, 1974: 22–23).

Compared with other countries of the world, Mexico is not remarkable for the numbers of women enrolled in higher education. Mexico is considered more progressive than Spain; yet in 1966, when both countries reported exactly the same number of university students, 154,289, Spain had 34,936 women studying at the university level while Mexico reported only 26,758 (U.N., 1970: 728, 734). Mexico also lags behind many other Latin American countries. In Costa Rica, Argentina, Chile, Colombia, and Peru at least 34 percent of the students enrolled in all institutions of higher education are women. In fact, of all Latin American countries excluding the Caribbean states, only Honduras reports a lower percentage (Ruddle and Odermann, 1972: 174). It is clear that Mexico has a long way still to go before women move far enough ahead to sustain a movement toward full equality of education with men.

Ratios of students to teachers of the same or opposite sex suggest significant differences in the experience of males and females. In the primary grades, where students are evenly divided between male and female, 89.6 percent of the teachers are women. Thus most girls have women teachers. However in the intermediate years the situation changes. For all intermediate education, in which 25 percent of the students are female, the percentage of female teachers declines to 33 percent. In the general secondary (college-preparatory) program, 28 percent of the students, but only 21 percent of the teachers, are female. Matters get worse in the vocational schools, where 48 percent of the students are female, and only 28 percent of the teachers are women. Even in normal school, where 63 percent of the students are female, only 40 percent of the faculty are women (Ruddle and Odermann, 1972: 146, 159, 170). While the number of women in professional schools at the National University increased from 16.9 percent in

1959 to 22.4 percent in 1969, the number of women professors grew from 7.8 percent to 12.5 percent during this period. There was also a noticeable increase in the number of women researchers in the University's various centers of scientific research (Gonzalez, 1974: 22).

It is easy to see from these statistics the odds against women being taught by women at any point after primary school. Evidence supports the view that Mexican parents are reluctant to have their female children taught by males. Within the indigenous groups this is a particularly strong taboo.

Mexico has been at the forefront in the development of nontraditional educational programs. Immediately after the Revolution of 1910 Rural Cultural Missions, composed of teams of young men and women, and similar to the United States' Peace Corps or Vista, were sent out into the villages. These teams taught carpentry, tanning, domestic science, music, masonry, along with reading and writing, in isolated villages to which they had been invited, often turning the rural school itself into a community center. A number of women linguists and educators have played key roles in establishing, supervising, and evaluating bicultural, bilingual programs and have been instrumental in involving community women, whose quickness, flexibility, and native intelligence were notable in spite of the great cultural adaptations that they often had to make (Araña de Swadesh, 1968; Modiano, 1973; and others).

Table 3 Latin America: Percent Literate in the Population Aged 15 Years and Over, by Sex, Urban, and Rural Areas Around the 1960 and 1970 Censuses

Country and Year	Total		Urban		Rural	
Mexico	Men	Women	Men	Women	Men	Women
1960	70.5	62.7	83.7	76.2	57.4	47.3
1970	79.5	73.1	87.8	82.0	67.8	58.9

Source. Organization of American States, 1975: 30

Health. It is crucial at the outset to point out Mexico's—and all of Latin America's—alarming birthrate, which both aggravates and is aggravated by the overall health picture. Mexico has an annual population growth rate of 3.5 percent, one of the highest in the world (Leñero Otero, 1968a, 1971: 868). During the 1950s Mexico began massive campaigns to wipe out the most deadly communicable diseases; these were largely successful and resulted in the saving of thousands of lives. As a consequence the population of Mexico has doubled in the past 25 years, going from 26 to 58 million, with estimates—if the present rate of growth continues—of 71 million in 1980 and 151 million in 2000 (*The New York Times,* May 27, 1974: 4). Slightly less than half the population is under 15 years of age, imposing a tremendous dependency burden (Nortman, 1973: 30). The rate of population increase, together with other socioeconomic factors, has limited the effect of the government's efforts to improve the quality of life. Although the Ministry of Education has been allocated up to 24.6 percent of the federal budget and many states contributed as much as 42 percent of their budgets for educational purposes, Mexico has not been able to alleviate its overall illiteracy, which remains at 27 percent for women and 21 percent for men (Nortman, 1973: 30; Navarrete, 1969, 1973: 74). Similarly, investments in medical services have often been counterbalanced by the greater demands of the higher population; today nearly half of the people still do not have access to medical care.

Despite the magnitude of the population growth Mexicans, both at a personal and a government level, have been slow to recognize and take steps to correct the problem. However Mexico has reacted faster than many other Latin American countries. The *marianismo–machismo* syndrome predisposes Mexican men to want a large family as a manifestation of their virility and influences women to have many children as means of elevating their status. For many, children are the greatest source of happiness and for women often a kind of social security for their old age. The Mexican family has an average of 6.9 children, and a high percentage of Mexicans, 40 percent of those interviewed in one survey, believe that eight or more children were necessary for the family to be considered large (Elu de Leñero, 1969: 77, 89). Until recently the government denied that Mexico had a population problem. Pioneer efforts in the 1950s to establish family planning clinics met with great opposition from the Church and were closed down on several occasions by the government. Although the government has liberalized its attitudes toward the distribution of contraceptives, it has claimed that Mexico could sustain a population as large as 200 million.

Although some support for family planning exists, a low percentage of the population practice it. A survey of 2500 couples conducted from 1966 to 1968 showed that only 11.5 percent knew about, accepted, and used contraceptive methods that were not approved by the Church. Slightly more than one-third of the population had no knowledge of contraceptive techniques other than rhythm and abstinence. More encouragingly, two-thirds of the couples questioned approved the idea of limiting the size of their families, although only one-third do anything about it. Those in urban environments are more likely to practice birth control than those in rural areas. Moreover in 57.5 percent of the families the husband and wife together reported that they made the decisions regarding family size, while men made the decisions in only 20 percent. This indicates that men were not unilaterally imposing large families (Leñero Otero, 1968a, 1971: 198, 328–29). The men have much more information about various methods of birth control than do women. The number of men cognizant of condoms and coitus interruptus was twice that of women (Elu de Leñero, 1969: 94).

The Mexican government has gradually come to realize the implications of the country's birthrate and in mid-1972, with the personal support of President Echeverria, embarked on a national family planning program, *Paternidad Responsable,* to make family planning services available in the Ministry of Health and Social Security Systems. In June 1973 Mexico reported 910,000 users of the family planning services—13.1 percent of married women between the ages of 15 and 44 (Nortman, 1973: 87). Members of the Mexican Catholic hierarchy have endorsed some of the measures taken by the government to promote responsible parenthood (Murphy, 1974: 33). However the government still refrains from using the terms *birth control* or *population control* and emphasizes that the program's goal is to enable couples to determine the number of children they want, rather than to reduce the size of the population (Nortman, 1973: Table 6). Even this program has provoked criticism from the pro-Catholic National Union of Heads of Families. Nevertheless the publicity and efforts of the national program to offer, free of charge, inclusive family planning services, with the exception of sterilization and abortion, in public clinics and hospitals, constitute a big step forward. The fact that Antonio Carillo Flores, one of Mexico's outstanding statesmen, served as the chairman of World Population Year, is further evidence of Mexico's new attitude. In the future Mexico's national family planning program may have some impact on the birthrate and on the overall health of Mexican women and their families, but only if women are consulted and included at every level. At the World Conference of the International Women's Year, held in Mexico City in the summer of 1975, many Latin American women, independently of their governments' population policies, insisted on their right "to control their own fertility as a central constituent of their demands for equal rights, opportunities and responsibilities" (Germaine, 1975: 235). Mexican women, as well as those from other Third World countries, spoke out strongly in favor of family planning, and Mexico sponsored a resolution which went far beyond its earlier limited platform of "responsible parenthood."

The high rate of abortion (primarily self-induced) in Mexico demonstrates the desire of women to limit their families. Self-induced abortion is still one of the leading causes of death among Mexican women, with a high percentage of patients in maternity hospitals being treated for complications following induced abortions. The official statistic is one abortion for every eight live births (Ordoñez, 1970; Leñero Otero, 1968a, 1971: 98). Several Latin

American countries have higher rates of abortion and related medical complications for women.* One study of over 2000 women in Ecuador that took into consideration the view of the Latin American woman points out the importance of the concepts of shame and modesty in family planning clinics or medical facilities (Scrimshaw, 1973: 17, 18).

Social and Political Involvement. As early as the 1850s there were stirrings of feminist movements in Mexico concentrating on work and educational rights. In the 1880s women joined men in the first labor strikes and subsequently organized their own strikes (Macias, 1971: 6). Early in the reign of Don Porfirio a few journals timidly suggested that more rights should be accorded women. In 1904 Mexico's first woman doctor, a lawyer, and a schoolteacher began a feminist monthly, La Mujer Mexicana (Macias, 1971: 4–5). Two years later a group of women joined together to form a feminist organization, "The Admirers of Jurarez," to diffuse ideas about women's rights, but the group seemed to arouse more ridicule than support (Morton, 1962: 2). When the Revolution of 1910 began, peasant women with their children went to war alongside the men. Some were integrated into the armies, became officers, and actually commanded battalions. Consequently after the Revolution women demanded the right of political participation, a change that was opposed by most influential men. Women's greater involvement in Mexican national life during World War I further stimulated their demands for political participation. The Constitution of 1917, adopted at the end of the Revolution, included several articles and provisions legally supporting the rights and privileges of women. However the Federal Election Law, passed in 1918, specifically excluded women from the franchise in federal elections, and it was not until 1953 that women were granted full suffrage. The fact that women were given very liberal socioeconomic and medical benefits under the new constitution but were denied political equality engendered a new impetus for organizing for specifically feminist purposes.

This delay in according political rights to women resulted from the fears of Mexico's male political leaders that women would be a conservative political force and that their entry into politics would threaten the progressive gains of the Revolution and the stability of the political order. Many of the liberal and radical politicians assumed that the Roman Catholic Church would be able to exert considerable influence over the female vote and would therefore use the women's vote as a political tool to elect candidates from the conservative opposition parties. The growing women's suffrage

*CELADE research showed 48.7 abortions per 100 pregnancies in Argentina in 1968 (Moore-Cavar, 1974: 612).

movement failed to convince members of the governing Institutional Revolutionary Party (PRI) that women had developed a revolutionary conscience. Individual presidents were often sympathetic to women's demands, but they would not risk their political fortunes by pushing through a constitutional amendment enfranchising women. When in 1937 President Cardenas managed to persuade both houses of parliament to vote in favor of such a reform and then had the measure ratified by a requisite number of states, the looming strength of the conservative opposition in a forthcoming national election led congress to put aside the amendment by intentionally failing to count the votes and neglecting to declare the reform approved (Morton, 1962). By waiting until 1953 to grant women full political rights, Mexico fell behind other Latin American states. Women voted in Mexican national elections for the first time in 1955 to elect representatives to the Chamber of Deputies and did not vote in a presidential election until 1958.

The discrepancy between the postrevolutionary constitution's ideals and the actual rights it accorded to women stimulated considerable feminist political activity. Two organizations that originated during this period were the Congress of Women Workers and Peasants, and the Feminist Congress of the Panamerican League of Women. The Congress of Women Workers and Peasants, which held national meetings in 1920 and 1931, took up such questions as the distribution of land to women peasants, equality for women in labor union struggles, and the broadening of popular education. The Feminist Congress discussed issues relating to birth control, free love, and the political and social rights of the Mexican women. Perhaps more significantly, all over the country housewives, workers, women scholars, and farm wives openly sought greater social and political rights (Encuentro de Mujeres, 1972a: 27).

Contrary to what one would be inclined to believe, the provincial areas have shown greater acceptance of women entering the political arena. The peninsula of Yucatan, isolated from the controls of Mexico City and falling more under the influence of Europe and the United States, has often gone its own way, even threatening secession. Its worldwide *henequen* trade and large population of Mayan Indians have made it both more and less traditional than the rest of Mexico, with an unbelievable autonomy in government policy decisions. Yucatan enfranchised women and granted them the right to hold office as early as 1922, only to rescind the measure in 1924. In 1924 one of the four congresswomen in the state legislature of Yucatan ran for the national congress from San Luis Potosi and won. The final vote was 4576 to 56, but she was not allowed to take her seat (Gruening, 1928: 629). For instance in 1958, at the suggestions of the wife of the governor, the state government signed an agreement to import donations of CARE milk, a measure that had been refused for five years at the national level (Elmendorf,

1971, and field observations, 1952–1960). Three of the primarily Indian communities south of the state capital had women mayors in 1972. Chiapas, also an isolated Mayan area, vested women with complete political equality in 1925 (Morton, 1962: 11).

Since being granted full suffrage in 1953, women have increased their representation in the federal congress from 1 seat in the first years to 4 in the next congress, then to 8, and finally to 12 in 1964. It has remained at that number since then (Navarrete, 1969, 1973). In 1969 the congresswomen, many of them lawyers, prepared a handbook on the rights of rural women which was widely distributed in the rural areas and is still used as a reference by villagers. The 12 seats held by women comprise 5.8 percent of the total congress—which means that women are more fairly represented at the national level in Mexico than in the United states, and they are even more conspicuous in top positions in the civil service and government appointments. Women have held many significant political offices, including senator, mayor, judge, first magistrate of the supreme court of the federal district and territories, magistrate, minister, ambassador, and government representative to international organizations. Women have also served in the different ministries, including health, education, welfare, social work, nursing, social security, agrarian reform, economic planning, Ministry of the Interior, and so on (Navarrete, 1969, 1973: 119–120; Gonzalez, 1974: 13). Some women have achieved political power through family connections and others on their own merit. All this is not to say that there has been little resistance to women taking political office.

Women's circumscribed social and political involvement is the result of specific limitations placed on women by Mexican culture. The tendency to consider politics as within men's sphere of activities and to define women's rightful concerns as those relating to the family discourages political participation by women. For this reason women candidates in Mexico usually stress their fulfillment of traditional feminine virtues: devotion to their home and husband and their many children, even though this may have little actual basis (Stevens, 1973a: 316). Thus women politicians in Mexico, just as in Chile and Peru, usually cast themselves in the role of the *supermadre* to minimize conflicts between traditional role definitions and their untraditional political activities (Chaney, 1973).

The fears of many male Mexican political leaders that women would be a very conservative political force susceptible to considerable Church influence has not been borne out by actual developments. For example, the 1958 electoral results indicated that the conservative, proclerical opposition party, the Partido de Accion Nacional (PAN), did not receive a disproportionate number of feminine votes, and in subsequent elections the governing PRI has continued to win easily.

The most common types of voluntary organization that Mexican women belong to are those that concentrate on charitable works related to the Church. Professional groupings, such as women doctors, and international and Pan-American groupings of women, are also of long-standing duration, some of them dating back 40 years or more. A number of United States clubs, such as the Junior League and the YMCA, organized early in Mexico as well. Mexico's counterpart of the American Association of University Women was founded in 1925. In all of these organizations women act as the office-holders and the organizers. In other situations a women's club is complementary to the original men's organization, such as the Damas de Leones. Associations such as Planned Parenthood, Mental Health, and Crippled Children have both men and women board members and officers.

The major Mexican political parties have separately organized women's sections (Scott, 1959: 169). Peasant women and labor groups also have organized for political action. However in the dominant political party, the PRI, and to a lesser extent in the opposition PAN, most women party officials are relegated to certain quota positions in posts where they will be limited to performing traditional feminine work of nurturing and protecting the young and the disadvantaged, for example, distributing toys and food, and administering women's programs (communication with Evelyn Stevens, 1974).

One of the major issues today rests on a link between the feminist movement and various socialist movements advocating the restructuring of society. One of the most vocal consciousness-raising groups in Mexico is Encuentro de Mujeres, literally "women's encounter." The following excerpt* prepared for them by Grupo 7, which includes some students and faculty members of the National University and other educational institutions in Mexico, indicates the character of their demands:

> Until now women dissatisfied with their situation have tried to enter the world of men and some have had success, but the fact that some workers have become capitalists has not abolished exploitation, just as the fact that there have been women astronauts has not ended sexist society. We insist either there is a solution for all women or there is no solution for any women. This presupposes a change in structures, a radical struggle directed at the roots of oppression [Encuentro de Mujeres, 1972b: 39].

Even the more radical women strongly believe that the women's problem should take second place to the Indian problem, the development problem, and the population problem. At the same time, however, they feel an urgent need for women to be more involved in resolving these basic concerns of Mexico.

*Part of a background paper, "Women and Work," used at a workshop held in Mexico City, November 26, 1972.

In sum the contemporary political role of Mexican women both reflects the general character of the Mexican culture and in turn affects its future evolution. Often women adopt a style within the stereotype of accepted female behavior. Sometimes they use the inside political route effectively. A group of young women lawyers, Las Jovenes Revolucionarias, claim that they went straight to the President of the Republic with their draft of needed revisions for legal reforms and that he used this for his recommendation for congressional reform.* Social workers have been involved in organizing domestic servants and prostitutes and in reorganizing their own schools and curricula. Other groups have worked around specific issues such as day-care centers, better working conditions, higher paying jobs, and so forth.

The last few years have seen the beginning of a women's movement in the sense that some Mexican women are redefining both their roles as women and their potentials as activists for social change. These women do not seem to think of themselves as following the North American model, which many reject as "a sign of the sickness of consumer society." They seem to be following a Mexican pattern—a pattern that goes back to the nunnery strikes during the seventeenth century, the strikes in the textile factories during the 1880s, the battalions of women during the Revolution, and the early legislation for equal rights and equal pay, as a part of their country's continuing revolution. Further political modernization in Mexico depends on the achievement of greater equality for all women—urban and rural.

As Mexico prepared to host the World Conference of the International Women's Year held in June and July of 1975, planning sessions were set up in the provincial capitals, as well as in Mexico City, to bring together previously dispersed and uncoordinated groups. Their discussions of mutual concerns about women—related to equality, development, and peace—undoubtedly strengthened the total effectiveness of the efforts of women in Mexico.

More than 2000 Mexican women of all classes participated actively in this unusual conference. Approximately 10,000 people from various political, social, economic, and national backgrounds worked together to reach consensus on equal rights, opportunities, and responsibilities for women. Together with other Third World women Mexican women stressed the need for unity and harmony between men and women who together must face common problems of illiteracy, unemployment, poverty, dependency, and underdevelopment.

*Conversation with Caroline Ware, participant at National Symposium on the Status of Women in Jalisco, February 15, 1975.

CONCLUSION

Writing 10 years after the Mexican Revolution, Ernest Gruening concluded that not much had been done for the emancipation of women and warned that the Revolution could not achieve its purposes while one-half of the Mexican population remained to be freed. According to Gruening, the Mexican woman "represents one of the conspicuous wastes of the Mexican heritage: for the considerable contribution she could make to Mexico's social, economic, and spiritual progress is still unutilized—obliterated by the shroud of persistent custom" (Gruening, 1928: 631). Almost 50 years have elapsed since Gruening's evaluation, and for the most part the situation remains the same today. Women still play a secondary part in the life of the society, and their roles are largely limited to those sectors considered suitable for women.

Mexico is a paradox. It has a reputation as one of the most progressive countries in Latin America, but notwithstanding the ideology of the Mexican Revolution, Mexico lags behind many other Latin American countries in the percentage of women who go on to higher education. On the other hand it has been a pioneer in nonformal education and a leader in bilingual, bicultural programs, which have benefited many women. Women's participation in secondary and vocational education has also been increasing. The participation of women in the labor force, particularly in the nonagricultural sectors, is the lowest in Latin America, which in turn has the lowest crude female labor activity rate of all the regions of the world, 13.6 percent in 1960 and 14.7 percent in 1970. That rate increased in Mexico from 8.7 percent in 1950 to 11.6 percent in 1960, but it is still one of the lowest in the region, along with those in Cuba, Guatemala, and Nicaragua. On the one hand the proportion of women in the service industries—nearly half of them in domestic service—is double that of Canada and the United States; on the other the percentage of women employed in professional and technical jobs in both Mexico and Latin America in general is far greater than that of men, a fact that is consistent with the educational statistics and that appears to reflect a tendency for those women who do find employment to aim for the top (Bowen, 1975: 5, 46–48; Ruddle and Odermann, 1972: 99).

In the years since the Revolution women's options have slowly expanded in almost all sectors of society. Educational opportunities, particularly at the lower levels of the educational system, have increased for all. However the benefits have accrued disproportionately to middle- and upper-class urban women. The exceptional middle- and upper-class women willing to flout social conventions prescribing that a woman's place is in the home have expanded professional and economic horizons. Most working women, however, do so out of economic necessity created by patterns of family disorganization and are engaged in domestic service or the more menial manufacturing jobs. Moreover it is possible that economic development has limited the employment prospects and perhaps even the status of many rural women.

The persistence of pre-Revolutionary norms regarding the role of women, and the soaring rate of population growth limit the options for Mexican women. The *machismo–marianismo* syndrome makes female subordination a sign of male virility, and male irresponsibility a keynote of male–female relationships. For the middle- and upper-class women who have had the benefits of higher education, the culture prescribes that they remain at home as adornments of their husband's success rather than pursue careers in their own right. To enhance their status, secure their place within the family, and ensure their future security, women have been inclined to have many children. Combined with the decrease in mortality following the introduction of improved medical practices, this has produced one of the highest rates of population growth in the world. In turn the high birthrate both confines many women to a continuous cycle of childbearing and childrearing, and imposes a heavy burden on educational and social services.

The report of the presidential commission on the status of women has prompted President Luis Echeverria to contemplate sweeping reforms to end discrimination against women. On September 1, 1974, in his fourth State of the Union address he made the statement that, "It is necessary to break the barriers that impede women from achieving their total development within the political, economic, and social life, and which obstruct the integral advancement of Mexico" ("Mexico Acts to Aid Women," 1974: 12). At the same time he warned that laws alone could not achieve equality for women. Thus even if these reforms are passed it remains to be seen whether the dawning sense of consciousness among Mexico's women will produce significant efforts on their part to enlarge their opportunities. As one social scientist has predicted, the change in women's attitudes and their refusal to endorse the continuation of the present cultural patterns may await further industrialization which, in Mexico as elsewhere, will be accompanied by the virtual disappearance of household servants. With this change will come the breakup of the extended family. Middle- and upper-class women will lose their built-in baby-sitters and the mother-goddess models traditionally provided by the older generation of women in the household. As long as the Indian sector remains marginal, this will be delayed, but when that sector does finally join the mainstream of Mexican society, women may be motivated to seek and develop a new life-style (Stevens, 1973b: 318).

Another social scientist reminds us that Mexican women are not more conservative than Mexican men in their attitudes toward family life, culture, work, and politics. In the IMES study already referred to, more than 60 percent of the 2953 women and the 2457 men interviewed expressed views that showed marked progressive tendencies in their attitudes and aspirations about their lives and their society. In Mexico, *feminine* is not synonymous with conservative nor *masculine* with progressive (Elu de Leñero, 1969: 46–69).

In the many worlds of Mexico who can say what shapes these new emerging women will take.

BIBLIOGRAPHY

Acosta, Marie Claire. 1973. "Los estereotipos de la mujer mexicana en la cultura de masas: el caso de las fotonovelas" (The Stereotype of the Mexican Woman in the Mass Culture: The Case of the Photonovels). Paper presented at the Conference of the American Association for the Advancement of Science and the Consejo Nacional de Ciencia y Tecnología. Mexico City, June.

Adams, Richard N., et al. 1960. *Social Change in Latin America Today.* New York: Random House.

Aguirre Beltran, Gonzalo. 1967. *Regiones de refugio: El Desarrollo de la Comunidad y el Proceso Dominical en Mestizo* (Regions of Refuge). Mexico. Instituto Interamericano Indígena.

Alba, Alejandra Jaidar de. 1973. "Lucha Femenil Contra la Discriminación" (Feminine Fight Against Discrimination). *Excelsior.* June 29.

Alegria, Rosa Luz. 1975. "Women and Education in Mexico." Paper prepared for the National Symposium on the Status of Women, Jalisco, February. Mexico: mimeo.

Almond, Gabriel A., and Sidney Verba. 1965. *The Civic Culture: Political Attitudes and Democracy in Five Nations.* Boston: Little, Brown and Co.

Araña de Swadesh, Evangelina. 1968. "Formas de aprendizaje entre las indígenas del estado de Oaxaca" (Forms of Learning among the Indians of the State of Oaxaca). Paper Presented at the Congress of the American Education Research Association.

Arizpe, Lourdes. 1972. "Rostros Indígenas" (Indian Faces). *Dialogos* **48:** 15–18.

———. 1975. *Indígenas en la Ciudad de Mexico: El Caso de las Marias* (Indian Women in Mexico City: The Case of the Marias). Mexico: SEP/Setentas.

Armanda Alegria, Juana. 1974. *Psicología de las Mexicanas* (The Psychology of Mexican Women). Mexico: Samo, S.A.

Arnold, Marigene. 1973. "La Madre Abnegada: One Role Among Many." Unpublished Ph.D. dissertation. University of Florida, Gainesville.

Beals, Ralph. 1965. *Social Stratification in Latin America: Contemporary Cultures and Societies of Latin America.* New York: Random House.

Bermúdez, Maria Elvira. 1955. *La Vida Familar del Mexicano (Family Life of the Mexican).* Mexico: Antigua Librería Robredo.

Blough, William. 1972. "Political Attitudes of Mexican Women: Support for the Political System among a Newly Enfranchised Group." *Journal of Interamerican Studies and World Affairs* **14** (May): 201–224.

Brenner, Anita. 1929, 1970. *Idols Behind Altars*. Boston: Beacon Press.

Calderon de la Barca, Frances. 1943, 1970. *Life in Mexico*. London: Aldine Press.

Castellanos, Rosario. 1973. *Mujer que Sabe Latin* (Women Who Know Latin). Mexico: SEP/ Setentas.

Chaney, Elsa M. 1973. "Women in Latin American Politics: The Case of Peru and Chile." In *Female and Male in Latin America: Essays*. Edited by Ann Pescatello. Pittsburgh: University of Pittsburgh Press, pp. 103–139.

——, and Marianne Schmink. 1974. "Going from Bad to Worse: Women and Modernization." In *Sex and Class in Latin America*. Edited by June Nash and Helen Safa. New York: Praeger, 1976; Mexico: SEP/Setentas, 1975.

Chiñas, Beverly. 1973. *The Isthmus Zapotecs*. (Case Studies in Cultural Anthropology). New York: Holt, Rinehart & Winston.

Cline, Howard F. 1963. *Mexico: Revolution to Evolution: 1940–1960*. New York: Oxford University Press.

Collier, Jane Fishburne. 1973. *Law and Social Change in Zinacantan*. Stanford: Stanford University Press.

Corona, Vargas Esther. 1973. "Sex Education." Paper presented at the Conference of the American Association for the Advancement of Science and the Consejo Nacional de Ciencia y Tecnología. Mexico City, June.

Cosio Villegas, Daniel, et. al. 1973. *Historia Mínima de México* (The Minimum History of Mexico). Mexico: El Colegio de Mexico.

Deere, Carmen Diana. 1975. "The Division of Labor by Sex in Agriculture: Peasant Women's Subsistence Production on the Minifundios." Ph.D. Research Essay, Department of Agricultural Economics. Berkeley: University of California.

Diaz, May N. 1967. *Tonala: A Mexican Town in Transition*. Berkeley: University of California Press.

Diaz-Guerrero, Rogelio. 1967. *Estudios de Psicología del Mexicano* (Studies of the Psychology of the Mexican). Mexico: Trillas.

——. 1973. "La mujer y las premisas histórico-socio-culturales de la familia mexicana" (The Woman and the Historical-Social-Cultural Premises of the Mexican Family). Paper presented at the Conference of the American Association for the Advancement of Science and the Consejo Nacional de Ciencia y Tecnología. Mexico City, June.

Durand, John D. 1971. "Regional Patterns in International Variations of Women's Participation in the Labor Force." Mimeo.

Elmendorf, Mary. 1971. *Role of Women as Agents for Peaceful Social Change*. Ottawa: Society for International Development, mimeo.

——. 1972. *The Mayan Woman and Change*. Cuernavaca, Mexico: Centro Intercultural de Documentacion, CIDOC Cuaderno No. 81.

——. 1973. *La Mujer Maya en el Cambio*. Mexico: SEP/Setentas No. 85.

——. 1976a. *Nine Mayan Women: A Village Faces Change*. New York: John Wiley.

——. 1976b. "Dilemmas of Peasant Women: A View From a Village in Yucatan." In *Women and World Development*. Edited by Irene Tinker and Michèle Bo Bramsen. Washington, D.C.: American Association for the Advancement of Science, Overseas Development Council.

Elu de Leñero, Maria del Carmen. 1969. ¿Hacia dónde va la mujer mexicana? (Where Is the Mexican Woman Going?) Mexico: Instituto Mexicano de Estudios Sociales.

————. 1971. *Mujeres que hablan* (Women Who Talk). Mexico: Instituto Mexicano de Estudios Sociales.

————. 1973. "Socio-familial Aspects of the Working Woman." Paper presented at the Conference of the American Association for the Advancement of Science and the Consejo Nacional de Ciencia y Tecnología. Mexico City, June.

————. 1974. "El Trabajo de la Mujer y la Fecundidad," (Woman's Work and Fecundity). Paper presented at the Conference on Feminine Perspectives in Social Science, Research in Latin America, Buenos Aires, March. In *Sex and Class in Latin America*. Edited by June Nash and Helen Safa. New York: Praeger, 1976; and Mexico: SEP/Setentas, 1975.

Encuentro de Mujeres (Women's Encounter) (Grupo 7). 1972a. "La Mujer en Mexico" (Woman in Mexico). *Punto Critico* **8** (August): 26–32.

————. 1972b. "La Mujer y el Trabajo" (Women and Work). *Punto Critico* **12** (December): 36–39.

Flora, Cornelia Butler. 1973. "The Passive Female and Social Change: A Cross-Cultural Comparison of Women's Magazine Fiction." In *Female and Male in Latin America: Essays*. Edited by Ann Pescatello. Pittsburgh: University of Pittsburgh Press, pp. 59–85.

Friedlander, Judith. 1974. *Montezuma's Legacy—The Reality of Being Indian in Hueyapan*. New York: St. Martin's Press.

Fromm, Erich, and Michael Maccoby. 1970. *Social Character in a Mexican Village*. Englewood Cliffs, New Jersey: Prentice Hall.

Gamio, Manuel. 1916. *Forjando Patria* (Forging a Nation). Mexico: Pomia.

Germaine, Adrienne. 1975. "Women at Mexico: Beyond Family Planning Acceptors." *Family Planning Perspective* **7** (October): 235–238.

Giele, Janet Zollinger, 1972. "Centuries of Womanhood: An Evolutionary Perspective on the Feminine Role." *Women's Studies,* Vol. 1. Great Britain: Gordon and Breach Science Publishers, pp. 97–110.

Gillin, John. 1959. "Changing Depths in Latin America." *Journal of Latin American Studies* **I:** 379–389.

Gonzalez Cassanova, Pablo. 1965. *La democracia en México* (Democracy in Mexico). Mexico: ERA.

————. 1968. "Mexico: The Dynamics of an Agrarian and Semicapitalist Revolution." In *Latin America, Reform or Revolution*. Edited by James Petras and Maurice Zeitlin. New York: Fawcett World Library.

Gonzalez Salazar, Gloria. 1971. *Problemas de la mano de obra en México* (Problems of the Labor Force in Mexico). Mexico: Universidad Nacional Autónoma de México.

————. 1972. *Subocupación y estructura de clases sociales en Mexico* (Underemployment and the Structure of Social Classes in Mexico). Mexico: Universidad Nacional Autónoma de Mexico.

————. 1974. "La Participacion de la Mujer en la Actividad Laboral de Mexico" (The Participation of the Woman in the Mexican Labor Force). Paper presented at the Conference on Feminine Perspectives in Social Science Research. Buenos Aires, March. In *Sex and Class in Latin America*. Edited by June Nash and Helen Safa. New York: Praeger, 1976; Mexico: SEP/Setentas, 1975.

Gruening, Ernest. 1928. *Mexico and Its Heritage*. New York: Century Company.

Gutierrez, Emma S. 1955. "Generation of Rebels." *Mexico This Month* **I** (June).

Hanke, Lewis. 1967. *Mexico and the Caribbean: Modern Latin America, Continent in Ferment,* Vol. I. New York: Van Nostrand Reinhold Company.

168   **Mary Elmendorf**

―――. 1968. *Contemporary Latin America: A Short History.* New York: Van Nostrand.

Hellbom, Anna-Britta. 1967. *La Participación Cultural de las Mujeres* (The Cultural Participation of Women). Stockholm: The Ethnological Museum.

Heredia, Bertha. 1973. "La Valoración Social de la Mujer, Mito y Realidad" (The Social Value of the Woman: Myth and Reality). Paper presented at the Conference of the American Association for the Advancement of Science and the Consejo Nacional de Ciencia y Technología. Mexico City, June.

Herman, William. 1973. "La Virgen de Guadalupe: As she lives in the town of Culhuacan." Mexico: National Institute of Anthropology and History, mimeo.

Hernandez, Susana. 1971. "Unas características de la mujer mexicana de clase media" (Some Characteristics of the Mexican Middle Class Woman). *Revista Mexicana de Ciencia Política* (July–September).

Herrick, Jane. 1957. "Periodicals for Women in Mexico During the 19th Century." *The Americas* **14** (October): 135–44.

Hiriart, Rosario. 1973. "America's First Feminist." *The Americas* **25** (May): 2–6.

Illich, Ivan. 1968. "Outwitting the 'Developed' Countries." Cuernavaca: CIDOC publications.

Inda, Caridad. 1975. "The Professional Woman: An International Perspective." Paper presented at Kirkland College, May, mimeo.

Jaquette, Jane. 1973. "Women in Revolutionary Movements in Latin America." *Journal of Marriage and the Family* **35** (May): 344–354.

Johnson, Allan. 1972. "Modernization and Social Change: Attitudes Toward Women's Roles in Mexico City." Unpublished Ph.D. dissertation: University of Michigan.

Kayberry, Phyllis M. 1939, 1973. *Aboriginal Woman.* New York: Gordon Press.

Kahl, Joseph A. 1968. *Comparative Perspectives on Stratification: Mexico, Great Britain, Japan.* Boston: Little, Brown and Company.

Keremitsis, Dawn. 1974. "The Expendables: Women in the Textile Industries of Mexico, Chile and Colombia." Paper presented at Latin American Studies Association, Fifth National Meeting, San Francisco.

Kinzer, Nora. 1973. "Priests, Machos and Babies, or Latin American Women and the Manichean Heresy." *Journal of Marriage and the Family* **35** (May): 300–312.

Knaster, Meri. 1976. "Women in Latin America: The State of Research, 1976." *Latin American Research Review* **XI** (1): 3–74.

Larguia, Isabel, and John Dumoulin. 1971. "Hacia una ciencia de la liberación" (Toward a Science of Women's Liberation). *Casa de las Americas* **10** (March-June): 37–55.

Lattes de Casseres, Virginia. 1972. "Home Management Consumer Education in Latin America." Rome: FAO, Document No. 5 in Nutrition Series.

Lavalle Urbina Maria. 1964. *Situación de la mujer en el derecho de familia latino americano.* (Status of Women in Family Law in Latin America). Bogota.

Lavrin, Asuncion. 1972. "Values and Meaning of Monastic Life for Nuns in Colonial Mexico." *The Catholic Historical Review* **LVIII** (3): 367–387.

――― 1975. "In Search of the Colonial Women in Mexico, XVII and XVIII Centuries." Unpublished paper.

Leñero Otero, Luis. 1968a, 1971. *Investigación de la familia en México.* Mexico: Galve.

―――. 1968b. "The Mexican Urbanization Process and Its Implications." *Demography* **V** (2): 866–873.

Leon-Portilla, Miguel. 1958. "La mujer en la cultura indígena" (The Woman in the Indigenous Culture). *Nicaragua Indígena* **21** (July–August): 6–8.

Lewis, Oscar. 1959. *Five Families: the Anthropology of Poverty*. New York: Basic Books.

Linton, Sally. 1973. "Woman the Gatherer: Male Bias in Anthropology." In *Women in Perspective: A Guide for Cross-Cultural Studies*. By Sue-Ellen Jacobs. Urbana: University of Illinois.

Lomnitz, Larissa. 1973a. "La mujer marginada en México" (The Marginal Woman in Mexico). Paper presented at the Conference of the American Association for the Advancement of Science and the Consejo Nacional de Ciencia y Technología. Mexico City, June.

————. 1973b. "The Survival of the Unfittest." Paper presented at the International Congress of Anthropological and Ethnological Sciences. Chicago, September.

Loreto Hernandez, Margarita. 1961. *Personalidad de la mujer mexicana* (Personality of the Mexican Woman). Mexico: Galve.

Macias, Anna. 1971. "Mexican Women in the Social Revolution." Paper presented at the American Historical Association Conference. New York.

———— 1973. "The Mexican Revolution Was No Revolution for Women." In *History of Latin American Civilization: Sources and Interpretation,* Vol 2. Edited by Lewis Hanke. New York: Little, Brown & Co., pp. 459–469; Cuernavaca, Mexico: CIDAL.

McGinn, Noel F. 1966. "Marriage and Family in Middle Class Mexico." *Journal of Marriage and the Family* **28** (3) (August): 305–313.

Martinez Alier, Verena. 1974. "The Women of Rio das Pedras." Paper for Buenos Aires Conference on Feminine Perspectives in Social Science Research. In *Sex and Class in Latin America*. Edited by June Nash and Helen Safa. New York: Praeger, 1976; Mexico: SEP/Setentas, 1975.

Mendieta de Alatorre, Maria de los Angeles. 1972. *Margarita de la Maza de Juarez: Epistolario, Antología, Iconographía, y Enfemérides*. Mexico: Comisión Nacional del Centenario del Fallecimiento de Don Benito Juarez.

"Mexico Acts to Aid Women." 1974. *Washington Post*. September 2.

"Mexico Offers Family Planning Help." 1974. *The New York Times*.

Modiano, Nancy. 1973. *Indian Education in the Chiapas Highlands*. New York: Holt, Rinehart & Winston.

Moore-Cavar, Emily Campbell. 1974. *International Inventory of Induced Abortions*. New York: Columbia University.

Morton, Ward M. 1962. *Woman Suffrage in Mexico*. Gainesville: University of Florida.

Murphy, Francis X. 1974. "Starving Children and the Catholic Church." *The New York Times*. May 31, p. 33.

Myers, Sarah K. 1973. *Language Shift Among Migrants to Lima, Peru*. University of Chicago, Department of Geography. Research Paper #147.

Nash, June. 1973. "Resistance as Protest." Paper presented at the International Congress of Anthropological and Ethnological Sciences. Chicago, September.

————, and Helen Safa, Eds. 1975, 1976. *Sex and Class in Latin America*. New York: Praeger, 1976. Spanish edition entitled *La Mujer en América Latina*. Mexico: SEP/Setentas, 1975.

Navarrete, Ifigenia Martinez de. 1969, 1973. *La mujer y los derechos sociales* (The Woman and Social Rights). S.A. Mexico: Ediciones Oasis.

Nortman, Dorothy. 1973. *Population and Family Planning Programs: A Factbook*. New York: Population Council.

Ordoñez, Blanco Raquel. 1970. "La población materno infantil, aspectos cuantitativos y cualitativos en México" (The Mother-Child Population, Quantitative and Qualitative Aspects in Mexico). Mexico: Fundación para Estudios de la Población.

————. 1973. "Investigación epidemiológica sobre el aborto inducido" (An Epidemiological Investigation of Induced Abortion). Proposal for a grant.

Organization of American States. 1975. "Women in the Latin American Labor Force." Paper prepared for the CEER/CIM Conference, Caracas, May, 1975. Washington, D.C.: OEA/SER L. 11.4.

Otero, Rosa Maria Lombardo. 1944. *La mujer tzeltal* (The Tzeltal Woman). Mexico: Privately printed.

Palavicini, Felix. 1910. Problemas de educación. (Educational Problems). Mexico: Sempere y Cia, pp. 54–64.

Paul, Lois. 1974. "The Mastery of Work and the Mystery of Sex in a Guatemalan Village." In *Woman, Culture and Society*. Edited by Michelle Z. Rosaldo and Louise Lamphere. Stanford: Stanford University Press, pp. 263–281.

Paz, Octavio. 1961. *Labyrinth of Solitude: Life and Thought in Mexico*. New York: Grove Press.

————. 1972. *The Other Mexico: Critique of the Pyramid*. New York: Grove Press.

Pellicer de Brody, Olga. 1973. "El Acercamiento de México a América Latina: Una Interpretación Politica" (The Rapprochement of Mexico to Latin America). Fourth International Congress of Mexican Studies, Los Angeles.

Peñalosa, Fernando. 1968. "Mexican Family Roles." *Journal of Marriage and the Family* **30** (November): 680–689.

Petersen, Frederick A. 1962. *Ancient Mexico*. New York: Capricorn Books.

Piho, Virve. 1973. "Life and Labor of the Female Textile Worker in Mexico City." Paper presented at the International Congress of Anthropological and Ethnological Sciences. Chicago, September. In *Women Cross-Culturally: Change and Challenge*. Edited by Ruby Rohrlich-Leavitt. The Hague: Mouton, 1975.

Poston, Richard. 1962. *Democracy Speaks Many Tongues*. New York: Harper and Row.

Pozas, Ricardo, and Isabel H. de Pozas. 1971. *Los Indios en las clases sociales de México*. (Indians in the Social Classes of Mexico). Mexico: Siglo XXI.

Rivera Marin, Guadalupe. 1955. *El Mercado de Trabajo*. Mexico: Fondo de Cultura Economica.

Ruddle, Kenneth, and Donald Odermann. 1972. *Statistical Abstract of Latin America*. Berkeley and Los Angeles: University of California Press.

Sanchez, Aurelia Guadalupe, and Ana E. Dominguez. 1974. "Women in Mexico." In *Cross Cultural Perspectives on Women*. Edited by Ruby Rohrlich-Leavitt. Paris and The Hague: Mouton.

Schaeffer, Wini. 1973. "Sisters Writing a Book on Sexism." *The News* (Mexico). June 7.

Schmink, Marianne. 1974a. "Survey of Anthropological Approaches to the Analysis of Sex Roles: Latin America." Presented at the 22nd Annual Meeting of the Rocky Mountain Council for Latin America. Lubbock, Texas.

————.1974b. "Dependent Development and the Division of Labor by Sex." Paper presented at Latin American Studies Association, Fifth National Meeting. San Francisco.

Schwartz, Lola Romanucci. 1962. "Mortality, Conflict and Violence in a Mexican Mestizo Village." Unpublished Ph.D. dissertation, University of Indiana.

Scott, Robert E. 1959. *Mexican Government in Transition*. Urbana: University of Illinois Press.

――――. 1965. "Mexico: The Established Revolution." In *Political Culture and Political Development*. Edited by Lucian W. Pye and Sidney Verba. Princeton: Princeton University Press, pp. 330–395.

Scrimshaw, Susan. 1973. *¡Lo de Nosotros!: Pudor and Family Planning Clinics*. New York: Columbia University, International Institute for the Study of Human Reproduction.

Smith, Margo Lane. 1973. "Domestic Service as a Channel of Upward Mobility for the Lower Class Woman: The Lima Case." In *Female and Male in Latin America: Essays*. Edited by Ann Pescatello. Pittsburgh: University of Pittsburgh Press, pp. 191–207.

Stavenhagen, Rodolfo. 1970. "Classes, Colonialism and Acculturation." In *Masses in Latin America*. Edited by I. Horowitz. Oxford: Oxford University Press.

Stevens, Evelyn P. 1965. "Mexican Machismo: Politics and Value Orientations." *Western Political Quarterly* **18** (December): 848–857.

――――. 1973a. "Marianismo, The Other Face of Machismo." In *Female and Male in Latin America: Essays*. Edited by Ann Pescatello. Pittsburgh: University of Pittsburgh Press, pp. 89–101.

――――. 1973b. "The Prospects for a Women's Liberation Movement in Latin America." *Journal of Marriage and the Family* **35** (May): 313–321.

――――. 1973c. "Machismo and Marianismo." *Society* **10** (September 10): 57–63.

――――, personal communication, 1974.

Sundel, Alfred. 1967. *A History of the Aztecs and the Mayas and Their Conquest*. New York: Macmillan Company.

Tienda, Martha. 1974. "Economic Development and the Female Labor Force: The Mexican Case." M.A. Thesis, University of Texas.

Torres-Rioseco, Arturo. 1947. *Sor Juana Inez de la Cruz*. Mexico: Revista Iberoamericana.

Tozzer, Alfred M. 1941. *Landa's relación de las cosas de Yucatan* (Landa's Account of Things in Yucatan [around 1566]). Cambridge, Massachusetts: Peabody Museum.

Turner, Frederick C. 1967. "Los efectos de la participación feminina en la revolución de 1910" (The Effects of Feminine Participation in the Revolution of 1910). *Historia Mexicana* **16** (April–June): 603–620.

United Nations. 1970. *Statistical Handbook, 1969*. New York: United Nations Publications.

Uzeta, Arnulfo. 1974. "Reforma el Articulo 123 en Favor de la Mujer" (Reform of Article 123 in Favor of Women). *Excelsior*. September 24, pp. 1, 9, 19.

Vasquez de Knauth, Josefina. 1973. "La enseñanza de las ciencies sociales, un aspecto de reforma educativa" (The Teaching of Social Sciences, One Aspect of Educational Reform). Paper presented at the Fourth International Congress of Mexicanists. October.

Viel, Benjamin. 1973. "The Demographic Explosion in Latin America." In *Population and Family Planning in Latin America, Fall*. 3–7. Washington: Victor Bostrum.

Villa Rojas, Alfonso. 1969. "The Maya of Yucatan." *Handbook of Middle American Indians*, Vol. 7. Austin: University of Texas.

Ware, Caroline. 1975. "Woman and Society." Paper presented at the National Symposium on the Status of Women. Jalisco, February 1975, Mexico: Mimeo.

Wolf, Eric. 1959, 1964. *Sons of the Shaking Earth*. Chicago: University of Chicago Press.

Womak, John. 1969. *Zapata and the Mexican Revolution*. New York: Alfred Knopf.

Youssef, Nadia H. 1972. "Differential Labor Force Participation of Women in Latin America

172   Mary Elmendorf

and Middle Eastern Countries: The Influence of Family Characteristics." *Social Forces*, **51** (2): 135–153.

———. 1973. "Cultural Ideals, Feminine Behavior and Family Control." *Comparative Studies in Society and History* **15:** 326–347.

———. 1974. *Women and Work in Developing Societies.* Berkeley: University of California, Population Monograph Series, No. 15.

Chapter Five

GHANA: FROM AUTONOMY TO SUBORDINATION

Audrey Chapman Smock

SOCIOLOGICAL AND HISTORICAL BACKGROUND

Precolonial Ghana.   The contemporary boundaries of Ghana, which was formerly known as the Gold Coast, as elsewhere in Africa, were set during the colonial period. Consequently, they incorporate disparate ethnic groups that, prior to the imposition of British rule, differed considerably in their social structure and cultural norms. Some 200 separate political units existed at the time of colonization. These traditional sociopolitical systems can be grouped into four basic organizational types: the Akan, the Ewe, the Ga, and the Northern. Of these, the Akan predominated and characterized not only the Akan-speaking states, which include the Fanti, the Ashanti, the Akim, and the Akwapim, but in modified form influenced the organization of other groups as well. The roles of women, as might be anticipated, varied among these groups. Women had the highest status, greatest independence, and the most significant positions under the Akan and Ga systems. Today the Akan and Ga-Adangme peoples, who reside in the southern part of the country, comprise somewhat more than half of the total Ghanaian population.

The precolonial period encompassed hundreds of years—from the settlement of diverse ethnic groups in the area of Ghana until the imposition of the colonial British system. Although small portions of coastal regions came under Portuguese, Dutch, or British control much earlier, most of what constitutes contemporary Ghana became a British colony at the beginning of the twentieth century. The distinction between the precolonial and colonial periods is very arbitrary, and the concepts of precolonial and traditional should not be considered synonymous. Some Ga and Fanti coastal settlements had fairly regular contacts with Europeans dating back to 1488, when the Portuguese built a fort at Elmina, whereas some groups in the North had little sustained interaction with Western culture until long after the formal establishment of British rule. Moreover many aspects of the traditional patterns of social organization still persist.

As with other preliterate societies, our knowledge of traditional Ghanaian social systems depends on reconstructed oral histories, legends, and the writings of foreign visitors. Systematic anthropological observation and analysis began only during the colonial period, hence most anthropologists attempting to reconstruct the precolonial order have studied communities that had already undergone varying degrees of change.

Although the norms defining women's place in society differed among the indigenous communities, women had considerable independence and economic power among all of the groups. Irrespective of the pattern of inheritance or the prevailing social organization, women performed key economic functions. None of Ghana's constituent ethnic units limited women's roles to serving as wives and mothers. As one anthropologist has commented, "The typical African woman thinks of herself as a cultivator or trader as well as a wife and mother; her occupational role is part of her self-image" (LeVine, 1970: 175). This was particularly true of the traditional societies of Ghana. The scope of women's economic activities, except in the North, was perhaps unsurpassed in Africa, and the value of the goods women produced did not vary significantly from male members. Women's freedom and autonomy also derived from the sexual mores, which did not place a high value on female chastity, and from the existence of institutions that supported women's corporate interests. The relative lack of concern with female sexual virtue meant that women were not subjected to extensive regulation or kept isolated from men.

The high status of women among the Akan groups derived in part from their matrilineal patterns of descent and inheritance. The Akan state was structured hierarchically, with the most basic unit being the matrilineage. Under the matrilineal system men still retained paramount political authority, and in many ways the mother's brother assumed the roles that the father exercises in a patrilineal system. The male head of each lineage represented his group in the village council, which was presided over by the village headman. A group of villages fell under a subchief, who in turn served as an elder on the state council of the paramount chief. Nevertheless the determination of kinship connections through the female line of descent and the belonging of all children to the mother's family elevated women's importance and contributed to their sense of self-respect and dignity.

Moreover, despite male political predominance, women held significant social and political roles and came close to achieving equality in many respects (Fortes, 1950: 256). Male lineage heads frequently had female counterparts to supervise female matters, adjudicate family quarrels, advise on matters of genealogy, and supervise certain key rituals. At higher levels of state organization the queen-mother, the most prominent female member of the royal lineage, had even greater power, for she nominated the new chief, advised him about his conduct, and acted as an expert on ritual and genealogy. Although the chief outranked the queen-mother, a capable woman filling that office could command considerable authority in her own right. On occasion Akan women even served as chiefs (Rattray, 1929; Busia, 1951). Yaa Asantewa, for example, an Ashanti woman, led the Ashanti warriors in the final Anglo-Ashanti war of 1900–1901.

The non-Akan ethnic groups in Ghana followed the more usual pattern of patrilineal descent. However among the Ga, the coastal people who traditionally inhabited the Accra area, the usual patrilineal system was modified in several respects, and women wielded considerable power within the society. Despite the emphasis on patrilineal descent a woman's property, which could be as extensive as a man's, was inherited in the female line. In the small, decentralized city-states of the Ga, several key positions were reserved for women, including the ritual town offices and such religious offices as the mouthpieces of the gods (Manoukian, 1950; Field, 1940). Since some anthropologists believe that the Ga originally had a theocratic form of government (Field, 1937: 3), women's religious roles must have accorded them even greater significance in the earlier part of the precolonial era.

Under the Ewe and Northern systems women had more limited social roles than among either the Akan or the Ga. Most Ewe states were organized around a hierarchy of lineage headmen and chiefs, roughly comparable to the Akan system but on a smaller scale. One major difference between the Akan and Ewe systems, however, lay in the positions that women assumed, because the Akan institutions copied by the Ewe were imposed on a society in which women had a far more subordinate status. Therefore the Ewe did not adopt offices comparable to the Akan woman lineage cohead or the queen-mother (Nukunya, 1969; Manoukian, 1952). Most of the Northern groups adhered to a common pattern based on the moral and religious authority of a priest-king, who presided over a locality by virtue of his presumed ability to mediate between the population and the deities inhabiting the area. It was considered inappropriate among most northern groups for women to assume leadership roles. Women were excluded from the council, which shared political authority with the priest-king and consisted of the elders, male lineage heads, and sometimes a secular chief (Manoukian, 1951; Fortes, 1945; Tait, 1961).

Ghanaian precolonial societies depended on a sexual division of labor in which women performed essential economic functions. The general pattern was for married women to be economically active in their own right and not merely as auxiliaries for their husbands, for them to have their own sources of income, and for them to assume part of the burden for the support of the household. Women commonly cultivated specific crops, engaged in petty trading, and sometimes produced handicrafts; and income that they earned was usually theirs to keep or dispose of as they wished (Fortes, 1949: 102–103; Manoukian, 1950: 71; Manoukian, 1951: 35; McCall, 1961: 286; Nukunya, 1969: 149; Tait, 1961: 197–198). Women usually farmed independently of their husbands on their own plots of land, and although men cleared the fields for them, women did not have a reciprocal obligation to help their husbands cultivate their crops. With the exception of certain Northern groups in which the men produced grains and yams, and the women vegetables, women could grow the same crops as men. The presence of the tsetse fly in the southern part of the country prevented men from raising livestock, which in some African societies is a male prerogative. Restrictions on women, such as the limitations on the items Akan women could trade, often related to the prerogatives of the royal lineage and not to the sexual division of labor (McCall, 1961: 288).

Women's having their own income and property accumulated from their earnings conferred a considerable degree of independence. Among all groups women engaged in petty trading, selling part of their own crops, the surplus of their husband's (often for a fixed commission), and sometimes handicrafts or goods they had made. Among the Ga and the Ewe, whose economy depended heavily on fishing, women handled the curing and selling of the fish (Manoukian, 1950: 71; Nukunya, 1969: 149). Women had control over their own property; even in the North, where a man could beat his wife with relative impunity, he dared not utilize her property without her consent (Fortes, 1949: 103). Although the patrilineal patterns of inheritance usually excluded women and the matrilineal order of precedence ranked them after the male members of the matrilineage, under both systems the access of women to land for cultivation, which was owned corporately by the kinship group, and their ability to control their earnings compensated for this. These laws of inheritance, as well as the instability of marriages among many of the groups, doubtlessly contributed to women's reluctance to work jointly with their husbands.

Regardless of whether the women's place was considered to be substantially equal to that of the male members, as among the Akan, or subordinate, as among the Ewe or Northern groups, men rarely interfered with or attempted to regulate directly women's conduct. In all these societies men and women had separate spheres of activity with their rights and duties deriving from them. Sex separation did not give rise to limitations on women's freedom; quite the contrary, it accorded them considerable independence. Among many of the groups women lived apart from men, further increasing their chances to develop a corporate sense of identity and social networks. The Ewe, Ga, and Akan women all had institutions embodying women's corporate sense of identity (Folson, n.d.: l, 5; Field, 1940: 6–8; Manoukian, 1952: 36).

Marriage entailed a much looser relationship than in many other cultures and in some ways resembled a business partnership. The payment of a bride price and the completion of the prescribed rituals established for both partners a series of rights and duties, some of which grew out of the sexual division of labor. The man received exclusive domestic and economic services; in return the woman had rights to sexual satisfaction, to maintenance for herself and her children, to care during illness, and among many of the groups, to decide whether the husband could take another wife (Fortes, 1950: 280). When either partner did not meet these obligations, the other could withdraw from the union. Women had just as much right to initiate divorce as men. As a consequence the divorce rate apparently was fairly high among many of the groups.

Women's ability to cope with marital instability reflected two factors: these societies did not place a high premium on female chastity, and women retained their place in their own kinship group. Ghanaian traditional societies accorded women considerable premarital sexual freedom and did not severely punish women's adultery (Tetteh, 1967: 203–204; Manoukian, 1951: 46). In cases of proven adultery the male offender paid the husband a fine, with the amount depending on the status of the aggrieved party (Vellenga, 1971: 132–133). The husband also accepted paternity of any child born of an adulterous union. Usually the wife escaped direct punishment from the society and was left to receive divine retribution for her conduct. At least among the Ewe the disproportional assignment of guilt reflected the belief that the woman was usually the passive victim (Nukunya, 1969: 111). Therefore there existed much less of a sexual double standard than inheres in most cultures. Equally important in comprehending the nature of marriage, kinship bonds could and apparently often did conflict with marital ties, and when this occurred, kinship obligations usually prevailed. Matrilineal societies were more prone to this, because the wife and children belonged to a different lineage than the husband, but even among the patrilineal groups women were not assimilated into their husband's lineage but instead retained strong links with their own kin and invariably returned to them in their old age (Fortes, 1950: 262–272; Fortes, 1949: 251; Nukunya, 1969: 57).

Ghana's constituent ethnic groups all practiced polygamy although at any given time probably only a small proportion of men had the means to afford more than one wife. It would be erroneous to assume, however, that the existence of plural marriages necessarily lowered women's status. Polygamy first and foremost represented the manner in which men could display wealth (Paulme, 1971: 8). Having more than one wife also increased the number of children available to work with the father and therefore enhanced his economic prospects. Polygamous unions often had advantages for women as well, by enhancing the prospects for independence and reducing the work load (Pool, 1972: 251–252). Since marriage did not usually involve a romantic attachment, the implications for the wife of having a permanent competitor were not the same as in a Western marriage based on an emotional tie. Therefore many women probably welcomed a second wife to share the burden of work or to raise the status of the family (Tait, 1961: 163). Moreover relationships within a polygamous family bore no resemblance to Western images of a harem in which a contingent of women slavishly strove to please the whims of a single man. Irrespective of how many wives a man had, each woman went her own way. Doubtlessly when the wives lived in close proximity, the presence of more than one wife gave rise to some discord, particularly in patrilineal societies over the precedence of the children, but this dissension had more repercussions for relationships among women than for the relative status of men and women.

Women frequently were the paramount figures within the family. The emotional bond between mother and child was the strongest and often the most satisfying relationship in the social system. This enduring attachment between mother and child has, of course, characterized all human society, but in the Ghanaian groups it did not coexist with a hierarchical authority structure that subordinated women to men within the family. Among the Akan the father's position was further weakened by his lack of legal prerogatives over his children and by the precedence of kinship bonds over marital ones. Even in the patrilineal systems, though, the moral authority of the mother counterbalanced to some extent the influence of the father's lineage.

The assessment of one woman anthropologist with regard to the place of women in African society that "whatever the system may be, the position of women within it is neither superior nor inferior to that of the men, but simply different and complementary" (Paulme, 1971: 6), applies fairly well to the Ghanaian precolonial social order described above. Within the traditional societies people would not have thought to rank two different and complementary social roles in a hierarchical manner, just as we would find it strange to order apples and oranges. Some observers of African mores have assumed that the practice of sex separation and the presence of rules of etiquette in which women deferred to men attest to women's subordinate status. Comtemporary anthropological research also has documented expressions of male superiority (Nukunya, 1969: 155), but such statements or inferences from codes of conduct may reflect the impact of colonial rule.

Although any efforts after the passing of precolonial society to measure female status in them obviously cannot be conclusive, Peggy Sanday's theory of the dimensions of female status in the public domain provides a starting point. According to Sanday, in simple societies four variables determine female status in the public domain: female material control, demand for female produce, female political participation, and female solidarity groups devoted to female political or economic interests (Sanday, 1974: 192). Without exception females in all Ghanaian precolonial societies had substantial material control of produce and crafts beyond the domestic unit. Female produce also had a recognized value beyond the localized family unit, a value which in most cases did not differ substantially from that of male produce. Only among the Akan did females have the ability to participate politically on a regular basis, but the consensual decision-making patterns commonly inhering within the lineage meant that among the Ga and the Ewe, as women grew older, their views were often heard and taken into account as well. With varying degrees of effectiveness, females grouped together to protect and represent their interests. Thus although males dominated all groups politically and militarily, female status rested on a firm base. Akan women had the most power and could command the greatest respect, but even in the North women were not devoid of the economic attributes of high status.

The Colonial Period.   The colonial period formally began in 1902, more than 400 years after the establishment of the first Portuguese forts on Ghana's Atlantic coast. In that year the British government passed three Orders in Council establishing the British Colonies of the Gold Coast and Ashanti, and the British Protectorate of the Northern Territories, covering what were to become the three major constituents of Ghana. Colonial policies had a rather important influence on sex role definitions and opportunities for women. Christian missionaries and colonial administrators brought with them Victorian conceptions concerning the place of women in society. Generally they did not appreciate the significant contributions frequently made by women and their sense of independence. The British tended to cast all African societies into the single mold of a patriarchy ruled by an all-powerful chief. Even when anthropologists provided evidence of the true role of women among many of the groups, prejudices prevented any application of this knowledge. Moreover British male researchers often shared the biases of colonial administrators. One of the classical works on the Ashanti, which was originally commissioned by the colonial administration, for example, mentions that its matrilineal principles bring "results which appear to us either unnatural or grotesque" (Rattray, 1929: 23).

In Ghana, as elsewhere, some groups had far greater access to schooling and to the new economic opportunities by virtue of their proximity to and their willingness to cooperate with missionaries and the colonial power. Largely by the accident of history and geographic location, the ethnic groups in which women held the highest status were the ones that benefitted most. Some groups, particularly the Fanti (Akan) and the Ga, were producing university graduates to fill responsible positions by the second part of the nineteenth century, whereas the North continuously lagged behind the remainder of the country because of the exclusion of Christian missionaries and its separate administration. Thus women's circumscribed roles in the traditional sphere there have been further limited by their limited access to education and jobs in the modern sector.

The spread of education, primarily under the aegis of missionaries, adversely affected the relative position of women more than did any other factor. Ghana's humid, tropical climate and the prevalence of malaria discouraged any permanent European settlement and predisposed the colonial office and European companies to training local personnel to fill all clerical and some middle-level posts. Since the missionaries and administrators assumed that it was the natural pattern everywhere for men to assume economic roles, they recruited African men to fill these posts. For this reason the education of men at all levels was accorded much higher priority than the education of women. Beginning in the colonial period, as one observer has commented, "Education appears to have become the basis for a kind of social and economic sexual inequality from which Ghanaian society has previously been free" (Griffiths, 1974: 13). Women were never completely excluded from Western education, but their education in Ghana, as in Europe during the same period, was oriented toward domestic skills rather than intellectual concerns until well into the twentieth century. The perceived need to provide educated young men with educated wives provided much of the impetus for the development of female education. Thus girls' schooling did not enable them to go on to higher levels of the educational system and, because it frequently emphasized domestic skills appropriate for an English housewife, it tended to be largely irrelevant to the needs of their society (Graham, 1971: 71–93).

Although the colonial educational system offered considerably greater opportunities to men, in the first half of the twentieth century, proportionately more women were probably educated in Ghana (followed by the Gold Coast) than in any other colonial African country. Ghana's relative affluence, based on the export of cocoa, provided a better base for the expansion of the educational system of schooling than did that of any other black African territory (Foster, 1965: 171). The first women's secondary boarding school opened in 1881 and taught academic subjects as well as needlework and scripture (Graham, 1971: 144). Some indication of the magnitude of disparities found in the education of boys and girls comes in the educational statistics for 1918, which show that in the government and Wesleyan mission schools there was one girl respectively for every six and seven boys, whereas the Basel Mission, which showed more concern for the provision of education for women, had one girl for every three boys (Graham, 1971: 150). Beginning in the mid–1920s, under the governorship of Sir Gordon Guggisberg, the government and the missions made more of an effort to close the gap. On the eve of independence, the ratio of girls to boys in Ghana's primary and middle schools, which together encompassed the first 10 years of education, stood at approximately 1 to 2.2 (McWilliam, 1962: 20).

Perhaps even more important than the total numbers of children of each sex who received some education, the colonial education system produced a predominantly male elite. The proportion of men increased at each succeeding level of the educational system. Particularly at the secondary school level, where boarding schools have been the training ground for Ghana's elite, many more quality educational institutions were opened for boys, and at the coeducational institutions most of the places were reserved for male students. Until the end of World War II all students seeking a university education had to pursue their studies in Europe or in the United States, and more scholarships were available for men than for women.

In addition to the imbalance in educational opportunities, several other aspects of the colonial legacy should be noted here. Ghana's pattern of economic development, which differed significantly from that of most other African territories, enabled women to participate in the cash economy in two respects: through cash cropping and through marketing. The early growth of the cocoa industry arose through small-scale African farming and did not entail the opening of plantations or the involvement of government agricultural extension workers, both of which generally exclude women (Boserup, 1970). Nevertheless, even though women traditionally grew many of the food crops, men have predominated in the cocoa sector. Little systematic research has been done to determine why this occurred, but it is possible to piece together some data. These indicate that cocoa farming frequently involved emigration from the village to find suitable land; women were more constrained than men from leaving the village to settle in another region. Moreover the companies formed by the male migrants to purchase the land from the chief rarely permitted women in their own right to join. When women did establish cocoa farms, and many did if suitable land in their traditional farming area was available for planting cocoa trees, at their death ownership probably reverted to male members of the family because of the inheritance patterns (Hill, 1963: 11, 39, 42, 65, 116–117). At the present time in the most productive cocoa-growing area, the Brong-Ahafo region, women own one-ninth of the farms and actively assist their husbands on the remainder (Addo, 1971a). Whether this reflects a long-standing division in this particular area or represents the pattern in other cocoa-growing areas is difficult to determine. Since the cocoa industry in the Brong-Ahafo region was developed by migrants from other parts of Ghana, women probably do at least as well in the other cocoa-growing areas.

Women's most significant economic advance during the colonial period came through the growth of the retail sector. The greater law and order provided by the colonial administration enabled many women in the rural areas to expand their trade to more distant markets, and gradually the limitations on the items women could deal in, some of which had been reserved for members of the chief's retinue, disappeared. In the urban areas the largely uneducated women migrants found petty trading the most suitable economic activity because it did not demand much capital, education, or restriction on time. The popularity of such trading is shown by the estimates of one researcher that in 1952 in Koforidua, a southern Ghanaian town, 70 percent of the female population engaged in selling on a more or less full-time basis (McCall, 1961: 292). The establishment of central markets in the towns enabled women to rent stalls and regularize and expand their enterprises. Over time women were able to monopolize the sectors of the wholesale and retail trade that were Ghanaianized. Thus urbanization did not result in widespread displacement of women from the economy, as happened in some other African territories. Contrary to prevailing patterns elsewhere, it frequently increased the woman's independence from her husband.

The pattern of urbanization in Ghana also did not result in a substantial imbalance in the sex ratio, as was common in other parts of Africa. Short-term urban migration exclusively by males, with the intention of accumulating enough resources to enable them to return permanently to the families they had left behind in their rural villages, has been the practice only of Northern groups. Urban migrants consistently have retained strong ties with their kin in the home villages and often visit them, particularly on specific ceremonial occasions. Nevertheless urban settlement has generally represented a long-range commitment by an entire family unit. The censuses of 1931, 1948, and 1960 indicated that more males than females lived in the towns (as was true in all areas), but that the extent of the difference was not considerable. In 1931 10.03 percent of the males and 8.63 percent of the females in the total population were urbanized; in 1948, 13.39 percent of the males and 12.32 percent of the females; and in 1960, 23.38 percent of the males and 22.55 percent of the females (Addo, 1971b: 57). This has meant that Ghanaian women have had greater access to educational institutions and wage employment, both of which tend to be disproportionately available in towns, than have women in many other countries in Africa. The influx of women to towns also facilitated the expansion of the scope of women's trading and other commercial enterprises.

Colonial rule affected the status of women in subtle and less direct ways as well. European traders who established the small settlements along the coast, missionaries, and colonial administrators all sought to deal with Ghanaian men, and over a period of several hundred years this both conferred advantages on the men involved and communicated the unsuitability of women for conducting affairs of substance. Missionaries and educators consciously or unconsciously sought to cast social relationships and mores in a European mold. Christian missionaries, usually unsuccessfully, sought to alter marriage patterns from the polygamous mode in which the husband and wives went their separate ways to a European-type, monogamous, nuclear family in which the wife was subordinate to the husband and devoted herself primarily to her husband and children. Furthermore as Ghanaians became educated and aspired to acceptance by Europeans as their equals, they began to imitate Western habits and practices. As one historian of the period has noted, "Often the imitation was unconscious, simply because the model was there. Europeans had, in fact, become a 'reference group' for patterns of behavior among those Africans who came in contact with them" (Kimble, 1963: 133). Men of the elite encouraged their wives to dress in European style and to act like Victorian ladies (Kimble, 1963: 134); and since Victorian ladies had more limited economic and social roles than did Ghanaian women, such imitation could only have affected adversely the place of these women in Ghanaian society.

Thus the colonial interlude affected the condition of women in Ghana by changing the balance in the societies through education, urbanization, economic development, and religious conversion. Although individual women achieved high positions, for the most part women's status declined because new opportunities were offered primarily to men. Nevertheless the inverse relationship between women's roles and development perceived by Boserup and others in many parts of Africa was less true of Ghana (Boserup, 1970; Economic Commission for Africa, 1974). Women were usually more successful in upholding their prerogatives because of a variety of factors, including their strong traditional roles, the growth of cash cropping independent of efforts by colonial extension agents, the early movement of women into the retail trade, the opening of some schools for women, and the relatively even balance between the sexes in urban areas.

WOMEN IN THE FAMILY

As described in the preceding section, the traditional societies were based on kinship units in which the extended family rather than the individual was the principal focus. Marriage represented an alliance between two kinship groups for the purpose of procreation, and was sealed by the payment of a bride price and the completion of prescribed ritual. Although women commonly had little choice in the selection of their first husbands, the arrangement was made more acceptable because marriage entailed a loose relationship in which the two partners each had their own spheres of activity and social networks. In an intolerable situation women could usually initiate divorce, and they often played a greater role in choosing a second husband. Moreover the close tie between mother and children, not the relationship between the wife and husband, provided the major emotional satisfaction for women.

As might be expected, Christianity, Western education, urbanization, and economic change all have affected and continue to affect the nature of marriage and family life in Ghana. Nevertheless the break with the past should not be exaggerated. Ghanaians still live in a world in which they owe allegiance to their larger kinship group and identify with their ethnic origins. Accommodation rather than conflict characterizes the relationship between the so-called traditional and the modern (Brokensha, 1966: 268–269). Exposure to modernizing influences has not necessarily induced change or precipitated irreconcilable conflicts between previously held beliefs and new systems, but instead enables people to choose their style of life from a wider range of alternatives. This is particularly true of marriage relationships.

One of the by-products of Christian missionary activity during the colonial period was the creation of new forms of marriage. To set their converts apart from the remainder of the community, missionaries petitioned the British government to introduce a pattern of binding monogamous marriage with inheritance rights for the wife and children comparable to those in Western society. Although at first the colonial authorities were reluctant to cooperate for fear of the repercussions of disturbing traditional social systems, they eventually passed the Marriage Ordinance for Christians. At the present time prospective marriage partners may choose to contract a valid marriage in the customary manner, under the Ordinance, or in a Christian or Muslim religious ceremony. The form used to validate the marriage determines whether the man can take another wife, how the marriage can be dissolved, and which laws of inheritance apply. Nominally some 44 percent of the population identify themselves as Christian and 12 percent as Muslim, but religious affiliation does not necessarily determine the kind of marriage elected (Gil, Aryee, Ghansah, 1964: *lxxxv*).

Today customary marriage, the form still followed by the vast majority of Ghanaians, involves a series of ceremonies performed over a period of time, just as in the precolonial era. The man makes several presentations or gifts, some of them to the family and some of them to the girl he proposes to marry, in accordance with the established norms of his community. The presentations usually come in three stages: the first to establish the acceptability of the suitor; the second and most important, sometimes referred to as the engagement, to validate the marriage and to enable the couple to live together; and the third, the bride price, which is given to the bride rather than the family, to complete the formalities. As in precolonial times, the gifts consist of liquor and money, and the amounts depend on the general affluence of the locality and the status of the girl. Now the level of education of the girl also counts for a great deal in determining the size of the bride price she can command. Total payments range from the equivalent of $10 in the poorest areas to many hundreds of dollars for an educated girl from a substantial family in Accra. By contracting a valid marriage, the man acquires exclusive sexual rights over the woman, and the wife reciprocally receives the right to maintenance and sexual satisfaction. If either party fails to uphold his or her part of the bargain, customary marriages can easily be dissolved by a council of the two families. Whether the bride's family has to refund part or all of the gifts depends on the circumstances leading to the divorce.

In a customary marriage the traditional inheritance laws of the particular community prevail and, as noted above, although a woman's share varies somewhat in matrilineal and patrilineal systems, this generally means that male members of the extended family are entitled to most of the estate. Under Ghanaian law a man married according to traditional procedure can still circumvent predetermined inheritance patterns by writing a will before his death to specifically designate a portion of his acquired property for his wife and/or children. However, with the exception of some of the elite coastal families among whom individual ownership of property emerged early, few men have opted to do so (Tetteh, 1967: 205–206; Oppong, 1974; Brokensha, 1966: 219–235).

In the second marriage alternative, marriage under the Ordinance, the provisions of the Marriage Ordinance (Cap. 127 of the Law of Ghana) rather than customary practices determine the respective rights of the parties. An ordinance marriage provides the wife with greater security by discouraging divorce, by precluding polygamy, and by securing for the wife two-ninths of her husband's estate. Divorce requires a court action rather than a decision of a family council. When a person married under the Ordinance dies intestate, two-thirds of his or her property is distributed in accordance with the provisions of English law, thus assuring the wife a fixed share, and the remaining one-third is inherited in accordance with customary law. However the very permanence of this form of marriage makes it less attractive since most Ghanaians, probably more men than women, prefer to preserve the option of dissolving their marriages easily and relatively inexpensively (Tetteh, 1967: 206–207; Vellenga, 1971: 136).

The third form of marriage involves a religious ceremony performed either in a Christian church or by a recognized Muslim official. In addition Muslim marriages must be registered in the office of a District Commissioner to be recognized as valid. The Marriage of Mohammedans Ordinance (Cap. 129 of the Law of Ghana) stipulates that marriages contracted in this manner are subject to Muslim laws of inheritance and divorce. Most Christian marriage ceremonies take place in conjunction with a customary marriage by couples seeking the blessing of a church for their union. A blessing in the church following a customary marriage generally does not alter the divorce or inheritance provisions of customary marriage. Some of the churches, particularly the Presbyterian Church, have their own regulations regarding the disposition of property, but these church rules are not legally binding (Tetteh, 1967: 207).

According to the 1960 census results, customary marriage remains the usual form of marriage in Ghana. The vast majority of the persons interviewed in the 1960 postenumeration survey, 86 percent of the total, had contracted a customary marriage. Many of the remainder had fulfilled the course of presentations and rituals prescribed for customary marriage and then followed it with an ordinance marriage, a church ceremony, or both. A combined church and ordinance marriage in which the couple had also completed the customary procedures was chosen by 2.3 percent of the males and 1.2 percent of the females. Ordinance marriage by a registrar in conjunction with customary procedures accounted for about 1 percent. Muslim marriages comprised a further 5 percent (Gil, de Graft-Johnson, Colecraft, Vol. VI, 1971: 215). The 1960 post enumeration survey also indicated that the incidence of polygamy is declining. Although polygamy is still permitted, three-fourths of all married males were in monogamous unions, and in the urban areas the expense of maintaining more than one wife reduced the figure to considerably lower than the national average (Gil, de Graft-Johnson, and Colecraft, 1971: 225–227).

In addition to those living in one of the three forms of valid marriage, studies of Ghana have shown that a sizable proportion of the population, 4 percent of the males and 5.6 percent of the females in the 1960 postenumeration census tabulation (Gil, de Graft-Johnson, and Colecraft, 1971: 215), and 19 percent of the urban and 6 percent of the rural women in a sample of 400 women in a 1965–1966 survey (Pool, 1972: 244), live in a mutual consent union in which neither of the parties is protected by the rights inherent in the legal forms of marriage. Although this type of arrangement has traditional precedents, it probably reflects as well the greater sexual freedom prevalent in contemporary Ghana. During the precolonial era girls in most ethnic groups were permitted to have intercourse once they had undergone the puberty rites which took place almost immediately after their first menstruation. Some of the groups, such as the Ashanti and the Krobos, also had recognized customs enabling couples to cohabit without performing the requisite customary rites. However these common consent unions were considered to be temporary situations that would lead to a more permanent customary marriage either with that partner or with another. This expectation does not hold in many of the contemporary relationships, and some of the women in the urban areas go from living with one man to another. In the towns the tendency to postpone marriage, but not sexual activity, to a later age, the greater independence of the individual from the social controls of his kinship group, the availability of men and women temporarily separated from their spouses, the difficulty of obtaining a divorce from ordinance and Christian marriage, and the desire on the part of some women to have a man support them so that they can enjoy a higher standard of living all contribute to the higher incidence of mutual consent unions. Contrary to the beliefs of some, though, the increase in sexual freedom does not result primarily from urbanization. The 1960 postenumeration survey, which was based on a carefully drawn representative sample, showed that cohabitation with a person of the opposite sex without the formalities of marriage took place more frequently in the rural areas of four of the regions than in Accra, the national capital (Tetteh, 1967: 203–209).

Ironically, greater sexual freedom and its concomitant promiscuity and adultery have come about to a considerable extent through the work of the very Christian missionaries who sought to create a new type of marriage modeled on Victorian family life. Conversion to Christianity, which nominally involves slightly less than half of the population, has weakened traditional agencies of social control without substituting new ones in their place; becoming a Christian is thought to free the convert from the consequences of violating traditional taboos, particularly from the possibility of some form of mystical retribution for committing adultery. Men who legally accept monogamous marital relationships, therefore, frequently compensate for this curb on their traditional sexual prerogatives by having frequent affairs. The incidence of premarital pregnancy also has risen somewhat because some men will not contract an ordinance marriage, which is difficult to dissolve, unless the woman can prove that she is capable of bearing children. Although women in both traditional and contemporary Ghana have been much less subject to a double standard regarding sexual conduct than in most cultures, women today face more problems than men. Children born from a temporary liaison do not bear the stigma of illegitimacy, but the woman cannot expect that she will receive financial support from the father to assist in their upbringing. Moreover evidence suggests that educated women, far more than their male counterparts, seem to have adopted many of the European and Christian values associated with marriage. Thus more women consider themselves bound by the ideal of extramarital chastity in a society in which few men are similarly inclined (Nukunya, 1969: 183–185; Tetteh, 1967: 203–211; Brokensha, 1966: 231–235).

Theoretically all three legally binding forms of marriage have equal validity, but they carry quite different prestige. Because it is not traditional for women to assume their husband's names, women married solely according to customary procedures are referred to as Miss or Madam, whereas a woman married under the ordinance is addressed as Mrs., making it easy to discern the form of marriage. A woman contracting an ordinance marriage not only has the advantage of greater security, but also is considered more modern and progressive, and other women sometimes regard their own situations as inferior. The desire they express to be a "wedded" wife or a "Mrs." implies that their own type of marriage does not confer full legality. The government has contributed to this confusion. The socialist ideology and modernizing thrust of the Nkrumah regime, which remained in power for the first nine years after independence, led to the favoring of monogamous ordinance marriage as the wave of the future. Under some circumstances only those married under the Ordinance were eligible to receive government gratuities meant for married persons. This led to the erroneous belief that the government did not recognize customary marriages (Vellenga, 1971: 136).

To clarify the confusion and eliminate some of the legal entanglements resulting from the parallel systems of marriage, the government set up an Inheritance Commission in 1959 to consider how the customary provisions for inheritance might be modified. Disagreements among members of the Commission, which included legal experts, representatives of the churches, and representatives from the Federation of Ghana Women, prevented the Commission from issuing any recommendations.

Two years later the government again confronted the issue when an attempt was made in parliament to amend sections of the criminal code that dealt with offences related to the marriage ordinance. This stimulated the formulation of a white paper on the subject and then a draft bill. The provisions of both were so complex that some people perceived them as favoring polygamy while others interpreted them as encouraging monogamy. In its final form the draft bill allowed men to register all their existing wives, but stipulated that in the future a man could register only one. If a man died intestate, only the registered wife would be entitled to a share of his property, although children from other unions would be eligible for a share equal to that of the children of the registered wife. Under the proposed law the surviving marriage partner (the registered wife or husband) would inherit one-third of the self-acquired property and all of the children of the deceased would share the remaining two-thirds of the estate. The divorce provisions in the bill resembled customary procedures in that the judge or magistrate petitioned to grant a divorce would first appoint a panel to attempt to reconcile the parties ("White Paper on Marriage, Divorce, and Inheritance," 1961).

The proposed bill aroused opposition from several different groups. Many women criticized the draft bill on the grounds that men would continue to practice polygamy and that the provision permitting a man to register only one wife would leave his other wives without protection. The educated, elite women, represented by the National Council of Ghana Women, the successor to the Federation of Ghana Women, feared that the bill would encourage polygamy. Representatives of the churches eventually requested that the bill be withdrawn because it contravened traditional practices too much and might give rise to concubinage rather than monogamy. The government finally dropped the measure when the Sarbah Society, a group of leading legal experts, wrote a memorandum indicating that the bill might undermine customary laws regarding inheritance. A law reform committee continued to work sporadically on a new law until a coup in 1966 dislodged the Nkrumah regime (Vellenga, 1971: 141–145).

Although women have been vaguely dissatisfied with their legal status and particularly disturbed by the disparities in their rights under customary and ordinance marriage, they have not actively sought legal reforms to rationalize inheritance provisions and divorce procedures since the matter was shelved 11 years ago. Thus women's groups have championed the cause of marriage reforms whenever the opportunities presented themselves, but they have not sought to create these opportunities. The lack of pressure by women to reconsider the issue probably results from several factors. Women disagree among themselves about the advisability of monogamy and the penalties that should be imposed for the continuation of polygamous relationships. Generally women today exhibit much less sense of corporate solidarity across ethnic boundaries than they did traditionally within their own communities; consequently women's organizations have usually been weak and incapable of organizing large numbers of women to do anything. Furthermore many educated Ghanaians realize that reform of personal status laws is but one aspect of the general unification and rationalization of the Ghanaian legal system, which suffers perpetual conflicts arising from the differences among the systems of customary law and from the differences between the customary laws and adopted English statutes. Nevertheless the passage of a bill enabling men to register all of their wives under a marriage ordinance and according all wives equal protection and security would probably receive broad support.

Several trends in Ghanaian family structure and marriage relationships are observable across the different forms of marriage. As with many other types of social change, many of these are more common among families living in urban areas and among those in which the husband and wife are highly educated. Nevertheless virtually no part of Ghana remains unexposed to modernizing influences, and it is more accurate to describe rural communities as being at a different point along a continuum than to emphasize the contrasts between rural and urban Ghana. First, the nuclear household seems to be gaining greater autonomy from the extended family and some concomitant independence in decision-making. Second, although women retain considerable economic independence, an erosion in the sexual division of labor has brought greater involvement of husbands in household and family matters. Third, women's status in society now depends to a considerable extent on their husbands' success rather than on their own activities, and this has led to a greater subordination of the wife. Fourth, marital instability seems to be on the ascendance.

The nuclear or conjugal family remains intricately interwoven into the social fabric of the kinship group but in its day-to-day living patterns has greater autonomy. Several factors have promoted this trend in Ghana as they have elsewhere in the world: migration, education, changes in living patterns, spread of private prosperity, and economic development. The high rate of internal migration—in 1960 at least half of the population in two-thirds of the local authority areas originated elsewhere—means that Ghanaians frequently live apart from their kinship groups in both rural and urban environments (Gil, Aryee, and Ghansah, 1964: *xliv*). The important part that schools play in the socialization of the child, particularly in the South, where school enrollment is very high, also decreases the influence of the extended family. The family no longer provides a total context for living, and the individual is increasingly linked to the wider society. As a consequence of factors already mentioned, the act of marriage has become more an expression of personal preference than an alliance between two kinship groups. Because of the current mobility, prospective mates are likely to come from outside the traditional locality that parents and elders formerly surveyed to choose an appropriate partner and may even be from a different ethnic group. While people rarely marry without the approval of their families, the initiative in the choice of a spouse now comes more frequently from the couple themselves. As elsewhere men play the more active role, but women are not passive recipients of their family's will. A recent survey of 4000 rural and urban women showed that three-fourths of them believed that sons should have the freedom to choose their own wives, and slightly less than half (49 percent) would accord the same privilege to their daughters. Interestingly, urban and rural women did not differ in their responses, indicating that urban women do not have a monopoly on modern ideas (Pool, 1971: 241). The likelihood of autonomy of the conjugal family increases for spouses who come from different kinship groups and/or who live at a significant distance from the home community. Nevertheless even in the rural villages the constituent units within the extended family now frequently live apart in their own households and usually work separately.

The fact that husband and wife now usually live together in the same household also contributes to the strengthening of the nuclear family. Formerly women often remained with their own families or maintained a separate residence in the husband's community. According to census results, despite the high rate of internal migration about two-thirds of the married women and men were living with their spouses. Joint households were more the norm in rural than in urban areas (Gil, de Graft-Johnson, and Colecraft, 1971: 254). As a corollary of the situation shown by these figures, one-third of all married Ghanaian women head their own households, and although this may be a lower proportion than traditionally was the case among certain of the groups, it shows that a considerable number of women still fend for themselves. Moreover women who head independent households probably have more responsibilities and less support from their own kinship group.

In those households in which the husband and wife co-reside, the quality of the relationship has not changed significantly. In the conjugal family the relationship between husband and wife still tends to lack the intimacy, emotional bonds, and shared interests and activities characterizing Western family life. The emergence of the nuclear family as a more autonomous social unit has not transformed the attitudes of its members, and the similarity to the Western family comes more in form than in substance. Even among the urban, educated elite, husbands and wives go out together perhaps only once a month and rarely engage in recreation or socializing as a family with husband, wife, and children (Caldwell, 1968b: 72). Both spouses maintain strong ties with their own extended families, including providing relatives with financial aid and living accommodations. In a national survey of 1757 school children at all levels of the educational system conducted by the author in conjunction with the Ministry of Education in 1972, an overwhelming percentage of the students believed it was wrong under any circumstances to refuse assistance to a relative, showing that this is one traditional value that has not been undermined by Western education.

When both the husband and wife are well-educated, an element of companionship may be present in their relationship, but regardless of the living arrangements the woman foremost in a man's affections is still more likely to be his mother than his wife. The inherent conflict between the demands of the husband's kin and his commitments to his conjugal family constitute a continuing source of domestic friction (Oppong, 1974; Lloyd, 1967: 177–179). In terms of their own security and well-being, therefore, women may at least in the short run be giving up more than they are gaining in the transition to the nuclear household pattern. They now receive less protection and support from their own kinship group, thus reducing their independence, while they gain little in the form of greater marital stability or a more satisfying marital relationship.

Women's overall role within the family is changing from independence in the domestic sphere to subordination. Previously women enjoyed autonomy within the domestic domain because of the sexual division of labor, the social separation of the sexes, and their control of their own property. Although contemporary women, as is shown in the section on economic activity, still are not confined to serving as wives and mothers, their earning power is now lower in relationship to their husband's income than it was formerly. This means that even though women regularly contribute to the family's maintenance, the husband usually provides a far greater portion. The economic leverage of the husband, his higher status (which reflects differential access of the sexes to schooling and to wage employment), and the emergence of the nuclear family all have brought about increasing involvement of men in domestic matters that were once reserved for women.

Men now make decisions on such issues as how the family income should be apportioned, where the children should be educated, and what style of life the family should have.

As an illustration of these trends, a slight majority of students at two Ghanaian universities who were surveyed on an open-ended questionnaire by the author described the domestic power relationship between their mother and father as that of a superordinate father and a subordinate mother; only 17 percent considered their relationship to be one of equals. When asked to define the subjects on which their mothers made decisions for the family, 48 percent listed topics concerning the internal organization of the household, 19 percent said only on food, and only 10 percent mentioned matters relating to the upbringing of children; a small minority replied that their mothers made no decisions for the family. These responses cannot be considered representative of the Ghanaian population for two reasons: the university student bodies from which the samples were drawn, hence the samples themselves, were disproportionately male, and the families of most of the students were somewhat elitist.

Although the breakdown of the traditional sexual division of labor has probably worked to the disadvantage of Ghanaian women in their efforts to uphold their domestic prerogatives, these trends should not be exaggerated. Ghanaian women at all levels of society still retain considerable economic independence and substantial control over their own income and property (Caldwell, 1968b: 68–70; Field, 1960: 30). As long as this pattern continues, women can resist being made fully subordinate.

Another accompaniment of the emphasis on the nuclear family and the intrusion of Western concepts of marriage is the dependence of the wife on the husband for her status in society. The fact that elite women carry their husband's name symbolizes other aspects of their relationship. Traditionally spouses operated within such separate spheres that the activities of one only indirectly affected the position of the other, but now among the elite the woman is seen more in the Western perspective as an extension of her husband and her status depends on his success (Little, 1972: 276; Lloyd, 1967: 171). This pattern of reflected status results as well from the greater access of men to higher education and prestigious types of employment. Even in the most elite circles few wives have attained an educational level equivalent to that of their husbands, and in many marriages the disparities between husband and wife are quite considerable. Doubtlessly this new form of dependence has repercussions on the domestic relationship; it becomes more difficult for a woman to demand equality within the home when society accords a higher rank to her husband.

All available evidence points to greater marital instability. This instability manifests itself in two different forms: a higher rate of dissolution of marriages and a lower rate of acceptance of traditional obligations. No accurate figures exist on the proportion of marriages that end in divorce. Census questionnaires ascertain the number of divorced persons still unmarried at the time of the interview, but fail to enumerate how many people have ever been divorced. The figure published in the census report, 5.2 percent of all adults, does not accurately indicate the frequency of divorce because most divorced men and women soon remarry (Gil, de Graft-Johnson, and Cole-craft, 1971: 206). Ghanaians themselves acknowledge the prevalence of marital instability and, at least among the elite, register disapproval of it (Caldwell, 1968b: 72). One study on the average percentage of time lived in conjugal unions showed that between the ages of 20 and 44 years, when according to social custom virtually all Ghanaians should be married, rural males spent 23 percent of the time, and urban males 36 percent of the time, outside of conjugal unions; rural and urban women in the same age span were similarly without a partner for 16 and 18 percent of the period (Caldwell, 1967b: 73). When the respondents in that survey were asked about the number of conjugal partners they had ever possessed, in the age group of 50 and over, rural males averaged 3.5 mates and rural females 2.1, while the comparable rates for urban males and females were 2.5 and 1.4, respectively. All rural men over 25 averaged more than two partners, and all other males and females somewhat more than one (Caldwell, 1967a: 71). One important conclusion to be drawn from this analysis of conjugal biographies is that the unstable marriage patterns are more prevalent in rural than urban areas.

Women in customary marriages also seem to be having greater difficulty in asserting their traditional rights. Previously most cases in the customary courts dealing with marriage were brought by husbands claiming damages from men who had committed adultery with their wives. Studies of two communities in southern Ghana show that the claimants now tend to be women suing their husbands for maintenance (Brokensha, 1966: 220–235; Vellenga, 1971: 150). Moreover when a prospective wife has already been married and divorced, a man often does not feel obliged to perform all of the customary rites to validate the marriage. This leaves the woman without legal recourse to traditional procedures for enforcing her rights. As the woman grows older, her bargaining position to insist on the performance of the customary procedures becomes weaker, and she is forced to accept a common consent union on the man's terms (Tetteh, 1967: 209).

Elite women and uneducated women confront different types of problems in marriage, but both find their position made more difficult by current trends. Elite women usually have greater security in marriage than their less educated sisters because they more often contract ordinance marriages and because divorce is frowned on among their class. Nevertheless their marital situation is not enviable; they have been thrust into a new pattern of relationships in which the wife is increasingly likely to become an appendage of her husband and in which her autonomy and independence have been reduced without a concomitant gain of a more satisfying relationship with her husband. Although any efforts to draw inferences from the data must of course be highly speculative, it would seem that elite women, who have absorbed many European and Christian ideas concerning marriage, must find it difficult to accept a marriage in which the husband's loyalty to his mother outweighs his commitment to his wife and conjugal family, and in which monogamous marriage goes hand in hand with frequent male infidelity. Those women socialized in Ghanaian cultural patterns probably balk at being subordinated to the husband within the household and being considered inferior by society. Because rural and uneducated women are less influenced by changes in the relative status of men and women resulting from differential access to higher education and prestigious occupations, they probably encounter fewer problems in maintaining their autonomy and independence within marriage. However they must cope with the consequences of marital instability and insecure inheritance rights under customary law.

Much has been written indicating that economic development may adversely affect the economic roles of women. The foregoing would indicate that in countries like Ghana, where women traditionally enjoyed relatively high status, the changes accompanying modernization may in the long run even more drastically undermine the social position of women. The Western model of development may lower women's security and status as well as reduce their economic options.

EDUCATION OF WOMEN

The Nkrumah regime, under which Ghana achieved its independence, was committed to the modernization and radical restructuring of society along socialist lines. With these objectives in mind, the government expanded the educational system and eliminated school fees so that every child, regardless of sex, would be able to receive 10 years of education. In 1948 only 4 percent of the population had received any schooling (Caldwell, 1967b: 48). By 1960, three years after independence, 27 percent of the population aged six years and older had been to school. Ten years later, in 1970, the percentage of persons having some education rose to 43.2 percent (*1970 Population Census*, Vol. II: *xxlv*). In assessing the magnitude of the educational expansion, one should keep in mind that it was accomplished despite high rates of population increase.

The greater equality of educational opportunity has increased girls' attendance, often at a slightly higher rate than boys', but it has not ended the educational disparity between the sexes. Almost all public primary and middle schools, which provide the first 10 years of education, are coeducational, and all children follow the same curriculum established by the national Ministry of Education. Nevertheless, as Table 1 indicates, a smaller proportion of the girls than boys begin school. At each succeeding level of the educational system, girls constitute a lower and lower percentage of the total number of students. The dropout rate for girls within any given level of the educational system also tends to be significantly higher than it is for boys (*Educational Report, 1963–1967*, 1968: 4).

Table 1   Percentage of Female Enrollment at all School Levels, 1968–1969

Total primary enrollment	44
Primary one	46
Primary six	42
Total middle school enrollment	36.7
Middle form one	40.5
Middle form four	30.7
Total secondary school enrollment	25.8
Forms one through five	26.4
Form six	16
Total university enrollment	8.5
University of Ghana (premier institution)	14.4
University of Science and Technology	5.3
University of Cape Coast (teacher training)	10.6

Source.   Educational Statistics, 1968–1969, 1971: 13, 36, 50–51, 68–70.

Educational trends indicate that an increasingly larger proportion of women are receiving some education, but that at the upper reaches the percentage of women remains fairly constant over time. Thus in the 10 years between 1960 and 1970 the percentage of females 6 years and over who had never been to school declined from 83 percent to 66 percent. In the compulsory school-age group of 6 through 14, the change was even more dramatic: girls' attendance went from 33.3 percent to 58.4 percent, whereas for boys the figure was 66.5, up from 53.5 percent (*1970 Population Census,* Vol. II: *xxiv*). At the time of the 1960 census, women comprised 17 percent of those above the age of 6 who had attended some secondary school, 32 percent of those who had completed the sixth form of secondary school (a prerequisite for admission to the university, comparable in level to the first year of American university training), and 18 percent of those with a university education (*1960 Population Census,* Vol. III, 1964: 38). The 1968–1969 educational statistics show that women constituted almost 26 percent of the students in secondary school. At the sixth form and university levels, though, women's relative position declined; only 16 percent of the sixth form students were women, and at Ghana's three universities only 8.5 percent of the student body was female (*Educational Statistics, 1968–1969,* 1971: 50–51). Hence one could conclude that the expansion of higher educational facilities had disproportionately benefitted men.

Comparative education statistics indicate that Ghana's record for women's education is not exceptional, even for Africa. Statistics compiled by the Economic Commission for Africa of the United Nations rank Ghana as ninth out of 37 African countries with respect to the percentage of girls among students in primary schools, thirteenth out of 27 with regard to the percentage of enrollment in secondary schools, and twentieth out of 31 at the university level (Economic Commission for Africa, 1974: 13, 33–34). Ghana's educational system has a better record for women at the earliest stages of education but falls behind many other African states in providing opportunities at the secondary and university levels. Furthermore Ghana's educational expansion, which began earlier than those of other African states, has probably peaked.

The continuing imbalance in the education of men and women results both from attitudes toward education and from the structure of the educational system. Most Ghanaians have a utilitarian approach to education; they value it as an instrument to improve access to good jobs rather than as a source of enlightenment and intellectual stimulation. Since girls are supposed to marry and have children, many parents evidently assume that they will make less use of their education and will be less inclined to pursue their career advancement. They consequently consider it a better investment to support their sons. Despite the elimination of school fees for primary and middle school, parents must still pay a considerable amount of money for the required school uniforms and books, and fees for secondary schools are very steep. Because they feel that education is less important for girls than for boys, mothers also feel less inhibited about keeping their daughters at home to help with household chores and to care for younger siblings. The oldest daughter in the family is particularly disadvantaged by the demands her family is likely to place upon her. According to a survey of students the author conducted in conjunction with the Ministry of Education, at each rung of the educational ladder girls in school had better-educated parents than did the boys at the same stage. Since education and income are usually related, this demonstrates that when parents can afford to finance the education of only some of their children, they usually choose their sons over their daughters. It also indicates that as the population becomes better educated, some of the prejudices against educating women may pass away.

The structure of the educational system affects women's educational opportunities in several respects. Modeled on the British system, the Ghanaian educational system has a decreased number of students at each succeeding level, with a sharp divide in attendance between public middle and private secondary schools. Advancement from middle school depends on receiving a good score on a national examination and then being admitted to a secondary school. The competition for secondary school places is very keen because there are not enough vacancies to accommodate all students who pass the examination. Much like American high school seniors, students apply directly to the schools of their choice and gamble on being accepted by one of the better schools. Secondary schools vary considerably in quality, and most of the elite schools were established during the colonial period. For most students this competitive process is repeated after completion of the fifth form of secondary school, because only a small number of schools have sixth form facilities and students from other institutions reapply for transfer to them. Once students finish the sixth form and pass another nationally administered examination, they virtually automatically gain entrance to one of Ghana's universities. At the university level, in contrast with the secondary schools, the government subsidizes the cost, and all Ghanaian students are given scholarships.

In this system women are disadvantaged by the high cost of secondary school, particularly at the elite institutions that require that students be boarded. Moreover at the secondary school level fewer places are available for women, particularly at elite institutions. This is particularly true of the sixth form. Because their schooling is likely to be of inferior quality, the women who do have the chance to attend secondary school are also not as well prepared for the examinations and for university work. Since the era of educational expansion is drawing to a close, it does not seem likely that many more facilities will be provided for women.

Women's interest in education in Ghana has been documented. For example, on the survey conducted by this author twice as many female secondary school students as male students revealed that if they were free to be trained for any job they liked, they would choose one that required at least the equivalent of a secondary school education; slightly less than half of the girl students chose a profession versus 24 percent of the boy students. Other surveys of secondary students have demonstrated similar aspirations and have also shown that the girls knew that few of them would have the opportunity to realize their ambition (Foster, 1965: 261–291). If given a fully equal opportunity, girls would doubtlessly improve their educational records.

Ghana's educational system is producing a large number of educated women, but the kind of education most of them are receiving does not prepare them for any career. As in other countries in Africa, the liberal arts orientation of the curriculum instills a contempt for farming and other forms of manual labor without imparting skills for a vocation other than working the land. In this author's survey results, girls exhibited at least the same disinclination as their male counterparts to remain as farmers in rural communities. Few of the clerical jobs that were once available to school dropouts with a primary or middle school degree still remain open. Post-middle school vocational institutes for women exist, but they are privately operated for profit and most of them charge high fees. Moreover most of them concentrate on sewing and cooking in a European style, and there are few occupational uses for fancy embroidery, knitting, and pastry making.

At the university level most women elect general liberal arts programs. For example, during the 1968–1969 academic year 42 percent of the women at Ghana's premier university, the University of Ghana, were enrolled in liberal arts degree programs, a figure not very different from that of their male counterparts, 40 percent of whom chose a similar course. However a greater proportion of the male liberal arts students qualified for an honors program. Similarly the largest number of women in any faculty at the University of Science and Technology was 27, in the Faculty of Art. Approximately one-third of the total female enrollment at that institution, and 70 percent of women students at the University College of Cape Coast, had elected the Faculty of Arts to study for a preliminary arts degree or a B.A. in education (*Educational Statistics, 1968–1969,* 1971: 68–70). Previously the civil service was the best employment opportunity for liberal arts graduates, but the number of vacancies left to be filled has declined considerably. In Ghana liberal arts graduates are beginning to have problems finding jobs, and the concentration of women in liberal arts does not augur well for the employment prospects of these university graduates.

WOMEN AND EMPLOYMENT

Disparities in education as well as increasing competition for scarce jobs have restricted women's access to employment. A high proportion of women in Ghana remain economically active but, as Table 2 indicates, the sectors in which women participate the most heavily—trading and farming—are those that do not require much education and have always attracted women. In 1970 61.1 percent of all Ghanaian women were engaged in some economic activity, a rise over the 53.7 percent reported in 1960. Between 1960 and 1970 female employment increased while male employment dropped, largely because more males over the age of 15 remained in school (*1970 Population Census of Ghana: xxiv*).

Table 2   *Women's Occupational Representation in Ghana, 1970*

Occupation	Percentage of Total Sector	Percentage of Economically Active Females
Professional, technical, and related	23.47	1.98
Administrative and managerial	5.17	0.04
Clerical	15.46	0.94
Sales (including petty trading)	87.81	25.66
Service (including domestic workers)	23.26	1.48
Agriculture, fishing, and related	42.91	64.53
Production and related	35.39	15.35

Source.   Calculations based on provisional census figures supplied by Division of Demographic and Social Statistics, Central Bureau of Statistics, Accra.

The question arises whether women will be able to retain a vital economic role in the future. According to the 1970 census results, more than half of Ghana's employed population (males 59.3 percent and females 54.6 percent) were still engaged in agriculture, fishing, and logging. This figure represents a decrease from the 1960 figure of 61.8 percent of the economically active population, and a further decline in the proportion of the population involved in primary production is anticipated (de Graft-Johnson, 1974: 483–485). It seems unlikely that major technical innovations will displace women from farming, but the high rate of population growth may create a land scarcity that would make it more difficult for women to maintain their own farms. This may already be taking place. Preliminary 1970 census figures show a decrease in the proportion of self-employed females in agriculture and a concomitant increase in the percentage of female family workers between 1960 and 1970. Surveys of particular agricultural communities also verify this transition from the more traditional pattern of separate cultivation on individual plots to women working on their husbands' farms as family workers, particularly in cocoa-producing areas (Oppong, Okali, and Houghton, 1975; Fuchs-Carsch, 1975: 35–39). Since women's autonomy has traditionally derived from their independent economic roles and their own sources of income, this shift from separate to joint cultivation, because it entails the loss of control by women over the profits realized from the farming, most likely will affect women's position in the family and in the community. As women become more integrated into production in a family unit, they very probably will become more economically dependent on the male head of the household.

The dichotomy observed by Boserup (1970) and others (Economic Commission for Africa, 1974) between women's involvement in subsistence farming and men's domination of cash cropping does not fully apply to Ghana. The situation in Ghana is more complex, in part because only a small proportion of Ghana's farmers, about 17 percent, produce solely for subsistence (Fuchs-Carsch, 1975: 35). Therefore many more female farmers than in other African countries produce a surplus for sale. Moreover, as noted earlier, women have never been excluded from cocoa farming, Ghana's principal cash crop.

Nevertheless the gap in the productivity of female and male farmers characterizing many other countries occurs in Ghana. The available evidence, which includes detailed surveys of several agricultural communities, suggests that female holdings are usually smaller than males' and that a significantly larger proportion of women than men are engaged in subsistence or near subsistence foodcrop farming (Fuchs-Carsch, 1975: 35). Data on cocoa-growing regions also demonstrate that women have far less opportunity to develop their own cocoa farms, both because land ownership is more restricted to men and because women have more responsibilities that drain their energy and resources (Oppong, Okali, and Houghton, 1975: 4–7). Migrant women farmers who cannot rely on the assistance of their male relatives seem particularly vulnerable to serving in subsidiary roles in agricultural production as laborers for their husbands (Oppong, Okali, and Houghton, 1975: 11).

Since women have such a strong hold over the small-scale wholesale and retail trade, it seems doubtful that the growth of large-scale enterprises will dislodge them in the future, especially since the attempts of the Ghana National Trading Corporation to take over food marketing have not been very successful. However it seems unlikely that market women will be able to go beyond trading into large-scale ventures because they tend to be uneducated and usually reinvest only a portion of their profits. Market women prefer to utilize their additional profits to improve the life-style of their families, particularly by increasing the opportunities for their children through supporting their education (Sai, 1971).

Women with a primary and middle school education seem disinclined to pursue the types of economic activity in which women in Ghana have been traditionally engaged since they consider farming and trading unsuitable for educated women. These attitudes are understandable because of the low status of such occupations and the low incomes they bring most women. The greatest unknown with respect to employment prospects for women is what will happen to these women. Few women are able to combine steady wage employment with family obligations, and those who do rarely advance to higher levels of responsibility. Moreover, although a husband rarely interferes with his wife's own business, he may attempt to control the spending of a salary.

A high proportion of the educated female population already resides in urban areas (41 percent in 1960 as against 23 percent of the total female population), where they have been attracted by hopes of further education and employment. Population estimates project that Ghana's rate of urbanization, approximately 28 percent now, will continue to accelerate (Addo, 1971b: 73). Female migrants to towns have sought jobs as clerks, typists, seamstresses, domestic servants, bakers, and industrial workers. None of these avenues of employment, however, is expanding rapidly enough to absorb the job applicants. Women also are attracted to opportunities for self-employment, because such situations are easier to combine with marriage and childrearing than is outside employment. The occupation of seamstress has become increasingly popular for young women, who obtain qualification through training in a vocational institute, because it enables them to be self-employed and has a higher status than trading, but there are obvious limitations on growth opportunities (Addo, n.d.: 14). Since factories do not maintain day nurseries and there are few public nurseries, most women in factory work are young, literate, and unmarried, and they view their factory employment as temporary (Peil, 1972: 36, 41).

Evidence exists that employers give preference to males in hiring policy, particularly in industrial employment. One major factor accounting for this is Ghana's employment code, which requires very liberal maternity benefits and other provisions that make employment of women expensive (Peil, 1972: 109). Ironically legislation passed to protect women now serves to exclude them from consideration for many jobs. More specifically, the Ghana Labour Decree prohibits employers from employing women to do certain types of jobs, including mine and underground work, because working conditions of such occupations are not considered conducive to a woman's health. A pregnant working woman receives three months of maternity leave at half salary. To protect her health, after the fourth month of pregnancy a female worker cannot be reassigned to a new location. For nine months after the baby is born, a woman is entitled to one hour off each day to nurse the baby, taken either at two spaced intervals or at one time. She is not allowed to work overtime during the first eight months after delivery. The Ghanaian Labour Code also endorses the principle of equal pay for equal work, which means that it is illegal to hire a woman at a lower base pay to compensate for the additional cost of these benefits (Chinery-Hesse, 1971: 7–9).

Women's economic contribution in the future will depend on their access to new sources of employment. Between 1960 and 1970 women's positions in technical and professional occupational groups improved somewhat. A 1968 manpower survey indicated that women comprised 25 percent of the middle level subprofessional and technical workers and 9 percent of the high level and skilled professionals. The 1970 census figures revealed an increase from 18 percent of professional and subprofessionals in 1960 to 24 percent. The 1970 census also showed that women's share of the high level managerial posts had risen from 3 percent to 5 percent. The most significant rise in female employment between the 1960 and 1970 censuses occurred in production and manufacturing, where women's share went from 3 to 35 percent of the total sector.

The government is the most important employer in Ghana, and its attitude toward women has an important effect on their overall economic standing. Although the government never has adopted a systematic policy regarding the employment of women, its practices could be described as being non-discriminatory while at the same time not encouraging fuller participation of women. The liberal provisions of the government labor code regarding the employment of women have already been mentioned. Ghanaian constitutions have guaranteed equality for women and have opened all offices in the civil service and political system to them. As is the case in most other countries, women tend to be employed at the lower levels of the administration and the public corporations, and their promotions seem to occur at a slower rate than those of their male counterparts. However during the Nkrumah period an effort was made to attract a group of highly qualified professional women to government service; some of these women and others who joined the public service prior to independence have attained very responsible positions, including ambassador, associate justice, principal secretaries (in the Ministries of Finance and Foreign Affairs, among others), and magistrates. Proportionally, however, the record is disappointing, and since the government does not intend to actively recruit more women, it seems unlikely, particularly in light of the much smaller number of vacancies occurring now than in the postindependence period, that the sexual imbalance at the high levels will be reduced.

The long-range prospects for women to achieve economic equality with men do not seem very encouraging in Ghana. Today, despite the significant economic roles that women traditionally assumed, the gap between women's and men's economic contribution and status is substantial. As already mentioned, this trend began during the colonial period and reflects the continuing disparity in educational opportunities, particularly at the higher levels. Another factor relates to the tendency for many people to accept what was originally the accidental exclusion of women from many sectors of the modern economy as being the inevitable and natural course of affairs, so that past and present occupational practices become the basis of a new tradition of sexual division of labor. The sexual division of labor inhering in most industrialized societies does not correspond with the economic roles in Ghanaian precolonial systems; with certain exceptions, such as men's monopoly over fishing and women's over the curing and selling of fish among the Ga and the Ewe, women and men engaged in similar economic tasks. The disproportionate congregation of women today in occupations considered particularly suitable for the European feminine nature results largely from the prejudices of colonial administrators and educators and the system they established. Unfortunately many of their Ghanaian successors are assuming similar attitudes. Even Kwame Nkrumah, who professed to be a radical, envisioned the expansion of employment opportunities for women in the modern sector primarily through such traditionally female vocations as nursing and teaching (interview, Michael Bentil: May 9, 1973). Some elite men have begun to state that "woman's place is in the home," a categorization that reflects neither past nor present economic activities of women and, it is hoped, will not represent the model of the future.

THE POLITICAL ROLE OF WOMEN

Women played very little part in either the independence movement or the postcolonial political system. When the expansion of suffrage took place during the colonial period, women attained universal adult suffrage at the same time as men, and women have never been legally excluded from any high position in the government. In spite of this, women have held few significant political offices.

The commitment of the Convention People's Party (CPP) of Kwame Nkrumah to a radical reordering of Ghanaian society along socialist lines predisposed the CPP regime, under which the country came to independence in 1957 and which governed for the next nine years, to seek equality for women. Although Nkrumah did not accord improvement in the status of women high priority, a number of measures that he undertook to modernize or mobilize Ghana benefitted women. Perhaps the most important of these was the expansion of the educational system and the elimination of school fees. In the 1962 draft party program the CPP was forced to take a stand because of the impending revision of the marriage laws. It stated that "The Party stands for complete equality of the sexes and complete equality is, strictly speaking, incompatible with polygamy" (quoted in Vellenga, 1971: 144). Nevertheless the CPP backed down and eventually shelved the marriage reform act, and it never undertook any concerted program to elevate the status of women and bring about equality of the sexes.

In the political sphere Nkrumah sought to redress the imbalance in political representation by co-opting more women into the parliament; no women had been elected in the 1954 or 1957 parliamentary elections based on universal adult suffrage. For that purpose a 1960 law provided for the nomination and election of 10 women to the National Assembly by the existing members of that body (Harvey, 1966: 36–37). Nkrumah also appointed a woman to the cabinet, first as Undersecretary for the Ministry of Education and then as Minister of Social Welfare.

As part of his overall design to centralize the direction of voluntary associations and subordinate them to the CPP, Nkrumah had the Federation of Ghana Women disbanded. In its place the CPP sponsored the formation of the National Council of Ghana Women as an official party wing. Although Nkrumah was vaguely committed to women's activism, the major purpose in establishing the National Council of Ghana Women was to take over and politically neutralize the Federation of Ghana Women, an umbrella organization for women's voluntary associations that he believed to lean toward the political opposition. The Federation of Ghana Women claimed to be politically neutral and did not engage in overt political activities on behalf of the opposition. However because its leadership was drawn from the same elite social class as that of the opposition party and because the woman heading it was not subservient to party directives, the organization was suspect. The ostensible purpose of the National Council of Ghana Women was to organize and mobilize women to participate in development, but it never fulfilled this function. Like other party auxiliaries, it suffered from the absence of capable leadership, poor organization, inadequate resources, and the lack of explicit directions from the CPP (Card, 1972).

In the regimes that have followed the ouster of Nkrumah by a military coup, women have played even less significant political roles. No women have held cabinet appointments. Two women members, one of whom was also a member of the opposition's shadow cabinet, sat in the parliament elected in 1969 under the Constitution of the Second Republic. Seven other women sought election in 1969 and were defeated (Danquah, n.d.). The Presidential Council of State of the Second Republic, a largely ceremonial body, also included two women. The women's auxiliaries attached to the political parties that succeeded the CPP have been little more than the paper organizations established on the eve of the 1969 election, only to pass into oblivion once the votes were counted.

Several factors have contributed to women's limited political roles. First, political leadership has tended to fall to those with high education, and in any period there have been fewer women with such qualifications. This was particularly the case at the end of the nineteenth and beginning of the twentieth centuries when educated men began to articulate opposition to the colonial administration, and it is possible that this early monopoly by men established the tradition of male domination of modern politics. Second, in the precolonial political systems of Ghana men usually controlled important political offices. Moreover the almost incessant warfare in the century prior to the inception of colonial rule led to institutional modifications among some of the groups that elevated the importance of the exclusively male military companies. Third, for three years following the ouster of Nkrumah and in the years since the military coup of 1972, the military has governed Ghana, and in Ghana, as elsewhere, the military is a male institution. Fourth, the strongest women's voluntary associations have been those organized by the predominantly illiterate market women, not by the educated women. Various regimes have sought periodically to curry favor with the market women (Bretton, 1966: 72–73), and the market women's associations were invited to send delegates to the constitutional convention that framed the Constitution of the Second Republic. Although market women have occasionally resorted to strikes to gain their objectives, they have neither the inclination nor the ability to influence policy formation on a regular basis.

Evidence exists as well that women, even those with the same level of education as men, continue to have less interest in political matters. For instance, a national survey of 1757 school children, undertaken by this author in conjunction with the Ministry of Education, showed that Ghanaian girls compared with boys of their own age level consistently had less exposure to the mass media, lower political awareness, and less ability to answer questions relating to the political system. Neither increasing levels of education nor advancing age closed the gap.

Most women's voluntary associations have been religious, economic, or social welfare oriented rather than political in nature. The Nanemei Akpee (Society of Friends), one of the best-established women's organizations, with branches in several Ghanaian towns, is a combination of trading and mutual benefit society. It assists women with the establishment of trading enterprises, obtaining loans, and saving money, and also provides financial support from members' contributions for births, sicknesses, and funerals (Little, 1972: 281–282). Many of the women's organizations have a religious base, such as the Ghana Branch of the Anglican Mothers Union, which has as its goal the maintenance of the sanctity of Christian marriage (Greenstreet, 1972: 354).

The reconstitution of the Federation of Ghana Women in 1969 under the new name of the Ghana Assembly of Women has made this organization, which dates back to 1953, the most prominent national women's association. Like its predecessor, the Assembly serves as an umbrella organization, coordinating and servicing its affiliated women's associations. The national officers of the Ghana Assembly of Women, like their counterparts in the former Federation of Ghana Women, aspire to help women achieve a leadership role by helping them to realize their civic, social, and political responsibilities through various educational programs. Its Committee on the Status of Women supports changes in women's roles that will lead to a more active participation in national life at all levels of the social and political system, but little has been done by the Assembly or its Committee on the Status of Women. The affiliates of the Ghana Assembly of Women are typical of the kind of organization run by educated women. Most are apolitical and social welfare oriented, and many have a religious affiliation. None of these groups has as its objective improving the position of women qua women in Ghanaian society, raising the consciousness of women, or organizing large numbers of women for any purpose. Furthermore few of them bridge the gap between educated and uneducated women.

The prospects do not seem very good for greater social and political activism on the part of women and for the development of a women's movement in Ghana. Ghana will probably remain under military rule for the foreseeable future, thus limiting the possibilities for political participation on the part of women. Moreover it has not been possible to translate the corporate sense of solidarity existing in many of the constituent traditional societies into forms that will work in the modern political system. Women have been more divided than united. Educated women have exhibited little inclination to extend their horizons and organizations to include their un-educated sisters. The strength of ethnic identity in Ghana has inhibited women of one ethnic group from perceiving a community of interest with women from other ethnic groups. As indicated previously, women have disagreed among themselves over basic issues relating directly to women, such as proposed marriage law reforms and the future of polygamy. Fur-thermore, the elite women, from whom the leadership of any woman's movement would come, face little overt discrimination that would stimulate a sense of injustice and promote greater organization. Elite social norms downgrading women's independence probably have the additional effect, as well, of stifling women's social and political activism.

FERTILITY AND FAMILY PLANNING

In precolonial and colonial times the area of the west coast of Africa in which Ghana is located was referred to as "the white man's grave" because of the incidence of disease and the inhospitable tropical climate. Although the indigenous African population was more acclimated to the physical conditions of life there, the toll of disease was high for them as well. A confluence of factors—Ghana's relative affluence from the cocoa industry; the early development of education, making it possible to train doctors; and the socialist disposition of the Nkrumah regime—have led to major investments in health and social welfare that have considerably lowered the death rate and reduced infant mortality.

Improved health care has brought about a very high rate of population growth. Demographers calculate that the rate of natural increase ranged between 3.0 and 3.5 percent per annum between 1967 and 1969, which if maintained would result in a doubling of the population in 20 years. Ghana also has one of the higest rates of total fertility, between 6.5 and 7.5 children per woman on the average, and a very high dependency ratio. Surveys further indicate that the desired family size remains high: 94 percent of Ghanaian women want four or more children, and in many cases the preferred family size is the same as the actual number of living children (Gaisie, Jones, Caldwell, and Perkin, 1970: 1–2). This high rate of population increase has made it difficult for the government to maintain the present level of social services. Furthermore Ghana's stagnant economy has not been able to absorb the growing labor force, and the opportunities for gainful employment have progressively been reduced relative to the numbers of people seeking positions. The presence of greater numbers of people without economic expansion led to a decline in per capita income during the last ten years.

The realization that the burden of rapid population growth was overwhelming efforts to improve the quality of life led the government to adopt a national family planning policy in 1969 ("Population Planning for National Progress and Prosperity: Ghana Population Policy": 1969). Ghana's program, which was instituted the following year, is the only broad, government-supported, and subsidized family planning effort in sub-Saharan Africa. By 1972 the government had established 140 clinics and licensed over 600 chemical retailers selling subsidized contraceptives ("Ghana National Family Planning Programme Progress Report," 1972: 3). The number of acceptors by the end of 1972 totaled 30,500, slightly more than half of whom were using birth control pills (Nortman, 1973: 67).

It is difficult to predict population trends for Ghana. The number of participants in the family planning program, although consisting of approximately 25 percent of the women between 20 and 34 ("Ghana National Family Planning Programme Progress Report," 1972) still is not sufficiently large to have a significant impact on the rate of population growth. Since the median age of women using intrauterine devices and pills is 29.8 years, women apparently resort to contraceptives primarily to space rather than limit the number of their children (Nortman, 1973: 73). As is the case in most countries with a national family planning program, the couples most likely to know about and to be utilizing contraceptives are the more urban, the more educated, and those with conjugal partners employed in the modern wage sector (Pool, 1970; Caldwell, 1971). There is some evidence, though, that knowledge of modern means of contraception is beginning to spread, and there may even be an emerging trend toward a somewhat smaller desired family size among the urban elite (Caldwell, 1974). Surveys indicate that residents of rural areas that had experienced significant social and economic change demonstrate more interest in limiting the size of their families than respondents in areas that had remained less developed. Thus the continuation of the processes of rural social change and urbanization should gradually lower the national total fertility rate (Caldwell, 1968a: 102). However survey results show that even urban, educated women desire at least four children; education, urbanization, and the availability of contraceptives will not in and of themselves, without a change in attitudes, reduce population growth to manageable proportions.

In Ghana the desire for a large family seems to reflect the positive value of children rather than the dependence of women on children for their primary status and security. In contemporary Ghana, as in the precolonial era, there exist many channels other than childbearing for a woman to infuse her life with dignity and purpose. Nevertheless marriage and childbearing remain integral aspects of a woman's role definition, and few women, then or now, can envision a life-style devoid of raising children. Women, particularly those in a rural situation, probably value having many children, independently of societal pressures and kinship preferences. Children provide labor on their farms and can assist with petty trading. Especially among the groups with considerable marital instability, children confer security for women's old age. Moreover the strong bond between mother and child, which is the predominant family tie even in the patrilineal societies, brings with it an emotional satisfaction that women cannot derive from other relationships.

It would also seem that women's high rates of economic activity in Ghana have been compatible thus far with the maintenance of high fertility. Most women have been engaged primarily in traditional economic pursuits that do not interfere with childbearing and childrearing, and the availability of servants has made it possible for elite women to combine a career with a family. For employment to lead to a decrease in fertility it would seem necessary for a large number of women to move out of trading and farming into nontraditional avenues of employment that would be less easily reconciled with mothering, and the prospects for such a transition seem dim.

A decrease in fertility seems linked to changed attitudes toward children. This seems to be occurring in urban areas. It has been documented that fertility rates are 10 percent lower in Ghana's urban centers than in the rural areas (Caldwell, 1967b: 99). This is caused at least partially by differences in life-style and expectations with regard to children. In an urban environment children become something of an economic liability rather than an economic asset. The cost of raising children in accordance with new standards and of providing an education discourages very large families. Infant mortality also is usually lower in urban areas, and urban parents may be realizing, to a greater extent than their rural counterparts, that most of their children are now surviving past infancy. As more parents become cognizant of these trends and aware of the contraceptive devices that can enable them to determine the size of their families—all of which are very novel concepts for them to absorb—Ghanaians may alter their views regarding the number of children they want to have.

CONCLUSION

The considerable independence, economic power, and particularly among the southern groups, significant social and political roles, that women had in the precolonial social order have frequently been undermined by the course of Ghana's modernization. Ghanaian society seems to be moving away from the traditional separation of male and female spheres of work and social relations into a new and more sexually integrated situation in which women are less separate and less equal. Ghana's development has enlarged the range of options available to some women, but at the expense of eroding women's autonomy and increasing their subordination to men. Although many women now enjoy some of the fruits of Ghana's development, including the opportunity to receive a primary school education, the social position and status of women relative to men has declined.

During the colonial period, the introduction of Western education and the spread of the cash economy disproportionately benefited male members of the society. This trend, common to many colonized territories in which women had had economic and social roles at variance with the division of labor then inhering in European societies, affected women in Ghana to a lesser extent than it did women in other places in Africa. The indigenous development of the cocoa industry, with women's participation in it, the large-scale movement of women into trading, and the availability of Western education to at least a small number of women blunted the detrimental impact of colonialism. Women continue to be economically active and resist efforts to make them solely mothers and housewives. Although women still have less access than men to higher education and prestigious employment opportunities, they are not being excluded through cultural or legal norms.

The danger for women in Ghana is that the present sex role division, which largely reflects women's limited access to education during the colonial period and the continuing imbalance in the opportunities for higher education, will become crystallized and accepted as the natural order of things. Ghana's stagnant economy, combined with its high rate of population growth, have reduced the number of jobs available for members of either sex. Moreover the large number of vacancies in the civil service that arose in the early postindependence years have disappeared, and the present incumbents are relatively young. Although women do not face discrimination now, as the scarcity of new employment sources grows and male unemployment rises, employers may give preference to male applicants, particularly in the high status openings.

The trend in social relationships seems to be for women to assume a less equal role. The relatively equitable traditional pattern in which each marital partner assumed certain responsibilities and received in exchange specific rights appears to be giving way to a new imbalance. Among the urban elite the husband provides a disproportionate share of the family income and usually commands a higher status than the wife by virtue of his education and employment. This situation, combined with exposure to European norms of family life, has eroded the wife's autonomy and independence. Elite women are caught in a web of conflicting obligations and ideals that gives them neither the advantages of the traditional marital relationship nor the security usually conferred on the wife in the European family. The condition of the less-educated woman is problematical in another way. In the rural environment the relative contributions of the husband and wife to the welfare of the family remain more equal, but men are less inclined to fulfill their traditional responsibilities and relationships frequently are unstable. This confluence of changes, therefore, renders the rural woman even less secure than her urban counterpart.

It is difficult to predict future trends with regard to the future roles and status of women. If the present trends of high fertility and slow economic growth are continued, a curtailment in educational and economic opportunities will probably follow. Because women are presently excluded from the top levels of management in all sectors of the society, it will be difficult for them to avoid a disproportionate share of the burden of limitation.

BIBLIOGRAPHY

Addo, Nelson. 1971a. "Some Demographic Aspects of Urbanization in Ghana, 1931–1960." *The Ghana Social Science Review* I (May): 50–82.

———. 1971b. "Some Aspects of the Employment Situation on Cocoa Farms in Brong Ahafo in the Pre and Post-Aliens Compliance Era." Unpublished paper presented at African Population Conference. Accra, December.

———. n.d. "Some Structural Aspects of Internal Migration in Southeastern Ghana: Their Implications for National Development Policies." Unpublished paper. Legon: Institute of Statistical, Social, and Economic Research.

Assessment of Manpower Situation—1971. 1971. Accra: Manpower Division, Development Planning Secretariat.

Bentil, Michael. 1974. Personal interview, May 9.

Boserup, Ester. 1970. *Woman's Role in Economic Development.* London: George Allen and Unwin Ltd.

Bourret, F. M. 1970. *Ghana: The Road to Independence, 1919–1957.* London: Oxford University Press.

Bretton, Henry L. 1966. *The Rise and Fall of Kwame Nkrumah: A Study of Personal Rule in Africa.* New York: Frederick A. Praeger.

Brokensha, David W. 1966. *Social Change at Larteh, Ghana.* Oxford: Clarendon Press.

Busia, K. A. 1951. *The Position of the Chief in the Modern Political System of Ashanti: A Study of the Influence of Contemporary Social Changes on Ashanti Political Institutions.* London: Oxford University Press.

Caldwell, John C. 1967a. "Population: General Characteristics." In *A Study of Contemporary Ghana,* Vol. 2. *Some Aspects of Social Structure.* Edited by Walter Birmingham, I. Neustadt, and E. N. Omaboe. Evanston, Illinois: Northwestern University Press, pp. 17–77.

———. 1967b. "Population Change. In *A Study of Contemporary Ghana,* Vol. 2.: Pp. 78–110.

———. 1968a. "The Control of Family Size in Tropical Africa." *Demography* **5** (2): 598–619.

———. 1968b. *Population Growth and Family Change in Africa: The New Urban Elite in Ghana.* Canberra: Australia National University Press.

———. 1971. "Some Factors Affecting Fertility in Ghana." In *Proceedings of the International Population Conference, London 1969,* Vol. I. Liege: International Union for the Scientific Study of Population, pp. 751–759.

———. 1974. "The Study of Fertility Change in Tropical Africa." Paper presented at the Meetings of the Population Association of America. New York, April 18–20.

Card, Emily Watts. 1972. "The Politics of Underdevelopment: From Voluntary Associations to Party Auxiliaries in Ghana." Unpublished Ph.D. dissertation. Columbia University.

Chinery-Hesse, Mary. 1971. "Background Paper on Ghana." Prepared for United Nations Seminar on the Participation of Women in Economic Life. Libreville, Gabon.

Danquah, Moses. n.d. *The Birth of the Second Republic.* Accra: Editorial and Publishing Services.

Economic Commission for Africa. 1974. "The Changing and Contemporary Role of Women in African Development." Mimeo.

Educational Report, 1963–1967. 1968. Accra: Ghana Publishing Corporation for the Ministry of Education.

Educational Statistics 1968–1969. 1971. Accra: Ministry of Education.

Field, M. J. 1937. *Religion and Medicine of the Ga People.* London: Crown Agents.

———. 1940. *Social Organization of the Ga People.* London: Crown Agents.

———. 1960. *Search for Security: An Ethno-Psychiatric Study of Rural Ghana.* Evanston, Illinois: Northwestern University.

Folson, B. D. G. n.d. "The Traditional Political System." Mimeo, Legon: University of Ghana.

Fortes, Meyer. 1945. *The Dynamics of Clanship among the Talensi.* London: Oxford University Press.

———. 1949. *The Web of Kinship among the Talensi.* London: Oxford University Press.

———. 1950. "Kinship and Marriage Among the Ashanti." In *African Systems of Kinship and*

Marriage. Edited by Radcliffe-Brown and Daryll Forde. London: Oxford University Press, pp. 252–283.

Foster, Philip. 1965. *Education and Social Change in Ghana.* London: Routledge and Kegan Paul.

Fuchs-Carsch, Marian. 1975. "The Small-Scale Farmer in Ghana." In *Women and National Development.* Edited by Jeanne North. Accra: U.S.A.I.D. Mimeo.

Gaisie, S. K., S. B. Jones, J. C. Caldwell, and Gordon W. Perkin. 1970. "Ghana." Country Profile. New York. Issued by the Population Council and the International Institute for the Study of Human Reproduction, Columbia University.

"Ghana National Family Planning Programme Progress Report." 1972. Accra: National Family Planning Programme..

Gil, B., A. F. Aryee, and D. K. Ghansah. 1964. *Population Census of Ghana, Special Report 'E', Tribes in Ghana.* Accra: Census Office.

———, K. T. de Graft-Johnson, and E. A. Colecraft. 1971. *1960 Population Census of Ghana,* Vol. VI. *The Post Enumeration Survey.* Accra: Census Office.

Graft-Johnson, K. T. de. 1974. "Population Growth and Rural–Urban Migration, with Special Reference to Ghana." *International Labour Review* **109** (May–June): 471–485.

Graham, C. K. 1971. *The History of Education in Ghana: From the Earliest Times to the Declaration of Independence.* London: Frank Cass and Company, Ltd.

Greenstreet, Miranda. 1972. "Social Change and Ghanaian Women." *Canadian Journal of African Studies* **VI** (2): 351–355.

Griffiths, John. 1974. "On Teaching Law in Ghana and Related Matters," *Law Center Bulletin* **21** (1): 4–28.

Harvey, William Burnett. 1966. *Law and Social Change in Ghana.* Princeton: Princeton University Press.

High Level and Skilled Manpower Survey—1968. 1971. Accra: Manpower Division, Development Planning Secretariat.

Hill, Polly. 1963. *Migrant Cocoa Farmers of Southern Ghana.* Cambridge: Cambridge University Press.

Hurd, G. E. 1967. "Education." In *A Study of Contemporary Ghana,* Vol. 2. *Some Aspects of Social Structure.* Edited by Walter Birmingham, I. Neustadt, and E. D. Omaboe. Evanston, Illinois: Northwestern University Press, pp. 217–239.

Kimble, David. 1963. *A Political History of Ghana: The Rise of Gold Coast Nationalism 1850–1928.* London: Oxford University Press.

Lebeuf, Annie. 1971. "The Role of Women in the Political Organization of African Societies." In *Women of Tropical Africa.* Edited by Denise Paulme and translated by H. M. Wright. Berkeley and Los Angeles: University of California Press, 93–119.

LeVine, Robert A. 1970. "Sex Roles and Economic Change." In *Black Africa: Its Peoples and Their Cultures Today.* Edited by John Middleton. New York: The Macmillan Company, pp. 174–187.

Little, Kenneth. 1972. "Voluntary Associations and Social Mobility Among West African Women." *Canadian Journal of African Studies* **VI** (2): 275–288.

Lloyd, P. C. 1967. *Africa in Social Change: Changing Traditional Societies in the Modern World.* Baltimore: Penguin Books.

McCall, D. 1961. "Tradition and the Role of a Wife in a Modern African Town." In *Social Change in Modern Africa.* Edited by Aidan Southall. London: Oxford University Press, pp. 286–299.

McWilliam, H. O. A. 1962. *The Development of Education in Ghana: An Outline.* 2nd ed. London: Longmans and Green and Co., Ltd.

Manoukian, Madeline. 1950. *Akan and Ga-Adangme Peoples.* London: International African Institute.

———. 1951. *Tribes of the Northern Territories of the Gold Coast.* London: International African Institute.

———. 1952. *The Ewe-Speaking People of Togoland and the Gold Coast.* London: International African Institute.

North, Jeanne, Editor. 1975. *Women in National Development in Ghana.* Accra: U.S.A.I.D. Mimeo.

Nortman, Dorothy. 1973. *Population and Family Planning Programs: A Factbook.* New York: Population Council.

Nukunya, G. K. 1969. *Kinship and Marriage Among the Anglo Ewe.* London: The Athlone Press.

One-Year Development Plan, July 1970 to June 1971. 1970. Accra-Tema: Ghana Publishing Corporation.

Oppong, Christine. 1974. *Marriage Among a Matrilineal Elite: A Family Study of Ghanaian Civil Servants.* Cambridge: Cambridge University Press.

———, Christine Okali, and Beverly Houghton. 1975. "Woman Power: Retrograde Steps in Ghana. Paper presented at the African Studies Association, San Francisco.

Paulme, Denise. 1971. "Introduction." In *Women of Tropical Africa.* Edited by Denise Paulme and translated by H. M. Wright. Berkeley and Los Angeles: University of California Press, pp. 1–16.

Peil, Margaret. 1972. *The Ghanaian Factory Worker: Industrial Man in Africa.* Cambridge: Cambridge University Press.

Pool, D. I. 1969. "Conjugal Patterns in Ghana." *The Canadian Review of Sociology and Anthropology* **5** (4): 241–253.

———. 1970. "Social Change and Interest in Family Planning in Ghana: An Exploratory Analysis." *Journal of African Studies* **4** (2): 207–227.

Pool, Janet E. 1972. "A Cross-Comparative Study of Aspects of Conjugal Behavior Among Women of Three West African Countries." *Canadian Journal of African Studies* **VI** (2): 233–259.

1960 Population Census of Ghana, Vol. III. Demographic Characteristics. 1964. Accra: Census Office.

1960 Population Census of Ghana, Vol. IV. *Economic Characteristics.* 1964. Accra: Census Office.

1970 Population Census of Ghana, Vol. II. *Statistics of Localities and Enumeration Areas.* 1972. Accra: Census Office.

"Population Planning for National Progress and Prosperity: Ghana Population Policy." 1969. Accra-Tema: Ghana Publishing Corp.

Rattray, R. S. 1929. *Ashanti Law and Constitution.* London: Oxford University Press.

Sai, Florence. 1971. "Market Women in the Economy of Ghana." M.A. Thesis, Cornell University.

Sanday, Peggy R. 1974. "Female Status in the Public Domain." In *Woman, Culture, and Society.* Edited by Michele Zimbalist Rosaldo and Louise Lamphere. Stanford: Stanford University Press, pp. 189–206.

Statistical Yearbook for 1964. 1964. Accra: Central Bureau of Statistics.

Statistical Yearbook for 1965–1966. 1966. Accra: Central Bureau of Statistics.

Tait, David. 1961. *The Konkomba of Northern Ghana*. London: Oxford University Press.

Tetteh, P. A. 1967. "Marriage, Family, and Household." In *A Study of Contemporary Ghana*, Vol. II. *Some Aspects of Social Structure*. Edited by Walter Birmingham, I. Neustadt, E. N. Omaboe. Evanston, Illinois: Northwestern University Press, pp. 201–216.

Vellenga, Dorothy Dee. 1971. "Attempts to Change the Marriage Laws in Ghana and the Ivory Coast." In *Ghana and the Ivory Coast*. Edited by Philip Foster and Aristide Zolberg. Chicago: The University of Chicago Press, pp. 125–150.

"White Paper on Marriage, Divorce, and Inheritance." 1961. Accra: Government Printing Office.

Chapter Six

JAPAN: HISTORICAL AND CONTEMPORARY PERSPECTIVES

....

Susan J. Pharr

HISTORICAL CHANGE IN THE STATUS OF WOMEN IN JAPAN

Early History to the Feudal Period (Earliest Times to 1185). Much of Japanese history until the fifth century is not in sharp focus, and only in the sixth and seventh centuries does recorded history truly begin. For that reason it is difficult to offer a precise account of early developments bearing on the status of women. This is unfortunate because evidence that does exist suggests that Japanese women occupied a high position in prehistorical and early historical society, and it would be extremely valuable in the study of women's status and roles to know more about the position of women in earliest times, and how and why it changed. We do know from a reliable early Chinese document written before 297 A.D. that Japan at that time was divided into some one hundred "countries" or tribes, some ruled by kings and others by queens. Leading authorities speculate that Japan then may have been passing through a transitional stage from matriarchy to patriarchy (Reischauer and Fairbank, 1958: 463). The same Chinese document describes a powerful, unmarried queen named Himiko who ruled a number of the early tribes. That she existed is fairly well substantiated by Japanese records, archaeological evidence, and other available data on early society.

Undoubtedly the most important evidence of women's high status in earliest times is derived from analysis of Japan's rich mythology, which became the basis for Shinto, the native religion of Japan still practiced today. In early mythology a central figure of the pantheon was Amaterasu Ōmikami, the Sun Goddess from whom the present imperial line traditionally claims its descent and thus its right to rule. Women figure prominently in mythology, and early recorded accounts of their comings and goings suggest that societies that could have evolved these myths must have accorded women high status. For example, when marriage is first described in mythology, it is the woman, not the man, who makes the proposal of marriage (Mason, 1939: 22). That mythology reflected contemporary customs is suggested by anthropological evidence of matrilocalism in marriage practices well into the historical period. Even today in certain remote parts of Japan signs of matrilocalism remain in local customs (Omachi in Dorson, 1963).

Throughout the early centuries of Japanese history there is much evidence that women's status remained high relative to subsequent periods. Between 572 and 770 half the rulers of Japan were women (Reischauer and Fairbank, 1958: 484). Well into the feudal period, which dates from the twelfth century, women had property rights, rights of inheritance, and much higher status in the family system than was accorded them in later centuries. Over the entire prefeudal period, however, women's standing in society faced pressures that were gradually to undermine and alter it.

Some of the new forces affecting the status of women were internal in origin; others resulted from influences on Japan from abroad. The internal pressures were those generated by political changes from the middle of the third century, which saw the development of numerous ruling families, organized into lineage groups called *uji* and headed by patriarchal chiefs. But external influences speeding the demise of matriarchy were perhaps of even greater significance. These originated from contact with China beginning in the sixth century. China, in one of its great periods of empire under the T'ang Dynasty from the seventh to the tenth centuries, was the most advanced culture in the area and one from which the Japanese were eager to learn. Cultural missions dispatched to China in the seventh and eighth centuries initiated contact that eventually led to the adoption of a new legal code for Japan based on the Chinese model, a code that, at least in the principles it set out, wholly reshaped the legal and governmental structure of Japan.

There is little doubt what these new influences from China meant for the status of Japanese women. China already had a highly developed patriarchal society, where concubinage and foot-binding were to appear by the late T'ang period. Under the new code whatever remained of the matriarchal system of clan organization was replaced by a patriarchal system embodying the Confucian precept of the inferiority of women, and numerous discriminatory measures affecting property, marriage, and divorce were introduced into the laws (Ackroyd, 1959: 32). The code from China, at least as it affected women, was much delayed in its impact, probably because customs favoring women were then too strong in Japan. Some of the worst abuses of the Chinese system, such as foot-binding, were never adopted in Japan, and even various civil legal measures introduced from China were in practice by-passed in favor of local ordinances that accorded women more favorable treatment under the law. Nevertheless the reforms dealing with women's rights set clear precedents that were to be followed rather than reversed for more than a thousand years.

It was not only legal influences from China that affected women's status. Even more significant perhaps in their long-term impact were Chinese religious and ethical systems entering Japan during the same period of cultural borrowing. As already suggested, in the mythology closely linked to Japan's native religion of Shinto, women undoubtedly were accorded a position of great importance. Shinto itself, though, is a primitive religion without a moral or ethical code, and thus Shinto has little to say one way or another about women's moral or social status. Buddhism and other moral and ethical doctrines arriving from China in the seventh and eighth centuries, however, made no such omission. Various schools of thought in Buddhism came to the forefront over the long prefeudal period, but it is fairly safe to say that none accorded women a high status in the moral order, and most offered an ethical and religious rationale for any loss of status women were suffering in society. Even in the Heian Period, when elite women were creating literary masterpieces, the Buddhist sutras "[left] no doubt about [women's] inferior spiritual status" (Morris, 1964: 121). Buddhism did not replace Shinto in Japan; the two religious systems coexisted. But the influence of Buddhist and Confucian precepts and values from China on Japanese religious thought appears to have been a major, long-term force in undermining the position of women in Japanese society.

Before we consider changes that occurred after the twelfth century, one particular period in the prefeudal era must be singled out. This is the Heian Period, at its high point from the middle of the tenth to the middle of the eleventh century, which represented a golden cultural era that Morris has called "the world of the shining prince" (Morris, 1964). In the court life centered in the old capital at Kyoto, women enjoyed high standing and dominated the literary life of the country. Why this was so had much to do with the political system of the times. With various key families vying for power, the main route to influence was through "marriage politics," that is, extending the family influence by marrying daughters well. One particular family—the Fujiwara—managed to become the leading family of much of the Heian Period through skilled manipulation of this method. Through marrying their women into the imperial line, the Fujiwara were able to control the emperor and thereby secure and extend their own position. This system gave noble women considerable importance in court life, an importance reinforced by the kind of inheritance and property rights then in effect, which provided women with an independence they lacked in later ages. Heian noblewomen put these legal rights to good use in a period in which the political system had strengthened their position. Many had extensive landholdings in the provinces and had personal administrative staffs to manage their financial affairs. It is remarkable indeed that most of the best-known writers of the Heian Period were women; that women not too far before the beginning of the feudal period enjoyed rights of property and inheritance which they were able to maneuver to increase their literary, social, and economic role; and that women were important in the operation of the political system at a time when Japanese civilization was at one of its highest points.

It would be a mistake, however, to leave a discussion of the long period from prehistorical times until the twelfth century without offering some remarks to balance this rather favorable portrayal of women's early status in Japanese society. It is hard not to exaggerate women's position in early centuries simply because their status later on, after the feudal era was underway, was so low. It should also be pointed out that after 770, before which time numerous women came to the throne, women effectively ceased to rule. However central they may have been in the "marriage politics" of the Heian Period, they had little real power in their own right. Even then, in an era of many women notables, women can be seen as pawns in a game played by the men who held the real power. In addition, although what evidence we have points to considerable social, religious, and political authority on the part of women in earliest times when Japan was matriarchal, all through recorded history Japan was a patriarchal and patrilineal society. Although women kept property and inheritance rights throughout the prefeudal period, family authority and responsibility resided in the male family head, and this was increasingly true as the institution of primogeniture, which began to spread in the Heian Period, became general (Fréderic, 1972: 54).

Even in citing the literary achievements of Heian noblewomen as a sign of women's high status in that day, further remarks must be added to balance the picture. Ironically these great achievements of women arose as the unlikely by-product of discriminatory educational attitudes in the Heian Period. Women then were barred from the study of Chinese, which was considered to be the "intellectual" language of the day, and were limited to use of native Japanese syllabaries for their writing. While Heian noblemen wrote ethical and philosophical essays in Chinese, Heian noblewomen wrote in the Japanese language, elevating it to new heights of expression and creating a new literary genre, the novel. Their literary contribution was thus born in a highly discriminatory situation.

One final factor should be considered as we evaluate the status of women in the prefeudal period. Even though women retained substantial rights in such matters as inheritance, property rights, and divorce, many laws embodied inequalities and the double standard. For example, in the Heian Period, women, unlike men, could not legally take additional husbands, and in extreme cases the law sanctioned a husband killing a wife found *in flagrante delicto*. Further inequalities in women's status are reflected in punishments for such crimes as wife-beating—punishment for that offense was two grades lower than that imposed for an assault on anyone else (Morris, 1964: 207).

It is difficult, then, to arrive at a balanced perspective on the position of women in the prefeudal period. By many indices, and particularly if compared to later periods, women occupied a favorable position in the legal, economic, political, and social worlds of prefeudal Japan. But these positive factors must be weighed along with evidence of numerous inequalities in society.

Feudal Period (1185–1867). Before recounting how women's status changed over the feudal period, we must describe how the political system of Japan had been evolving. By the end of the ninth century local authority had reasserted itself at the expense of central governmental institutions which had been adopted as a result of Chinese influence. During the Heian Period a few successive families like the Fujiwara managed to gain hegemony over what remained of the central government and dominate the court life of the capital at Kyoto. During this period, however, provincial nobles grew in strength and number, took up arms, and eventually, after much infighting, took control of the capital and, finally, the whole country. By the end of the twelfth century, one particular clan, headed by the historic figure Yoritomo, was able to set up a military dictatorship, or *bakufu*, establish his retainers over estates in the countryside, and try to rule. These changes are considered to have ushered in the feudal era, which is usually dated from 1185, and also to have brought on the era of the *samurai*, or warrior class. For the next four centuries the *bakufu* attempted to keep order, but the effort to maintain central authority gradually failed, and during much of that period the country was torn with fighting and bloodshed. Then finally, at the beginning of the seventeenth century, a strong government under the Tokugawa family took power and established a system of centralized feudalism capable of keeping the peace. This system, in which the political power was held by the *samurai* elite under the authority of the *shōgun*, was in force for the next three-and-a-half centuries until it at last crumbled on the eve of the modernization period in the mid-nineteenth century.

Over the long feudal period, from the time Yoritomo came to power toward the end of the twelfth century until the system fell apart in the 1860s, it is widely agreed that the status of women suffered major declines. To be sure these changes occurred gradually. In the Kamakura period (1185–1333) women continued to retain something of the favored legal status they held during the prefeudal age. But as one authority notes, by the Sengoku period in the fifteen and sixteenth centuries when feudalism is considered to have reached its peak, the subjugation of women had also "reached its peak in practice" (Ackroyd, 1959: 67). Finally, over the long Tokugawa period of centralized feudalism (1600–1867), the discriminatory practices of the preceding age were provided with a sound moral and philosophical basis (Ackroyd, 1959: 67). Why did all these changes come about? Political, economic, and religious factors are considered in turn.

Political factors seem particularly crucial. Four centuries of warfare from the twelfth to the early seventeenth centuries elevated to power the warrior class. In contrast to the peaceful "marriage politics" of earlier centuries which had made daughters important, the military politics of the feudal period made it essential to have sons who could fight. As the feudal period progressed, women of the warrior class often became little more than chattel in the political machinations of the day. In some cases daughters were relinquished to seal feudal military compacts or were given to the heads of enemy clans as hostages (Takemure, 1966; Ackroyd, 1959).

The nature of the political system in the feudal period also had a devastating impact on the status of women within the family. Under feudalism the primary bond valued in society was between lord and vassal. A man's feudal obligations took precedence over any other responsibilities and loyalties in his life, such as those to his wife and offspring. The wife came to occupy the lowest rung on the entire social ladder; she was subordinated within the feudal hierarchy and within the family hierarchy as well. The structure of the family system itself did not change; even back in the Heian Period, authority had resided in the male family head. However in the feudal period, particularly within warrior families from the fourteenth century on, this authority appears to have been made absolute, and wives were gradually excluded from even informal participation in decision-making (Fréderic, 1972: 53–54).

The economic ramifications of political factors put women's status in even further jeopardy, particularly weakening the legal basis for that status connected with property and inheritance rights. Civil unrest, rivalry for land and wealth carried on by military means, and the ever-increasing importance of the military class—all these political factors made it important that land, the basis of wealth and power in an agricultural society, be in the hands of those who could defend it. Since daughters could not fight to defend inherited property, they gradually lost their rights to inheritance altogether. Another reason for this loss was that families feared that their daughters, if they inherited the family lands, would lose control of them after marriage, possibly to a rival family (Fréderic, 1972; Morosawa, Vol. I, 1970: 155–200).

Finally we may consider the impact of religious factors on women's loss of status in the feudal period. Religious influences became particularly important during the long Tokugawa period, which dates from the early seventeenth century, when society at last turned away from warfare and gave its attention to normal life, including the scholarly pursuits that had been so long neglected. When the country renewed its interest in religious doctrine, the status of women was dealt a further blow. This was mainly caused by the growth of the influence of Confucianism, in particular, the Neo-Confucian philosophy of Chu-Hsi, which was supported by the teachings of Buddhist orders such as the Tendai and Shigon sects. These sects held that women had no hope of attaining any of the five states of spiritual existence to which men could aspire. Writings of the period instructed a woman to regard herself as an "agent of the devils sent to destroy the teaching of Buddha" (quoted in Ackroyd, 1959: 55).

The collective impact of social, economic, political, and religious influences over the feudal period, then, was to confirm woman's low estate from every side. Her legal position during the feudal period put her wholly at the mercy of her husband, who had full legal responsibility for her actions. Primogeniture became the rule, so women lost all rights to inherit property in favor of the sons they bore. During the Tokugawa period it was stressed that wives functioned primarily as vessels to bear the family heir (*hara no karimono*). A wife's adultery, by the Tokugawa period, was widely punishable by death, and it was considered to be fully within the husband's rights to kill both his wife and her lover in such cases. A woman could be divorced for any one of seven reasons: for failing to produce an heir, gossiping, stealing from her husband, jealousy, loose conduct, or disease. These laws had all been on the books since the eighth century, when they had been brought from China, but it was really not until the Tokugawa era that they were applied. All the laws, of course, applied only to women. Adultery was socially approved for men, and women of the *samurai* class had no acceptable grounds for divorcing husbands (Ackroyd, 1959: 58–62).

The inequalities that developed in the social system during the feudal period had far more impact on women in the upper classes then those in the peasantry (Fréderic, 1972). Partly this was because, as described earlier, much of the legal and religious influence that resulted ultimately in a loss of status for women came from China, and those in the capital, who were attentive to influences from abroad, were far more affected than were peasants in the countryside. To cite one example, Buddhist and other Chinese moral writings were adapted with far greater interest and fervor by the tiny elite of the country who could read; meanwhile, in the countryside, the peasantry ordered their lives with the rituals of their native Shinto religion, in whose rich mythology women played such an important role. Political change, too, was felt far more slowly in the countryside. Thus the rise of a martial class, and the value changes that resulted from it, had little initial impact on the women—or men—in the fields.

Beginning in the Tokugawa era, however, a new trend can be noted. With society firmly under the control of the *samurai* class, and Japan, by government policy almost totally closed to foreign influences, the laws and conventions of the military elite began to seep down to all ranks of society far more than had ever been the case. For women the most important new factor was the increasing adoption of the family system of the military class as a model for the rest of society. During the Tokugawa period society came to be stratified into four rigid classes; in descending order of importance they were the *samurai*, who constituted 5 to 6 percent of the population, and far below them the farmers, artisans, and merchants.

The experience of women in the merchant class is particularly noteworthy. Despite their low rank in the official ideology, merchants became increasingly prosperous in the Tokugawa period, but for women of that class prosperity appears to have been a mixed blessing. On the one hand numerous benefits arose from their role in the functioning of an increasingly well-to-do class. Compared with *samurai* women, who generally were tied to a feudal estate, women of the merchant class enjoyed far greater mobility and contact with society at large. They benefited from the pleasures of town life and, because they often had a hand in running the family business, frequently had more leverage in family and business matters as well as freer use of family money. Also, because merchants had easily divisible capital rather than land as the basis of their wealth, they could provide daughters with dowries, thus strengthening their daughters' position in the bridegroom's family (Ackroyd, 1959: 63; Murakami, Vol. I, 1970: 254–312).

On the other hand, however, prosperity appears to have had certain negative effects on the status of merchant women. As the wealth, hence the power, of the merchant class increased, well-to-do merchants held an advantageous position in their dealings with the *samurai* class, which for all their power and prestige in society were increasingly suffering from impoverishment because of worsening agricultural conditions in the Tokugawa era. As the *samurai* turned to merchants for loans, the two classes were brought more closely together. Gradually the wealthier merchants could even entertain hopes of buying their way into the lowest ranks of the *samurai,* and the merchant class as a whole took to imitating the conduct of the class that was still considered the elite class of society. For merchant women this gradual change in class distance had unfortunate ramifications, because it was the *samurai* woman above all others who had been affected by the political changes of the feudal period and who was held most closely in check by her class's stringent codes of moral conduct. Wives and daughters of merchants came to read the same books of ethics as women of the *samurai* class. Almost certainly one result of this increased contact was the spread of *samurai* values regarding women to the merchant class, thus in some ways impairing the sense of independence of merchant women.

Elite culture undoubtedly permeated less deeply into the lives of women of the peasantry, but even they found their lives increasingly touched by the moral values of the *samurai* elite once the Tokugawa period was under way. *Samurai,* in their role as officials, held heads of households responsible for all family members, and the codes increasingly reflected the moral values of the military clan. The *samurai* set out strict regulations governing marriages among peasants; these rules were not always enforced, but the degree of control from above in the lives of peasants was greater than ever before. That peasant women suffered from inferior social status within their own stratum of society is suggested in the practice, which arose during the Tokugawa period when agricultural conditions were deteriorating, of poor farmers selling daughters as prostitutes.

Over the feudal period, then, the status of women deteriorated to some extent in every class and on every front—social, political, economic, and religious. On the eve of modernization women had been stripped of virtually all the perogatives they had enjoyed in the prefeudal period, when Japan was evolving with the imprint of its matriarchal origins.

Early Modernization (1868–1945). In the late 1850s and early 1860s an increasingly weak Tokugawa government could no longer hold together a crumbling feudal structure, and a group of ambitious *samurai*, declaring that Japan should open itself to the West and modernize, took power. The old feudal caste system was abolished, and the *samurai* who led the country through the period of rapid modernization that followed denounced many of the privileges of their own former caste. After four centuries of isolation the Japanese elite began the eager study of what had been going on in Western societies as they sought the know-how to modernize and industrialize the country. An industrial structure, a communications and transportation network, a modern military establishment, a rationalized bureaucracy with competitive entrance exams—all of this arose over a brief span of less than fifty years. Political parties appeared, and by 1889 Japan had a constitution. A modern society was emerging.

During much of the feudal period education had been available mainly to men of the *samurai* class. As the Tokugawa period had progressed, this situation had changed somewhat, and by the later part of that period education had become somewhat more accessible to the lower classes and, to a limited extent, to women. One scholar estimates that at the onset of the modern period in 1868, about 40 percent of all Japanese boys and some 10 percent of Japanese girls were getting some type of formal education outside the home (Dore, 1965: 254). During the Tokugawa era most *samurai* women had received some instruction at home in the basic skills of reading, writing, and simple arithmetic. Their main education, however, was thought to be the training they would receive from their mother-in-law once they married and became part of their husband's family. On the whole, educational opportunities for women had been extremely limited in the feudal period.

The new Meiji school system corrected this deficiency by providing for public education for women. However their curriculum in a separate girls' track reflected attitudes from the previous age. The elite academic track in the new educational system established in 1886 was reserved for males. After the third year of elementary school girls moved into their separate girls' track. After six years of elementary schooling girls who wanted to go further could attend separate four- or five-year secondary schools. However one writer estimates that only 8 percent of the girls graduating from elementary school went on to attend the secondary schools (Hall in Hall and Beardsley, 1965: 404). The curriculum for girls reflected the attitudes of the previous period. The academic standards were lower than those of the academic track and women's homemaking skills were stressed (Anderson, 1959: 38; Fukaya, 1966).

There were no universities for women. A limited number of postsecondary training programs existed in teaching, nursing, dentistry, and so on, but otherwise women seeking advanced education either went to one of the 60 private girls' colleges established prior to World War II or in a few cases sought special permission to attend the national universities established for men, where they were allowed to audit courses but not to take examinations (Hall in Hall and Beardsley, 1965: 404). Although modernization efforts in the Meiji period made new educational opportunities available to women, the degree and type of education available to them were hardly on a par with those available to men.

Changes in the industrial sector similarly had both positive and negative impacts on women's status. On the one hand, with industrialization women for the first time participated in economic life outside the family unit. Before the Meiji period the women involved in productive life outside the home were mainly entertainers, servants, music teachers, hairdressers, midwives, and the like; but during the Meiji era increasing numbers of women became a part of the new economic activity in a modernizing country. After 1880, great numbers of women were employed in textile mills. Soon women held between 70 to 80 percent of all textile jobs and were also working in numerous other kinds of factories, mines, and fisheries as well. Women were also swept into the new communications industries that came with modernization. Beginning in 1899 women began to be hired as telephone operators and soon were employed in other communications work. As merchandisers and retailers appeared on the scene, some hired women for sales jobs. The new plans for public education called for a vast number of teachers, and by 1872 there were 2500 women employed in primary schools, representing 3 percent of the total number of primary teachers (Yanagida, 1957: 250).

Undoubtedly it was a step forward for women to find their way into the productive life of the country during the early stages of modernization. But it should be noted that their entry into almost every sphere was met with discriminatory practices, and in many cases exploitation and oppression of the worst kind. When women were hired as telephone operators, they were crowded together at the switchboard and were kept from contact with the public (Yanagida, 1957: 250). Oppressive working conditions existed in mines, fisheries, and other industries where they took jobs. The worst forms of exploitation appeared in the textile mills where women made up a high portion of the total work force. Many were sent to work by their fathers, generally lower-class, impoverished farmers, who could borrow in advance against their salaries. Since women could be hired at lower salaries than male workers, factories competed for the services of women and sometimes practically kidnapped them for jobs in the spinning mills (Taira, 1970). Statistics for cotton-spinning mills in 1901 show that more than half the female workers were under 20 (Shibusawa, 1958: 315–317). Working and living conditions in most factories were deplorable. Dormitories housing young women workers were frequently walled in to keep the occupants from running away. Industrialization, if it meant the opening of new life possibilities for women in the economic world, also made women victims of some of the most brutal forms of exploitation of workers in Japanese history (Taira, 1970; Shibusawa, 1958; Hosoi, 1954).

Within the family unit it is more difficult to assess how women fared in the new era. It is certainly true that the influx of Western ideas during the Meiji period made the Japanese highly conscious of how they were viewed by the outside world. As a result an attempt was made in numerous superficial ways to "modernize" women. For example, during the feudal period married women had generally blackened their teeth with a special dye preparation and plucked or shaved their eyebrows, measures regarded in the feudal period as enhancing to a woman's beauty. In the new era, however, there were fears that these practices would be regarded as "quaint" or "uncivilized" by foreigners, so women were encouraged by the government to change their customs (Shibusawa, 1958: 35).

But women's status in the family did not undergo major changes in the wake of modernization. The typical pattern of family life, particularly in cases where her new husband was the eldest son and thus the family heir, was one in which the bride went to live with her husband's family and was expected to adapt to the ways of his house. In the type of three-generation household considered the ideal before the war, the new bride had the lowest status of all family members and was expected to be obedient to the authority of her mother-in-law. The moral code that became widespread during the Meiji period enjoined the wife to be the first up in the morning, the last to go to bed, to take her bath only after her husband and all his family members had bathed, and to devote herself in every way to her husband and his family. As in the feudal period among the *samurai* class, adultery was widely tolerated for the male but strictly forbidden for the wife. A man could divorce his wife simply by sending her back to her parents with a brief explanatory note, while women in all but the most exteme cases were not considered to have the right of divorce. Marriages were generally arranged either by the families themselves or through the offices of a go-between, and young people's wishes were considered to be of minor importance in the final decisions.

Variations occurred in this pattern according to class, of course. During the Meiji era just as in the feudal period, moral codes were most stringently enforced among the upper classes. There is considerable evidence that in rural areas young people were allowed far more latitude, especially in such matters as sexual conduct before marriage. "Trial marriages" were common in the countryside, where premarital sex was socially accepted as long as it was handled discreetly; among upper-class families, however, the same conduct was wholly condemned for daughters who in many cases had little contact at all with men outside the family (Embree, 1939). But in general the trend of change in the family system was toward increased standardization throughout society of moral and social values relating to the family and to the conduct of female family members.

It was probably in the area of political rights that the least accommodation was made for a possible role for women in shaping the major changes going on in society. Women were largely untouched by changes going on at the political front. When universal suffrage was declared in 1925, it applied only to males over 25. In the period before World War II women were thus wholly excluded from the political process. An embryonic women's suffrage movement appeared intermittently after the turn of the century, but its gains seem modest indeed. Describing changes in Japan in the early 1920s, one prewar woman activist writes in English for foreign readers,

> After a few years, as a result of their earnest work, notwithstanding prejudice all around, a law was passed and the regulation preventing women from listening to political lectures was taken away [Kawai and Ochimi, 1934: 125].

It is difficult to offer a balanced assessment of the effects of modernization on women's role and status in the period prior to World War II. Reviewing the Japanese experience, the most positive changes were probably in the area of education. Though the educational opportunities that were opened to women were inferior to those that became available to men, they were nevertheless crucial to eventual change in women's lives. One may ask why women benefited so little from the modernization process. The main factor, it appears, was the basic social conservatism of the modernizing elite who, though they made many changes to improve the economic life of the country, perpetuated the moral values that had had such a stifling effect on women of the samurai class during the feudal period. This moral code, it might be added, took on religious significance when it was incorporated into State Shinto, the quasireligious doctrine so important in the prewar period.

As Japan in the 1930s began its policy of expansionism and moved closer to war, these same Confucian codes became moral enjoiners to elicit the full cooperation of the Japanese population in the war effort. Women, linked to the great "family" of Japan with the emperor at its head, played their part in that effort. All were required to join the Women's National Defense Association in which they prepared supplies for soldiers, tended the wounded, helped the families of soldiers, and engaged in a wide variety of similar activities. By 1943 numerous girls' higher schools were turned into factories for making military uniforms (Anderson, 1959: 46), and most women were involved in war preparations in some way. As the defeat in World War II brought the period of early modernization to its disastrous close, women in Japan were fully a part of national life. However on a great many counts their status in society and the family had made only limited gains as a result of the modernization process, and in certain respects they can even be said to have lost ground.

JAPAN TODAY

Legal change.　Japan's surrender in 1945 ended a war that had brought the normal life of the country to a standstill. Soon after the surrender, Japan became an occupied country under General Douglas MacArthur, Supreme Commander for the Allied Powers (SCAP). The policy of the occupying force was to carry out the mandate of the Potsdam Declaration of July 26, 1945: to oversee "the revival and strengthening of democratic tendencies among the Japanese people," and to ensure that "freedom of speech, of religion, and of thought as well as respect for the fundamental human rights" would be established. (SCAP, 1949: 413). In 1952 the Occupation formally ended, but by then it had set in motion economic, social, and political changes that had a major impact on many areas of Japanese life.

Those in the Occupation believed that once the legal and structural basis for a democratic system were laid down, democracy as they understood it would take root. In a number of instances the Occupation view proved wrong; some of its measures were rescinded after the occupying forces left, and certain other provisions were left on the books but ignored or bypassed in practice. Nevertheless, on balance, the Occupation represented a remarkable experiment in guided social change, and a great many of the reforms it introduced have been lasting ones.

Many measures introduced by the Occupation had an incalculable impact on women's status and role. The new Constitution of 1947 specifically forbade "discrimination in political, economic or social relations because of race, creed, sex, social status or family origin," thus giving Japanese women a more explicit constitutional guarantee of equality than provided for in the American Constitution (SCAP, 1949: 672). The new Constitution also made explicit provision, in Article 24, that "marriage shall be based only on the mutual consent of both sexes" and on the "equal rights of husband and wife." The same article went on to guarantee that "with regard to choice of spouse, property rights, inheritance, choice of domicile, divorce, and other matters pertaining to marriage and the family, laws shall be enacted from the standpoint of individual dignity and the essential equality of the sexes" (SCAP, 1949: 672). These provisions make the Constitution of 1947 one of the most progressive in the world in the setting down of guarantees for women's equality in society and the family.

The Constitution also established the basis for equal educational opportunities for women by stipulating equal education for all according to ability (Article 26, SCAP, 1949: 672). In the School Education Law and the Fundamental Law of Education, which followed in the same year, the terms of the new educational policy were made more explicit. A new single-track, 6-3-3-4 system (6 years of elementary school, 3 years of junior high school, 3 years of senior high school, and 4 years of university) was established to replace the prewar multitrack system that had relegated women to their inferior girls' track (Passin, 1966: 292–303). The second of these follow-up laws gave specific support for coeducation: "Men and women shall esteem and cooperate with each other. Coeducation, therefore, shall be recognized in education" (SCAP, 1949: 302–303), thus opening the way to a public school system that has become largely coeducational.

The Labor Standard Law enacted in April 1947 set the basis for fair treatment of women workers (SCAP, 1949: 877–878). While some of these measures, modeled on the kind of women's labor laws then in force in the United States, fall in the category of protective legislation rather than measures for securing equal work rights, there is little doubt that the new law led to vast improvements in the working conditions of the female work force.

New provisions introduced into the Civil Code further implemented the constitutional guarantee of women's equality in family life. Prewar provisions in the Civil Code concerning marriage, divorce, property rights of married women, and other matters coming under family law, had consistently favored the husband. The basic unit under the old law was the house, that is, the extended family organized and duly registered under a head of household who assumed full legal responsibility for all family members. Upon marriage, a woman became subject to the authority of her husband's family head, generally her father-in-law. The system had devastating consequences for a woman's legal position, for in virtually all matters coming under civil law, she could act only with the approval of her husband's family. Since the children she bore were viewed as family heirs, she generally lost custody of them to her husband in the event of divorce. Adultery constituted legal grounds for divorce only if committed by the wife. And since a woman was under the legal authority of her own family head until she married, quite literally the law placed her in a position of total dependency throughout her life (George in Hall and Beardsley, 1965: 509–514).

In the postwar reform of the Civil Code this situation was remedied, and husbands and wives were given legal parity in the marriage relationship. Today both can terminate marriage on the same grounds, "for acts of unchastity, desertion, continued absence, mental illness, or any other grave reason for which it is difficult . . . to continue the marriage" (George in Hall and Beardsley, 1965: 515). Family courts were set up to intervene in such matters as child custody and property disputes in cases in which divorce is under consideration. Women can now negotiate contracts without their husband's consent. And marriage itself can be entered into on consent of both parties without parental permission when both have reached legal age (18 for males, 16 for females). Whereas under the old code a woman had to be registered under either her own family head or that of her husband, today she may apply for her own registration (George in Hall and Beardsley, 1965: 514).

Since the democratic system of the United States was the natural model for the American Occupation, the legal basis for the Japanese woman's participation in the national life is similar to that of the American woman. In fact, in some ways, particularly in their explicit constitutional guarantee of equality, Japanese women are far ahead of women in many countries, including the United States. It might also be added that certain legal problems faced by women in other highly developed countries have not been a problem in Japan. For example, the obtaining of credit has not been a major woman's issue there because most business and sales transactions are conducted in cash.

The pressure from women on the legal structure has been directed mainly at laws regulating work. Women have taken to court a number of cases in which they have charged that a company's employment policies and practices were in violation of women's constitutional guarantee of equality in economic life. Most of these cases have disputed the right of companies to force the early retirement of women for various reasons not applying to men, for example, at marriage, childbirth, or a set age earlier than the retirement age for men (Akamatsu, 1970). The most important case so far involved the complaint of a woman who had been dismissed from her job at a cement factory upon marriage. A Tokyo District Court in 1966 ruled that the cement company's policy was null and void because it violated the constitutional provision for equality of the sexes and for freedom of marriage, in addition to violating public order (Akamatsu, 1967). A number of cases involving women and the labor law have come to court in recent years and in most decisions have favored the women plaintiffs.

The pressure applied to the legal system from women, as in the cases cited above, generally is not toward changing the laws, but toward ensuring their enforcement. Legal guarantees today give women a full legal basis for equality, but the nature of family life, educational attitudes, and informal policies and practices in the employment world all make it difficult to mesh legal norms with social reality. The main barriers for Japanese women are not the legal ones, but those rooted in customs and general societal norms affecting women.

Work.   In 1972 women constituted 38.2 percent of Japan's total work force of 51,820,000. Almost half (47.8 percent) of the women of working age were in the labor force (Japan, Ministry of Labor, Women's and Minors' Bureau (WMB), 1972: 4).

The postwar trend has undoubtedly been toward greater work force participation in the modern sector on the part of women. Over the last few years the rate of work force participation for both males and females has declined slightly, but much of this has been caused by the rising prosperity in postwar Japan which has made it possible for more young people to seek a higher level of education, thereby delaying their entry into the work force. In 1960, 49.7 percent of women in the 15 to 19 age group were working, whereas by 1970 the figure had dropped to 33.6 percent because more young women stayed in school (Japan, Ministry of Labor, Women's and Minors' Bureau, 1971a: 47).

Two further trends are particularly striking. First is the substantial increase in the number of women entering or returning to the work force in their forties and early fifties after bringing up their children. In 1960, 55.3 percent of women in the 40 to 54 age range were working, but by 1970 the figure had climbed to 61.8 percent (Japan, Ministry of Labor, Women's and Minors' Bureau, 1971a: 47). A second trend is the decrease in the number of working women in the 25 to 29 age range, in which childbearing is concentrated in Japan. It appears that postwar prosperity has made it possible for growing numbers of young mothers to quit their jobs and stay home with their young children. There also has been a steady increase in the number of married women entering the work force. By 1972, 46 percent of all female workers were married women, a figure that has more than doubled in the last 15 years (Japan, Ministry of Labor, Women's and Minors' Bureau, 1973: 13).

If we look at the occupational distribution of women workers set forth in Table 1, it is clear that Japanese women, like women in most countries,

Table 1 Percent Women Workers, by Occupation

Occupational category	1955	1960	1965	1970
Professional and technical	30.1	35.9	37.6	40.7
Managers and officials	2.7	4.3	3.4	3.8
Clerical	33.5	36.3	39.9	46.9
Sales	41.0	34.2	37.0	32.7
Farming and fishing	20.0	24.7	23.7	23.8
Mining	6.1	5.7	5.0	10.0
Communications and transportation	3.9	13.5	12.0	10.0
Operatives	25.2	25.7	24.9	25.9
Laborers			31.5	33.2
Service	59.4	58.2	54.7	56.2

Source. Japan, Ministry of Labor, Women's and Minors' Bureau, 1971a: 52.

continue to do mainly nonprofessional and menial jobs. In 1970 women made up only 3.8 percent of those in the category of managers and officials. At the opposite end of the scale, women occupied 56.2 percent of jobs in the service category. Figures for the past 15 years, however, show a number of changes in occupational patterns of Japanese women. For one thing, increasing numbers of women have found their way into jobs in the "clerical" and "professional and technical" categories. This change, however, should not be taken as a direct sign of women's entry into types of work generally done by men, though there are some signs of a trend in that direction. Women's professional activity continues to be concentrated in the "women's" fields of nursing and public school teaching.

The Labor Standards Law enacted in 1947 affirms the principle of equal pay for equal work. However there are striking disparities in pay received by women as compared with that earned by men. Women's average wage in 1972 was only half that received by male workers (Japan, Ministry of Labor, Women's and Minors' Bureau, 1973: 18). In none of the major job categories does the average wage received by women approach that received by men. Women in transportation and communications work fared better in comparison with their male fellow workers than women in any other job category, but the average pay they received in 1972 was still only 65.7 percent of that received by men in their category (Japan, Ministry of Labor, Women's and Minors' Bureau, 1973: 18).

As mentioned in the section dealing with legal change, the Labor Standards Law includes a number of measures aimed at improving working conditions for women. The law provides for a maternity leave of six weeks before and after delivery and allows mothers to nurse babies on the job, granting them two extra 30-minute rests per day for nursing (SCAP, 1949:

877–878). A new law passed in 1972 further strengthens the provisions of the original law.

Because measures in the Labor Standards Law of 1947 affecting women were designed, under pressure from the American Occupation, to do away with the abuses of the past, a number of provisions fall into the category of protective legislation. For example, with certain exceptions women cannot be employed for night work in industry and commerce, and limits are set on the amount of overtime they can be required to work. Similarly women cannot be engaged in specified jobs that are classified as dangerous or that involve heavy work (SCAP, 1949: 877–878). In 1971 and 1972, I interviewed a number of Japanese women in clerical and assemblyline work, as well as several women in high positions in major unions and the Labor Ministry. In general I found very little opposition to measures in the labor law that would be considered protective by American standards. Most thought that there would be few concrete gains for women in terms of better jobs or increased pay if such measures were eliminated; indeed, most felt that many of these provisions were still essential for protecting woman workers from exploitation by employers.

One of the main problems of the working woman in Japan, as in the United States, is child-care. There are growing demands in Japan for an increase in the number of public day-care facilities because present facilities are wholly inadequate. As of September 1969, there were 13,300 day-care centers in Japan, approximately two-thirds public and one-third private, accommodating around one million children. But in 1971 there were almost 400,000 children on waiting lists and many others whose mothers would seek placement if facilities were available (Government of Japan, 1971: 53). Present facilities are being used almost exclusively by working-class mothers and divorced or widowed mothers who are heads of families. The view of most Japanese I talked to, including several administrators and nurses in day-care centers, was that public day-care should be reserved for the poor. This attitude arises out of a deeply felt belief (which is one of the most formidable, psychological barriers faced by the middle-class mother who wants to work) that only in the direst of circumstances should a mother turn over the care of her young children to strangers.

The traditional alternative to day-care for children in Japan was provided by grandparents or other relatives. In the extended family system traditional in Japan, grandparents generally lived under the same roof with the young couple, so there was usually someone around to tend the children when the mother was away. In today's large urban centers, however, the extended family is fast disappearing, and most working mothers must make provisions for outside day-care. Only upper-middle-class, well-to-do families seek domestic help. Even if such help were financially within the reach of middle-class and working-class wives, there is no real tradition in Japan for any but the well-to-do to have domestic help. Even relatively wealthy families in Japan are unlikely to have more than one helper, often a young woman who lives with the family and is treated more or less as a family member. Most working mothers either rely on relatives for child-care where that is possible, or look for public or private day-care facilities.

Work patterns for women, of course, vary with social status and economic class. Most working-class women, who work primarily for economic reasons, enter the work market directly after graduation from junior or, increasingly, senior high school, and many spend much of their adult lives in and out of the labor market. Their problems as working women are manyfold: low pay, access mainly to the lower categories of industrial work requiring minimal skills, a marginal employment status offering little job security, problems associated with having to do double duty as wives and workers, child-care problems, and so on. Women in the agricultural sector, who in 1972 constituted 52 percent of all farmworkers (Japan, Ministry of Labor, Women's and Minors' Bureau, 1973: 28), follow a similar educational pattern. Since their work and home lives after marriage are closely integrated, certain problems, such as outside child-care and wage disparities, do not arise. The main difficulty of the farm wife has come as the result of larger postwar changes in the agricultural sector, which increased the number of male family heads and younger family members seeking part-time or full-time work in the cities, thus leaving the burden of farmwork on those still at home, particularly the wife and grandparents.

Some level of higher education, often undertaken in junior colleges or women's colleges, is becoming increasingly accessible to women of the middle class. Their work pattern typically involves a short work span of from two to four years after their formal education and before marriage. Unless she is involved in one of the "women's" professions, such as nursing or public schoolteaching, the middle-class woman today usually quits her job upon marriage, often voicing satisfaction that in a prosperous postwar society she can devote all of her time to her home and family. Only in her late thirties or early forties is she likely to consider returning to the work force. For those who do want to work after marriage and have no special skills, the problems are numerous: low pay that barely covers the costs of child-care; the negative attitude of employers toward hiring married women for white-collar work; and most difficult of all, the psychological barrier posed by the attitude of society, and many husbands, to a wife's working when there is no dire economic necessity.

The same educational pattern applies to the upper-middle-class woman, though she is somewhat more likely to attend a four-year college or one of the better coed universities. Though a tiny minority of women from well-to-do families seek professional training leading to a career, most upper-class women still gravitate to "women's" majors and thus enter the job market without special skills. Their work pattern follows the one for the middle class, but as one study indicates, they are probably somewhat more likely (see Table 2) to work after marriage, at least until they have children.

Table 2   Tokyo Married Women: Employment According to Education

	High School: nongraduate	High School: graduate	College: nongraduate	College: graduate
Percent of graduates that are working wives	33	24	43	69

Source.   Blood, 1967: 149. Based on a study of 444 Tokyo suburban dwellers.

Family.   Three major forces have probably done the most to alter the nature of family life in Japan and to change the status of women within the family system. The first of these was the democratization process described earlier; the Occupation fortified woman's position within the family with basic legal and constitutional guarantees: the right to inherit property, the right of free choice of her marriage partner, easier recourse to divorce, and so on. A second force is urbanization. Women's inferior standing in the prewar family system was anchored in the low status of the wife vis-à-vis her husband and his family members in an extended family arrangement. But in the postwar period more and more young people have deserted the countryside for city life, with the result that family ties have loosened. Certainly many signs of strong family solidarity and extended family arrangements remain in modern Japan, but the trend toward city living is of tremendous significance in a country that in 1970 was 72.2 percent urban. Urban migration, along with other factors, has meant that the average size of a household in Japan has decreased from 5.08 persons in 1930 to 3.72 persons in 1970 (Japan, Ministry of Labor, Women's and Minors' Bureau 1971b: 40). Within the nuclear family common today in urban areas, the values and attitudes surrounding marriage itself and the wife's role in the family are changing. Whereas in the extended family the wife's chief function traditionally was to bear an heir to preserve family continuity, increased value is placed on companionship and mutual understanding in the marriage relationship.

A third factor bringing about change in women's role and status in the family has been prosperity. Increased material comfort has greatly simplified housework and relieved women of much of their previous drudgery, thus freeing them for other pursuits. Prosperity has also provided more financial resources for leisure activities. Young married couples today are far more likely than in the past to have money for an occasional dinner out, a family outing, or a vacation. Increased family resources have meant that parents today feel able financially to educate daughters as well as sons. And finally, despite recent economic setbacks, prosperity in the postwar period overall has brought new employment opportunities, thus providing growing numbers of women with an independent economic base within marriage.

Let us now look more closely at some of the key areas in which changes in the family system can be observed. An important area of change is in the mate selection process itself. In the prewar period the extended family exercised control over family members by playing the decisive role in choosing their marriage partners. In the system of arranged marriage (*miai-kekkon*) the family or a go-between weighed family credentials of the young people concerned and ultimately decided the match. Marriages were also made as a result of "love matches" (*renai-kekkon*), in which the couple themselves made an independent decision to marry, but these were much less common and were socially disapproved among middle- and upper-class families. Loving someone was not thought to be strong grounds for considering the prospect of marriage.

Throughout the early postwar period arranged marriage continued to be the main method of mate selection. A study in the mid-1950s showed that 73 percent of marriages in large cities and 86 percent of those in farming areas were still arranged (Koyama, 1961: 43). But the number of love marriages has been increasing rapidly over the last two decades. Figures released in 1971 show that "love" marriages comprise 60.3 percent of all matches in large cities, 59.5 percent of those in medium-sized cities, and even 35.8 percent of those in villages (Japan, Economic Planning Agency, 1971: 30). The arranged marriage system itself has changed in the postwar period. Today many Japanese see it as little more than a method of introduction that brings together young people of carefully matched backgrounds who can decide for themselves whether they will marry.

In the postwar period the rate of marriage itself has been increasing. In 1955 the rate was 8.0 (per 1,000 population), whereas by 1970 it had risen to 9.9 (Japan, Ministry of Labor, Women's and Minors' Bureau, 1971b: 44). As the marriage rate has increased, so has the divorce rate, which has risen from 0.84 (per 1,000 population) in 1967 to 0.93 in 1970 (U.N. Demographic Yearbook, 1971). Interestingly enough, the divorce rates for Japan in the early modernization period were far higher than today's, almost as high as the United States rate in the 1970s (Kawashima and Steiner, 1960: 214).

The high divorce rate in the early modern period is attributable to the frequent initiation of divorce by the husband on a wide variety of grounds, all reflecting his superior position in the family, such as the wife's failure to bear an heir or her inability to get along with his parents. Since the postwar period the number of divorce suits brought by the wife is increasing, and also rising is the number of cases brought by her on such nontraditional grounds as the husband's unchastity. These trends in Japan are far more significant than changes in the divorce rate itself.

We may still ask why it is that the divorce rate itself is remarkably low compared to that in most modern societies. One answer, certainly, is the solidarity of the family unit in Japan. Divorce continues to be considered an extreme solution to problems in marriage. Another factor relates to the problems a divorced woman faces. Japanese civil law makes no provision for alimony, and the amounts of money awarded for child support tend to be extremely small. Some public assistance is available for divorced women, but again, amounts are minimal. Because wages for women are generally low, the divorcée often faces economic hardship—not to mention criticism from a society that places high value on family harmony. These factors undoubtedly contribute to the low divorce rate.

Within the marriage relationship itself it is more difficult to pinpoint how things have changed in the postwar period. Certainly the growth of the nuclear family, the improved educational attainment of women, and the increase in the number of married women who work have had their effects on the family system, and that impact has been in the direction of greater communication and companionship in the marriage relationship (Blood, 1967). However, the basic pattern of marriage continues to be one in which the worlds of the husband and wife are kept separate and distinct (Vogel, 1963; Dore, 1958; Blood, 1967). The husband's world revolves about his work, and he shares far less of that world with his wife than does the husband in the United States, for example. Not only may he tell her very little of what goes on at the office, but the Japanese husband tends to spend a great deal of his leisure time with his male co-workers in a social life that does not include wives. In the company of fellow workers he often stops off at bars or restaurants after work, and he is likely to enjoy playing mahjong or golf with men from the office in his off-hours (Plath, 1964). For her part the wife usually develops her own life centering on the home and neighborhood. Though the pattern is altering somewhat, she is far less involved in outside activities such as volunteer work or civic groups than are women in the United States and focuses most of her energies on the home itself. Within that circumscribed sphere her authority is undoubtedly great. She generally has full responsibility for managing the family budget and makes most of the decisions relating to her children. Since her role satisfaction depends heavily on how well she manages the home sphere, she generally does not ask for or expect help with household chores from her husband, though this too is changing somewhat.

Certain class differences appear in this pattern. White-collar workers, for example, are more likely to help their wives with housework than are farmers or manual workers (Dore, 1958: 175). Conversely, farmers and others working in rural areas, who may be traditional on many counts, are more likely to share their social lives with their wives than many "modern" couples in Tokyo, who find themselves living in separate worlds not only because of custom, but because of structural economic factors beyond their control, such as an employment system which requires that a man fraternize after-hours with co-workers if he wants to get ahead.

The family system in Japan is changing on many fronts. Though the typical pattern continues to involve considerable role separation for husbands and wives, recent writers have commented on the increasing tendency for wives to join civic activities, such as support groups for local politicians, and for young husbands, who today are somewhat more critical of values surrounding the work world in Japan, to spend more time with their wives and families (Vogel, 1970; Pharr, forthcoming).

Education. The educational system that came under the scrutiny of the Occupation in the early postwar period had long since succeeded in its major goals of making some level of education widely available in society and of educating the leaders of a rapidly modernizing nation. Virtually the entire population had achieved literacy by the end of the Meiji period (1868–1912) (Passin, 1966: 4), and the groundwork for a modern mass educational system had been laid in the prewar period. The main concerns of the Occupation were, first, to change the content of education to eliminate all ideas and values regarded as antidemocratic, and second, to unify the system, making education available to all on the basis of ability.

The changes instituted by the Occupation to achieve both goals had profound impact on women. Reform of educational content included eliminating the prewar required "morals" course which had idealized the traditional family system within which women had had low status. The morals course was replaced with a social studies course designed to educate young Japanese in the ways of democracy. Like the postwar constitution itself, the new course was aimed at introducing democratic values into society at all levels and consequently gave strong support for the democratization of family life and for the equality of women. Similarly, reforms aimed at making education available to all on the basis of ability had incalculable impact on the status of women. No major group benefited more than they, for it was women who had constituted the principal segment of society excluded from the upper reaches of the educational system in the prewar period.

The key to implementing the new principles of democratic mass education was to secure acceptance for coeducation from the Japanese public. This has been achieved today, but the gains have come only gradually. Though educators and the public were quick to accept coeducation at the lower levels, many educators argued that "during the ages of 15 or 16 to 17 or 18 in the upper secondary school . . . pupils' feelings are unstable" and that coeducation at those levels was therefore undesirable (Report of the Japanese Education Reform Council, cited in Anderson, 1959: 54). As a result of such opposition, coeducation was made compulsory only through the lower secondary school level, and optional for the upper secondary level.

In the immediate postwar period many upper secondary schools did not go coeducational; thereafter, however, coeducation spread rapidly as it won public acceptance. Though a few coed upper secondary schools have reconverted to separate education, the great majority of schools today are coeducational.

Coeducation has meant that girls today have the same study options as boys. Also as a result of the equalization of educational opportunity, they can now pursue their education for as far as their ability and desires—and family financial resources—permit. To study how women's status in the field of education is changing, then, there are really two major questions we should ask. First, to what extent have women taken advantage of their equal access to the educational ladder; that is, how far are they going in the schools in comparison with male students? Second, to what extent are they utilizing their equal study options; that is, once girls reach a level in the schools where they can elect their field of concentration, what are they choosing to study?

There is no question that women's enrollment in education at all levels has increased at a remarkable rate throughout the postwar period. In 1955 only 47.4 percent of girl students advanced beyond compulsory education to enter upper secondary schools, whereas 55.5 percent of the male students continued their schooling. By 1970 the rate of advancement for girls had exceeded that for boys: 82.7 percent of the girls went on, as compared to 81.6 percent of the boys (Japan, Ministry of Labor, Women's and Minors' Bureau, 1971a: 6). The movement of women into higher education has been increasing at a phenomenal rate. In 1955, 14.9 percent of female senior high school students entered higher education, whereas by 1970 the figure had increased to 23.5 percent. (The comparable figures for males are 20.9 percent in 1955 and 25 percent in 1970.) (Japan, Ministry of Labor, Women's and Minors' Bureau, 1971a: 6).

These figures indicate that ever-increasing numbers of women are climbing the educational ladder. They do not mean, however, that educational patterns for males and females are now congruent. Though they now advance to higher education, a high percentage of women attend junior colleges rather than four-year institutions. In 1970 women made up 82.7 percent of the enrollment in junior colleges but only 18 percent of the enrollment in four-year institutions (Japan, Ministry of Labor, Women's and Minors' Bureau, 1971a: 6). Even these figures do not tell the whole story, for the percentage of women in the prestigious national universities is still lower. It also should be taken into account that a high percentage of women in four-year schools are enrolled in private women's colleges rather than in public or private coed institutions.

How can we interpret these trends? A principle seems to operate in Japan whereby parents educate sons before daughters, but will educate daughters as well if financial resources permit (Tomoda, 1972: 262). Prosperity in the postwar period has thus meant that families increasingly are able to send daughters up the educational ladder—but generally to a lower rung than the one to which they send sons. This is undoubtedly a large part of the explanation for the higher enrollment of women in junior colleges than in four-year institutions. But a financial explanation only goes so far. It particularly falls down when we try to say why so few women are enrolled in the prestigious national universities. In Japan the best education available is practically free; parents spend far more sending daughters to private institutions than to the top universities in Japan. Admission to the best universities is by competitive examination, and the competition is fierce. But why relatively few women try for admission to these schools goes to the heart of many of the problems surrounding the status of women in education. Many parents—and many daughters as well—continue to feel that the education of daughters has goals totally different from those of a son's education, and some of these goals of women's education are thought to be compromised by a tough, competitive coed environment. In Japan I interviewed a number of women students at Tokyo University, Japan's top-ranking institution, and was told by many that they had encountered serious opposition at home when they had announced their intention to try for admission to the best university in Japan. Parents had expressed fears, not that their daughters would fail to gain admission, but that they might succeed—and thereby hurt their marriage chances or cause themselves to be viewed as "hard" or unfeminine. The parents of many of these top students would have preferred to send them to expensive four-year women's colleges rather than see them receive an education that might become a handicap to marriage. When we evaluate the degree to which women have taken advantage of their equal access to education in the postwar period, there is no doubt that the overall trend points in the direction of ever-increasing enrollments at all levels and an increasing willingness of parents to see their daughters through some degree of higher education. But when the pattern of women's education is examined, it is clear that many problems remain which bear closely on the status of women.

Similar findings recur when we look at the kind of education women are receiving today in an educational system that gives them a wide variety of study options. Just as before the war, when girls studied subjects thought suitable for them, there is still a pronounced tendency for them to steer their educational course somewhat differently than boys. In upper secondary school the majority take a general education course whether or not they plan to go on to college. Few women prepare for technical jobs that bring good pay. Instead those who choose a vocational course take home economics to prepare themselves to become wives and mothers; others enter the commercial course so that they can find clerical jobs after graduation. The general pattern, then, is one in which a great many girls take the general course without any special plans to go beyond a high school education. Boys, in contrast, take the general education course with further education in mind, or else enter a special vocational course so that they will leave high school with a skill (Tomoda, 1972).

In higher education the tendency of women to elect study options different from those of male students and to gravitate to "women's" majors over majors that lead more directly to careers is even more pronounced (See Table 3). The great majority of women major in literature. The number of

Table 3   Percent Women Students by Department in Four-Year Institutions of Higher Learning (1972)

Department	As percent of total enrollment
Literature	54.1
Law, politics, economics, and industrial management	5.9
Science	13.5
Engineering	.7
Agriculture	7.2
Medicine, dentistry, pharmacy, nursing	38.5
Home economics	99.5
Teacher training	54.1
Arts	57.1
Others	19.4

Source.   Japan, Ministry of Labor, Women's and Minors' Bureau, 1973: 7.

women in literature combined with those in home economics constitutes well over half of all women students in higher education (Japan, Ministry of Labor, Women's and Minors' Bureau, 1973: 7).

Today the goals of the Occupation in the field of education largely have been achieved. Mothers of the present generation of young Japanese women are overwhelmed at the educational options and possibilities open to their daughters. Naturally, when parents who attended school before the war offer direction to their children, they often steer them toward paths most familiar to them. At the same time daughters, looking to mothers as models for their own lives, are drawn to fields of study that their mothers—and society at large—still see as most appropriate for women. But even if this general principle still applies, a vast amount of change is occurring on the educational front, and the pace shows no signs of slowing.

Fertility and Family Planning.   The average life expectancy for Japanese women is one of the highest in the world. In 1971 it stood at 75.58 years, as compared to 70.17 for males (figures released by the Ministry of Health and Welfare in July, 1972, Japan Times, 1972a: 2). As average life expectancy has increased, the death rate has shown a corresponding decrease. At the same time the birthrate declined and stabilized in the postwar period. The average number of children born to each family was 5.14 in 1940, whereas by 1967 it had dropped dramatically to 1.69 (Government of Japan, 1971: 9).

Why is it that Japan has been so successful in keeping its population size so well in hand? One answer certainly is the responsiveness of the Japanese to changes in government population policy. Another is the widespread availability of both contraceptive measures and legal abortion. The main contraceptive device in use in Japan is the condom. According to a survey on birth control conducted by the Prime Minister's Office in the early 1970s, contraception by condom and the rhythm method accounted for 90 percent of preventive efforts, and the IUD for 10 percent (Japan Times, 1972b: 4). The pill is not available as a contraceptive measure in Japan. Authorization has been withheld by the Ministry of Health and Welfare for the official reasons that "it may cause thrombosis as a side effect" and that "its safety has not been proven" (Japan Times, 1972b: 4). Beyond this official view is a feeling among many policy-makers, expressed to me in an interview with a high-ranking official of the Liberal Democratic Party, that the pill is conducive to lax morals among young people and that it is unnecessary in Japan anyway since abortion is legal, safe, and inexpensive. (Interview with policy spokesman for the Liberal Democratic Party, Party Headquarters, Tokyo, April, 1972).

Abortion, long accepted in Japan, is undoubtedly the main method by which the country has been able to keep its population growth in hand. The cost of abortion is covered under the National Health Insurance program, and clinics handling abortions are numerous. For those covered by health insurance, the cost is minimal. With the absence of any moral or religious traditions in conflict with the practice, abortion appears to be a common method of ending unwanted pregnancies for women of all ages in Japan. Recently a measure has come before the Diet several times to limit the availability of abortion by eliminating "economic reasons" as a legal grounds for one. The proposed revision of the existing law has been widely protested by women's groups, the Japan Medical Association, the Family Planning Federation of Japan, and numerous other civic groups, and thus far has been defeated each time it has come before the Diet.

The foregoing discussion might indicate that there are few problems of birth control in Japan today, and the ready availability of abortion, so slow to gain acceptance in many countries, might make it seem that government policy is quite liberal. However, many members of Japanese women's groups point out that present methods of limiting population control have a conservative bias, for they restrict the sexual freedom of women, particularly unmarried women. Abortion, no matter how inexpensive and available, is an unpleasant experience which may endanger a woman's later childbearing capacity if repeated too often, and thus it is unsatisfactory as a normal method of birth control. These women, and a growing number of authorities and groups concerned with population control, argue that the pill should be legalized in Japan, but thus far the government has been unresponsive.

Political Action, Volunteerism, and the Women's Movement. A women's suffrage movement appeared in Japan during the prewar period, but since it failed to achieve its goal, its impact on the lives of most Japanese women was fairly limited. Of all their human rights women's right to free political expression and participation was probably the least recognized by the government and society at large in the prewar period.

In 1945, with the arrival of the Occupation, all this changed dramatically. With one stroke the Occupation granted full political equality to women, and in the first election of the postwar period, held on April 10, 1946, over 20 million women went to the polls for the first time. Perhaps in no other area of change was the handiwork of the Occupation so visible in such a short period of time. Other measures introduced in the early postwar period to improve women's status socially and economically have had lasting impact, but the change in most areas was diffuse and long-term. Changes affecting women's political status, in contrast, were sudden and dramatic.

In that first postwar election the percentage of women who turned out to vote was considerably below the level for men. Only 66.97 percent of eligible women voters cast their ballots, as compared to 78.5 percent for men (Japan, Ministry of Labor, Women's and Minors' Bureau, 1971b: 65). Over the last several decades, however, the voting rate of women rose steadily in relation to that for men. Since 1968, in fact, the voting rate for women in national elections has exceeded that for men. If we look at how various age groups voted, the effects of postwar change on a younger generation of women voters can be readily noted, for it is the younger women—particularly those in urban areas, where the impact of change has been greatest—who are mainly responsible for the increase in the voting rate for women. It is among the electorate under the age of 50 that the voting rate for women exceeds that for men, with women in the youngest age group, 20 to 29, leading the way (Japan, Ministry of Labor, Women's and Minors' Bureau, 1971b: 18). It is primarily among voters in the countryside and among voters over 50—the most traditional segments of society—that the men outvote the women (Japan, Ministry of Labor, Women's and Minors' Bureau, 1971b: 18; Watanuki, 1972).

In areas of political participation other than voting, however, women in Japan, like women in virtually all countries of the world today, are still strikingly underrepresented in the effective political life of the country. Women generally have held around 20 seats in the Diet at any time since the war, but this represents less than 3 percent of the total membership (Japan, Ministry of Labor, Women and Minors' Bureau, 1968: 2–3). In other elective bodies they are even further underrepresented. In 1971 women made up only 1.0 percent of the membership of prefectural assemblies. In municipal assemblies they held only 1.7 percent of the seats in the same year. And in the traditional countryside, they had the least representation of all: in town or village assemblies across Japan women were elected to only 0.4 percent of all seats (Japan, Ministry of Labor, Women and Minors' Bureau, 1973: 4).

As far as appointive offices in the national government are concerned, women had notable representation mainly in those bureaus and commissions bearing directly on "women's" concerns. For example, in 1972 some 34 percent of all mediation commissioners of the family courts, and 32 percent of all public and child welfare commissioners, were women (Japan, Ministry of Labor, Women's and Minors' Bureau, 1973: 4). As of 1972 two women had served in the cabinet, one as Health and Welfare Minister in 1960 and one as Director General of the Science and Technology Agency in 1962–63, but both were token, short-term appointments.

In terms of elective and appointive office-holding, then, women are clearly underrepresented. In the area of private organizational life, however, Japan has a fairly extensive network of activities, including women's political groups. All five major political parties have women's groups attached to them, and Japan has a rather well-developed club life including many of the kinds of groups found in the United States, such as the League of Women Voters and the Association of University Women. A great many farm women are at least nominal members of the National Women's Organizational Council of the Agricultural Cooperative Union, which has a membership in the millions. One of the most active of the postwar women's groups is the Housewives' Federation (*Shufu Rengōkai*), which has branches all over Japan and has been active in consumer protection activities. Most of these organizations are concerned with political and social issues in which women are thought to have a particular stake: consumer issues, inflation, the price of rice, the banning of nuclear testing, and in the case of political groups, support of candidates thought to forward these ends.

The "women's movement" (in the sense of a movement to improve women's status) that exists today can probably be said to have at least five major sources of support: (1) organizations of older women, often professionals, with goals similar to those of the National Organization of Women in the United States, that is, improving women's position in the work world and in society at the legal and institutional level; (2) organizations of younger women, including many associated with the New Left, who believe in equality of the sexes and sexual freedom who in many cases explicitly identify themselves as "women's lib" (*ūman ribu*), and who collectively take political positions on issues relating to women; (3) informal groups of college women or white-collar workers that function much like consciousness-raising groups in the United States (for example, one such group I encountered in Tokyo had 12 members, all students at a major private university, who met once a week in a group that had started out to talk over the experiences that a number of the members had had with abortions); (4) study groups organized at a great number of colleges and universities to do research on various women's issues, often publishing their findings (for example, one such study group at Tokyo University was researching the problem of prostitution in Okinawa); and (5) activist movements specifically aimed at conditions affecting women, such as groups concerned with improving day-care facilities. Since a great many of these groups do not see themselves as part of a wider movement, it is difficult to speak of a "women's liberation movement" in Japan in the way that such a term is used in the United States to encompass a wide variety of disparate groups that are identified with a common cause. But certainly the number of groups concerned with women's problems has been increasing, partly in response to media coverage of women's movement activities in other countries, and it seems likely that the interest will continue.

To summarize, women today—especially younger, urban women—have a higher voter participation rate than men and an interest in politics that appears to be increasing. Women are greatly underrepresented in active political involvement at the level of holding elective or appointive office. Most women in Japan undoubtedly continue to think of politics as a male activity and do not consider becoming actively involved. If they did so, social attitudes would set many barriers in their way to participation at the highest levels. A great many of those women who do manage to achieve political note are from political families or are "political widows" who serve their husbands' constituencies after their deaths. Most women limit their political participation to voting and, in some cases, to joining a women's auxiliary to one of the political parties or a particular politician's support group. These latter activities appeal to women of different classes, depending on the political party or politician involved. For example, a woman joining a group supporting the Liberal Democratic Party, which draws its vote heavily from business and agricultural interests, is likely to be a businessman's or farmer's wife. Supporters of the Japanese Communist Party's women's auxiliary are likely to be working-class women or, in some cases, wives of writers, intellectuals, and professionals, some of whom have such status in their own right.

Middle-class women are only beginning to join social and political organizations. Until recently, for the most part their participation was limited to such groups as the Parent-Teachers' Association. Japan has no strong tradition of volunteerism for charitable causes, perhaps because Japanese traditionally have looked to their families or, as a last resort, to the government bureaucracy to support needed services. Volunteer work for charitable causes thus attracts relatively few women in Japan. However recently a number of "citizens'" groups have been trying to effect change in such areas as consumer issues and environmental protection. Growing numbers of women, including many urban middle-class women, are joining such movements, and if the trend continues, participation patterns for women in the middle class may undergo a major change.

CONCLUSION

Although constitutional and legal reforms enacted by the Occupation following the war have not assured equality, they have facilitated an improvement in the status of women by eliminating prewar legal provisions that restricted the freedom, rights, and range of opportunities open to women. Japan's phenomenal economic growth, together with rapid social change and urbanization in the postwar period, has brought increased access to higher education for women and has provided them with new employment opportunities outside the home. Today growing numbers of women take advantage of the new life possibilities. Of those who do so, however, most continue to plan their lives with the primary goal of becoming wives and mothers. Japanese society still judges the adult woman primarily on the basis of her performance in the wife-mother role. The major forces impeding the improvement of women's position in society derive from Japan's cultural traditions. In a Ministry of Labor survey conducted in 1949, more than 75 percent of the women questioned stated their belief that the persistence of "feudalistic" customs and the attitude of men toward women constituted the greatest barriers standing in the way of women's progress (Koyama, 1961: 146). The situation now, some 25 years later, remains very much the same.

Polls consistently show women's strong support for improving their status in society. In a study in 1955, only 18 percent of those questioned believed that women's position in society was satisfactory, whereas an overwhelming 70 percent considered that further improvement of that position was necessary (Koyama, 1961: 73). It was among younger and more educated women that support for change was strongest, suggesting the degree to which opportunities opening up to women since the war have had their impact on the postwar generation and have led to a revolution of rising expectations.

Trends set in the postwar years appear to be continuing. The high enrollment rates at all levels of education, women's increased entry into the labor force, their growing desire to play the decisive role in choosing a marriage partner—all these and many other signs point to the ever-increasing desire of women for higher status, greater opportunity, and more independence. The remarkably high voter turnout among women, higher today than that of male voters, is undoubtedly another reflection of the Japanese woman's desire to participate actively in society. That the women themselves see strong links between increased social and political participation and their overall social status appears to be the reasonable inference to be drawn from a recent poll of 1000 persons—more than half of the women questioned said that women's political participation led to an improved status for Japanese women (Sankei Shimbun, 1972: 225). Many problems for women remain in the customs and attitudes of a country where a great many of the forces changing woman's role are recent ones. But the desire for improving their position in society is widely felt among women, and trends point to change in almost every direction.

BIBLIOGRAPHY

Ackroyd, Joyce. 1959. "Women in Feudal Japan." *Transactions of the Asiatic Society of Japan* **VII:** 31–68. Tokyo.

Adams, Don. 1970. *Education and Modernization in Asia*. Reading, Massachusetts: Addison-Wesley.

Akamatsu Tadashi Hanami. 1970. "New Problems Facing the Protective Labor Law." *Japan Labor Bulletin*, Part I (May): 7–10; Part II (June): 5–8.

———. 1967. "The Retirement Age System in Japan." *Japan Labor Bulletin*. (October).

Anderson, Ronald S. 1959. *Japan: Three Epochs of Modern Education*. Washington, D.C.: Department of Health, Education, and Welfare, Bulletin No. II.

Arichi Toru. 1971. *Fujin no chii to gendai shakai* (The Position of Women and Contemporary Society). Tokyo: Noritsu Bunkasha.

Ariga Kizaemon. 1956. "Contemporary Japanese Family in Transition." *Transactions of the Third World Congress of Sociology* **4:** 215–221. Amsterdam: International Sociological Association.

———. 1948. *Nihon koninshiron* (A Study of the History of Marriage in Japan). Tokyo: Nikko Shoin.

———. 1954. "The Family in Japan." *Marriage and Family Living* **16:** 362–368.

Beard, Mary. 1953. *The Force of Women in Japanese History*. Washington, D.C.: Public Affairs Press.

Bellah, Robert N. 1957. *Tokugawa Religion*. New York: Free Press of Glencoe, Illinois.

Benedict, Ruth. 1946. *Chrysanthemum and the Sword*. Boston: Houghton Mifflin Co.

Bennett, John W., Herbert Passin, and Robert K. McKnight. 1958. *The Japanese Overseas Scholar in America and Japan*. Minneapolis: University of Minnesota Press.

Blood, Robert O., Jr. 1967. *Love Match and Arranged Marriage: A Tokyo–Detroit Comparison*. New York: Free Press.

Borton, Hugh. 1955. *Japan's Modern Century*. New York: Ronald Press.

Brinkley, F. A. 1915. *A History of the Japanese People from the Earliest Times to the End of the Meiji Era*. New York: Encyclopedia Britannica.

Brown, Delmar M. 1955. *Nationalism in Japan*. Berkeley: University of California Press.

Burton, Margaret. 1914. *The Education of Women in Japan*. New York: Fleming H. Revell Co.

Cressy, Earl. 1955. *Daughters of Changing Japan*. New York: Farrar, Straus, and Cudahy.

DeVos, George, and Hiroshi Wagatsuma. 1961. "Value Attitudes towards Role Behavior of Women in Two Japanese Villages." *American Anthropologist* **LXIII:** 1204–1230.

Dore, Ronald. 1958. *City Life in Japan*. Berkeley: University of California Press.

———. 1965. *Education in Tokugawa Japan*. Berkeley: University of California Press.

———, Editor. 1967. *Aspects of Social Change in Modern Japan*. Princeton: Princeton University Press.

Dorson, Richard M., Editor. 1963. *Studies in Japanese Folklore*. Bloomington, Indiana: Indiana University Press.

Embree, John. 1939. *Suye Mura: A Japanese Village*. Chicago: University of Chicago Press.

Fairbank, John K., Edwin O. Reischauer, and Albert Craig. 1965. *East Asia: The Modern Transformation*. Boston: Houghton Mifflin Co.

Fréderic, Louis. 1972. *Daily Life in Japan at the Time of the Samurai, 1185–1603*. Translated by Eileen M. Lowe. New York: Praeger.

Fujimoto Taizo. 1916. *The Story of the Geisha Girl*. London: T. W. Laurie.

Fujita Taki. 1954. *Japanese Women in the Post-War Years*. Twelfth Conference, Institute of Pacific Relations, Kyoto, Japan.

Fukaya Masashi. 1966. *Ryōsai kenbo shugi no kyōiku* (Education to be a Virtuous Wife and Wise Mother). Tokyo: Reimei Shobō.

Groot, Bernard J. 1951. *The Prehistory of Japan*. New York: Columbia University Press.

Hall, John W., and Richard K. Beardsley. 1965. *Twelve Doors to Japan*. New York: McGraw Hill.

Harada Tomohiko. 1965. *Nihon josei shi* (History of Japanese Women). Tokyo: Kasui Shobō Shinsha.

Hearn, Lafcadio. 1902. "A Woman's Tragedy: The Dairy of a Japanese Woman." *Transactions and Proceedings of the Japanese Society*. (October). London.

Higa Masako. 1971. *Onna no tatakai* (Women's Struggle). Tokyo: Nippon Jitsugyō Shuppansha.

Hiratsuka Raicho. 1955. *Watakushi no aruita michi* (The Road I Walked). Tokyo: Shin Hyōronsha.

Hosoi Wakizō. 1954. *Jokō aishi* (A Tragic History of Girl Operatives). Tokyo: Iwanami Shoten.

Ishimoto Shizue. 1935. *East-Way, West-Way*. New York: Farrar and Rinehart.

Isomura Ei-ichi, Kawashima Takeyoshi, and Koyama Takashi, Editors. 1955–1956. *Gendai kazoku kōza* (The Structure of the Contemporary Family). 6 Volumes. Tokyo: Kawado Shobō.

Jansen, Marius, Editor. 1965. *Changing Japanese Attitudes towards Modernization*. Princeton: Princeton University Press.

Japan, Economic Planning Agency. 1971. *Kokumin seikatsu hakusho* (Report on National Life). Tokyo.

Japan, Government of. 1971. *Seminar in Public Administration Officers on Women's Problems 1971 Fiscal Year* (sic). Tokyo.

Japan, Ministry of Education. 1971. *Educational Standards in Japan 1970*. Tokyo, March.

———. 1961, 1971. *Gakkō kihon chōsa* (Basic School Survey). Tokyo.

———. 1961, 1971. *Zenkoku gakkō sōran* (National School Report). Tokyo.

Japan, Ministry of Health and Welfare. 1970. *Vital Statistics*. Tokyo.

Japan, Ministry of Labor, Women's and Minors' Bureau. 1971a. *Fujin no genjō* (The Condition of Women). Tokyo.

———. 1971b. *Me de miru no ayumi* (A Look at Women's Progress). Tokyo, April.

———. 1972. *Fujin rōdō no jitsujō* (The Status Quo of Women Workers). Report No. 130. Tokyo.

———. 1973. *The Status of Women in Japan*. Tokyo.

Japan Times. 1972a. July 21, p. 2.

———. 1972b. July 4, p. 4.

Kawai Michi and Ochimi Kabushiro. 1934. *Japanese Women Speak*. Boston: The Central Committee on the United Study of Foreign Missions.

Kawashima Takeyoshi. 1954. *Kekkon* (Marriage). Tokyo: Iwanami Shoten.

———. 1950. *Nihon shakai no kazoku-teki kōsei* (The Familistic Structure of Japanese Society). Tokyo: Nihon Hyōron Shinsha.

——— and Kurt Steiner. 1960. "Modernization and Divorce Rate Trends in Japan." *Economic Development and Cultural Change* 9 Part 2, 213–239.

Kitakoji Satoshi, et al. 1967: "Gakusei undō no genjō to tenbō" (The Present Condition and Future Prospects for the Student Movement). *Shisō no kagaku*, no. 62 (May).

Koyama Takashi. 1961. *The Changing Social Position of Women in Japan*. Paris: UNESCO.

Kuchler, L. W. 1885. "Marriage in Japan." *Transactions of the Asiatic Society of Japan* 13 (July): 114–137.

Lifton, Robert Jay. 1964. "Individual Patterns in Historical Change: Imagery of Japanese Youth." *Journal of Social Issues* **20** (October): 96–111.

———. 1967. "Woman as Knower: Some Psychohistorical Perspectives." In *The Woman in America*. Edited by Robert Jay Lifton. Boston: Beacon Press.

Maki, John M., Editor. 1964. *Court and Constitution in Japan*. Seattle: University of Washington Press.

Mason, J. W. T. 1939. *The Spirit of Shinto Mythology*. Tokyo: Fuzambo.

Mishima Sumie. 1941. *My Narrow Island*. New York: J. Day Co.

———. 1953. *The Broader Way, A Woman's Life in the New Japan*. New York: J. Day Co.

Moore, Barrington. 1966. "Asian Fascism." In *Social Origins of Dictatorship and Democracy*. Boston: Beacon Press.

Morisaki Kazue. 1970. *Makkura: Jokōfu kara no kikigaki* (Darkness: Notes from Interviews with Women Mineworkers). Tokyo: Gendai Shichōsha.

Morosawa Yōko. 1970. *Onna no rekishi* (History of Women). 2 Volumes. Tokyo: Miraisha.

Morris, Ivan. 1964. *The World of the Shining Prince: Court Life in Ancient Japan*. New York: Alfred A. Knopf.

Morris, J. 1885. *Kotaka: A Samurai's Daughter*. London: Wyman.

Murakami Nobuhiko. 1970–1972. *Meiji josei shi* (The History of Meiji Women). 3 Volumes. Tokyo: Rironsha.

Murasaki Shikibu. 1925. *The Tale of Genji*. Translated by Arthur Whaley. London: Allen and Unwin.

Nakano Takashi. 1962. "Recent Studies of Change in the Japanese Family." *International Social Science Journal* **14** (3): 527–538.

Nishio, H. K. 1972. "The Changing Japanese Perspectives and Attitudes Towards Leisure." *Humanitas* **VIII** (3) (November): 367–388.

Ōmori, Annie S., and Kōchi Doi. 1920. *Diaries of Court Ladies of Old Japan*. Boston: Houghton Mifflin Co.

Passin, Herbert. 1962. "Sources of Protest in Japan." *American Political Science Review* **56** (June): 391–403.

———. 1966. *Society and Education in Japan*. New York: Teachers' College, Columbia University.

Pharr, Susan J. 1975. *Sex and Politics: Women in Social and Political Movements in Japan*. Unpublished doctoral dissertation, Columbia University.

———. Forthcoming. "The Japanese Woman: Evolving Views of Life and Role." In *Japan—The Paradox of Progress*. Edited by Lewis Austin. New Haven: Yale University Press.

Plath, David W. 1964. *The After Hours: Modern Japan and the Search for Enjoyment*. Berkeley: University of California Press.

Reischauer, Edwin O., and John K. Fairbank. 1958. *East Asia: The Great Tradition*. Boston: Houghton Mifflin Co.

Sakata Yoshio and John W. Hall. 1956. "The Motivation of Political Leadership in the Meiji Restoration." *Journal of Asian Studies* **XVI**: 31–50.

Sano Chie. 1958. *Changing Values of the Japanese Family*. Washington, D.C.: Catholic University of America Press.

Sankei Shimbun. 1972. *Iken to ishiki no hyakkajiten: Sankei shimbun 1000-nin chosa kara* (Encyclopedia of Thought and Opinion: From Sankei Shimbun's Survey of 1000 Persons). Tokyo: Sankei Shimbun.

Sansom, George B. 1960. *A History of Japan to 1334*. Stanford: Stanford University Press.

———. 1943. *A Short Cultural History of Japan*. New York: D. Appleton-Century.

SCAP (Supreme Commander for the Allied Powers) General Headquarters, Government Section, 1949. *Political Reorientation of Japan, September 1945 to September 1948*. 2 Volumes. Washington, D.C.

Sei Shōnagon. 1949. *The Pillow-book of Sei Shōnagon*. Translated by Arthur Waley. London: Allen.

Shibusawa Keizo. 1958. *Japanese Life and Culture in the Meiji Era*. Translated by Charles Terry. Tokyo: Obunsha.

Smith, Thomas C. 1959. *The Agarian Origins of Modern Japan*. Stanford: Stanford University Press.

Stead, Alfred, Editor. 1904. "Women's Education" in *Japan by the Japanese*. London: William Heinemann.

Stoetzel, Jean. 1955. *Without the Chrysanthemum and the Sword: A Study of Attitudes in Post-War Japan*. New York: Columbia University Press.

Sugimoto Etsu Inagaki. 1925. *A Daughter of the Samurai*. New York: Doubleday, Page and Co.

Taira Koji. 1970. *Economic Development and the Labor Market in Japan*. New York: Columbia University Press.

Takemure Itsue. 1966. *Zenshū: Josei no rekishi 1, 2* (Collected Works: History of Women. Parts I and II). Volumes 4 and 5. Tokyo: Rironsha.

Tamura Kenji and Tamura Makie. 1961. *Anata wa dare to kekkon shiteru ka* (Who Is Your Marriage Partner?) Tokyo: Sekkasha.

Tanaka Sumiko and Hidaka Rokuro. 1969. *Fujin seisaki: Fujin undō* (Women's Political Approach: The Women's Movement). Vol. 1 of *Gendai fujin mondai kōza*. 6 Volumes. Tokyo: Aki Shobō.

Tomoda, Yasumasa. 1972. "Educational and Occupational Aspirations of Female Senior High School Students." *Bulletin of the Hiroshima Agricultural College* **4** (3) (December).

Totten, George O., III. 1966. *The Social Democratic Movement in Prewar Japan*. New Haven: Yale University Press.

Tsunoda Ryusaku, W., Theodore de Barry, and Donald Keene. 1958. *Sources of Japanese Tradition*. New York: Columbia University Press.

Tsurumi Kazuko. 1970. *Social Change and the Individual*. Princeton: Princeton University Press.

Uno Riemon, Editor. 1912. *Shokkō mondai shiryō* (Data on the Problems of Factory Operatives). Osaka: Kōgyō Kyōiku-kai.

U. N. Demographic Yearbook. 1967 and 1971. New York.

Vogel, Ezra. 1970. "Beyond Salary: Mamachi Revisited." *Japan Interpreter* **6** (Summer): 105–113.

———. 1961. "The Democratization of Family Relations in Japanese Urban Society." *Asian Survey* **I** (June): 18–24.

———. 1961. "The Go-Between in a Developing Society: The Case of the Japanese Marriage Arranger." *Human Organization* **20:** 112–120.

———. 1963. *Japan's New Middle Class: The Salary Man and His Family in a Tokyo Suburb*. Berkeley: University of California Press.

———, and Susanne H. Vogel. 1961. "Family Security, Personal Immaturity and Emotional Health in a Japanese Sample." *Marriage and Family Living* **23** (May): 161–166.

Wagatsuma Hiroshi and George DeVos. "Attitudes Towards Arranged Marriage in Rural Japan." *Human Organization* **XXI:** 187–200.

Wagatsuma Sakae. 1950. "Democratization of Family Relations in Japan." *Washington Law Review* **25:** 405–426.

Ward, Robert E. 1956. "The Origins of the Present Japanese Constitution." *American Political Science Review* **50:** 980–1010.

———, and Dankwart A. Rustow. 1964. *Political Modernization in Japan and Turkey.* Princeton: Princeton University Press.

Watanuki Joji. 1972. "Social Structure and Political Participation in Japan." *Research Papers of the Institute of International Relations.* Series A-9. Tokyo: Sophia University.

Yamamura Yoshiaki. 1971. *Nihonjin to haha* (The Japanese and Their Mothers). Tōyōhan Shuppansha.

Yanagida Kunio. 1957. *Customs and Manners in the Meiji Period.* Translated by Charles Terry. Tokyo: Obunsha.

Chapter Seven

FRANCE: CONTRASTS IN FAMILIAL AND SOCIETAL ROLES

Catherine Bodard Silver

HISTORICAL AND CULTURAL BACKGROUND

The position of French women in today's society is characterized by surprising contrasts. Women in France today have one of the highest levels of participation in the economy among Western nations, and the proportion of working women who are married is increasingly large. French women have largely succeeded in implanting themselves in the educational and administrative sectors of the nation, roles that in France carry an aura of prestige and authority. In education women have achieved equality of representation with men—at least abstractly defined—since they make up nearly 50 percent of the students in lycées and universities. At the same time French women have maintained the traditional cultural ideals concerning the role of woman as wife and mother. French women do not widely conceive of work as intrinsically liberating, and only reluctantly do they commit themselves to a full professional career. Also they are more likely to experience the complementarity rather than the opposition between the domestic world and the occupational sphere, between the arena of "masculinity" and that of "femininity." These characteristics of French women cannot be understood independently of the forces that have shaped women's role and image in French society.

Historical considerations are primary to an understanding of the legal status and position of women today, for deep-seated continuities in French civilization and legislation render an understanding even of the recent past impossible without taking them into account. The mere fact that France is the oldest territorially organized polity in Europe sets the stage for these continuities; to understand the persistence of key doctrines concerning women's role throughout periods of abrupt or gradual political and economic change, these continuities must be grasped.

In the early Middle Ages, before the collapse of the Frankish state, the family was not so central as it became during the nineteenth century. It was not a major center of loyalties or of the transmission of property. Wife and husband were two independent economic agents managing their property independently and enjoying roughly equal rights as members of a household. Through the work of legal and social historians (Duby, 1953, 1962; Pirenne, 1936; Ariès, 1971) we know that at the beginning of the Middle Ages the family did not play a key role in the life of individuals compared with the roles played by other types of associations such as the guild, compagnonage, parish, and village community.

Duby, in his analysis of the Mâcon region between the ninth and the thirteenth centuries, shows that strong human relationships, blood ties, and links of dependency were not necessary for protection or survival. During that time the family consisted of a very loose network of relationships without strong obligations among family members. The relative weakness of blood ties, a high degree of "diffuse sociability," and restricted obligations went hand in hand with relatively equal status of husband and wife inside the family and with economic independence outside the family. According to Duby this state of affairs was partly accounted for by the power and organization of the Frankish state, which could provide physical and economic security. Similar analyses by Pirenne and Ariès of the relationship between the status of women and the organization of the family suggest that a strengthening of blood ties as a basis of social organization is usually accompanied by a weakening of women's rights and status.

With the collapse of the Frankish state, blood ties took on a new importance as a basis of social organization, primarily through the strengthening of lineal solidarity. At the same time new institutions emerged to replace the weakened state: vassalage, the seigneury, the manor. The feudal and manorial systems, which promoted economic and social ties of mutual dependency, reflected a new need—extending to both noble and peasant groups—for mutual protection and support.

Of course feudalism and manorialism were not exclusively French, but their manifestation in France was stronger and longer lasting than in other Western countries. Just as the Frankish state represented the most developed territorial polity of the epoch, so did its decline stimulate the fullest and most pervasive development of feudal institutions (Bloch, 1939). These deeper and slower rhythms of French history, underlying the manifold course of social change, may help to account for the distinctively long-lasting traditionalism of women's role in France, even as France developed many of the structures of a modern governance, economy, and society.

The strengthening of blood ties led to a new form of property ownership: joint ownership by husband and wife as a means of family protection. Joint ownership became common practice among noble families. From this point on property was managed jointly, buying and selling no longer being done separately by each spouse. As an additional protection of family property, joint ownership was extended to the children, who were thus prevented from obtaining any advance on their inheritance. "There was a prolonged integration in the family home and under the ancestor's authority, of descendants destitute of all personal wealth and of all economic advantages" (cited in Ariès, 1962: 354). This type of joint ownership, described in the institution of the *Frereche*, applied mostly to knightly families. The *Frereche* did not usually last more than two generations, but even after the division of the estate the "line" maintained collective rights over the divided estate (Mousnier, 1975: 52–53). The spread of joint ownership regulated by collective interest was accompanied by a strengthening of male authority, which protected the property of the family as a whole. At the same time the independence of the wife and of the children were correspondingly curtailed. Thus joint ownership had enduring consequences for the organization of the family and the role of the father.

With the security of the state once again achieved under the Capetian kings in the middle of the thirteenth century, the development of new forms of monetary transactions, and the extension of the "personality," the nuclear family once again became independent of larger social units. Families among the nobility, however, never reverted to the loose links of the twelfth century family.* Among the noble and merchant classes the nuclear family maintained and increased the power and the authority of the father. In the Mâcon region the law of primogeniture spread rapidly among noble families, giving the father the right to pass on all family property to his eldest son. The wide acceptance of the law of primogeniture by the nobility sustained paternal authority in dealing with everyday matters and eventually strengthened the relationship between a father and his children. The concentration of authority in the father was accompanied by a gradual decline in the independence of the wife and of the children. The legal rights of the wife were gradually curtailed. During the Middle Ages, however, she never became incapacitated. She could replace the husband in the event of his sickness, madness, desertion, or arrest; she had some control over her own property and was expected to share in the responsibilities of managing the household. She already owed obedience to the head of the household and needed his approval to sign contracts legalizing her own property, but contracts signed without her husband's authority were not considered invalid; they would only take effect after the dissolution of the marriage (Petiot, 1955: 14).

The shift from individual property to joint ownership and to primogeniture is linked to the concentration of power in the father-husband and the weakening of status of the wife-mother. The principle of economic subordination found in the "order of nature" itself a reflection of a divine order based on divine principles. Conservative and reactionary thinkers of the eighteenth and nineteenth centuries used the same idea, reevaluating the function of the family after the collapse of the *ancien régime*. What began as a measure of expediency became a principle of social organization rooted in human nature. Thus although at the beginning of the Middle Ages woman's economic rights put her in a position of domestic equality with her husband in the context of a weak nuclear family, by the end of the Middle Ages the relationship was reversed. She had lost her independence and she owed obedience to the husband. Her status *in the family* would determine the

---

*What we have said of noble families does not apply equally to peasant families. The organization of peasant families in the manor was much looser; the ties between family members were weak and women retained longer their economic and legal independence.

extent of her civil rights and her ability to act as an independent agent *outside the family* (Mousnier, 1975: 149).

It is worth noting that while the status and position of women in the household were gradually being undermined, she took on new attributes in the eyes of men. The *roman courtois* glorified her beauty; she became a subject of adoration for ardent young knights. Chivalrous love became the center of their lives, which had to be devoted, risked, or lost for her own sake and beauty. In the *Roman de la Rose*, Guillaume de Lorris pressed young men to devote their lives to the service of the *dames*. Chivalrous love appeared among nobles at a time when the family was not the center of attachment and loyalty. Love sentiments were not expected from spouses but were present in relationships outside the family.

It was during the sixteenth century that new codes regulating the relationship of spouses and the organization of the family were adopted. These show a real decline in the position of women from that of feudal times—a position that had already eroded but still recognized the married woman as a partner to her husband, *socia mariti,* who had limited rights but was not legally incapacitated. Renaissance legislation left married women with no legal rights. Anything performed by a married woman without the authority of her husband was null. This new legislation was based on Roman laws concerning family organization and on church ideas about the nature of women and the institution of marriage. The combination of canon laws and Christian ideology led to a view of the married woman as incapable, fragile, dangerous, and sinful; marriage was presented as a debased form of association, a concession to the flesh, and an obstacle to sanctity; the family as an institution could only be tolerated on the basis of a principle of subordination, which was to regulate all family relationships. It is thus no surprise to learn that the wife no longer could replace her husband in the household or do anything without his authorization. She was incapacitated, treated as a minor.

These codes were in force during the *ancien régime*. The Revolution of 1789 did not alter them substantially despite the efforts of Condorcet, the representative Cambacères, and Olympe de Gouges to introduce a *déclaration du droit des femmes* (declaration of women's rights). The Revolution of 1789 introduced divorce and put an end to the law of primogeniture. But despite the solidarity between men and women in the fight to overthrow the *ancien régime,* in the name of *liberté, egalité,* and *fraternité,* despite the new universal rank of *citoyen* and *citoyenne,* the position and rights of women in the household were not altered. Married women remained under complete authority of the husband and without legal capacity.

While the legal position of women had deteriorated, their contribution to the development and diffusion of art and science was flourishing (Tuchman, 1975). The role of women as an agent of high culture had been a traditional one in the seventeenth and eighteenth centuries—above all in the famous Parisian salons, which were centers of political, cultural, and intellectual activities. The two centuries that produced the classical culture of France also produced a series of women who were eminent as both sponsors and creators of high culture. Beside such sames as la duchesse de Rambouillet, la marquise de Lafayette, la marquise de Sévigné, Madame de Maintenon, Mademoiselle de Lespinasse, and Madame de Staël, corresponding figures in Anglo-American culture, Jane Austen and Emily Dickinson, for example, are comparatively pale late-comers. French women helped shape the values and language that have become essential to the substance of French culture. Such women, of course, were few and highly privileged, belonging to both the aristocracy and the *haute bourgeoisie,* and all flourished in the setting of an aristocratic social order.

After the Revolution paternal authority was further defined and codified by the Napoleonic Code, published in 1804, which was to determine the status of French women until the twentieth century. The *Code Napoléon* showed continuity with the previous codes. It combined doctrines from Roman law with strong anticlerical feelings and increased even further the concentration of power in the hand of the father. The Napoleonic Code defines the father's roles as head of the household (*chef de famille*) and chief of family property (*chef de la communauté*). These two functions gave him the supreme power in the family. They show very clearly the relationship between material power and power over the lives of others: control over the use and disposal of property on one hand, and control over family members in the household on the other.

The rise of commercial society in the nineteenth century demoted women from the highest reaches of cultural creativity and from their participation as key sponsors of culture. Balzac and Flaubert among others described the emergence of a new type of woman—a highly elaborate aesthetic object, the property of men, seeking expression as wife and mistress. "The destiny of woman and her sole glory," writes Balzac in his *Physiologie du Mariage,* "is to excite the hearts of men. Woman is a property acquired by contract; she is disposable property . . . in short, woman, properly speaking, is only an annex of man" (cited by de Beauvoir, 1949: 187).

Such a family could not function adequately and efficiently unless united and directed by one person and one person only—the father. Under this doctrine the use and management of family property, as well as that of wife and children, contribute to the welfare of the family. The father became solely responsible for the organization of the household and was made the sole repository of family property and values. The education of the children, for example, became his responsibility, especially that of the male children, who would inherit the property and carry on the family name. The Napoleonic Code, seeking to strengthen family continuity, reintroduced differential treatment of children, with the possibility of one-half of the family property being inherited by one child. Only the man, partaking in both the world of work and the world of the family, could bridge the gap between the two and ensure the welfare of the family. Women, especially bourgeois women, were further separated from the world of money and finance, and their domain was increasingly that of the household, where they had little to do and contribute. Until about the middle of the eighteenth century, bourgeois and aristocratic women had little or nothing to do with such matters. On the whole they neither reared children nor administered households; these tasks were discharged by servants, nurses, and tutors under the ultimate direction of the husband. The married woman was left with no legal rights over her own person, property, or children. The husband's decisions about the moral and physical well-being of the family could not be challenged in court, because the wife was treated as a minor with no legal claims.

The Code's anticlericalism did not lead to an abolition of traditional doctrine regarding the family but to a transfer of the burden of its administration from church to state. The state became the regulator of such matters as marriage and family relations. The Civil Code was an attempt to use the family as a new basis for the creation of a stable social order. The Revolution of 1789 had destroyed the aristocracy and weakened the church. These institutions could not serve as a sufficient basis for the Restoration's ideology of social stability. The renewed importance given to the family was a way of compensating for the lack of support from such corporate groups. The family, as organized by the Civil Code, was to ensure the support of the state and the continuity of a stable society.

The Civil Code promoted a form of family organization well suited to the needs of the growing and powerful bourgeoisie. At that time the economy experienced an increased volume of financial transactions, but land and real property were still predominantly in the form of small and medium-size enterprises and landholdings. The family was a major vehicle of capital accumulation and investment. Simultaneously the family became the repository of traditional values in a country still deeply influenced by Catholic ideas, even though secular laws governed family matters. As organized by the Civil Code, the family reflected a new social order in which the structure of law and sentiment corresponded to the family's roles as an economic unit in commercial society and as the moral cell of the social order.

It was in this period that a new image of the role of women was formed, under the pressure of conservative thinkers as well as of the Church. The role of women was upgraded, albeit in the setting of domesticity. She was seen as playing a new and important function in the household as its manager (maîtresse de maison) and as teacher (éducatrice); her teaching of la politesse was seen as most important for the future success of the children in both their career and life.

Older themes portraying woman as an idealized, erotic object finding fulfillment and power over a man through love outside marriage certainly persisted, but more significant by far was the new dominance of the domestic ideal which was associated above all with the most prosperous bourgeoisie. The focus of emotional life became the foyer—an idea for which home is a weaker equivalent. As an arena for women the foyer was focused and restricted, but it should not be considered solely as a decrease of women's power. On the contrary women's enhanced role within the family—the expectation of being loved, some responsibility for the rearing and education of the children—represented a significant improvement. Ironically in view of later developments, among the first conquests and achievements of higher-status women in France was the role of maîtresse de maison.

The attitude of the Catholic Church regarding the family also changed after the Bourbon Restoration. The family and marriage took on more positive features. The family was seen as a unit for the transmittal of religious ideas; it became a source of sanctification and stability. The role of mother was honored and encouraged by the Church. Her role in the family was further enhanced by her role as guardian of religious ideas (Lepatis, 1954). The strong concern of the French Church with the role of family stability and paternal authority reflected its search for new sources of social stability to compensate for the weakening of corporatist structures, civil and clerical, of the ancien régime. This represented a profound reversal of the Church's older attitude toward the family, which saw it as an untrustworthy or refractory partner in the propagation of the faith. This "retraditionalization of the family," in part through renewed religious interest in it, was a feature of Western European life in general in the nineteenth and early twentieth centuries, but it was particularly marked in France (Deniel: 1965). There the Church was continuously confronted by a lay state marked by strong anti-clerical features (Fogarty, 1957).

The new conception of the family was as a key social, moral, and sentimental entity, one in which members could invest their energies, resources, and loyalties. Such a view of the family was for the most part the product of one class, the bourgeoisie, and especially the haute bourgeoisie, who saw the family as the key unit of society, well adapted to promoting both continuity and wealth.

WOMEN, FAMILY AND SOCIETY

The result of this historical development was that womens' position in society-at-large was effectively determined by their position in domestic society. Throughout the nineteenth century a fundamental difference was presented in the civil rights of married and unmarried women. Unmarried women could work, participate in social and political activities, testify as witnesses, own and manage property; married womenn, on the other hand, were considered minors, without legal capacity. This difference reflects a strongly different set of ideas about women and the family. An unmarried woman was treated as an unattached individual whose actions could not jeopardize the family. But a married woman, as a member of a family, could no longer act independently as an individual. The interest of the family as a whole took precedence over her individual rights. The underlying assumption was that the family is a unit under the sole leadership of the husband.

A striking illustration of this difference in concept is seen in the Senate debates on the enfranchisement of women. It was suggested that the vote be given to single women, but not to married women. That is to say, marriage was seen not as a sign of political maturity, but as a reflection of the subordination of the wife to the husband. The assumption was that the husband's vote would represent the family and that the prospect of political disagreement between spouses was subversive of family solidarity and the husband's authority. The vote was given to all women only after World War II, legitimized in part by the heroic roles that women had played in the Resistance.

While the legal status of married women was inferior to that of single women, their social status was superior. Single women in France, their legal rights notwithstanding, were seen as unusual and socially inferior. In the French mind unattached individuals, above all women, are seen as potential sources of instability and disruption. The discrepancy between the legal and social rights of married and single women shows the extent to which the issue of women is not so much one of sex—being a woman—but of family organization.

The legal status of women in France did not change until after World War I, when the integration of bourgeois women into the world of work began. Indeed it was not until 1938 that women began to regain legal capacities that they had lost in the sixteenth century! Legislation enacted that year modified women's legal incapacity and repealed Article 213 of the Civil Code, which stated that the wife owed complete obedience to her husband. She now could appeal in court against her husband's choice of a residence or against his opposition to her taking a job. Nonetheless the husband was still the *chef de famille,* as manifested by the very circumstance that the wife had to have legal recourse to participate in fundamental family decisions with which she did not agree.

Although he could no longer automatically administer his wife's property, the husband was still solely responsible for the material and moral direction of the family as a whole. He alone was responsible for the administration of the family's property and he alone embodied parental authority (Kallai, 1950: 48). A husband was able to decide the fate of his wife and the children, because as chief of the family he was the only one entitled to act in the name of the family's interest. The married woman was, in fact, still unable to oppose her husband's decisions concerning the education of their children and the choice of a residence; the husband's decisions regarding family matters always prevailed in court. The idea of the *interêt de la famille* meant that he had the legal power to override his wife's own interests and desires, the assumption being that he would always act in the family's interest. Changes in women's rights were to a great extent illusory.

Most of the changes introduced in the legal status of married women since the end of the nineteenth century dealt with their relationships to the world *outside* the family. Married women, for example, received the right to keep their own earnings, to have an old age pension, to have separate bank accounts, and to hold separate professional and personal property (Michel and Texier, 1964, Vol. 1: 78). Their position and status *in the family,* however, based on the principle of subordination to the husband in the family's interest, was changed only by legislation enacted in 1970. A law was then passed declaring that the husband was no longer the *chef de la communauté,* and thus his signature was no longer necessary for the wife to buy on credit, to start a new business, to take a job, and to open a bank account. He is no longer the *chef de famille;* now his paternal authority must be shared with the wife on matters of education and management of the household. This law repealed the principle of subordination, and egalitarian ideas, for the first time since the beginning of the Middle Ages, were incorporated into the laws governing the organization of the family. The laws of 1970 are of strategic importance because they touch on what has been for centuries the basis of family organization and functioning.

The ideology of the *femme au foyer* is a complex set of values and attitudes regarding marriage, the role of wife and mother, and the importance of the family in society. It has recently been described in the following way:

The ideology of the "mère au foyer" consists essentially in the enlargement of the role of mother as far as the education of her children is concerned. She is the only one capable of giving them security and affection, indispensable for their balance during the first years as well as during adolescence. At the same time, the mother finds a sense of fulfillment for herself in carrying out this mission [Charzat, 1972: 115].

Although there is no doubt that the ideology of the femme au foyer originated with the bourgeoisie, it nonetheless became a cultural model toward which all classes of society aspire. A 1958 study of working-class women in the Department of the Seine shows that the image of the femme au foyer is accepted as an ideal by working-class women, and thus a conservative attitude regarding the role of women in the home seems to flow from the bourgeoisie to the working class (Grégoire, 1961: 745).

It is important to point out that the French idea of the femme au foyer has a connotation very different from that of the English expression, "A woman's place is in the home." The role of the French woman in the home is primarily that of transmitting social and cultural ideals rather than perform-ing menial chores, which typically were discharged in bourgeois homes with the help of maids and other servants. The role of maîtresse de maison in a bourgeois home presupposes servants. In general, bourgeois women see domestic work as tiring and often involving meaningless tasks, things they do not like to do. Even though it is increasingly difficult to find servants, the percentage of bourgeois homes with servants is still very high.

It should also be noted that a woman's role in the household is seen as complementary—not as inferior—to that of the husband. The family, seen as a key institution able to promote stability and continuity in the social order, is organized around that conception of the role of the woman. The harmony of the couple in the French mind is based on the "complementarity of their roles." The sexual division of labor in the French household implies a clear division between roles and duties outside and inside the home. The author-ity of the father is the center around which the family is organized, but the wife has complete authority in her own sphere inside the household (Zeldin, 1973: 300).

Marriage and married life become comparable to having a career and assume complete devotion on the part of the married woman. She is exempted from any outside activity (Guélaud-Léridon, 1967). The career of married life involves important functions as wife and mother, functions that could not be carried out properly by any other institution. As a wife the woman plays a key role in the advancement and promotion of the husband's work, creating a social life attractive and adequate to the man's occupa-tional status. Above all, however, it is her duty as a mother to which her time and energies are devoted. The socialization and education of the children in the home are central to her life and to that of the family. What the children have to learn from her is immense: modes of life, manners, taste, cultural heritage, morals—in short, *l'éducation et la moralité bourgeoise.*

The importance of children in defining womens' role becomes clearer when we analyze the answers to a question asked in 1956 to a cross section of the French population: "Do you think that married women should stay at home or work?" No difference appeared in the answers of men and women. Three-quarters of both groups thought that the woman should stay at home. Significant differences were found between women with and without children. Among married women without children 68 percent said women ought to work, while among those with one small child 88 percent indicated that women should stay at home (Girard, 1961: 924). The education and socialization of young children take priority over occupational interests and careers.

The higher the social class, the more likely it is that a woman will accept a traditional role as wife and mother. Women from the *haute bourgeoisie* are most likely to have traditional attitudes toward their mission in the house-hold, to give priority not merely to domestic style but to their *career in the home* rather than their occupational *career outside the home.* Even though they are more likely to have pursued advanced studies, they are less likely to have a career than are middle-class women. Bourgeois women need the strong support and encouragement of their husbands to take a job or have a career. In the home a strict division of labor prevails between husband and wife; only rarely does the husband share in the household chores because to do so would be seen as a strong blow to his masculine role. As a corollary, a working woman is seen as a sign of her husband's failure in man's traditional role as sole provider of material support for the family. One of the strongest obstacles to the participation of bourgeois women in the economy comes from the opposition of the husband, who tends to be even more traditional than women of this group and who is less likely to perceive and accept change (Chombart de Lauwe et al., 1963).

Thus the very class whose cultural, economic, and social advantages render many of its women particularly qualified candidates for professional careers is that least disposed to approve and provide for womens' work outside the home (Silver, 1973: 848). The data are striking indeed—perhaps especially to American readers, who are likely to think of higher social status and education as implying greater acceptance of the equality of women. In France the percentage of women who play significant roles in decisions about the family budget is 15 percent among the *haute bourgeoisie,* 53 percent among the *classe moyenne (moyenne* and *petite bourgeoisie*), and 78 percent in the working class (Chombart de Lauwe et al., 1963: 158).

Working-class men are more likely than bourgeois men to help in domestic tasks, since most working-class wives work out of financial necessity and would only stop working if the cost of caring for their children became higher than their wages. Working-class aspirations, however, often include a household in which the woman would not have to work outside the home and could devote all her time to caring for her children and home. Working-class men aspire to see their wives staying at home "like the wives of the bourgeois." The relatively egalitarian organization of the working-class household is more the result of necessity than of an ideology of sexual equality.

WOMEN, EMPLOYMENT, AND THE FRENCH ECONOMY

Despite the presence of a strong familistic orientation in France, the level of women's participation in the economy is and has long been quite high. The proportion of women in the labor force, excluding the rural sector, was 34.8 percent in 1962, 36.1 percent in 1968, and 38.0 percent in 1972 (Annuaire Statistique de la France, 1970: 79; 1973: 64).* The participation of women in the nonagricultural labor force is higher in France than in Italy, Belgium, or England and about equal to that in Germany (Chaton, 1972: 15; "La proportion des femmes parmi les salariés ne cesse de croître," Le Monde, 1973: 22). Moreover the rate of participation of French women—the ratio of the female working population to the total female population—has been constant over the century: about one woman out of three is working. Comparing the female labor force to the *total* working population, we also see stability over the last century: the labor force has remained about one-third female. The stability of female employment demonstrates the continuity of social and economic forces affecting women.

Although the rate of female participation in various occupational sectors has varied over time—decreasing in industry, for example, and increasing in commerce and services—these shifts have reflected gradual changes rather than abrupt breaks. The French occupational and economic structure has shown little discontinuity in the way in which it affects women between traditional nineteenth century and industrialized twentieth century patterns. Despite very different social structures the level of female employment was virtually the same in 1866, 30.8 percent, as in 1962, 32.4 percent (both including the rural sector) (Guélaud-Léridon, 1964: 14).

The continuity in the social and economic forces affecting women's level

---

*All descriptive statistics not otherwise attributed have been drawn from a 5 percent sample of census data.

of participation in the French economy is in part a consequence of the importance of the rural sector, which is stronger in France than in other Western countries. In the rural sector 32 percent of women were working in 1866, as compared to 20.6 percent in 1962* (Guélaud-Léridon, 1964: 14). The French rural sector is characterized by the smallness and often the economic "backwardness" of its enterprises. France is a country of small and medium-size farms, marginally affected by the market economy and in some cases still organized as self-sufficient family units.

In the rural sector, and in farming in particular, the role of the women is essential for the functioning of the farm and the economic survival of the family; the farming woman is a partner to her husband, combining an occupational role with a domestic one. She has always had an important economic function as a producer of goods, and often she has also been in charge of the finances of the rural enterprise. She is essential to the farm as mother, wife, and worker.

The relative importance of the rural sector and the smallness of scale of rural enterprise reflect the fact that France did not experience the impact of the Industrial Revolution to the same extent as did Britain and Germany. In France the Industrial Revolution came more gradually; it did not as quickly destroy the old economic system, and it only slightly altered the social network on which that system was based. Before the rise of industry France had a rural economy based on self-sufficient small farms and an urban economy dominated by small merchants and craftsmen. Industrialization did not drastically change the organization of work, the family structure, or the relationship between country and towns. The Industrial Revolution in France did not involve a heavy concentration of capital and workers, and did not lead to a large-scale migration of rural workers to urban centers, as in England; it did not change the peasants, as a class, into rootless workers. In France, with the exception of a number of large manufacturing towns, most industrialization occurred in small workshops and in small-scale manufacturing enterprises located in the countryside, where a large labor force remained. Rural women were widely employed in such enterprises.

In addition cottage industries persisted in France well into the twentieth century. Men and women produced goods sold on the market either directly or through a merchant who provided them with raw materials and equipment. Since cottage industry was widespread in the rural sector, from which the labor force migrated only slowly, the transition from that form of industry

---

*The relative importance of women in agriculture is underestimated since women are considered active only if they declare that they are working. In the rural population, however, a high proportion of women do not perceive themselves as "workers" and are thus not included in the working population.

to small manufacturing enterprises did not require drastic changes in family organization and traditional values (Scott and Tilly, 1975: 40). When the first workshops and factories opened in the countryside, women quickly found employment in them, thus continuing in a different setting the same patterns of employment that had prevailed in peasant and cottage industry settings. The smallness of the manufacturers and their rural location meant that in most cases family members could continue working together.*

After World War II the decline in the rural population accelerated because of the mechanization of agriculture, the decline of small local industries, the concentration of the service sector in large urban centers, and the increasing difficulty small and medium-size farmers had in competing with larger and more efficient farming enterprises in other Common Market countries. The migration of women from the rural sector to the urban towns is more recent in France than in most Western nations. As late as 1968, 20 percent of the female labor force was in the rural sector, a proportion that had not changed much since the end of World War II; by 1972, however, this figure had dropped to 11 percent. Urban migration, which was once disproportionately masculine, is now a migration of young girls and women, among whom the rates of rural unemployment are highest. The migration of young girls to large towns also reflects aspirations for better marriages and a desire to escape the traditional and often backward style of life in the French countryside (Mendras, 1958).

The persisting location of industry in the countryside explains in part the high percentage of women working in industry, which in the mid-nineteenth century was already 30.6 percent; with industrialization the proportion increased until 1876, when 35 percent of women were working in industry. In 1921 it was still 31.4 percent, declining to 28.5 percent in 1962 and to 24.0 percent in 1972 (Guélaud-Léridon, 1964: 24). It is not widely known that a substantial proportion of women were already working in small-scale industries before the Industrial Revolution. Women formed the majority of workers in distillery, leather, metal, and ceramic work. The percentage of married women who worked in industry was higher at the beginning of the twentieth century than it is now, reflecting the organization of work in small industries, which allowed women to work with their children. In 1906, 20.2 percent of married women had jobs outside of agriculture, compared to 18.7 percent in 1936 (Guilbert, 1966a: 36).

Important changes have occurred in the industries in which women work.

---

*These patterns exemplify those postulated by Habakkuk (1955: 1–12) and Goode (1963: Chapter I), in which the location of industry is a function of family, social, and economic organization, not the other way around.

At the beginning of the twentieth century more than 75 percent of the female labor force was employed in textile and clothing industries, where their jobs were similar to traditional female domestic tasks. In 1962 the proportion of working women in such industries was only 34 percent, although women still comprised 67 percent of all the workers in this sector. The opposite trend holds for women working in the metal industry; although their proportion was very small in 1906, in 1962 it was 24 percent, with women representing 18 percent of that industry's labor force (Guélaud-Léridon, 1964: 24). Between 1906 and 1962 the proportion of women working in industry as a whole decreased, although the decrease in the more traditional industries of textile and clothing was in part compensated for by an increase in more modern types of industry—metalwork requiring precision, chemistry, food industries, and electrical industries. These industries, even though more modern, emphasize aspects of work that could be labeled "feminine"—involving precision and manual dexterity—or cover areas that are still in some ways linked to the household. Such industries have shown a high rate of growth in the last decade. This may explain the increase in the proportion of women in industry since the last census, after a decline of several decades. In 1970–1971 women made up 56 percent of the increase in the labor force working in industry. Between 1962 and 1968 the proportion of women in industry holding purely industrial jobs increased by 3.8 percent ("La proportion des femmes parmi les salariés ne cesse de croître," 1973). The decline of women in industry may be entering a new phase characterized by an increase of women in modern industrial sectors. Such gross trends, however, cannot be interpreted only as indicators of women's integration in the economy. They must also be interpreted as changes in the nature of the demand for kinds of jobs that remain distinctively "feminine."

The proportion of women working in the nonagricultural sectors has increased steadily since the beginning of the twentieth century with the growth of banking bureaucracies, commerce, and state institutions. In 1968 such workers comprised 32.5 percent of the female working population (Annuaire Statistique de la France, 1973: 64). Women in the nonindustrial sectors, however, are very heterogeneous, including professional and managerial, semiprofessional and technical, clerical, service, and household workers. The entry of women in these very different sectors has occurred at widely varying times. The two world wars, especially the first, opened the doors to the daughters of the bourgeoisie, who were able to work in the health department and state bureaucracy. Although during the wars working-class as well as middle-class women entered new areas of work, replacing men in service, after each war middle-class women were to a greater extent able to stay in the state bureaucracies and public institutions, while working-class women were forced back into the home. World War I benefited the women of the bourgeoisie much more than those of the working class.

The extension of the state bureaucracies has meant wider opportunities for bourgeois women to enter the civil service and to secure jobs that have some security and continuity, in addition to being prestigious and patriotic. In 1856 one woman out of five in the labor force was working for the government. Between and after the wars the extension of state-sponsored institutions—in health, social welfare, but above all, in education—enlarged employment opportunities for women. In particular, the existence in France of parallel but separate educational institutions for boys and girls, and the existence among teaching staffs of similar distinctions, has meant that special training schools had to be opened to women, who thus gained the large and important educational field as a source of employment.

The French government has played a very special role in the integration of women, mostly middle-class and bourgeois women, into the economy. This has often meant that qualified women were associated not with the more dynamic aspect of French life—the most modern industrial and professional enterprises—but with the state administration, a typically conservative force. Today, however, changes have occurred. State bureaucracies and public institutions continue to play an important role, but women in positions of high responsibility have been increasingly attracted by the private sector.

In the nonindustrial sector in 1970 women in the professions and in high managerial and administrative positions comprised 3.2 percent of the working female population, while 15.0 percent were in the *cadres moyens* (technicians, semiprofessionals, elementary schoolteachers, among others). The annual increases of women in these two categories have been among the highest, 4.1 percent and 7.9 percent, respectively (*Economie et Statistique,* 1972: 7). The proportion of women among the *cadres moyens* is quite high, 40.0 percent, compared to 16.0 percent among the *cadres supérieurs* (high managerial and administrative positions) and the professions. The changing role of women in France is especially felt through their participation in the *cadres moyens,* holding jobs that require professional training and responsibilities. Women have succeeded in integrating themselves into an important sector of the economy, where they share in about equal proportion with men increasingly important and dynamic positions. In a society oriented toward a service economy and a welfare state, the *cadres moyens* are certain to play a new and dynamic role, especially through the extension of social and economic planning and the involvement of the state in modern economic and social sectors.

The importance of the proportion of women among the *cadres moyens* should not obscure some trends in the participation of males in semiprofessions traditionally described as "feminine." In the last decades there has been a gradual increase in the ratio of male participation in several of these sectors. Because of the increasingly difficult economic situation and stronger competition for trained positions, fields such as librarianship, nursing, and education are slowly losing their all-female character.

The largest occupational group in the nonindustrial sector, however, is composed of unskilled and untrained women working as clerical and sales workers. This group in 1972 represented 30.2 percent of the female working population. With the larger importance of service-producing industries in the economy, this group has increased constantly since the beginning of the century, and today it is 60 percent female (Hugues and Peslier, 1969: 31).

Since 1971 women have constituted more than 75 percent of the increase in the working population. Women's work is increasingly seen as a normal state of affairs by private and public institutions, necessary for the achievement of a higher standard of living by an increasing number of French people.

The general level of the female working population has been stable for some time, but there have been important changes in the ages of females in the labor force. The rate of participation of women varies by age group.* It is lower for younger women (below the age of 19) and for older women (60 years old and above). The rate of participation is highest between ages 20 and 25 and between 45 and 60; it is lowest between ages 30 and 35, the time when a woman is most likely to have young children at home. The rate of female participation since the beginning of the century has *decreased* for women between 30 and 35 years old. Whereas 529 out of 1000 women between these ages were employed in 1906, only 385 were in 1962. At the same time the rates of participation of younger women and of women of age 45 and older have *increased* since the beginning of the century. Today more women work before their children are born and after they have grown up (Guélaud-Léridon, 1964: 17). Thus the trend in the participation rate of women in the economy seems to demonstrate the desire of French women to combine at different points in their life cycles the domestic role, especially the rearing of children, with an occupational commitment. The strong orientation toward the family in France thus does not appear to be a continuing obstacle to the participation of women in the economy.

A key element in the rate of participation of women in the economy is not marital status but the presence of children in a family. France has long been characterized by a high and increasing percentage of married women working. It is having children that changes the organization of the household, the

*The rate of participation by age group is the proportion of the working female population to the total female population in each age group.

allocation of time, the priorities. In 1962, 76 percent of married women in the labor force had no children below the age of 16, 13 percent had one child, and 10 percent had two children. The census of 1968 showed that 75 percent of married women without children were working. Among married women with one child 51 percent work; among married women with three children only 12 percent work (Chaton, 1972: 27). The presence of small children in the home is the strongest factor in keeping the mother out of the labor force. Although there are class differences—bourgeois women are more likely to stay at home with young children than middle-class or lower-class women—we find similar patterns in all classes.

It was in response to the needs of working mothers that several institutions were created to care for children. Among them are *pouponières, crèches,* and *garderies d' enfants* for children below three years old; *maternelles* and *jardins d' enfants* for children between three and six years of age. Although the types and number of institutions may look impressive, they are quite inadequate for the needs of working mothers. The ideology of social responsibility for motherhood is not sustained by sufficient resources. For example, in 1964 there were three available spaces for children in a *crèche* for 1000 working mothers. Only half of the children between the ages of three and six can be accepted in a preschool program (Guélaud-Léridon, 1967: 117). Most of these child-care institutions are paid for by public funds, usually collected at the local level; 67 percent of the institutions enumerated are state-sponsored, 24.5 percent are privately sponsored, and 7.5 percent are sponsored by private businesses and enterprises. The facilities mentioned vary as to the age of the children they care for and the quality of the education they provide. The *maternelles* have been especially successful in trying to be something more than custodial agencies. Most of these institutions, however, especially the *crèches*, tend to be used by working-class mothers only and are never seen as the best way of looking after children.

The high level of participation of married women in the economy can be further explained by the existence of an elaborate Code of Work. One of the earliest and most advanced in Europe, this code regulates and organizes women's work. Measures regarding maternity were accepted as early as 1936 in the Accords Matignon,* which initiated a series of measures and created a labor code to deal with these questions. Under pressure from the unions, motherhood was acknowledged as a social function, similar to the military service for men, that had to be financially supported by the whole community. The Labor Code is one of the most advanced in Europe regarding the treatment of pregnant women. An employer, for example, may not

*The Accords Matignon were the first agreements between the French state and unions regarding working conditions and levels of wages.

require a woman to work for 14 weeks before birth and may not break a contract for 6 weeks before and after birth. Pregnant women are given 8 weeks of paid leave. After giving birth, the working mother must be rehired without penalty. She is allowed to feed the child for an hour a day during the first year and must be given easier tasks without a change in her wages. More extensive maternity and motherhood benefits were included in collective bargaining contracts between employers and unions at the national and local levels. Above all the pregnant woman must not be given lower wages when she stops working, and often she receives partial or total reimbursement for the 14 weeks during which she is unable to work (Vieille-Michel, 1961: 875; Michel and Texier, 1964: 169). Thus in France working-class women have been encouraged to work through the extension of state institutions to take care of their children and through the far-reaching Code of Work, which acknowledges the social function of motherhood. These measures, however, reflect more the concerns of the unions and the state than an ideology stemming from women's desire for self-actualization or fulfillment through work.

Even though women, especially working-class women, are encouraged to work, they are far from equal to men in the wages they receive. Until 1935 women's wages were about one-half those of men. The Accords Matignon reduced the difference to 15 percent. Despite the Constitutions of 1946 and 1958, the convention of the International Bureau of Labor, ratified by France in 1952, and the laws of 1971 on collective contracts, the differences in the wages received by men and women still persist. These differences are greater among nonindustrial than among industrial workers (Michel and Texier, 1964: 150–151). In 1972, among professionals, high administrators, and managers the difference between the sexes in annual income was 34 percent, among semiprofessionals and technicians it was 26 percent, and among service workers 33 percent. Differences in earnings are further increased by state regulations that prohibit women to work overtime or at night (Roy, 1972: 15–17). Once again the wage differential between men and women points to the compensatory nature of women's work. The classic example, of course, comes from the war experience, at which time women's wages very closely approached men's, only to drop drastically after the war in order to minimize the competition between the sexes and to ensure women's return to the home.

In recent years the number of women looking for jobs has increased. In 1971 the proportion of women looking for jobs was double that of men, and the annual increase in the population looking for work between 1970 and 1971 was greater for women than for men (*Economie et Statistique*, 1972: 4). The increase of women looking for jobs is reflected in an increase in the unemployment rates of women. Changes and variations in the economy affect women and young people first. The level of unemployment among women in the last five years has been one of the highest. The way in which female labor has been used in the past and is still being used today reflects its compensatory nature in an increasingly dual economy. One sector of the economy, the stable working class, is protected by the unions and collective contracts. The other, comprising women, foreign labor, and the young, have little guarantee of stability and lack support from organized and powerful unions; it is this group who must compensate for variations in the state of the economy.

FRENCH WOMEN AND THE EDUCATIONAL SYSTEM

The high level of participation by French women in the economy is not in itself a measure of their accomplishments, since women are concentrated in unskilled and semiskilled industrial jobs and in middle-range positions in the public and private sectors. In any case understanding the position of women in the economy requires analyzing their participation in the educational system. Education is a prerequisite for any skilled job, and higher education is a necessity for entry into the professions.

The link between the educational system and the occupational world is a weak one in the case of French women. Education for most women—bourgeois as well as working-class women—is not primarily a step toward a job or a career. Time spent in educational institutions is more likely to prepare women for their future career *in the home* as wives and mothers than to train them in manual trades or professional occupations (Guélaud-Léridon, 1964: 61). Most bourgeois women go to the university to receive an education that is seen as necessary to a bourgeois way of life, that is, consistent with the traditional family structure. Knowledge of high culture—classical culture, language, and increasingly some knowledge of the social sciences—is perceived as a good preparation for a woman's future in the household. Thus while the bourgeoisie see higher education as a prerequisite for becoming a good wife and mother, the lower classes view the learning of household tasks in the schools as an important condition for the same end.

Access to education for women dates from the Third Republic, when, in 1880, efforts by Victor Duruy and Camille Sée led to the first system of public secondary education for women. This development was strongly opposed by the Catholic clergy, who stood to lose their monopoly over the education of women, which of course was religiously centered. The first *lycée, Lycée Fénelon,* was opened in 1883, followed by several others in the capital and in major urban centers. The clientele of such institutions were, of course, the daughters of the bourgeoisie, who were prompt to take advantage of this new opportunity. The *lycées* for women were not perceived as a threat to women's traditional positions or duties. On the contrary the bourgeoisie—emphasizing the acquisition of cultural values and classical culture—saw it as quite appropriate that their girls, before marriage, be taught the "French heritage."

For some time there existed two different systems of education for males and females. The *lycées* for women did not teach the same subjects as did those for men—there was less emphasis on science and little Latin. Despite the French taste for uniformity in intellectual matters, only in 1924 were the two curricula standardized. The creation of a separate set of secondary institutions for the education of girls had a further consequence—the need for a large number of women teachers. Bourgeois parents were not willing to permit their daughters to be taught by men, and as a consequence the first women's teachers' college, the Ecole Nationale de Sèvres, was opened in 1881. It remains one of the most famous women's teacher training schools. The creation of separate public education brought with it the opportunity for women in large numbers to enter the very prestigious occupation of *lycée professeur,* of whom 55 percent were women in the 1969–1970 school year. In all 17,037 women were *lycée professeurs,* constituting fully one-quarter of all women in the *cadres supérieures* (Chaton, 1972: 10). It is important to add, however, that most of the higher administrative positions within *lycées* are held by men.

Because a high proportion of elementary school teachers are women, the *écoles d'instituteurs* are also important. In 1962, 72 percent of such teachers were women (Ministère de l'Education Nationale, 1968–1969). Although certainly a high proportion, this figure is lower than the comparable figure in the United States, which is 90 percent. This difference suggests the higher status of elementary school teachers in France. As representatives of culture in a society that regards its culture as a national treasure, *instituteurs* have high prestige, especially in rural communes and small towns and villages. The *école d'instituteurs,* in addition to training elementary school teachers, also trains teachers to work in the *maternelles.* The teachers in the *écoles maternelles* are required to achieve the same educational level as *instituteurs,* and many have begun advanced studies (Berger and Benjamin, 1964; Berger, 1959).

Thus women participate heavily at all levels of the public teachers' training institutions. The *lycées* especially, which are sexually segregated both as to students and teaching staff, have offered women an entrée to prestigious and important positions among French professionals. The structure of education is especially important for the pattern of professional opportunities for women in France because the state educational system forms so high a proportion of professional opportunities, far more so than in the United States. Teachers' training in the *écoles normales supérieures* and in the *écoles d'instituteurs* has been a vehicle of social mobility for middle- and lower-class children, who have a much smaller chance of going through the regular channels of the university. Thus the French educational system has provided women with a great opportunity for advancement.

Lycée students themselves are in great majority the children of the bourgeoisie. Today 82 percent of the children of the bourgeoisie attend *lycées,* where the quality of education is generally higher than that offered by private schools, which are largely under religious auspices. The university, to a lesser extent than the *lycée,* caters to the children of the bourgeoisie. Indeed access to higher education in France is heavily a function of class inequality. In 1962 the *grande bourgeoisie* represented 4 percent of the total population but 29 percent of university students; the *cadres moyens* amounted to 7.8 percent of the population but 18 percent of the students; workers amounted to 38 percent of the population but only 6 percent of university students (Organisation de la Coopération et du Développement Economique, 1965: 292). Among women university students the proportion having a bourgeois origin is higher than among men. Thus higher education in France acts to consolidate the class position of the bourgeoisie more often among women than among men (Bourdieu and Passeron, 1964). The daughters of the bourgeoisie are more likely to go to universities than are the sons of nonmanual workers, let alone those of manual workers.

The distribution of women in the various disciplines shows that women are more likely to be found in the more traditionally "feminine" fields. In 1970, 60 percent of the students in the *facultés de lettres* (humanities, languages, and social sciences) were women compared to 58 percent in pharmacy, 32 percent in the sciences, 29 percent in law, and 16 percent in technical institutions. In the last five years the strongest increases in women's enrollment have occurred in pharmacy, law, and science. The increase in these less traditional fields reflects an increase in the university enrollment of children coming from the *cadres moyens* and lower classes. These students tend to enter scientific fields, while those from the bourgeoisie are more likely to enter law and the humanities.

The concentration of women in humanities and languages reflects the attitude of bourgeois women toward university education. We have noted that higher education and university training are not necessarily linked in women's minds to the idea of a career or of a vocation. This is shown very clearly by a 1969 study by the Association des Femmes Diplomées de l'Université on the role of higher education in the lives and careers of women. This study found that women who received university degrees believe that their attitudes toward marriage have changed. They take more time to choose their mate and are more confident about choosing to remain single. The more striking result, however, is that university degrees do not seem to affect their commitment to professional life or their attitude toward work. Women with degrees feel that university education helps them become a better *maîtresse de maison,* more efficient in the organization of the household and more capable of combining their domestic and occupational roles. The great benefit they experience is more a psychological satisfaction for having succeeded in obtaining a degree—acquiring in the process a better sense of personal organization and a greater self-confidence—than a sense of commitment to a career ("Les diplômes constituent-ils un facteur décisif d'intégration des femmes dans la vie contemporaine?" 1969: 12).

Women's participation in the *grandes écoles* is still very small. The *grandes écoles,* which are entered only after strenuous competition (*le concours*), are the prestigious French public institutions of higher education. They prepare the nation's elite for the highest positions of responsibility in military establishments, public offices in the ministries, and more generally for high positions of authority in the civil service, private bureaucracies, and industries. Until the last decade the *grandes écoles* were closed to women. The entry of women into the prestigious Ecole Nationale d'Administration dates only from 1970.

Some of the highly prestigious technical schools have only a token number of women students. For example, in *Central* and *Sub-de-Co,* two prestigious schools for engineers, 0.57 percent of the students are women; the number is less than 1 percent in the Ecole Supérieure d'Aéronautique, 3 percent in the School of Engineers, and 1 percent in the Ecole Supérieure d'Electricité. Only in the School of Chemistry do we find a higher proportion of women—20 percent in the Ecole de Chimie de Paris—but chemistry has long been a relatively "feminine" field.

In some of the *grandes écoles* the resistance to the entry of women was strongest among male students and faculty, a fact that led to the creation of separate institutions or programs for women. For example, the business school, Haute Etudes Commerciales, opened a branch for women in the hope of preserving the quality of education and the prestige of the diploma. Women who enter Hautes Etudes Commerciales pour Jeunes Filles (H.E.C.J.F.), are less likely to find jobs than men; their diploma, in theory equal, is not treated as such by public and private employers. Many women are employed in positions far below those corresponding to their qualifications. In France a pattern seems to emerge of creating separate programs for men and women to preserve the "quality" of male education.

The low level of participation of women in the professions and professional schools contrasts with their high level of participation in public administration. The high qualifications required and associated prestige of public administration in France lend it both the aura and substance of a professional career. Women first entered the ministries between the world wars, but only after 1945 were the highest administrative positions made accessible to them. As of 1962, 11.2 percent of the highest administrative positions—such as finance inspectors, members of the *Conseil d'Etat*—were held by women. The major significance of public administration lies in the *cadres moyens,* which in 1962 embraced 79,060 women and 168,700 men. Nonetheless whole ministries—Justice, Foreign Affairs, and Finance—have very few women in positions of high responsibility, and admission to some administrative careers remains formally closed. Women are still formally barred from the office of *préfet,* the extremely important representative of central government in the *départements* into which France is administratively divided. Women are wholly excluded from the *Ecoles des Mines, Ecoles du Génie Rural,* and the *Ecoles des Eaux et Forêts.* On the other hand their presence at responsible levels is significant in the Ministries of Education, Health and Labor.

Women's attempt to find work situations with which they can reconcile their domestic roles, combined with their proportions in the universities, may explain their relatively good position in the academic world. As we would expect, the proportion of full professors is very small—1.1 percent in law schools, 1.8 percent in medical schools, 3.7 percent in pharmacy, and 4 percent in the humanities. However below the professional rank, at instructional levels equivalent in rights and relative compensation to a rank below associate and assistant professor in the American system, the proportion of women jumps to 22 percent in law schools, 31 percent in medicine and pharmacy, 25 percent in the humanities, and 35 percent in the *facultés de lettres* (Michel and Texier, 1964: 163).

In addition to the *lycée* educational system, which prepares students for entry into the universities and professional schools, there exists a parallel system of education geared toward the lower middle class and the working class, a system that reflects and helps perpetuate class differences. This system of general and technical education has little prestige and recognition, and in no case does it open the doors of the university.

While France has been one of the most egalitarian countries regarding the entry of women into the *lycée* and university, the greatest inequality is found in the *collèges techniques* and *centres d'apprentissage.* In 1970–1971, 51.5 percent of the students in *lycées* were women, and about the same ratio is found at the university level, not counting the *grandes écoles.* In the technical schools, however, only 25 percent of the students in the *collèges techniques* and 37 percent of those in the *centres d'apprentissage* were women (Hugues and Peslier, 1969: 68). The greatest educational inequality between men and women is found in the working class, as seen especially in the technical schools. Women and girls in industry, as already noted, make up about 28 percent of the employed female labor force, but are characterized by a low level of qualification and consequently are more likely to receive lower wages. The lack of qualification in industrial skills reflects the lack of adequate technical education, especially for women; the existing system of education directs women toward skills that they will not use or that are not in demand.

Institutions that prepare women to enter the industrial world are very limited. In the technical schools men are allowed to learn more than 390 skills and trades, but women are limited to a choice of only 171. The technical education of women often teaches them skills that are of decreasing importance in industry. In the *centres d'apprentissage* 92.2 percent of women receive technical certification for sewing, although they form only 22 percent of the female labor force in the clothing industry (Isambert-Jamati, 1961: 910). Only 0.8 percent of women are trained in purely technical and industrial skills, but they form 15 percent of the female working population in the metal industry. Thus the educational and employment situation among working-class women is much worse than among those of the middle class and the bourgeoisie. While bourgeois women are, if anything, overeducated and overprofessionalized, working-class women show a lack of technical training, education, and skills that constitutes one of the strongest barriers to their achieving higher levels of qualification and equality with men.

In recent years considerable attention has been paid to the university system as a means of increasing social mobility and promoting equality. The university system, however, mainly serves the children of the upper and lower bourgeoisie, and it is the latter group that has benefited in recent years (Boudon, 1973). Fiscal difficulties and concern about overproduction of university-educated people may in fact lead to a decline of the university population. Moreover, as we have seen, the way in which bourgeois women use the university reinforces many traditional patterns of domesticity. Crucial areas for progress lie in the entry of women into the private professions and business—a much-neglected topic—and in the provision of skilled training to the large number of women in industry. Professions and businesses, of course, are expanding areas in a modern economy, and there at least an opportunity structure exists for the entry of the large numbers of educated women who are admitted to the universities, if not to many specialized faculties and the *grandes écoles*. It remains to be seen, however, whether the prospect of a new stratum of skilled women workers in industry would lead to a change in the severe scarcity of such positions. Moreover there is little in the ideology of the unions or of the culture of the working class to provide encouragement for such developments. Yet the disparity between the sexes in training and in occupational levels of qualification is greatest in the sector for which the least concern has been voiced: the industrial working class.

WOMEN, FAMILY PLANNING, AND BIRTH CONTROL

It is perhaps in the area of birth control and family planning that the French government and French women have shown the strongest resistance to change. It was not until 1967—much later than was the case in other countries—that contraceptives were freely and widely available in France. And it was not until December 1974 that the French National Assembly legalized abortion, thus creating for the first time the precondition for emancipation for millions of women and acknowledging the idea professed by Simone de Beauvoir more than 10 years earlier: "La liberté de la femme commence au ventre" (Women's freedom starts in the belly) (Weill-Hallée, 1960: 153).

That it took so long for the French nation to acknowledge the sexual rights of women was caused by a complex of attitudes, including a concern with declining birthrates, the doctrine of the Catholic Church and its impact on the laity, the lack of an organized position on the part of the political parties, the general traditional and conservative nature of the French population, especially in rural communes, the attitude of the government, and—reflecting all of these factors—the nature of the laws defining and regulating family relationships.

Since the end of the eighteenth century France experienced a slow but continuing decline in the birthrate, which abruptly decreased in the second half of the nineteenth century. Declining birthrates were a result of changes in the nation's social and economic structures, as well as a reflection of a change in attitudes toward sexual relationships. A distinction began to be made between sexuality and procreation. The bourgeoisie was the first group to limit the size of the family as well as to introduce new attitudes between spouses regarding sexual relations and a stronger attachment toward children. The bourgeoisie seems to have introduced more rational and methodical forms of behavior in all forms of interaction and management, including family relationships.

The tendency of the bourgeoisie to reduce the size of the family also reflected economic concerns. Since the family had become the center of economic as well as emotional life, the father was concerned with using it to transmit property to his male child. What the father wanted was not a large family, but a small one with at least one son who would continue the father's lifework. For the first time in history, economic, social, and emotional factors converged to create the necessary conditions for smaller families.

There were important differences between the social classes regarding the attitude toward sexuality and the organization of the family. The working class was less strict than the bourgeoisie and more likely to put a new emphasis on the conjugal relationship rather than on the parent–child relationship (Shorter, 1973). By the end of the nineteenth century the bourgeois morality had become a model followed to varying degrees by all classes of society. It consisted of a set of rules of social conduct and a certain ideology concerning sexuality (Barber, 1955). A striking feature of this morality was the double standard regarding sexuality for males and females, a standard that was applied to both spouses and children.

The conditions under which adultery was punishable and the sanctions imposed were different for men and women.* What was permissible sexual behavior for a man has been different from what was permissible for a woman. While men have been expected to learn about sexual life before marriage, chastity has been highly valued for women; while men have been using contraceptives for some time without exciting the opposition of the Church or the public powers, the thought of women using contraceptives has caused a different reaction. In the case of the male the role of neither the male nor the family was endangered. In the case of women sexual freedom was perceived as going against her own "nature" and was seen as dangerous for both the institution of the family and her position of subordination within it. It was not until her position in the family was altered that she could easily gain equal access to methods of birth control and thus obtain power over her own body. Historically the French woman regained her power and independence over her personal wealth, property, and children before she could succeed in regaining power over her body. The laws of 1970 regarding the legal status of women in the household, which brought back some equality between the spouses and abolished the concept of the man as *chef de famille*, led to the possibility of a woman exercising rights over her sexual life.

While the bourgeoisie was promoting economic Malthusianism at the level of the family, the Church was encouraging moral Malthusianism. It would be a mistake, however, to assume that the Church has always encouraged large families. For a long time the Church was not centrally concerned with the declining birthrate. It was not until the period between the two world wars that the Church took an active interest in promoting large

---

*The laws of adultery in the Civil Code show how the bourgeois morality used different standards for men and women. Although men could be found guilty of adultery only in their own home, wives could be sanctioned severely under any circumstances.

Catholic families. The encyclical of Pope Pius XI concerning the sanctity of marriage established the large family as a religious duty, and large families became a sign of religious fervor and commitment.

To some extent during the period between the two world wars, but expecially after World War II, the government adopted a series of regulations and policies designed to increase the declining birthrate. The old nineteenth century idea of the political economists that the power of a nation is measured by the size of its population was promoted in France well into the twentieth century. We have only to remember the remark made by Charles de Gaulle, who envisioned a France with 100 million Frenchmen in the year 2000! The policies of the government created a new ideology about population growth. It became patriotic to have large families, since the nation needed an expanding population to regain its power in Europe and to guard against attack from the enemy. Thus any use of birth control measures could be interpreted as an attack on the collective goal of the nation, whose interest would not be well served by strong individualistic interest centered around small families. It was no longer enough for the family to be a source of stability; the family—the large family—had to play a key role in the rebuilding of the French nation.

After World War II several policies were implemented for the purpose of increasing the birthrate among the French population. These included monetary allowances for families of at least three children, in which the family received a monthly allowance for each child until his or her majority. The larger the family, the greater was the allowance per child. This measure, known as *allocations de familles nombreuses,* applied to all families, whatever their income. Housing policies were also designed to encourage large families. The creation of housing complexes to provide young married couples with apartments and the *allocation logement,* a system of government financial assistance to young couples to rent or to buy apartments, were intended to create better conditions in which to raise families. The government established an allowance called the *salaire unique* for nonworking mothers who stayed at home looking after their children, an allowance that was intended to compensate for the wife's foregone income. This policy was designed both to encourage large families and to persuade mothers to stay at home. The cost of keeping women at home was lower than that of creating child care facilities, training teachers, and paying administrators to run them.

Government policies aimed at rewarding large families were related to government attitudes toward birth control and family planning. France is one of the few countries in Western Europe that has consistently officially opposed the dissemination of modern contraceptive methods, even though, as we noted before, contraception has been widely practiced in the form of abstinence and coitus interruptus.

The law that until recently regulated the use and distribution of contraceptives was passed in 1920. It punished the distributors of either contraceptives or information about their use, expressly forbade the labeling of contraceptives as such, and allowed their sale only under very strict medical conditions. Performing an abortion or providing information about abortion to a pregnant woman was until recently a crime that was severely punished. Article 317 of the Penal Code imposed imprisonment of 5 to 10 years on both those who assisted in obtaining an abortion and those who sought assistance; usually the sentence has been greater for those who helped than for those who sought help.

The attitudes of the state and the Catholic Church against abortion fed on each other. The Catholic Church has always been opposed to abortion under any circumstances, on the theory that the fetus has a soul and that an abortion is the killing of an unbaptized child who is thus condemned to hell for eternity. If it became necessary to choose between saving the life of the child or that of the mother, the child's life was always given priority because the mother was already baptized while the child was not. The horror of abortion was met by the severity of the punishment: excommunication from the Church for both the mother and her accomplices. The Church remains opposed to abortion, but since 1973 has become somewhat more flexible regarding certain forms of birth control. In a strongly Catholic country where social and economic changes have occurred quickly, it is possible to imagine the strains and stresses among the many believing Catholics who may desire or need to use modern contraceptive methods, despite the official opposition of the Church. These stresses are more likely to be found among bourgeois women, since the interaction between religious values and family ideologies is greatest among the bourgeoisie.

A 1962 study of a group of professional women and wives of professionals showed that most were quite conservative on matters related to sexual activities, birth control, and abortion. To a question about whether or not they thought girls ought to remain virgins until their marriage, 60 percent replied that they should. Regarding contraceptive devices, most of these women were opposed to their use. To the question, "Do you think that abortion is a homicide?" 66 percent of the women answered "yes," but at the same time they thought that abortion should be legalized for difficult medical and social cases (Andrieux, 1962: 360–61).

In 1970 only 6 percent of French women were using contraceptive pills, compared to 46 percent in England. The IUD has only been legally allowed since 1967. In 1963 two women out of three did not use any modern contraceptive devices (Michel and Texier, 1964: Vol. 2, 152).

Modern contraceptive devices are more likely to be used among other classes of society, especially the *classes moyennes,* than among bourgeois women. The bourgeoisie, together with peasants, laborers, and unskilled workers, is the group with the highest number of children. The *classes moyennes* have the smallest families of all, along with the group of small property owners.

The problems of birth control and abortion have not been items on the French political agenda, and this has been true for all parties, from Conservatives to Communists. The Socialist and the Communist parties did not support women's fight for the free distribution of contraceptives and for legalized abortion until 1973, despite both parties' theoretical commitment to the "liberation of women," as part of the larger liberation of all workers from bourgeois ideologies.

In 1967 a first step toward liberalization of birth control policies was taken with the passage in the National Assembly of the *loi Neuwirth,* which annulled the previous law of 1920. From then on contraceptives could be labeled as such, bought in pharmacies with a doctor's prescription, and made available to adolescents under 18 with authorization of the parents. The distribution of information about contraception was no longer a crime. Abortion, however, was still considered a crime and severely punished. The Church, the public powers, and the political parties all were against abortion.

The struggle to liberalize birth control policies started in France with the *mouvement du planning familial,* which first attempted to disseminate ideas and methods of birth control in 1961. The movement was condemned as illegal until 1967; even in 1972 it was not accepted as an Institution of Public Interest, a legal status that would allow it to receive help and subsidies from the Ministry of Health. The strength of the *planning familial* movement spread rapidly, however, and it soon began giving advice and performing illegal abortions throughout France. The creation in 1973 of a *Conseil National Supérieur de l'Information Sexuelle, de la Régulation des Naissances et de l'Education Familiale* was a turning point in the attitudes of both professional groups and political parties. The issue could no longer be avoided and had to be openly discussed. The support of the leftist parties in the Assembly made it possible to present a law legalizing abortion, but this advancement materialized only because small and militant groups of women and professionals (doctors and lawyers) brought the issue into the public forum. The pressure they exerted on the political parties and on public opinion was largely responsible for the successful passage of a liberalized abortion law in December 1974 after long months of heated debate. The Minister of Health, Mme. Simone Veil, presented and strongly supported the law at the Assembly, where it received a large majority of votes despite strong opposition from the conservative parties and from the Church.

In 1974 French women had achieved a great victory, only four years after they had regained their power in the home. Despite the acceleration of

changes concerning the status of women, and the far-reaching consequences these changes may have, a large proportion of the French remain
very conservative in these matters, and the decision of the Assembly in some
ways does not reflect the spirit of the nation. In 1974 French women had
regained most of the basic rights already granted to men. In a country that
praises itself for its universalism and rationality it remains to be seen to what
extent such far-reaching changes will affect the status and position both of
women and of a whole country engaged in a new process of modernization,
expansion, and self-scrutiny.

WOMEN AND POLITICAL PARTICIPATION IN FRANCE

In France, as in several so-called Latin countries, politics and political
participation are perceived as exclusively masculine domains. This ex-
clusionary attitude toward the role of women in politics covers a complex
set of values, among them the acceptance of an idea of femininity based on
specific physiological and psychological attributes, the definition of the role
of motherhood, and the acceptance of the family as the basic and most
important unit through which to promote social stability.

These ideas were widespread in nineteenth century France among conservatives and radicals alike. Bonald, one of the most influential conservative social thinkers of the period, had the following to say about the proper
relationship (or lack thereof) between women and politics: "Women belong
to the family and not to the political society; nature has made them for
domestic chores and not for public functions" (cited in de Beauvoir, 1949:
186). At the other end of the political spectrum Proudhon, perhaps the most
indigenously French founder of the European Left, was an equally fervent
misogynist. Even among some of the early supporters of women's cause,
such as the Fourierists and the St. Simonians, women were never acknowledged as having a potential function as political agents. For them women
had moral qualities that were much superior to those of men but incompatible with politics (Maitron, 1954: 84 ff.).

Politics, of course, take place in the public arena outside the home. The
exposure to forces outside the family was seen as a direct threat to a
woman's functioning in the home. Between the world wars such ideas were
still being expressed in the debates that took place regarding whether to
grant women the vote. Among the reasons put forward for not giving the vote
to women were the following: the influence of the Church is too great on
women (a reason given by radicals and left deputies); there is a basic
incompatibility between political life and women's mission in the home;
women's nature is not suited for political activities; women do not have
enough political maturity, and their political participation may introduce

conflict in the family; women are not interested in politics (Dogan and Narbonne, 1955: 11–14).

The strongest consequence of the entry of women into the political arena in 1946 through their vote and their participation in elected bodies was the introduction of a conservative force that in some ways has been an obstacle to the advancement of feminist ideas. Such a consequence of women's participation in the political process had not been clearly anticipated by the nation itself and even less so by the deputies debating the question. Women as voters have been more likely than men to support conservative and moderate, rather than leftist and liberal, candidates for office. In the presidential election of 1965, when François Mitterand, a leftist candidate, was running against the incumbent, Charles de Gaulle, the support of women enabled de Gaulle to win the election by a small margin. A study conducted by *Information Française d'Opinion Publique* (IFOP) just before the second round of that election showed that 52 percent of the men and 38 percent of the women supported Mitterand, while 48 percent of the men and 62 percent of the women supported de Gaulle.

It would be inaccurate to say that women have no influence in the political life of the country, but their strongest impact is felt in elected positions held by women at the local level of the *commune,* the smallest administrative unit in France. At the national level women are barely represented. In 1968, for example, 2 percent of the members of the National Assembly were women. Their number has decreased since 1946, the year they were given the vote, when there were 40 women at the Bourbon Palace. In 1951 there were 23 women in the National Assembly compared to 19 in 1956, 6 in 1958, 8 in 1962, and 10 in 1972. The tiny minority of women at the national level are most likely to represent socialist and communist groups. In 1946, 40 percent of the women in the National Assembly belonged to the Communist Party.

At the local level, however, the role of elected women and their social and political roots are very different. Whereas men see election at the local level as a first step toward election at the national level, women see their participation at the local level as an end in itself, as something they can accomplish without doing violence to their duties as wife and mother. Although the participation of women at the local level may seem at first to be an indicator of their relative emancipation, the fact is that their integration into the local political apparatus is perceived as not threatening to their traditional domestic roles and is thus encouraged by the majority parties as a source of stability. Local politics and the management of the commune have become for public opinion an extension of the home.

In the municipality (the smallest elected political body in France) an increasing number of women have been elected to political office with the approval of moderates, the conservatives, and even the Church. Women are known to be capable in administrative positions and are considered unlikely to try to change the social structure. Elections to the various positions in the municipality are conducted on the basis of slates presented by each party, the electorate voting for a slate as a whole. There has been increasing pressure to include women on the slates, and all parties, especially those on the left, have increasingly done so. The administrative positions of the municipality, though reflecting political interests, are not considered by many to be political positions.

By an ironic turn of history the very same arguments used to oppose the entry of women into politics—namely, the incompatibility between political life and women's "mission" in the home, women's feminine nature, and above all their moral delicacy and indifference to politics—have more recently been used to integrate women into the political apparatus at the local level. In the small communes with fewer than 5000 inhabitants, 10,711 women hold municipal positions, comprising 85 percent of those elected; in the larger communes of more than 5000 inhabitants, however, women make up only 15 percent of elected officials. Among the women elected only a scant few are found in the highest positions of responsibility. Only 0.4 percent of the women elected were mayors; the great majority were found in middle-range political administrative positions. "She is to charm, console, understand. Her role is that of helpful, available assistant, but without initiative. She exists essentially in relation to others." Thus does a sociologist, summing up contemporary research findings, describe the model image of women in France (Chombart de Lauwe et al., 1963: 120). The image of woman and her role in the domestic world is thus being transposed as such to the political world at the local level, where she is asked to use the same qualities of understanding, supportive help, and good management.

The social background of the women who enter the political world is revealing. Among the women who were mayors and aides to mayors in 1965, more than half did not work and did not have a profession, while a third belonged to the rural population and were rural landowners. This pattern is even more characteristic of the middle-range administrative levels, where the percentage of women without a profession is even higher. Women working in the political apparatus are more likely to be defined by their "domestic mission," which is no longer seen as an obstacle to their participation in the public life of the community. More than men they have the time and often the social position and conveniences to engage in time-consuming, and often poorly paid, official activities. It has also been suggested that women's participation in the administration of the *commune* is a legitimate means for them to break away from the isolation and boredom characteristic of family life in small provincial towns.

The traditional orientation of women in political and social matters has a long history in France. The importance of the radical clubs and women's associations that emerged with every revolutionary upheaval—in 1789, 1848, and 1870—must not be underestimated, but their action was usually spontaneous and not based in any well-defined and lasting organizational apparatus. Well-organized women's associations have existed since the nineteenth century and became especially strong under the Third Republic. These groups were likely to reflect the interests of bourgeois women, and their membership demonstrated their links with the political ruling elites. Women's associations played a major role in opening the universities to women and in their struggles for recognition within the educational system on the basis of equal treatment with men.

France is currently characterized by an unusual number of women's associations, some of them directly linked to unions or to political parties, others not officially linked with any political organization but supporting strong political interests. The striking feature common to all these associations—with the exception of the feminist *Mouvement de Libération de la Femme* (MLF), created in the 1970s—has been the promotion of the traditional domestic women's image and policies favoring population growth. In these matters the differences between political parties are small. For example, the Communist Party as well as the conservative parties are promoting the traditional role of the *femme au foyer,* organized around the complementarity and subordination of roles in the household, and until very recently both were encouraging policies favoring population growth. The great majority of the nonpolitical women's associations are Catholic and conservative. These include, for example, the *Centre Féminin d'Etudes et d'Information* (CFEI), and the *Conseil National des Femmes,* nonpolitical organizations that are primarily engaged in defending the traditional family structure, in which they believe a woman can flourish by being a good mother, a good *citoyenne,* a good patriot.

Thus the many women's organizations in France have been used to reinforce domestic ideals and family stability around the father. The most advanced ones, like the *Mouvement Démocratique Féminin* (MDF) and the Club Louise Michel, have supported equality and democracy in the home, the workplace, and in the mores in general but have not questioned the basic ideas underlying the status of women in society. Women's associations in France, because of their long conservative tradition, have been more of an obstacle than a help in the liberation of women. It was only after the events of 1968, which shook the French social structure, that the "woman question" began to emerge. And it was only after left and moderate political parties had changed their attitudes toward the role of women in society that existing women's organizations began to be more active in the defense and promotion of women's interests. These changes were partly responsible for the important votes in the National Assembly in 1970 and 1974 regarding the legal status of the wife in the household and the legalization of abortion.

Women's participation in the electoral process has always been smaller than that of men. French women constitute the majority of the electoral vote, and they represented 53 percent in 1972. But the rate of abstention for women is higher than that for men. In the 1968 elections 22 percent of the women abstained, compared to 14 percent of the men; in the referendum of 1962, 27 percent of the women abstained compared to 17 percent of the men (Charzat, 1972: 18).

Women's higher rate of abstention may reflect the fact that women are less likely to be interested in politics than are men. To the question asked in 1968 by the *Information Française d'Opinion Publique,* "Are you interested in politics?" 47 percent of the men said "yes," compared to 31 percent of the women. The high rate of abstention and the low level of interest on the part of French women may reflect a social reality in which the man in the family is defined as being politically responsible for the family as a whole. French women are characterized by a strong political comformity with their husbands; 85 percent of voting women vote the same way as their husbands (Charzat, 1972: 61).

With the exception of small and very active groups of militant women, French women have been a conservative force in the trends that have affected their position in society. The traditional images of women as uninterested in politics and as psychologically and biologically unable to function as political agents are still widespread in French public opinion. The conservatism and lack of political interest of French women, however, have created the conditions that have helped them reintegrate the political machine. Their "feminine" attributes and their "higher sense of morality" may ultimately give them a larger say in the political process. Now that women have achieved equality in the home, it is very likely that they will assume a much greater part in the running of the nation.

CONCLUSIONS

In France women have succeeded in participating significantly, if unequally, in the cultural, economic, and political domains while occupying a legally inferior status in the household. It was easier to change the economic conditions under which women worked than the legal foundation of family organization. French women have been more concerned with obtaining equality in the economic, educational, and political spheres, while paying little attention to changes in the legal organization of the family.

The laws of 1967 and 1970, however, introduced drastic changes in the principles regulating family relationships and organization. Married women regained the legal capacity that they had lost at the end of the Middle Ages. The principle of the subordination of the woman to the man as the head of the household (*chef de la communauté*) was abolished and replaced by more egalitarian principles, whereby the husband and wife were jointly responsible for the administration of household property and the formal education of children. In view of the historical role played by the family as a source of social order and the long-established tradition of family organization centered around the father, such changes are extraordinary—all the more so because, however belated, they did not result from extensive struggle or agitation. This is not to say that these laws were not actively sought, sometimes militantly. The role of the political parties and unions—especially on the left—and the action of small but militant groups of professional women influenced their enactment.

These actions, however important, do not account for the more fundamental changes that had previously occurred in the society and that had prepared the ground for this legislation. Among the structural changes since World War II that changed the position and status of women, three seem of special importance: the changes in the occupational structure, combined with a high rate of growth in the economy; the expansion of the role of government in modern and dynamic sectors; and finally, the emergence of an increasingly important group—both numerically and culturally—that promotes a cultural definition of the role of women competing with that of the traditional, bourgeois domestic model.

Since World War II, but especially since the 1950s, France has experienced a strong rate of economic growth, one of the highest among Western nations. This expansion of the economy has affected the distribution of women in several economic sectors. As in all expanding industrial countries, the service sector has grown very fast. Women in the tertiary sector in France are numerically important, forming the third largest group in the working female population. They had one of the highest rates of occupational growth between the last two censuses (1954 and 1968), especially among the middle management and supervisors in the private sector; an increasingly large group do skilled and professional work that requires a certain level of training and expertise. This group of workers is labeled *cadres moyens* by the French census and includes semiprofessionals (nurses, medical aides, elementary and secondary teachers, librarians, pharmacists, social workers), technicians, middle management workers and the lower level of supervisors. The proportion of women in the category of *cadres moyens* is high, 62 percent, but not so high as to "feminize" these occupations to the extent that their status is thereby lowered (as with, for example, American librarians, schoolteachers, and social workers). They constitute a professionally dynamic group, involved in public and private sectors that have been steadily growing.

A second set of factors important in the understanding of the relatively high participation of women in the economy is the role played by the state apparatus. State institutions, especially educational institutions and administrative bureaucracies, have for a long time been a source of employment for women in France. France has one of the oldest and most extensive bureaucratic apparatuses in Europe, and women have done comparatively well within it, reaching high and prestigious positions of responsibility. Working for the government in France has a special prestige attached to it, and women have thus gained a certain aura of esteem.

Since World War II the role of the state in directing the economy and in extending its intervention in social matters has increased. For example, the extension of public medicine and health institutions, the role of the state in education, research, and the creation of more universities, as well as the spread of preschool institutions for children of working mothers, have increased opportunities for women. In partial competition with the traditional role of the state as the quasimonopolistic sponsor of culture, local authorities sometimes seek to organize such activities and are likely to call on women in doing so. In any event the technicians, professionals, and semiprofessionals working for state institutions constitute an active group of workers in the fight for better working conditions for civil servants.

In addition to the changes in the occupational structure and the expanding role of the government in French society, the transformations in the position and status of women reflect changes in the traditional bourgeois ideology of the *femme au foyer*. The bourgeois ideals of family organization reflected in the Civil Code and of woman's "mission" in the home have been somewhat weakened by a more democratic model of family organization. This new cultural model of the role of women in the organization of the household is the product of an upwardly mobile and growing middle class, including the *cadre moyens*, whose values differ from both the *bourgeoisie* and the working class (*ouvriers*).

It is among the *classes moyennes* that one finds striking cultural differences in the direction of greater equality. The *classes moyennes* are characterized by smaller families than are either the *bourgeoisie* or the working class. They have one of the lowest birthrates in the country and have more readily accepted the use of modern contraceptive methods. The women of the *classes moyennes* have one of the highest rates of participation in the economy among the working female population. They are more likely to resume working when their children are grown up and are more inclined to use preschool facilities in order to continue working. Work is accepted by both husband and wife as a normal state of affairs and as a contribution to the well-being of the family as a whole. The wife's income is increasingly important among upwardly mobile families for achieving or maintaining a higher standard of living. The man is more likely to help with household tasks on a daily basis and spends more time helping in the rearing of the children. Husbands in this class are less likely to be defined as the family's sole provider or as the ultimate source of authority.

In French society this group of upwardly mobile families, which is becoming increasingly important numerically, has succeeded in creating an alternate cultural model through which to define women's work and women's image. This is not to say that women in the *classes moyennes* have given up their role in the household. They still wish to stay at home when their children are very young, but they see no sustained incompatibility between the domestic and occupational worlds. They still regard the home as important in their lives, but no longer does it become a mission or career.

My impression is that it is the increasingly important role of the *cadres moyens* in the economy, together with the emergence of a new model of family organization based on a more equal division of sexual labor consistent with the legal changes, that explains the advantages that French women have witnessed in recent years. This is not to say, of course, that the majority of French women have accepted the new image of the role of women; they are still quite conservative.

In the long history of changes in the position of women in France, two important features emerge. First is the persistence to the present time of the society's strong orientation toward the family and the importance placed on the domestic role of women as contributing to the stability of the society and, in *bourgeois* settings, of cultural norms. Second is that most changes in the status of women in French society have not been preceded by large-scale feminist movements, as has been the case in the Anglo-Saxon countries. In France feminist ideas did not find a strong social basis, despite the avant garde role played by women like Simone de Beauvoir, whose ideas were so important in Anglo-Saxon countries in defining new images for women but did not affect French women until much later. With the important exception of access to education during the Third Republic, the struggle for women's rights has largely occurred within existing institutions and was often sponsored by political parties. Thus few purely "feminist" ideologies and organizations were developed. Today France is a country (not the only one, to be sure) that has succeeded in elevating the status of women and in providing for their greater economic participation within the context of a family-oriented society in which the basic goal is the better integration of domestic and occupational structures rather than the more fundamental reform of either.

BIBLIOGRAPHY

Andrieux, Cécile. 1962. "Idéologies traditionelles et modernes dans les attitudes sociales féminines." Thesis, Université de Paris.

Annales. 1972. "Economies, Sociétés, Civilisations." Special issue of Famille et Société 45 (July-October).

Annuaire Statistique de la France. 1969, 1970, 1973. Paris: Institut National de la Statistique et des Etudes Economiques.

Annuaire Statistique du Travail. 1967. Organisation Internationale du Travail.

Ariès, Philippe. 1962. Centuries of Childhood. London: Cape.

———. 1971. Histoire des Populations Françaises. Paris: Editions de Seuil.

Barber, Elinor. 1955. The French Bourgeoisie in the Eighteenth Century. Princeton: Princeton University Press.

Beauvoir, Simone de. 1949. Le Deuxième Sexe. Paris: Gallimard.

Berger, Ida. 1959. Les Maternelles. Paris: Centre National de la Recherche Scientifique.

———, and Roger Benjamin. 1964. L'Univers des Instituteurs. Paris: Editions de Minuit.

Bloch, Marc. 1939. La Société Féodale. Paris: Albion Michel.

Bonald, Louis de. 1864. "Du divorce considéré au XIXe siècle relativement à l'état domestique et à l'état public de société." In Oeuvres Complètes, Vol. 2. Paris: Magne.

Boudon, Raymond. 1973. Les Inégalités des Chances. Paris: Armand Colin.

Bourdieu, Pierre, and J. C. Passeron. 1964. Les Héritiers. Paris: Editions de Minuit.

"Les carrières féminines." 1965. Avenir (April-May).

Charzat, Gisèle. 1972. Les Françaises sont-elles citoyennes? Paris: Gonthier.

Chaton, Jeanne H. 1972. "Les femmes françaises en 1972." Tendances 75 (February).

Chombart de Lauwe, Paul-Henri. 1964. Images de la Femme dans la Société. Paris: Les Editions Óuvrières.

———, and Marie José, et al. 1963. La Femme dans la Société, son Image dans Différents Milieux Sociaux. Travaux du Groupe d'Ethnologie Sociale. Paris: Centre National de la Recherche Scientifique.

Comte, Auguste. 1848. Discours sur l'ensemble du positivisme. Paris: Mathias.

Deniel, Raymond. 1965. Une Image de la Famille et de la Société sous la Restauration (1815-1830). Paris: Editions Ouvrières.

"Les diplômes constituent-ils un facteur décisif d'intégration des femmes dans la vie contemporaine?" 1969. Le Monde, August 13.

Dogan, Mattei, and Jacques Narbonne. 1955. Les Françaises face à la politique, comportement politique et condition sociale. Cahiers de la Fondation Nationale des Sciences Politiques. Paris: Armand Colin.

Duby, Georges. 1953. La Société aux XIe et XIIe Siècles dans la Région Mâconnaise. Paris: Armand Colin.

———. 1962. Economie rurale et la vie des campagnes dans l'occident médiéval. Paris: Aubier.

Duverger, Maurice. 1955. La participation des femmes à la vie politique. Paris: UNESCO.

Economie et Statistique. 1972. 34 (May).

"L'Emploi féminin et son évolution depuis 1954." Etudes et Conjonctures (December).

Fogarty, Michael. 1957. *Christian Democracy in Western Europe, 1870–1953*. London: Routledge and Kegan.

Girard, Alain. 1961. "Les femmes sont-elles féministes? Travail féminin et participation sociale." *Esprit* (May).

Goode, William J. 1963. *World Revolution and Family Patterns*. New York: Free Press.

Grégoire, Ménie. 1961. "Mythes et réalités." *Esprit* (May).

Guélaud-Léridon, Françoise. 1964. *Le travail des femmes en France*. Institut National d'Etudes Démographiques, Travaux et Documents, Cahier No. 42. Paris: Presses Universitaires de France.

———. 1967. *Recherches sur la condition féminine dans la société d'aujourd'hui*. Institut National d'Etudes Démographiques, Travaux et Documents, Cahier No. 48. Paris: Presses Universitaires de France.

Guilbert, Madeleine. 1966a. *Les fonctions des femmes dans l'industrie*. Paris: Mouton.

———. 1966b. *Les femmes et l'organisation syndicale avant 1914*. Paris: Edition du Centre National de la Recherche Scientifique.

Habakkuk, H. 1955. "Family Structure and Economic Change in 19th Century Europe." *Journal of Economic History* **XV** (1).

Hugues, Philippe d', and Michel Peslier. 1969. *Les Professions en France, Evolution et Perspectives*. Institut National d'Etudes Démographiques, Travaux et Documents, Cahier No. 51. Paris: Presses Universitaires de France.

Isambert-Jamati, Vivianne. 1961. "Le choix du métier—réponse à une enquête." *Esprit* (May).

Kallai, Thomas. 1950. *La notion de chef de famille*. Paris.

Laslett, Peter, and Richard Wall, Editors. 1972. *Household and Family in Past Time*. Cambridge: Cambridge University Press.

Lepatis, Stanislas de. 1954. "Evolution de la pensée exprimée de l'Eglise catholique." In *Renouveau des Idées sur la Famille*. Edited by Robert Pringent. Institut National d'Etudes Démographiques. Paris: Presses Universitaires de France.

Maitron, Jean. 1954. "Les penseurs sociaux de la famille dans la première moitié du XIXe siècle." In *Renouveau des Idées sur la Famille*. Edited by Robert Pringent. Paris: Presses Universitaires de France.

Mendras, H. 1958. *Les paysans et la modernisation de l'agriculture*. Paris: Centre National de la Recherche Scientifique.

Michel, Andrée, and Geneviève Texier. 1964. *La condition de la Française d'aujourd'hui*. Paris: Collection Femme Gonthier.

Ministère de l'Education Nationale. 1968–1969. *Le personnel de l'enseignement public. Statistique des Enseignants*. No. 3 (1).

Mousnier, Roland. 1975. *La Famille, l'Enfant, et l'Education en France et en Grande-Bretagne du XVIe au XVIIIe*. Les Cours de Sorbonne. Paris: Centre de Documentation Universitaire.

Organisation de la Coopération et du Développement Economique. 1965. *Origines sociales des professeurs et instituteurs*. Paris: Direction des Affaires Scientifiques.

———. 1970. *L'emploi des femmes*. Paris: Séminaire Syndical Régional.

Petiot, P. 1955. "La famille en France sous l'ancien régime." In *La Sociologie Comparée de la Famille Contemporaine*. Paris: Colloque du Centre National de la Recherche Scientifique.

Pirenne, Henri. 1936. *Economic and Social History of Medieval Europe*. London: Routledge and Kegan.

"Population active au sens du recensement en mars." 1971. 1972. *Economie et Statistique* **34** (May).

Pringent, Robert, Editor. 1954. *Renouveau des Idées sur la Famille.* Institut National d'Etudes Démographiques, Travaux et Documents, Cahier No. 18. Paris: Presses Universitaires de France.

"La proportion des femmes parmi les salariés ne cesse de croître." 1973. *Le Monde,* (September 18), p. 22.

Roy, Janine. 1972. "L'égalité des salaires masculins et féminins." *Le Monde,* November 7.

Scott, Joan, and Louise Tilly. 1975. "Women's Work and the Family in Nineteenth Century Europe." *Comparative Studies in Society and History* **17** (January): 36–64.

Semaine de la Pensée Marxiste. 1965. *Femmes du XXe Siècle.* Paris: Presses Universitaires de France.

Shorter, E. 1973. "Female emancipation, birth control and fertility in European history." *The American Historical Review* **78** (3).

———. 1974. "Amour, sensibilité et classes sociales depuis 1750." *Annales* **4** (July–August).

Silver, Catherine. 1973. "Salon, foyer, bureau: Women and the professions in France." *American Journal of Sociology* **78** (4) (January).

Sullerot, Evelyne. 1968. *Histoire et Sociologie du Travail Féminin.* Paris: Gonthier.

Tuchman, Gaye. 1975. "Women and the creation of culture." *Sociological Inquiry* (Spring).

Van de Walle, Etienne. 1974. *The Female Population of France in the Nineteenth Century.* Princeton: Princeton University Press.

Vieille-Michel, Andrée. 1961. "Le status de la travailleuse française." *Esprit* (May).

Vimont, Claude. 1965. "Une enquête sur les femmes fonctionnaires." *Population* (January–February): 22–55.

Weill-Hallé, Marie Andrée. 1960. *La grand'peur d'aimer.* Paris: Julliard.

Wesley, Camp D. 1961. *Marriage and the Family in France since the Revolution.* New York: Bookman.

Zeldin, Theodore. 1973. *France, 1848–1945.* Vol. 1, *Ambition, Love, and Politics.* Oxford: Clarendon Press.

Chapter Eight

UNITED STATES: A PROLONGED SEARCH FOR EQUAL RIGHTS

Janet Zollinger Giele

Current efforts of American women to win greater public recognition have their roots in conditions of the colonial period as well as in the feminist movement of the nineteenth century. After near silence for 50 years feminism is again a viable movement in American society, not content this time to rest with any single victory but seeking instead a new organization of economic and social activity that will end discrimination against women and also open wider possibilities to men.

The search for equality took various shapes under different historical conditions. In the colonial period the major advances were primarily in the religious realm. Early in the industrial period women sought rights to control their earnings, to vote, and to get an education. In the advanced industrial society they search for more subtle and elusive forms of equality. They dare to aspire to political office, seek access to "men's" jobs, decry sex stereotypes in the school curriculum, and ask that men and the state help with women's traditional family responsibilities. As the society has become more complex and women's and men's tasks have become more inter- changeable, American women's search for equality has broadened and deepened so that it currently reaches into almost every corner of life.

HISTORICAL BACKGROUND

From the time of the initial settlement through the first years of the early republic, many people came to America for religious or economic freedom. Frontier conditions brought a certain rough egalitarianism to the conditions of women and men (Flexner, 1975: 9). Then rapid industrial expansion and new wealth allowed women to withdraw from production. In public life they took on ornamental and cultural roles, particularly among the middle and upper classes. The women's suffrage movement from 1848 to 1920 criticized this turn of events but in the end rested when it had won the vote.

Colonial Period and Early Republic (1600–1820). The colonial record does not show in any simple way whether the status of women was uni- formly high or consistently low. Instead a woman's status depended on the religious climate and laws of her region, her social position, and her particu- lar family history. Any one of these elements could limit or enlarge the privileges she was granted.

Religious groups that came to America in search of religious freedom brought wider opportunities to women as well. The Pilgrims who founded Plymouth Colony in 1620 gave men the final authority in family decisions, but on the whole their belief regarding proper conduct of husbands and wives was fundamentally egalitarian. They encouraged men and women to live together in harmony and not to speak abusively to one another. As far as we know they required no habitual signs of deference between the sexes (Demos, 1970: 95). Most divorces in the colony stemmed from adultery, which was severely punished in *both* men and women, although more concern was voiced about a woman's infidelity than about a man's. Wives were about as often as husbands accused of "abusive carriage," suggesting that they were not altogether meek and mild.

The Puritans of Massachusetts Bay Colony, founded in 1632, also had a family ethic with egalitarian elements. The Puritans believed that marriage should be based on rational choice between partners, taking into consideration equality of rank, God's will, and property interests. The relationship between husband and wife should be governed by *mutual* affection. Respect between husband and wife arose from the regard of each for the different but equally necessary functions of the other. Man was compared to Christ and woman to believer. Milton's lines can be used to express the relationship: "He for God only; she for God in him." Each was to be respected by children and servants; though the husband was "the Head of the wife," she was "an Head of the Family" (Morgan, 1944: 46). The husband's authority over his wife was strictly limited; he could not lawfully strike her nor could he command her to do anything contrary to the laws of God which were explicitly defined in the civil codes (Morgan, 1944: 45). In the Southern colonies, however, men had the right of chastisement (Spruill, 1938: 342).

Certain religious denominations such as the Quakers, Methodists, and some Baptists brought women into public prominence. In the mid-seventeenth century Quaker women traveled as missionaries to New England, New York, and Virginia. Several were imprisoned for their beliefs (Spruill, 1938: 245–254).

The Salem witch trials of Massachusetts Bay Colony in the 1680s became the most famous example of women's religious persecution in colonial America. Several decades earlier Quakers had been hanged on the Boston Common. In 1637 Anne Hutchinson, a woman who held private religious discussions in her home and espoused heretical beliefs, was banished from the colony. The Salem witch trials may have been a culminating effort on the part of Puritan leaders to quell such signs of inner spiritual direction, which was a threat to their theocratic rule and which curiously was so often found in women (Erikson, 1966). The Anglican Church was not subject to these excesses. However it maintained the view of St. Paul toward women—that they should keep silence in the churches, be subject to their husbands, and in no way serve as ministers or priests.

Colonial laws generally followed the English common law in matters of family property and women's rights to enter contracts. The governing principle was that of *femme couverte*, as expressed in this 1632 version published in London:

It is true that husband and wife are one person; but understand in what manner. When a small brooke or little river incorporateth with Rhodanus, Humber, or the Thames, the poor rivulet loseth her name; it is carried and recarried with the new associate; it beareth no sway; it possesseth nothing during coverture. A woman as soon as she is married is called *covert*; in Latine *nupta*, that is "veiled"; as it were, clouded and overshadowed; she hath lost her streame [quoted in Spruill, 1938: 340].

When a woman married, her property, unless secured by special agreement, passed under her husband's control. In return she had the right to be supported by him and she received back a third if she was widowed. Writing of the Southern colonies, Spruill said, "As a rule, she could not make a valid contract, bring suit or be sued in court, execute a deed, administer an estate, or make a will" (Spruill, 1938: 346).

There were exceptions to this general common law rule. When a husband failed to support the wife and ran away, a court ruling granted maintenance to a wife, a special legislative act granted women powers of contract, or other special arrangements were made to set aside the common law rule. Prenuptial agreements were sometimes made to keep a woman's property in her family after her death. Among tradesmen a wife could be made a sole trader, whereby she could enter contracts, collect debts, and neither be liable to her husband's debts nor he be liable to hers (Spruill, 1938: 343, 345, 362). In 1646 the General Court of Massachusetts passed a law requiring that women agree to the sale of land by their husbands. In Plymouth Colony both parents joined in the decision of placing their children in apprenticeship or in foster families (Demos, 1970: 84).

The most dramatic example of women's political leadership in colonial times is given by Mistress Margaret Brent of Maryland. For a brief period between 1638 and 1650 her name appears frequently in court records and public affairs. She, like some other wealthy landowning women of the period, had power of attorney to represent herself and others in court. She served as executor of Lord Calvert's estate and averted a civil war in Maryland. She asked for the right to vote in the Maryland assembly, but not having fully won the confidence of Lord Baltimore in England, was denied it (James et al., 1971, Vol. I: 236–237).

The rank of a woman in society had something to do with the opportunities afforded her. The early landed proprietors such as Margaret Brent or Lady Berkeley of Virginia could draw on an earlier feudal tradition brought from England that accorded them rights by virtue of their aristocratic position. They were educated, could travel, and were allowed to represent family interests in court. Special legal agreements assured them power of attorney and protection of their rights to land. At the other end of the social scale rough frontier women entered into the hard work of settling a new territory and achieved a ready expertise from this experience. In the Southern colonies a woman partly of Indian origin, Mary Musgrove, became advisor to Oglethorpe of Georgia in his plans for settlement (Spruill, 1938: 242). In the middle classes women plied their trades as part of small family enterprises. Before the Revolution in 1775 they were well represented in all colonies as innkeepers, merchants, seamstresses and artificers, nurses and midwives, and teachers of dame schools (Dexter, 1924).

By 1800, however, the activity of women in these occupations and in public affairs appeared to be on the decline. Greater affluence brought them the chance to be "ladies" and encouraged a withdrawal to less active occupations as a symbol of family success (Dexter, 1924: 139–162; Wilson, 1976: 373–374). The presence of indentured servants and slaves probably encouraged this development, making inactivity for the wife more possible while reinforcing the association between rank and women's ornamental functions.

The overwhelming majority of women, of course, had little opportunity to choose between cultural pursuits and public affairs. Their lives were subject to the simple demographic facts of life: they were born, they lived, and they died, often young, after early marriages and many pregnancies. Benjamin Franklin at the time of the Revolution estimated that the American population doubled every generation, and modern demography supports Franklin's estimate (Potter, 1965: 662). Such rapid growth meant that American women were bearing considerably more than the European average of 4 to 6 children, and more likely had 10 to 12 children. Infant mortality was high, so many of these children did not survive. The early and frequent death of women meant that many a husband had several wives and a number of children by each. Since common law placed the guardianship of these children in the husband's hands, there was also frequent occasion for injustice and ill feeling if a wife rather than a husband was the surviving partner (Spruill, 1938: 349).

Education for girls was meager. Only a third of women in Virginia before 1700 could read and write as compared to almost twice that proportion of males. When schooling became more common in the eighteenth century, girls were taught the 2 R's, reading and writing, while boys had access to 3 R's, reading, writing, and arithmetic as well. Generally, however, educational opportunity was patchy, depending on the availability of local dame schools organized through private initiative. In the South Georgia made some attempt at public education (Spruill, 1938: 191). In a Northern colony such as Massachusetts, girls were sent to dame schools for a few years but did not have much access to public shcools until well into the nineteenth century. In 1821 Boston provided for a public secondary school that would serve both boys and girls, and in 1852 Massachusetts passed the first compulsory school attendance law (Butts, 1973: 993). Before that, training through apprenticeship and family enterprise provided some women the opportunity of pursuing a trade, practicing as doctors and midwives, and exercising the power of attorney. These fields were later closed to women during the nineteenth century, when credentials were made dependent on meeting formalized and upgraded standards of training (Lerner, 1969: 5–15).

Industrialization (1820–1920). The amorphous egalitarian order that preceded the Revolution held certain possibilities for achievement by women who were fortunate enough to have access to education or family property. However rapid territorial and industrial expansion in the nineteenth century posed new threats. Industrialization created a split between work and family life that brought new job opportunities to women but also precipitated an integrative crisis in the legal, moral, and social rules that governed women's lives. The nineteenth century women's movement was a response; it sought new roles for women under changing social and economic conditions. Educational opportunities expanded rapidly; legal reform granted women property rights and eventually the right of suffrage; women formed their own voluntary associations and fought for social reform.

These changes occurred in a social context of both heightened individualism and increasing corporate complexity. Young women came from the farms of New Hampshire and Vermont to work in the textile mills at Lowell and Manchester. They were housed in dormitories and during the earliest years had their own self-improvement society with a publication, *The Lowell Offering,* that recorded their essays and poems. After working in the factory some married and some went West, where they became missionaries and teachers (Abbott, 1910: 141).

Early strikes for better working conditions and pay were spearheaded by women (Dublin, 1974: 11–21). Later, however, as mills adopted faster and larger machines and immigrant labor came to predominate during the latter half of the century, women were less active in the emerging labor unions.

Women were found in a great variety of occupations. By 1900 over half of those in manufacturing were concentrated in textiles, clothing industries, cigar-making, boots and shoes, and printing and publishing. Everywhere they were underrepresented as supervisors and foremen, and their pay for roughly comparable work averaged between 50 and 60 percent of men's (Abbott, 1910: 85, 312). The number of women in manufacturing represented only 22 percent of employed women. Census figures for 1910 show that domestic and personal service still claimed nearly a third of all gainfully employed women. By 1920, however, this figure had declined noticeably to about one-fourth, which was still slightly higher than the proportion of women in manufacturing (Woody, 1929, Vol. II: 16).

Access to the professions was more difficult. As early as the 1600s women had performed ministerial roles among the Quakers. They had been healers and midwives. A few had carried out some legal business. But higher educational requirements and formal licensing procedures made it hard for women, whose qualifications were based primarily on experience, to maintain a foothold in the emerging professions. Under the new standards women had to argue that they were capable and should be admitted to professional schools (Dexter, 1924: 224; Lerner, 1969). The nineteenth century saw a number of "firsts" among women who entered major professional occupations. Elizabeth Blackwell was denied admission to better known medical schools in the East, but in 1849 received a medical degree from the Geneva Medical College in upstate New York, gained experience at La Maternité in Paris, and then established the New York Infirmary for Women and Children in 1857. Her sister-in-law, Antoinette Brown Blackwell, was graduated from Oberlin, the first woman to earn a degree in theology, in 1851. The astronomer Maria Mitchell, self-educated in the whaling seaport of Nantucket, discovered a comet in 1847, achieved renown in the scientific world, and became one of the charter faculty members of Vassar College when it opened in 1865 (James et al., 1971, Vol. I: 158–165; Vol. II: 554–556).

A number of battles for education of girls and women were also fought during the nineteenth century. In 1821 Emma Willard opened her renowned seminary for girls in Troy, New York. Oberlin College opened in 1837 to become the first to admit women as well as men to a college program. Led by Mount Holyoke, which was founded in 1837, a number of colleges especially for women opened in the latter part of the nineteenth century: Vassar in 1865; Wellesley and Smith in 1875; and Bryn Mawr in 1885. The midwestern state universities were some of the first to admit women: Iowa in 1856; Wisconsin in 1860; Michigan in 1870 (Woody, 1929, Vol. II: 38–39). By the 1890s women could do graduate study under Harvard professors at Radcliffe College, and departments of graduate study at Yale and the University of Chicago admitted women. But the professional schools were slow to follow. Columbia law school still remained closed to women in 1920 (Woody, 1929, Vol. II: 334–337, 375). Not until the 1950s did Harvard Law School admit women.

Nevertheless by the end of the century enormous gains had been made in the general education of females. Girls benefited from the development of public education that began around 1830. By 1890 there were actually more girls enrolled in high schools than boys, and from 1900 to 1920 the proportion of high school graduates who were girls held steady at about 60%. Not until 1968 did the proportion of boys graduating from high school equal the proportion of girls (Women's Bureau, 1969: 13).

Before the Civil War the women's movement was intertwined with anti-slavery, suffrage, and temperance. The Seneca Falls Convention of 1848 marked the opening of the women's suffrage movement, which sought decision-making power for women at three levels of social life: first the home, then the local community, and finally, the nation at large.

Between 1830 and 1860 women's major reform accomplishments were concentrated on the home. They gained "women's rights": the right to hold property, make contracts, to sue and be sued, to serve as guardians of children. Established first in the Southern states, these reforms particularly aided the position of married women. Until that time a wife had no right under the common law to her own saved earnings or to retain her own property after marriage. Only special prenuptial agreements or contracts typically confined to the upper classes could assure her protection before the married women's property acts were passed (Beard, 1946: 133–156; Johnston, 1972: 15–57).

During the latter half of the century women's public reform efforts were most striking at the community level. The Civil War brought more women into community effort. Women nursed the wounded. In the South they fed and clothed an army and kept farms and plantations running (Flexner, 1975: 105–114; Scott, 1970). Two national suffrage organizations began a campaign for women's right to vote. Among their leaders were Susan B. Anthony and Elizabeth Cady Stanton. The National Women's Christian Temperance Union also sought the ballot for women to use for improving their local governments. In the 1880s the WCTU claimed a membership of several hundred thousand. A host of other women's clubs and cultural associations, missionary societies, and auxiliaries proliferated, and in 1890 they were gathered under the umbrella of the General Federation of Women's Clubs (Flexner, 1975: 182–196). While not particularly feminist, the women's clubs nonetheless were the primary vehicle by which many women took their first interest in public projects.

Women's major political accomplishments of the period were winning municipal suffrage and the vote for granting local option to sell alcoholic beverages (Giele, 1961: 143, 173, 205–206). Although the suffrage associations struggled hard, by 1900 only four Western frontier states—Colorado, Idaho, Wyoming, and Utah—had granted women the right to vote for federal candidates (Flexner, 1975: 228). It is often speculated that frontier society and the scarcity of women gave women a political advantage in the West. By contrast many Easterners and immigrants disdained both feminism and its likely companion, Prohibition. Not until after the turn of the century did suffrage sentiment prevail in the populous urban states of the Eastern seaboard.

The granting of the vote to women in 1920, through a federal amendment to the Constitution rather than by individual states, came on a wave of Progressive sentiment. Women reformers and club members had been active in efforts to deal with exploitive and unhealthy work conditions in factories. They had addressed the poverty of the new immigrants, prostitution, slums, the political corruption of big city government, child labor, and the rapacious practices of big business. Many women themselves promised—and their hearers believed—that the voices of a female element would reform government and hold it to higher standards. World War I also had an effect. Women who served as nurses and helped on the war front could not be denied the vote as easily as women who had been held in a dependent and protected state.

The industrial impulse initiated massive structural changes that brought a revolution in the status of women. It is fashionable now to question whether these changes did very much good. In the minds of women in 1920 there was certainly no doubt that they had come a long way from the limited choices open to them a century before. Changes in the law had guaranteed them the right to keep their own earnings, to make contracts, and to hold property. Their work could take place outside the home, independent of a family member's domination (though there might be other evils). Girls had a right to the same public education available to boys. A woman had the option not to marry, and the number of single women rose, particularly among the educated. When feminists won the right to vote, most women seemed to think that their equality was assured.

But the chinks in this foundation of accomplishment became apparent as time went on. Education was won at the lower levels but women were still underrepresented at college and professional levels. Work opportunities were still sex segregated and pay was unequal. Success at winning high elective and appointive office was not assured by women's vote. Though Calhoun, the American social historian of the family, noted in 1919 that men might push the baby carriage and build the kitchen fire, few raised the subtle questions of how to reorganize household work more efficiently or how to divide family chores between men and women more equitably (Calhoun, 1919: 120; O'Neill, 1969: 47–48). Women's rights to limit conception were still in question, and not even all feminists were in accord with the birth control movement (Reed, 1974). The existing sex-typed division of labor was accepted as natural and desirable. The major option by which women could pursue higher education and a career was to remain single.

We may ask whether women of all classes were affected in the same way by these changes. Almost certainly they were not, but it is difficult to describe major variations precisely. Women of the urban middle and working classes were most noticeably affected. Middle-class women who did not have paid employment participated in the glorification of womanhood and domestic values, while at the same time entering public life through membership in a church, club, reform group, or other voluntary association. Some working-class women such as Leonora O'Reilly of the Women's Trade Union League worked to get better working conditions and uniform labor standards. Rank and file working women were beneficiaries of the improvements that resulted. Rural women and immigrants had less opportunity for schooling. They probably also had fewer choices of work, yet gained a rough and ready training in the city as domestics or as factory workers. Upper-class women were a mixed lot. A substantial number clung to a conservative patriarchal ideology and were active in the Anti-Suffrage League. Others were beacons of reform, giving support to striking working girls through their efforts in the Women's Trade Union League or donating their time or money to the neighborhood settlement houses and other charitable activities founded by such women as Jane Addams in Chicago and Lillian Wald in New York.

Black women had the hardest lot. Newly emancipated from slavery, they struggled to keep families together, often living on the edge of survival on poor tenant farms or working as domestics at the lowest possible pay. In addition to suffering racial prejudice, they were constrained by poor opportunities for education and a narrow range of occupational choice. Yet as among white women there were outstanding pioneers among them—the famous Sojourner Truth, who spoke at the first Women's Rights Convention in 1848; Harriet Tubman, a fugitive slave and rescuer of slaves, who served in the abolitionist cause during the Civil War; and middle-class leaders and club women like Josephine Ruffin of Boston, who was active in welfare work, Negro rights, and the suffrage movement (James et al., 1971, Vol. III: 479–483, 206–208).

The Postsuffrage Era (1920–1960). Enfranchisement promised a new role to women in politics, but united feminist political action was derailed over the issue of protective labor laws and the Equal Rights Amendment. Social feminists such as Florence Kelley came from a broad spectrum of women's groups, ranging from the Women's Trade Union League to the YWCA, General Federation of Women's Clubs, and League of Women Voters. They believed for humanitarian reasons that women benefited from laws prohibiting night work or employment of women under certain working conditions.

However the National Women's Party, under the leadership of Alice Paul, disagreed and beginning in 1923 introduced to Congress year after year a constitutional amendment barring any distinction in legal rights of women and men (Lemons, 1973: 184–191). When in 1938 the Fair Labor Standards Act applied the same rules limiting wages and hours to men and women, the

ERA cause appeared to gain strength (Chafe, 1972: 131). By the end of the War, the Women's Party, so encouraged at the active role women had taken during the national emergency, believed that the amendment would be passed and ratified by 1948 (Rupp, 1974).

But instead, protective legislation hung on. Supreme Court decisions affirmed the famous *Muller v. Oregon* decision of 1908 that upheld an Oregon law limiting female labor to 10 hours a day (Purcell, 1974: 136). The patchwork of state laws imposing legal disabilities on women remained on the books to the end of this period except in Wisconsin, which in 1921 passed the only state Equal Rights Law (Lemons, 1973: 184–187).

The number of women holding political office rose markedly but never surpassed more than 2.4 percent of key federal offices, according to a study done in the early 1960s (Mead and Kaplan, 1965: 73). The number of women in state legislatures gradually rose to about 350 in 1961, then declined to less than 300 in 1970–1971 (Werner and Bachtold, 1974: 76). Women's voting rates were something of a disappointment. Approximately 60 percent of those registered to vote in Chicago during the first decade of women's suffrage were men and only 40 percent were women (Brecken- ridge, 1933: 249). More recent studies of voting turnout have shown, how- ever, that the ratio of women voters for President rose sharply between 1948, when 56 percent of a sample of women voted, and 1960, when 69 percent voted (Lansing, 1974: 8).

Women's most visible political impact came during the five-year period immediately after suffrage was granted and during the Depression years of the Roosevelt administration. Between 1920 and 1925, social feminists helped win progressive legislation providing health-care instruction to mothers with infants, consumer legislation regulating packers and stock- yards, reform in the citizenship requirements for married women, and civil service regulations that upgraded the merit system. But in 1924 they saw the defeat of a Constitutional amendment prohibiting child labor that they had strongly supported. From then on, their forces were in disarray, and they were swept under in the conservative tide that swamped the country until the enactment of powerful social welfare programs during the New Deal (Chafe, 1972: 27–29). During the Roosevelt years many women who had been leading social feminists were appointed to responsible posts adminis- tering the new programs. Frances Perkins held a cabinet-level post as Secre- tary of Labor. Florence Allen was appointed Judge of a U.S. Circuit Court of Appeal. Mary Dewson organized a powerful Women's Division in the Democratic Party. Eleanor Roosevelt herself stood as an inspiration to many (Chafe, 1972: 41–44).

The vagaries of the economic cycle dominated the period. The conserva- tive, business-oriented prosperity of the 1920s plunged to a crash in 1929, and Depression cut through the whole social structure, leaving one-third of the nation ill-clothed, ill-housed, and ill-fed. The adaptations that women made to the Depression and then World War II were hardly thought normal at the time. A woman whose husband was unemployed could take work during the 1930s (Komarovsky, 1940; Bakke, 1940). She might work in a war factory during the 1940s if her children were old enough or if her husband or son were away. The return to normalcy of the 1950s was supposed to let women go back to the home, much as the ideal had been during the 1920s. Yet employment of women throughout the 1950s continued to rise, even among mothers of young children.

Family life through these widely fluctuating periods showed a consistent trend toward a nuclear family form with strong sex-typed roles for husband and wife. Decline in household size had been going on since the founding of the nation (Glick, 1957: 22). The number of childless and one-child families increased markedly between 1890 and 1900, particularly in the professional and business classes (Thompson and Whelpton, 1933: 43). The Lynds found that all women of the business class in Middletown who gave information said that they used some form of birth control, but only half of the working classes did so (Lynd and Lynd, 1929: 123).

Since the turn of the century there had been a rise in both the marriage rate and the divorce rate. Sixty-five percent of females 14 years of age and over were married in 1950, as compared with fifty-eight percent in 1890 (Glick, 1957: 105). The divorce rate had nearly doubled from 1900 to 1930 (Ogburn and Tibbitts, 1933: 684; Lynd and Lynd, 1929: 120–121). William F. Ogburn, in his report to the President's Research Commission on Social Trends in 1933, suggested two major conclusions that could be reached from the variety of information then available on changing family life. First, there had been a decline in the institutional functions of the family, such as economic production and education. Second, the family's predominant function was now psychological support for individual personalities (Ogburn and Tibbitts, 1933: 661).

The Lynds's study of Middletown recorded the Midwestern small town ideals of husband and wife. A man was supposed to be primarily "a good provider." A woman was to be a "home-maker, child-rearer . . . and social pace-setter" (Lynd and Lynd, 1929: 117). As electricity, central heating, and indoor plumbing were introduced, women's household chores lightened, and their devotion to the personality functions of the family intensified. An electricity advertisement in Middletown distilled the feminine role ideal:

> . . . a successful mother . . . puts first things first. She does not give to sweeping the time that belongs to her children . . . . She delegates to electricity all that electricity can do. She cannot delegate the one task most important. Human lives are in her keeping, their fortune is molded by her hand and heart [Lynd and Lynd, 1929: 173].

Although working-class men and women shared some household duties in Middletown (Lynd and Lynd, 1929: 167) and Komarovsky (1940) showed that women helped support families in which the husbands were unemployed, the prevalent model of family life teamed a benevolent husband-provider with a wife who was both a cultured homemaker and an understanding mother. The model did not always work well. Sometimes the wife had no idea of the husband's income, or he could not provide the money that upward mobility demanded. Frequently there was little communication betweeen the pair (Lynd and Lynd, 1929: 120, 127, 168). Nevertheless the ideal persisted and was revived during the postwar period. During the 1950s wives put their husbands through school, returning to the home to have children and to serve as social assets to their husbands' careers (Whyte, 1956: 175).

Contrary to what one might suppose on the basis of such family norms, the actual number of married women in the paid labor force continued to rise after 1950. The trend was particularly striking among older women and among mothers of young children. The clearest explanation for the phenomenon comes from demographer Valerie Oppenheimer. She has shown that the greatest labor shortages after the war occurred in women's jobs. These jobs were in industries such as wholesale and retail trade and professional and related services. Great numbers of clerical and teaching jobs opened after the war. Yet the traditional female labor supply—single young women—was smaller than usual. More women were married; furthermore the number of young women was smaller than usual because of the drop in the birthrate during the Depression. These forces changed the definition of who could work. Prior to World War II hiring practices discriminated against married women, older women, and mothers. With heightened demand and short supply far greater numbers of older women entered the labor force. Their labor force participation rate rose from 15 percent in 1940 to 37 percent in 1960 (Oppenheimer, 1970: 20).

Women's unprecedented entry into the labor force gave rise to role conflict. During the 1950s women were encouraged to stay at home, embellishing their domestic chores with extra effort and investing time and attention in meeting the needs of their husbands and children. Betty Friedan's term the *feminine mystique* will forever characterize the mood of the era (Komarovsky, 1953; Friedan, 1963). Psychological literature emphasized the value of continuous mothering for children and suggested that a woman who worked not only risked injuring her husband's pride but might harm her children as well. Later social scientists would contend that working mothers do not harm children and that some healthy inattention might actually be good for both parents and children (Nye and Hoffman, 1963; Rossi, 1964).

These conflicting ideologies left their mark on women's educational attainment during the period. The number of girls completing high school surpassed the number of boys. In addition, the proportion of girls who graduated from high school had steadily risen. In 1920 one-fifth of all girls graduated; in 1960 two-thirds of all girls received their high school diplomas. But the percentage of women who received higher degrees did not show such a steady upward trend. A peak was reached in 1930 and 1940, when women received 40 percent of all bachelor's, master's, and doctoral degrees (Women's Bureau, 1969: 13, 16). A sharp decline occurred after World War II, as veterans swelled college and university admissions. Only in 1968 had women regained the proportion of bachelor's degrees that they had received in 1940. Only in the 1971–1972 academic year did their proportion of master's and doctoral degrees equal the share they had won in 1930, approximately 40 percent of master's degrees and 15 percent of doctoral degrees (Baker and Wells, 1975: 7).

WOMEN IN CONTEMPORARY AMERICAN INSTITUTIONS

Around 1960 the old order of sex roles began to be challenged, and by 1970 "Women's Lib" was a household phrase. The civil rights movement of the late 1950s and early 1960s had brought heightened self-awareness and protest tactics not only to students but also to women. Feminists' principal theme in relations between the sexes was to challenge male chauvinism and to substitute what Jessie Bernard (1971: 149–179) called the *shared-role pattern*.

The nineteenth century reinforced a two-sphere theory of sex roles. Men were the providers; women, the caretakers. In the latter half of the twentieth century, however, society became more urban and jobs more specialized. Machines now do most of the heavy physical work. Women have fewer children and children spend much of their time in schools. More than ever before in history it is possible for men and women to do each other's jobs. The repercussions of these changes are felt in every major institution of the society. In law, work, family, education, health, and cultural images, there is both an effort to establish rules that are fair to each sex and an effort to recover elements of female experience that were overlooked or undervalued in the past.

Law, Politics, and the New Feminist Movement. Soon after his election in 1960, President Kennedy appointed a Commission on the Status of Women. The Commission's report, issued in 1963, touched all the key issues that would dominate legal and social change during the next decade. A number of states treated women inequitably through their laws governing jury service, child custody, guardianship, property rights, and inheritance. Some protective legislation such as prohibitions against night work penalized women. The Commission found sex discrimination in employment, called for affirmative action by government, and noted the need for day-care services (Mead and Kaplan, 1965). Its summary of inequities in educational and employment opportunity, govenment programs, and social welfare provide a useful baseline against which succeeding reforms can be measured.

Since 1960 the single most outstanding development in the legal and political status of women is the rise of a new feminist movement. The National Organization of Women (NOW) was founded in 1966 to focus women's efforts and to provide a vehicle for orderly change of social institutions. An immediate purpose was to ensure enforcement of new anti–sex discrimination laws. Since the mid-1960s organizations such as NOW, the Women's Equity Action League (WEAL), and the National Women's Political Caucus have put life into newly enacted legislation and executive orders that bar sex discrimination. These organizations maintain pressure for enforcement, support court cases representing the feminist position, and keep a watchful eye on new legislation before Congress (Carden, 1974: 133–147; Sandler, 1973).

Another arm of the women's movement is represented by small consciousness-raising groups that grew among young women active in civil rights work during the early 1960s because they were excluded from leadership positions by male civil rights workers. These groups operate anonymously and informally and use a style of interaction found in leaderless groups and therapy settings; members speak their feelings, give each other support, and try to come to terms with individual and group problems (Carden, 1974: 59–70; Freeman, 1973). Although observers of these groups note that they are short-lived, continuing for no more than a few months or a year, their style and purpose appear to have passed into the general culture of participatory democracy. Informal "women's groups" now appear in almost every major business firm or academic setting and have even been reported in working-class neighborhoods. Sometimes they give rise to formal organizations that channel women's grievances with respect to hiring, promotion, or pay. They may work cooperatively with the local chapter of a major national women's organization such as NOW, WEAL, or another appropriate support group such as a trade union or religious association.

Opinion polls now suggest that feminist sentiment has had an effect on the wider population. In the spring of 1975 a Harris poll showed that 59 percent of women favored the aims of the women's movement and 28 percent opposed them. Only four years earlier 42 percent had favored and 41 percent had opposed them (*Women Today*, 1975: 72).

With the revitalization of feminism women seem to have gained a new interest in politics. More of them had begun to vote even before the new women's movement. Since World War II their participation has steadily risen. In the 1960 elections 69 percent of women voted, 11 percent fewer than men. In 1964 and 1968 there was only a 3 percent difference. In 1972, 70 percent of women voted as compared to 76 percent of men (Lansing, 1974: 8). Perhaps one interpretation of these changes is to be found in women's rising employment. A woman with considerable work experience is more likely to vote than is one without this background (Levitt, 1967). The impact of a person's sex on American voting should not be overrated, however. Of all the major background characteristics, such as race, region, education, or occupation, sex is now in the United States the *least important* in affecting whether or not a person will vote (Verba and Nie, 1972: 339).

Campaigning and officeholding are other avenues by which women participate in the political process. As late as 1972 men were more likely to have joined in a political discussion or helped in a campaign (Harris and Associates, 1972). Some encouraging signs of change came with the Democratic and Republican conventions of 1972, however. There for the first time the number of women approached parity with that of men. The 1974 election mobilized women in a new grass-roots type of campaign that catapulted an unprecedented number of women into political office. With little money but large volunteer armies of precinct workers, candidates like Barbara Mikulski of Maryland and Judith Petty of Missouri managed to rack up 40 percent of the vote against incumbent senators from their states. Ella Grasso of Connecticut became the first woman ever elected governor of a state in her own right. In 1975 a total of 51 women were serving in high state offices such as governor, lieutenant governor, and secretary of state, a gain of 36 percent over 1972. Progress was particularly evident in state legislatures. In 1969 there had been a total of 305 women, but by 1974 their number had increased to 599 (National Women's Education Fund, 1975). In addition, public opinion polls showed a steady rise in the willingness of the electorate to say that they would vote for a woman for President and for Congress (Kirkpatrick, 1974: 248).

Women's rising political visibility was very much tied to the women's movement. Feminism educates women to use political methods for accomplishing private goals in the family or local community. Recent feminist efforts at legal reform reveal women's interest in pressing not only for their own equality but also for social services that support their roles in work, family, and education.

In the last decade a solid foundation for sex equality has been laid in a series of new laws, court decisions, and enforcement procedures. Throughout the period organized women's groups have aided the governmental process by bringing actions, providing useful background reports, and disseminating new information or rulings when they became available.

Two major laws together with several Executive Orders have provided the primary tools to protest sex discrimination in employment. The Equal Pay Act of 1963 requires equal pay for jobs that require the same skills under similar working conditions. Title VII of the Civil Rights Act of 1964 contains a clause that forbids discrimination on the basis of sex in terms, conditions, or privileges of employment. Executive Order 11375, effective in 1968, prohibits sex discrimination by federal contractors. Executive Order 11478 enjoins affirmative action by federal agencies. Under these rulings a major victory came in 1973 with an out-of-court settlement between the government and the American Telegraph and Telephone Company. Women employees were awarded over $15 million in back pay which they had lost as a result of job discrimination.

Women have also maintained pressure on educational institutions to get some women teachers promoted to higher rank and to root out sexist features of the curriculum. They were hampered in their activity, however, because the Equal Pay Act did not cover professional employees and Title VII of the Civil Rights Act did not cover education. Until the 1972 Educational Amendments Act and the 1974 Women's Educational Equity Act, the primary feminist strategy in education had to be contract compliance. Under EO 11375 women sought withdrawal of federal contracts from institutions that engaged in sex discrimination (Sandler, 1973).

Legal breakthroughs came in other institutional areas through several landmark decisions of the Supreme Court. In 1965 state laws against contraception were struck down in *Griswold v. Connecticut*. In 1973 decisions in *Roe v. Wade* and *Doe v. Bolton* upheld women's constitutional right to abortion. In 1971 the Court struck down the practice of excluding mothers of preschool children from employment (*Phillips v. Martin Marietta*). In 1973, in *Frontiero v. Richardson* the Court ruled against armed services regulations that denied dependents of women members the same benefits as dependents of male members.

As in the 1920s, advocates of the Equal Rights Amendment argue that the inconsistent patchwork of state and federal regulation affecting sex equality can best be handled by a Constitutional amendment. Prominent reform groups such as the American Civil Liberties Union and Common Cause, as well as all the feminist organizations, have supported the amendment. The amendment was passed by Congress in 1972, but by the spring of 1976 four states had yet to ratify before it could be made part of the Constitution.

The ERA states "Equality of rights under the law shall not be denied or abridged by the United States or by any State on account of sex." Proponents of the amendment argue that a sure and consistent remedy is needed to right existing inequities. For example, protective labor laws that apply only to women may deprive them of needed jobs. Women who serve in the Armed Forces are not entitled to the same veteran's benefits as men. Women may have to be entirely responsible for children because no child support is provided by the father. At the moment there is no simple way by which such injustice can be redressed. The ERA would provide a uniform basis for designing fairer alternatives.

The general mood of the country will probably have as much to do with the success of women in government as the resurgence of feminism or the accumulation of equal rights legislation. The Watergate scandal made people cynical about big government. Women's success in the subsequent elections was in part caused by their open, direct manner and their identification with the "little guy." Continued emphasis on representative government and limited campaign spending will probably help women further. So too will a shift from heavy government spending on defense to more spending on human services. Government programs for health, education, and welfare will touch women directly by affecting their work and family life. The opportunity to institute more equitable practices in related government programs is just now becoming clear.

Woman in the Economy. By the early 1970s the proportion of American women in the labor force had risen to 44 percent. A number of observers have tried to explain the increase in women's employment. Household conveniences and the shorter childbearing period have liberated women from some of their traditional responsibilities. High demand for workers in female-labeled occupations such as teaching and office work also pulled women into the labor force. Yet the question remains: why do some women work while others do not?

For a time psychologists explored personality differences that made some women career-oriented. Now so many women work, however, that they find no single dominant personality type among them (Hoffman, 1974). Economists find that a woman's decision to work is based on a combination of factors related to job opportunities in the region and her own family and background characteristics. If she has a good education, if her children are older, or if her husband's income is not terribly high, she is more likely to work (Cain, 1966; Bowen and Finegan, 1969).

Most women who are employed are clustered in a very limited range of industries and occupations. In industry, for example, about 40 percent of all men are employed in secondary processes such as construction and manufacturing, while only 20 percent of all employed women are found there. Slightly over half of all males are employed in industries such as trade and services, while more than three-quarters of all women are so employed. Between 1960 and 1970 the percentage of women employed in private household services declined still further from 8.6 to 3.5 percent. On the other hand the proportion of women in professional and related services rose from 22.6 to 29.6 percent (see Table 1).

By occupational grouping we find 60 percent of all women employed in

Table 1   Percentage Employed in Industry Groups, by Sex, 1960 and 1970*

| | Males | | Females | |
Industry	1960	1970	1960	1970
Total employed	100.0	100.0	100.0	100.0
Primary industries	10.8	6.5	2.3	1.3
Agriculture, forestry, and fishing	9.3	5.3	2.1	1.1
Mining	1.4	1.2	0.2	0.2
Secondary industries	40.0	38.8	22.6	20.5
Construction	8.7	9.0	0.7	0.9
Manufacturing	31.3	29.8	21.8	19.6
Tertiary industries	49.2	54.7	75.0	78.2
Transportation, communication, and other utilities	8.8	8.6	3.8	3.9
Wholesale and retail trade	17.6	19.0	21.8	21.9
Finance, insurance, and real estate	3.5	4.0	6.1	6.6
Business and repair services	3.0	3.6	1.7	2.3
Private household services	0.4	0.2	8.6	3.5
Other personal services	2.2	1.9	5.1	5.2
Entertainment and recreation	0.8	0.9	0.7	0.8
Professional and related services	7.3	10.4	22.6	29.6
Public administration	5.5	6.1	4.5	4.4

Sources. Oppenheimer, Valerie Kincade, *The Female Labor Force in the United States: Demographic and Economic Factors Governing Its Growth and Changing Composition,* Population Monograph Series, No. 5, Regents of the University of California, Berkeley, 1970, p. 144; U.S. Bureau of the Census, Census of Population, 1970, Vol. 1, *Characteristics of the Population,* Part I, U.S. Summary—Section 2, Table 236.
*Percentages may not add up to 100.0 because of rounding.

nonmanual occupations, as compared to 40 percent of all men. Clerical work is the largest single female occupation claiming 34.9 percent of all women workers in 1970, while only 7.6 percent of men were so employed. Slightly over 10 percent of men are managers, as compared to less than 4 percent of women (see Table 2). Although the proportion of women in professional, technical, and related occupations was 15.7 percent in 1970, slightly higher than the proportion of men so employed, the representation of women in the most prestigious professions remains very low. Women constitute only 9 percent of physicians, 5 percent of lawyers and judges, and 28 percent of college professors and administrators (Council of Economic Advisors, 1973: 101–102). In every profession they are underrepresented in the higher ranks and receive lower salaries.

Table 2 Occupational Distribution of the Labor Force, by Sex, 1960 and 1970

| | Percentage Distribution* | | | |
| | Males | | Females | |
Major Occupational Group	1960	1970	1960	1970
Total	100.0	100.0	100.0	100.0
Farm occupations	8.1	4.5	1.7	0.7
Farmers and farm managers	5.3	2.8	0.5	0.2
Farm laborers and foremen	2.8	1.7	1.2	0.5
Nonfarm occupations	87.0	95.5	92.4	99.2
Manual occupations	53.3	55.5	39.4	37.5
Craftsmen, foremen, and kindred workers	19.6	21.2	1.2	1.8
Operatives and kindred workers	20.2	19.5	16.2	14.3
Laborers	7.4	6.6	0.6	1.0
Private household workers	0.1	0.1	7.9	3.8
Other service workers	6.0	8.1	13.5	16.6
Nonmanual occupations	33.7	40.0	53.0	61.7
Professional, technical, and kindred workers	9.9	14.3	12.5	15.7
Managers, officials, and proprietors	10.3	11.2	3.6	3.7
Clerical and kindred workers	6.8	7.6	29.1	34.9
Sales workers	6.7	6.9	7.8	7.4

Sources. Oppenheimer, Valerie Kincade, *The Female Labor Force in the United States: Demographic and Economic Factors Governing Its Growth and Changing Composition,* Population Monograph Series, No. 5, Regents of the University of California, Berkeley, 1970, p. 149; U.S. Bureau of the Census, Census of Population: 1970, Vol. I, *Characteristics of the Population,* Part I, U.S. Summary—Section 2, Table 222.
*Percentages may not add up to 100.0 because of rounding.

Why do women cluster in a few fields such as teaching and clerical work and stay at the lower rungs of the career ladder? A number of explanations have been offered. Some psychologists and economists have suggested that women may not invest as much of their human capital in occupational achievement because they prefer to invest time and effort in their families instead (Fuchs, 1971; Mincer and Polachek, 1974). Other analysts suggest that culture and socialization have associated sex labels with certain kinds of work. Women thus enter a few female-labeled professions. In 1970 one-fourth of all women were employed in four occupations—secretary, domestic, schoolteacher, and waitress (Hedges, 1970: 19–29). Because these professions are overcrowded, the pay scales are low (Bergmann, 1971).

Other economists have recently suggested a dual labor market theory to explain the present pattern of sex-typed employment. Some jobs are full-time, year-round positions in the core of major companies. These jobs carry fringe benefits, pensions, and security. On the periphery are to be found marginal, seasonal, and part-time jobs that come and go as demand fluctuates. Minority workers and women tend to be assigned to these marginal positions, perhaps because they are less well trained or are perceived as more likely to quit. The employer is reluctant to invest benefits and on-the-job training in these fringe workers. As a result they are at a disadvantage in security, promotions, and pay (Blau and Jusenius, 1976; Piore, 1971).

History shows remarkable consistency in the pay differences between men and women. In 1910 Edith Abbott noted that women were paid 50 to 60 percent of what men were paid for the same work. In 1971 the earnings of full-time year-round women workers were 66 percent that of males (Council of Economic Advisors, 1973: 103). Even in academia, where presumably the nature of men's and women's work is quite similar, a number of studies have reported not only unequal pay for women and men, but consistent failure to promote women to high ranks of administration and full professorship (Astin and Bayer, 1973).

Such continuity suggests that long-term structural conditions endemic in industrial society perpetuate women's second-class status in employment. The question is how these conditions can be changed. Principal alternatives are (1) enforcement of antidiscrimination laws; (2) restructuring of work schedules and production techniques; (3) provision of supports to women's familial roles; and (4) encouragement of women to reenter the work force by making available counseling services and retraining opportunities.

There are now on the books a number of legal remedies for sex discrimination in employment—the problem is inadequate enforcement. The Office of Federal Contract Compliance (OFCC) and the Equal Employment Opportunities Commission (EEOC), which administer the 1963 Equal Pay Act and 1964 Civil Rights Act, are grossly understaffed for meeting the backlog of cases they must handle. The OFCC in the Department of Defense alone must oversee contracts with 30,000 corporations. The EEOC is reported to have more than 50,000 cases waiting review. With staffs of only a few thousand people scattered throughout the country, full enforcement cannot be left to the time-consuming method of taking a complaint to court. Eventually new reporting and compliance procedures may be developed.

Restructuring of work has been tried in a few manufacturing plants. Some women professionals such as architects and teachers have experimented with sharing responsibility with a partner. Rather than working a fixed schedule, these workers agree on getting a job done by a certain time and so arrange their work as to meet the goal (Berkeley, 1972). The flexible working schedule that results encourages not only more autonomy and satisfaction on the part of workers but allows women to fulfill unexpected family emergencies as well.

Child-care services and maternity benefits are another means by which women can remain in the labor force. If women are to win promotions at an early age, they must be able to combine family responsibility with work. Several firms have tried making day-care available on the premises. In some instances maternity leaves and pregnancy have been defined as medical disabilities, thereby permitting women to receive benefits similar to those received by men in case of sickness. Eventually such practices may create a precedent that men will use to take leaves of absence in industry for their own purposes.

Finally, there is growing interest on the part of older women in counseling for job reentry. Even a woman with a good education and grown children may have skills that are ill fitted to actual job opportunities. There are few places to which she can turn for advice. One economist has suggested that there be a Maternal Bill of Rights, modeled after the GI Bill, to give women who wish to reenter the labor market financial help for training (Cook, 1975).

All such suggestions for reform ultimately call for a change in expectations about what roles women and men should perform in the economy. As long as women must be primarily homemakers they will be overburdened when they take a job. Only help by men or outside services such as child-care and home help can ultimately solve their problem.

At the same time the industrial and office routine may also become more flexible. Hours may be set by workers in accordance with their needs. Part-time work may be redefined as an asset that enriches the individual's expertise for a given job. Leaves of absence and job reentry may also be restructured so as to welcome the new knowledge and resources an individual can bring to a firm.

If all this can be done, eventually jobs may become less sex-typed. The flexibility that women in the past have tried to safeguard may be extended to men, and the rewards and status of the greater number of jobs enjoyed by men may eventually be shared with women.

Changing Sex Roles and Family Life. As record-breaking numbers of married women have entered the paid labor force, the traditional division of labor between the sexes has come into question. Not only that: the whole relationship of work life to family life is up for reconsideration. The split between production in the work place and consumption at home that occurred with the Industrial Revolution had been neatly associated with man specializing in the instrumental sphere and woman in the expressive sphere. Under present conditions that solution is coming undone.

At the same time two major demographic changes have taken place that affect the family life cycle and women's role within it. The childbearing period has been compressed, and adult women's average length of life has increased. As a result the typical American woman in this century bears fewer children and has her last child at the age of 26 or 27. That child leaves home when a woman is in her midforties, and she can still expect to live another 30 years. As recently as the turn of the century women were bearing their last child when they were 33, seeing their last child married when they were 56, and themselves living only another 10 or 15 years. In a matter of two or three generations the average woman's number of childfree years has doubled (Wells, 1973; Glick, 1957).

In part because marriage is earlier, because people live longer, and because the percentage of the population who marry is greater, there is now a higher divorce rate than in the nineteenth century. By current estimates nearly 40 percent of all first marriages made in the 1970s will end in divorce (Schoen, 1975). Yet the total number of marriages broken by death and divorce is about the same as at the turn of the century. While death decreased in certain age groups, divorce went up (Davis, 1972: 261).

Women's increasing employment, longer middle age, and greater likelihood of being divorced are affecting the structure of the family. Current change is indicated by (1) many husbands' and wives' efforts to work out a different division of labor; (2) emergence of new marriage forms; and (3) government efforts to devise new laws, policies, and services that will help the family carry out its functions when women are no longer full-time housewives.

In many families there is evident strain in the traditional division of labor between husband and wife. For women who have both jobs and young children there is the problem of providing adequate child-care after school. The working wife is typically also overburdened because she tries to carry out both her traditional domestic responsibilities and her duties at work. As a result an integrative crisis appears to be in process that results from competing work and family demands. It is no longer so universally accepted that a husband's career opportunity should take precedence over a wife's, or that direct care of the family is primarily the wife's obligation. Instead there is a potential competition between the life obligations to which each sex should give priority. The traditional rules have been thrown into question.

Now it seems likely that there will be a great deal more overlap or crossover between the work that a husband or wife will do. Whereas in the past a man's work ranked higher than a woman's because he was the provider, that priority will no longer be so clear. Whereas in the past a woman was given less pay or opportunity because it was expected that she would get married or drop out when she had a family, that expectation is no longer valid. There is now a potential for each member of a family to take over one function or another at different points in the life cycle. The husband may bring in the income at one point in the marriage; the wife, at another. Or the couple may share work and family functions more or less continuously. There are now also numerous examples of families in which work is so important to both husband and wife that they live at some distance from each other to pursue their careers, even though they are still married and in some instances have young children. Reduction of work time for both men and women is also a viable alternative. A household could survive on the earnings of several people working part-time rather than the earnings of one full-time wage-earner aided by one full-time home-worker (Sawhill, Ross, and MacIntosh, 1973: 13).

As a result of the integrative crisis that threatens the smooth interlocking of work and family functions, a number of solutions have been tried out by pioneer individuals on an ad hoc basis (Poloma and Garland, 1971; Holmstrom, 1972). Their solutions have now been repeated enough times that several patterns can be discerned. Among them are the following:

1. Living together without marriage.
2. So-called "marriage contracts" that spell out agreements about work and family obligations of husbands and wives.
3. A single job shared by one couple (this is most common among academics and professionals and often entails as well an assault on anti-nepotism rules).
4. Acceptance of separate living arrangements for a temporary period so that husband and wife can each pursue their careers in different regions of the country.
5. Willingness to accept alternation in the priority given a husband's or wife's job at different points in the life-cycle.

These inventive solutions appear largely confined to the highly educated. Among working-class people women without the services of a parent or other family member have been forced to go to work without adequate care for their children. Recently there has emerged a new pattern of husband–wife division of labor with a daily schedule that permits one parent to stay home while the other is at work. Instead of giving over care of their household or children to strangers, these couples apparently prefer to be self-sufficient by spreading their own work and family time over day and night. As a result there may be little time for interaction between the adults during their working hours (Lein et al., 1974). Nevertheless they have succeeded in managing both work and family obligations without breaking up the family.

Alongside these variations in the nuclear family, communes and new types of extended families also became more common in the late 1960s. While most rural communes reinforce traditional sex roles, the men and women in urban groups are likely to share household tasks and child-care. Communes are generally not long-lived, but nonetheless they may teach new possibilities to people in transition between marriage, young adults establishing their independence from parents, or singles wanting to join a community. Other forms may eventually prove more viable. One such is a large household of related persons who together contribute to a common income and share economies of scale. A study of 5000 families at the University of Michigan has shown that this structure is a powerful factor in the economic well-being of such family members (Morgan et al., 1974). In some academic communities another family form has emerged: two or more unpartnered women living together with their children and sharing household expenses and duties.

Divorce creates a state in which the household is, at least for a time, headed by a single parent. The number of such households headed by women has increased markedly since World War II. In 1960, 10 percent of all households with children were headed by women. By 1972 this number had risen to 14 percent. A particular cause for concern is the high proportion of female-headed households that fall below the poverty line, either because women are in low-paid occupations or cannot work or because they do not receive adequate support from other sources (Ross and Sawhill, 1975: 2).

New family forms and changing family roles of women have created pressures to redraft marriage, divorce, custody, and tax laws so that men and women are treated in more egalitarian fashion. A Task Force on Family Law and Policy took the position in a 1968 report that marriage is an economic partnership in which each spouse should have legally defined rights in the earnings of the other. Under this view property would be divided equally except in cases of deliberate misappropriation (Citizens' Advisory Council on the Status of Women, 1968; Kay, 1970). Alimony and child support would no longer automatically be seen as the primary duty of the father and custody the right of the mother. Throughout the country divorce settlements are beginning to change the traditional practice of awarding child custody to the woman and demanding support payments from the man. At least five states have now instituted true no-fault divorce laws, and nine others have adopted some other form of no-fault divorce. The new laws substitute the concept of no-fault for the older adversary procedure that assigned fault and based support and custody settlements on that. Settlements under the new law appear less likely to follow the sex-stereotyped pattern of support paid by the man and child custody assigned to the woman (Weitzman, 1974; Glick, 1975).

Income tax and social security legislation are also under review. Present regulations are based on the assumption that most married women are themselves occupied as wives and mothers and are supported by a wage-earner husband. The income-splitting and joint return provisions benefit the couple in which the wife is not engaged in paid work. To avoid penalizing couples with an employed wife the law will have to be changed to permit more liberal deduction of work-related expenses from taxable income.

At present social security benefits are figured on the assumption that most wives are dependent on their husbands. In 1971 nearly one-fifth of retired women workers found that benefits based on their own earnings were less than their benefits as dependent wives. The payments they received did not reflect the additional contribution that they had made as both wife-mother and employed worker (Kahne, 1975).

At the same time women who make an unpaid contribution to the family are subject to a disadvantage of another sort. If divorced from a man to whom they have been married less than 20 years, they cannot claim any social security benefits. Furthermore the contribution of women in the home, because it is unpaid, is not entered on the ledgers of national income accounting when calculating the Gross National Product (Kreps, 1971: 75). Nor is it otherwise recognized that unpaid housewives make a valuable contribution by maintaining the productivity and health of family members who in turn contribute to the economy. Some economists now suggest that an occupation of "consumer maintenance" be recognized to name this activity (Bell, 1975). Another possible solution is to treat the household like a firm in which the housewife's work is given credit as a labor cost when calculating deductible expenses for taxes (Lekachman, 1975).

In addition to pressure to reformulate family laws, there is also at the moment great interest in providing services to families so that they may fulfill their functions yet at the same time permit women to pursue outside activities. A number of programs have this effect: health care plans, care of the elderly, and provision of maternity leave. But the single most popular issue has been day-care. More mothers of young children are working, and many are not able to rely on a husband-provider. The number of children using day-care services rose from an estimated 16,600 in 1961 to almost 700,000 in 1970 (Keyserling, 1972: 73). Twice as many children were in kindergarten and nursery school in the second half of the 1960s as in the first half. As the day-care movement has continued to grow, more centers have been established in colleges, universities, and licensed homes. From over 4000 available centers in 1961 the number has grown to more than 140,000 in 1970 (Jusenius and Shortlidge, 1975: 78).

The net effect of all these changes has been to push government family policy toward equal treatment of the sexes. Family legislation of the 1930s provided aid to dependent children whose absent or incapacitated father was presumed to be the breadwinner and whose mother was presumed to be a dependent wife. Future policies will probably be designed to provide for family functions under conditions where such a traditional division of labor by sex can no longer be assumed.

Education.   Three-fourths of the high school-age population complete high school, and 50 percent of these graduates are girls. Yet only 40 percent of bachelor's and master's degrees go to women. At the doctoral level only 15 percent of the degrees conferred go to women (U.S. Department of Health, Education, and Welfare, 1972: 51, 69, 90). However between 1966–1967 and 1971–1972 there was a noticeable increase in women's share of higher degrees. The proportion of women receiving master's degrees rose more than 6 percentage points in those five years, and their proportion of doctorates rose more than 3 percentage points (see Table 3).

Table 3   Degrees Conferred in Institutions of Higher Education by Level of Degree and Sex of Student

	1966–1967		1971–1972	
	Number	Percent	Number	Percent
Bachelor's				
Men	324,236	57.7	503,631	56.3
Women	238,133	42.3	390,479	43.7
	562,369	100.0	894,110	100.0
Master's				
Men	103,179	65.3	150,085	59.4
Women	54,713	34.7	102,689	40.6
	157,892	100.0	252,774	100.0
Doctoral				
Men	18,164	88.1	28,095	84.2
Women	2,457	11.9	5,274	15.8
	20,621	100.0	33,369	100.0

Source.   Curtis O. Baker and Agnes Q. Wells. 1975. Earned Degrees Completed: 1971–72. National Center for Educational Statistics. Washington, D.C.: U.S. Government Printing Office.

Women undergraduate and graduate students cluster most heavily in fine arts, education, and the humanities, where they constitute 50 percent or more of the student body. About one-third of students in the social sciences, and one-fifth in the biological and physical sciences, are women (Carnegie Commission on Higher Education, 1973: 67). Women's grades are almost uniformly higher than men's (approximately half of all women students in the institutions of higher learning were in the top quarter of their high school class as compared to 35 percent of the men) (American Council on Education, 1971: 25, 33). However their attrition rates are much higher than men's. Such facts pose a simple and familiar question which Arlie Hochschild (1975: 48) phrases as follows:

Why at a public university like the University of California at Berkeley in 1972 do women compose 41 percent of the entering freshmen, 37 percent of the graduating seniors, 31 percent of the applicants for admission to graduate school, 28 percent of the graduate admissions, 24 percent of the doctoral students, 21 percent of advanced doctoral students, 12 percent of the Ph.D.'s, 38 percent of instructors, 9 percent of assistant professors, 6 percent of associate professors, and 3 percent of full professors?

The three major explanations for achievement differences between boys and girls are psychological functioning, early socialization, and a culture of educational institutions that generally rewards male rather than female role. Tests that measure differences in psychological functioning show that girls perform better on tests of verbal ability and boys do better on visual and spatial tasks. Such differences could account for girls' concentration in the humanities and boys' in the sciences. After a recent comprehensive review of the literature, however, Maccoby and Jacklin (1974: 366) concluded that the sexes are no different in their ability to learn. Early socialization may account for girls' relatively greater interest in interpersonal relations, marriage, and peer involvement, while boys show greater interest in task accomplishments (Boocock, 1972: 80).

The institutional reward systems that encourage boys and hamper girls are currently of greatest interest to those trying to improve educational opportunity for women. The following aspects of the established system are open to question: (1) current educational goals and values that are male-oriented; (2) sex stereotyping in the curriculum; (3) small proportions of women who are tenured faculty; (4) educational calendars and admissions policies that may hinder women; (5) educational reliance on outside institutions such as the family that may help men but hinder women. Associated with each of these topics is mounting research evidence showing implicit or explicit discrimination against women.

Feminist observers now assert that educational institutions are primarily geared to training men for their careeers. In teaching and in studying it has been claimed that faculty and students devote time to analyzing wars, aggressive deeds, and other inhumane acts; were they to value the roles of women more highly, men would be taught to care, give time to community service, and cooperate through sharing (Roby, 1972: 137–138). Schools would value more highly the nurturant qualities of schoolteachers, 85 percent of whom are women (Lightfoot, 1975: 116–120). University departments that now force women faculty and graduate students "inside the clockwork of male careers" would expand from "20 full-time men . . . to departments of 40 part-time men and women" (Hochschild, 1975: 74). The feminist alternative is not so much to replace the male pattern with a female one but to substitute a hybrid model that would better allow achievement by persons of each sex.

One of the most accessible objects for change is the content of teaching and the curriculum itself. Textbooks and basal readers typically devote much more space to male than to female characters and portray the few females whom they do picture outside the home in a narrow range of roles such as teacher or nurse. Vocational tracking typically channels girls into seventh grade home economics courses and boys into shop or vocational agriculture. While over 90 percent of all students registered in consumer and homemaking courses are female, over ninety percent of those registered in technical courses, such as metallurgy, engineering, oceanography, and police science, are male. Three-fourths of students training for office occupations are female, and nine-tenths of those in trade and industrial courses are male (Saario et al., 1973: 399, 408–409).

Removal of the obvious stereotypes may help change the ratio of boys to girls in vocational courses, sciences, and the humanities. Maccoby and Jacklin (1974: 366–367) also suggest that education should make a concerted effort to round out cognitive capacities of girls in the visual-spatial domain and those of boys in the verbal domain. Few women are in the scientific field in part because women try to avoid the mathematical preparation and reasoning on which such courses are based (Carnegie Commission on Higher Education, 1973: 64).

Introduction of women's studies is another means by which to alter the curriculum on behalf of sex equality. The number of women's studies courses taught in colleges and universities throughout the country mushroomed from approximately 110 in 1970, to 800 or 900 by the 1972–1973 academic year (Howe and Ahlum, 1973: 393–394). Such courses not only exhibit a great deal of intellectual "rigor," but also raise consciousness and usually carry a radical message—that much of established academic scholarship, particularly in the humanities and social sciences, is male-oriented.

A heavily female staff in the primary grades may be disadvantageous to boys. For girls the harm may come at more advanced levels, where in colleges and universities in particular the faculty and administration are overwhelmingly male (Boocock, 1972: 95). While 65 percent of the instructional staff in public schools are female, only 15 percent of the school principals are women (Dale, 1973: 393). Although 39.4 percent of the faculty in four-year colleges and universities are women, only 8.6 percent of the full professors are female (Carnegie Commission on Higher Education, 1973: 111).

Feminists have responded to women's underrepresentation in positions of high rank by a combination of legal actions and efforts to implement affirmative action plans. Because the Civil Rights Act of 1964 excluded educational institutions from its coverage, various indirect avenues of legal recourse had to be used until 1972, when the Equal Pay Act and the Civil Rights Act were broadened to bar discrimination against educational personnel. In the interim the Women's Equity Action League pioneered in using the Executive Orders to bring suits against a number of universities (Sandler, 1973: 441–442). Although no federal contract with a university has ever been canceled because of sex discrimination, there does seem to be progress in the hiring of women faculty as instructors and assistant professors. Between 1959–1960 and 1974–1975 the percentage of women instructors at four-year colleges had risen from 29.3 to 47.6, and the fraction of assistant professors rose from one-fifth to a fourth. But at the professorial level the proportion of women held steady at around 9 percent (Carnegie Council on Policy Studies in Higher Education, 1975: 20). Only time will tell whether the large cohort of young women at the instructor level will eventually rise to the top.

Reorganization of the educational institutions is another means by which women may be benefited. It is debatable whether women's colleges or coeducational institutions better promote student leadership among women. A recent survey of coeducational institutions found more women among student leaders than men (Carnegie Commission on Higher Education, 1973: 62). It does seem clear, however, that there are more science majors in a women's college like Mount Holyoke and more economics majors at Wellesley than in comparable institutions such as Radcliffe where classes are coeducational with Harvard.

The most profound challenge to the structure of existing school calendars and four-year institutions of higher education has come through the movement for continuing education. Such education permits women (and men, though they are fewer) to reenter college, take courses, and finish degrees that they began some years earlier. Under the auspices of adult education programs, extension courses, or "continuing education centers," many women have gained credentials that have enabled them to reenter the labor force or move to a higher-level job. By the early 1970s these programs were beginning to band together for mutual cooperation, to study their constituencies, and to evaluate their accomplishments (Campbell, 1973). The mobility and flexibility that such courses provide, as well as the mature and highly motivated students they attract, give them a great advantage. Women may also come to use volunteer work as educational preparation for paid careers (Loeser, 1974). In this rapidly changing society continuing education allows a student to gain new skills as they are needed. Women pioneers in these programs may eventually guide others to educational innovations that will meet the whole population's changing needs (Campbell, 1973; Huber, 1973).

Pressures that do not come from educational institutions are another aspect of women's unequal educational opportunities. Two factors have received particular attention: the differential impact of the family on women and men, and the difference in financial support available to members of each sex. Family responsibilities delay and obstruct women's progress through college and graduate training, for they still bear primary responsibility for homemaking services. For men, on the other hand, a wife becomes an asset, a member of a two-person career, or a cryptoservant to whom the educational enterprise can subcontract for personal maintenance services that facilitate the male student's advance (Hochschild, 1975: 48–50).

Financial support for women students, on the other hand, is more heavily derived from family sources than is that for men students. Roby (1973: 47–48) shows no significant sex differences in the level of *institutional support* to undergraduate and graduate students. But she does find men more dependent on their own efforts than women, through employment and use of savings or loans, while women are more dependent on family contributions either from parent or spouse. Probably as a result, the women who manage to continue are much more likely to come from financially comfortable families. A truer picture of other women's disadvantage would result from examining the careers of working and lower-middle-class girls whose further education is sacrificed because they cannot hope for such family support. Government help may also be crucial. One study of stipend support for doctorates found that 10 percent more men than women received help from the government, whereas 8 percent more women than men relied on support from savings, family, or spouse (Attwood, 1972: 9).

The Higher Education Act of 1972 through Title IX extended legal recourse against sex discrimination to issues of curriculum and program. It bars discrimination in educational programs, admissions criteria, and financial assistance, and thus gives legal basis for protest against unequal public investment in male or female sports, vocational education, and other facilities. Particularly controversial issues relate to athletics, fringe benefits, childbirth leave, admission to private undergraduate professional schools, and effects of the use of educational facilities by single-sex youth organizations. The Women's Educational Equity Act of 1974 calls for development of new and improved curricula, initiation of programs for women at all levels, improved counseling, women's resource centers, and community education programs on opportunities for women (*Women in 1973*: 12). Redesign of educational programs on behalf of women is thus now supported by these recent laws, but it is still too soon to say whether they will be effective in their aim.

Health. Since the 1920s, when demographers first noted that more and more deaths were caused by the diseases of middle and old age, the life expectancy of women has increased even further to the age of 81 (U.S. Commission on Population Growth and the American Future, 1972: 101). The birthrate has fallen to its lowest point, 15 per thousand people in 1973. The total fertility rate in 1973 stood at 1.9 children per woman—just half what it had been in 1957 (Glick, 1975: 16). The picture painted by these statistics shows that some of the most serious health and fertility problems of women are apparently "solved." What then are the contemporary health concerns of women in the United States?

Freedom of contraception and availability of abortion are uppermost in the minds of many, especially the young and unmarried, who may not be well informed or properly prepared for the sexual freedom they experience (Bengis, 1973: 62–63). Teenage illegitimate pregnancy rose markedly between 1940 and 1968, caused in large part by improvement in health and nutrition among the poor as well as by changing sexual mores. (Cutright, 1973: 90). Efforts by teachers, counselors, and social workers are invested in better sex education and in keeping the young mother in school until she can learn adequate skills and perhaps graduate.

Feminists have invested great energy in turning back efforts to introduce antiabortion legislation. Abortion clinics now operate freely enough to have removed much of the risk that until 1972 was entailed in having an illegal abortion (Lee, 1969). Laws prohibiting dispensation of birth control devices remained on the books in some states, such as Massachusetts, until recently. Informed women consumers now complain that warnings against dangerous side effects of the birth control pills have not been adequately advertised (Seaman, 1972: 244–245).

Adequate sexual functioning receives a great deal of attention in both popular and medical literature. The work of Masters and Johnson (1966) in treating sexual dysfunction reopened discussion of frigidity in women and put greater emphasis on the quality of the relationship between two people rather than on the individual capacity of a particular man or woman. Subsequent work by Mary Jane Sherfey and others has pointed out a fundamental bisexual capacity shared by males and females that is in later development differentiated in the two sexes (Miller, 1973). Work at the Johns Hopkins University on transsexuals has discovered three basic elements in the formation of sexual identity: hormones, morphology, and social assignment by parents or other close family members (Money and Ehrhardt, 1972: 1–23). Accompanying these changes in scientific and intellectual stance toward various sexual behavior has been a growing activity on the part of homosexuals in a movement known as Gay Liberation. Much more prominent than ever before in the women's movement is an open discussion of lesbianism and bisexuality (Bengis, 1973: 95–156; Carden, 1974: 68–69).

Aside from efforts to ensure free access to contraception and abortion, the women's movement's largest contribution to contemporary health care has been the formation of "women's health collectives." The Boston Collective in 1971 published a book *Our Bodies, Ourselves* that has been nationally distributed. It teaches laywomen a self-help approach to gynecologists, clinics, and the medical establishment in general. Like knowing how to discuss with a mechanic the inside of a car, women are encouraged to know about and take care of their own reproductive systems, rather than to passively hand over all responsibility to a doctor. They are also encouraged to value their own strength, to give birth without anesthesia, to nurse their babies, and generally to rely on their own powers as women (Seaman, 1972; Boston Women's Health Book Collective, 1971, 1973).

Mental illness among women has received more attention than the epidemiology of their physical complaints, particularly by social scientists. The relatively higher rate of depression in middle-aged women has been attributed to the loss of their children with no substitute activity to take their place (Bart, 1971). Married women have a greater risk of mental illness than either married men or single women, suggesting a factor in marriage that works to women's disadvantage (Bernard, 1972). Community surveys consistently find that 33 percent of adult females report three or more psychiatric symptoms, as compared to 25 percent of adult males, and the difference is not merely attributable to a response bias by females (Clancy and Gove, 1974). Higher rates of mental illness in women suggest that the stress of modern American society bears more heavily on them. On the other hand, women live longer, on the average three years longer, than men. A great deal more research must be done to ascertain the implications that should be drawn from the present data.

The most significant long-term impact of feminism on medicine may be in its emphasis on self-help, consumer knowledge, and preventive health care.

In an era of wider health insurance coverage and mounting costs, the preventive emphasis may prove attractive for other segments of the population as well.

Images. Over and above all the changes occurring in the institutional structure of society, there is a change in the cultural definition of the essential images of male and female. Religion, media, and the arts have shown a revolutionary willingness in recent times to question the old symbols and role models of masculine and feminine.

Change came earliest and most visibly to the all-male bastion of TV newscasters. The popular *Today* show introduced a woman as one of its three principals. A Supreme Court decision prohibiting the listing of employment advertisements by sex brought some self-awaremess to newspaper advertisers habituated to sex stereotyping.

Feminists themselves have had some success in their own publishing efforts. The feminist magazine *Ms.,* launched in 1972, now has a large circulation and covers all aspects of changing women's roles from health, child-care, work, and politics to religion. Feminist organizations have emerged to handle the growing demand for books and articles in the women's movement. Among them are KNOW, Inc., of Pittsburgh, established in 1969, and the Feminist Press, of Old Westbury, New York, which distributes materials for women's studies courses.

Fashion has shown greater acceptance of pants by women, even among the older generation. Women in sports or women "firsts" in unusual occupations for women, such as high-line telephone worker, baseball umpire, and miner, have received considerable news coverage. The portrayal of the women's movement itself has gradually become more sympathetic—less inclined to focus on bizarre acts and more concerned with easily understood grievances.

Language has also come under critical review. The generic use of the term *he* or *man* to refer to all persons is no longer considered acceptable by feminists. Substitution of such terms as *chairperson* for *chairman* is becoming more common, but few go so far as some radical feminists when they substitute the term "herstory" for "history."

In the whole symbolic revolution perhaps the most far-reaching changes have come in politics and religion. Political images are significant for what they communicate about who has power. National television coverage of the House Committee hearings on the Watergate affair brought into public view the competent style of women members of Congress such as Elizabeth Holtzman of New York and Barbara Jordan of Texas. The elections that followed in the fall brought a record number of women into high state and federal office.

Religious images project what is valuable and good in the whole society and connect the roles of men and women to a distinctive value domain. Religious change in the image of women is particularly striking in the work of Catholic theologian Mary Daly (1973), who calls for an end to male God-language and a substitution of terms that permit expression of the full male and female personality of God as Creator, Person, and Spirit (Reuther, 1974; Goldenberg, 1972). The irregular ordination of 11 Episcopal women to the priesthood in 1974 called into question the legitimacy of an all-male priesthood and the relegation of women to lower orders.

Several themes are apparent in the efforts to change both secular and religious images of female and male. First, there is an attempt to *broaden the content and range* of activity and personality associated with male and female so as to effect crossover in the types of opportunity open to each. Second, there is a concern to *provide positive role models.* If persons of high prestige and symbolic importance do not include women, it is felt that women of the future will not have adequate models to imitate. Third, there is an effort to *raise consciousness* by challenging the existing rules and showing that women are implicitly and unfairly linked with inferior or negative images.

Image, like culture, pervades all human activity. Images combine symbolic elements to become imbedded in books, film, fashion, and language. They may be closely connected with live people who are representatives and role models for a certain type of image. The contemporary women's movement in America has questioned both symbol and reality and sought a broader, more positive, and less stereotyped role for each sex (Heilbrun, 1973).

The search has penetrated into scholarship. Scholarly disciplines organize the cognitive components of culture and help society adapt to the challenges of the physical, social, and metaphysical world. To the extent that such scholarship ignores the experience of women or their point of view, it may actually prove maladaptive. Current feminist critics point out that much of history, sociology, and the arts has been conducted from a primarily male point of view about the experience of males. Male historians have written about war, battles, and kings. Male sociologists have written about "power, work, climbing the occupational ladder and sex—but not women, or women only as adjuncts to men" (Bernard, 1973: 785–786). Yet according to one woman historian, women have done important work. Women have been central to social mobility and family life, and "women have been prolific and effective builders of social structure beyond anything . . . previously realized" (Scott, 1972: 631).

The search for new and valid images of women has led into literature and the arts. Virginia Woolf, Anaïs Nin, and Kate Chopin have enjoyed a tremendous revival. The novels of Doris Lessing, the poetry of Anne Sexton, and the work of Sylvia Plath are all subject to heretofore unequaled popular interest (Spacks, 1971–1972, 1972; Moers, 1976). Women appear to be seeking usable images as they turn to women authors, poets, playwrights, and filmmakers to hear the secrets that result from their self-revelation and invention (Ausubel, 1974).

There is, however, a crisis in communication when standards of evaluation fail to bridge the male and female symbolic world. This is perhaps best illustrated in the visual arts. One feminist art historian, after reviewing the evidence, asked why there had been no great women artists (Nochlin, 1973). Women are greatly underrepresented in art openings and galleries, in official exhibits and acquistions by the great museums. The usual explanation is discrimination.

Yet at least one other explanation is available—that the *definition* of great art is really what is at issue. Women have long held a prominent place in the decorative arts—weaving, needlework, decorative painting. A priceless quilt made by a Negro woman of Georgia, probably born a slave, belongs to the Boston Museum of Fine Arts. If it is agreed that the aesthetic standards of this society are as much represented by its everyday clothing, textiles, baskets, pottery, and needlework as by its sculptures and paintings in museums, women will almost certainly be found among the important contributors to American art. If it is also understood that culture is created not just by artistic geniuses but also by the women who host the salons and run the symphony benefits, women will also be found among its creators (Tuchman, 1975).

CONCLUSION

Women in the United States share with men the benefits of a developed economy, good physical health, a high general level of literacy and education. They participate in all the major rights of citizenship characteristic of a Western democracy. Yet in a number of important dimensions there is still clear and consistent inequality in their status with men.

Legal disabilities remain in a number of states. The Equal Rights Amendment to the Constitution is still several states short of ratification. The number of women in public office still falls far short of parity with men. The pay that a full-time woman worker receives averages 66 percent that of a full-time male worker. Women are greatly underrepresented at the top of any administrative hierarchy. Although as many girls graduate from high school as boys, the number of women who receive professional degrees and doctorates is less than half that of men. Women who are single heads of families with children are twice as likely to be poor as are families with a male at their head. Women have higher rates of mental illness than men.

The feminist movement of the nineteenth century fought some of the grossest forms of inequality—the exclusion of women from the vote and from admission to institutions of higher learning. The American feminist movement of the twentieth century now presses for removal of more subtle barriers to equality.

The recent changes appear to encourage females to adopt a male pattern of achievement more than to upgrade traditional women's jobs or encourage men to enter them. Yet the logic of interchangeability of men's and women's tasks calls for recognition of value in women's traditional functions as well as in men's. Otherwise there is a danger that more women will leave their nurturant roles in the family and their charitable roles in the community for paid jobs and public recognition, and neither men nor other women will replace them. If movement across sex roles boundaries occurs in only one direction, the quality of life will be endangered, cultural and emotional life may suffer, and the noneconomic and private dimensions of social experience will be submerged.

Whether sex equality is possible under the present social system is a question that lingers just below the surface. Feminists active in health collectives advocate reorganization of the entire system to put more emphasis on self-help and preventive care. Feminists active in academia, the church, and the media press for deep reorganization of knowledge, symbolic forms, and images to raise female elements in human experience to a place of greater importance. These events perhaps foretell a time when the female experience will be more highly valued and will exert as much pull on humane and thoughtful men as the male pattern now exerts on ambitious and accomplished women.

The full development of sex equality in America is still incomplete. Considerable change has been accomplished: the role options for both men and women are noticeably broader than a century ago. Nevertheless, we have yet to see whether the movement will ultimately reorganize the American experience at a deeper level.

BIBLIOGRAPHY

Abbott, Edith. 1910. *Women in Industry.* New York: D. Appleton.

American Council on Education. 1971. *The American Freshman: National Norms for Fall 1971.* Washington, D.C.: ACE Research Reports **6,** (6) December.

Astin, Helen S., and Alan E. Bayer. 1973. "Sex Discrimination in Academe." In *Academic Women on the Move.* Edited by A. Rossi and A. Calderwood. New York: Russell Sage Foundation, pp. 333–356.

Attwood, Cynthia L. 1972. "Women in Fellowship and Training Programs." Project on the Status and Education of Women. Washington, D.C.: Association of American Colleges.

Ausubel, Bobbie. 1974. Personal Communication. (Ausubel is director of the experimental Caravan Theater that produced *How to Make a Woman.*)

Bailyn, Bernard. 1960. *Education in the Forming of American Society*. Chapel Hill: University of North Carolina Press.

Baker, Curtis O., and Agnes Q. Wells. 1975. *Earned Degrees Conferred: 1971–72*. National Center for Educational Statistics. Washington, D.C.: U.S. Government Printing Office.

Bakke, E. Wight. 1940. *The Unemployed Worker*. New Haven: Yale University Press.

Bart, Pauline. 1971. "Depression in Middle-Aged Women." In *Woman in Sexist Society*. Edited by Vivian Gornick and Barbara K. Moran. New York: Basic Books, pp. 163–186.

Beard, Mary R. 1946. *Woman as Force in History: A Study in Traditions and Realities*. New York: Collier Books.

Bell, Carolyn Shaw. 1975. "The Next Revolution." *Social Policy* **6** (September–October): 5–11.

Bengis, Ingrid. 1973. *Combat in the Erogenous Zone*. New York: Bantam Books.

Bergmann, Barbara. 1971. "The Effect on White Incomes of Discrimination in Employment." *Journal of Political Economy* **79** (March/April): 294–313.

Berkeley, Ellen. 1972. "Women in Architecture." *The Architectural Forum* **137** (September): 46 ff.

Bernard, Jessie. 1971. *Women and the Public Interest: An Essay on Policy and Protest*. Chicago: Aldine.

———. 1972. *The Future of Marriage*. New York: World Publishing.

———. 1973. "My Four Revolutions: An Autobiographical History of the ASA." *American Journal of Sociology* **78** (January): 733–791.

Blake, Judith. 1974. "The Changing Status of Women in Developed Countries." *Scientific American* **231** (September): 136–147.

Blau, Francine D., and Carol L. Jusenius. 1976. "Economists' Approaches to Sex Segregation in the Labor Market: An Appraisal." *Signs: Journal of Women in Culture and Society* **1** (Spring, Part 2): 181–199.

Boocock, Sarane S. 1972. *An Introduction to the Sociology of Learning*. Boston: Houghton Mifflin.

Boston Women's Health Book Collective. 1971, 1973. *Our Bodies, Ourselves: A Book By and For Women*. New York: Simon and Schuster.

Bowen, William G., and T. Aldrich Finegan. 1969. *The Economics of Labor Force Participation*. Princeton: Princeton University Press.

Breckinridge, Sophonisba. 1933. *Women in the Twentieth Century: A Study of Their Political, Social and Economic Activities*. New York: McGraw-Hill.

Butts, R. Freeman. 1973. "Education, History of. United States." *Encyclopedia Britannica* **7**:990–997. Chicago, Encyclopedia Britannica, Inc.

Cain, Glen G. 1966. *Married Women in the Labor Force: An Economic Analysis*. Chicago: University of Chicago Press.

Calhoun, Arthur W. 1919. *A Social History of the American Family*. Vol. III. *Since the Civil War*. Cleveland: Arthur Clark Co.

Campbell, Jean W. 1973. "Women Drop Back In: Educational Innovation in the Sixties." In *Academic Women on the Move*. Edited by A. Rossi and A. Calderwood. New York: Russell Sage Foundation, pp. 93–124.

Carden, Maren Lockwood. 1974. *The New Feminist Movement*. New York: Russell Sage Foundation.

Carnegie Commission on Higher Education. 1973. *Opportunities for Women in Higher Education*. New York: McGraw-Hill.

Carnegie Council on Policy Studies in Higher Education. 1975. *Making Affirmative Action Work in Higher Education.* San Francisco: Jossey-Bass.

Chafe, William. 1972. *The American Woman: Her Changing Social, Economic and Political Roles, 1920–1970.* New York: Oxford University Press.

Citizen's Advisory Council on the Status of Women. 1968. *Report of the Task Force on Family Law and Policy.* Washington, D.C.: U.S. Government Printing Office.

Clancy, Kevin, and Walter Gove. 1974. "Sex Differences in Mental Illness: An Analysis of Response Bias in Self-Reports." *American Journal of Sociology* **80** (July): 205–216.

Cook, Alice H. 1975. *The Working Mother: A Survey of Problems and Programs in Nine Countries.* Ithaca, New York: Cornell University, New York State School of Industrial Relations.

Council of Economic Advisors. 1973. "The Economic Role of Women." *Economic Report of the President.* Washington: U.S. Government Printing Office, pp. 89–112.

Cutright, Phillips. 1973. "Illegitimacy and Income Supplements." In *Studies in Public Welfare.* Part I. The Family, Poverty and Welfare Programs: Factors Influencing Family Instability. Washington, D.C.: U.S. Government Printing Office, pp. 90–138.

Dale, Charlene. 1973. "Wanted More Women: Where are the Superintendents?" In *Women's Educational Equity Act of 1973, Hearings before the Subcommittee on Education of the Committee on Labor and Public Welfare.* U.S. Senate, October 17 and November 9, 1973, pp. 389–396.

Daly, Mary. 1973. *Beyond God the Father: Toward a Philosophy of Women's Liberation.* Boston: Beacon Press.

Davis, Kingsley. 1972. "The American Family in Relation to Demographic Change." Berkeley, California: Population Reprint Series, Reprint No. 425. Reprinted from Charles Westoff and Robert Parke, Jr., Editors, *Demographic and Social Aspects of Population Growth,* pp. 237–265.

Demos, John. 1970. *A Little Commonwealth: Family Life in Plymouth Colony.* New York: Oxford University Press.

Dexter, Elizabeth Anthony. 1924. *Colonial Women of Affairs: A Study of Women in Business and the Professions in America before 1776.* Boston: Houghton Mifflin.

Dublin, Thomas. 1974. "Women, Work, and the Family: Women Operatives in the Lowell Mills, 1830–1860." Paper presented at the Berkshire Conference on Women's History. Radcliffe College, October 26.

Erikson, Kai. 1966. *Wayward Puritans: A Study in the Sociology of Deviance.* New York: Wiley.

Flexner, Eleanor. 1975. *Century of Struggle.* Cambridge: Harvard University Press. Revised edition.

Frank, Lawrence K. 1933. "Childhood and Youth." In *Recent Social Trends.* Vol. II. President's Research Committee on Social Trends. New York: McGraw-Hill, pp. 757–800.

Freeman, Jo. 1973. "The Tyranny of Structurelessness." *Berkeley Journal of Sociology: A Critical Review* **XVII** (1972–73): 151–164. Reprinted in *Ms.* (July 1973), pp. 76–78 ff.

Friedan, Betty. 1963. *The Feminine Mystique.* New York: W. W. Norton Company.

Fuchs, Victor. 1971. "Differences in Hourly Earnings between Men and Women." *Monthly Labor Review* **94** (May): 9–15.

Giele, Janet Zollinger. 1961. *Social Change in the Feminine Role: A Comparison of Woman's Suffrage and Woman's Temperance, 1870–1920.* Unpublished doctoral dissertation, Radcliffe College.

Glick, Paul C. 1957. *American Families*. New York: Wiley.

———. 1975. "A Demographer Looks at American Families." *Journal of Marriage and the Family* **37** (February): 15–26.

Goldenberg, Judith Plaskow. 1972. *Women and Religion*. Proceedings, American Academy of Religion. Available from CSR Executive Office, Waterloo Lutheran University, Waterloo, Ontario.

Harris, Louis, and Associates. 1972. *The 1972 Virginia Slims American Women's Opinion Poll*.

Hedges, Janice N. 1970. "Women Workers and Manpower Demands in the 1970's." *Monthly Labor Review* **93** (June): 19–29.

Heilbrun, Carolyn G. 1973. *Toward a Recognition of Androgyny*. New York: Harper.

Hochschild, Arlie Russell. 1975. "Inside the Clockwork of Male Careers." In *Women and the Power to Change*. Edited by Florence Howe. A volume of essays sponsored by the Carnegie Commission on Higher Education. New York: McGraw-Hill, pp. 47–80.

Hoffman, Lois. 1974. "Psychological Factors." In *Working Mothers*. Edited by Lois Hoffman and Ivan Nye. San Francisco: Jossey-Bass.

Holmstrom, Lynda Lytle. 1972. *The Two-Career Family*. Cambridge: Schenckman.

Howe, Florence, and Carol Ahlum. 1973. "Women's Studies and Social Change." In *Academic Women on the Move*. Edited by A. Rossi and A. Calderwood. New York: Russell Sage Foundation, pp. 393–424.

Huber, Joan. 1973. "From Sugar and Spice to Professor." In *Academic Women on the Move*. Edited by A. Rossi and A. Calderwood. New York: Russell Sage Foundation, pp. 125–135.

James, Edward, Janet W. James, and Paul S. Boyer. 1971. *Notable American Women, 1607– 1950: A Biographical Dictionary*. 3 vols. Cambridge, Massachusetts: Harvard University Press.

Jennings, M. Kent, and Richard G. Niemi. 1974. *The Political Character of Adolescence: The Influence of Families and Schools*. Princeton: Princeton University Press.

Johnston, John D., Jr. 1972. "Common Law, Women, and the Property Curriculum of American Law Schools." AAAS Symposium on Women and the Law. New York University, October 21–22. (American Association of Law Schools.)

Jusenius, Carol, and Richard L. Shortlidge. 1975. *Dual Careers: A Longitudinal Study of Labor Market Experience of Women*. Columbus, Ohio: Ohio State University, Center for Human Resource Research.

Kahne, Hilda. 1975. "Economic Perspectives on the Roles of Women in the American Economy." *Journal of Economic Literature* **13** (December): 1249–1292.

Kay, Herma Hill. 1970. "A Family Court: The California Proposal." In *Divorce and After*. Edited by Paul Bohannan. Garden City, New Jersey: Doubleday.

Keyserling, Mary Dublin. 1972. *Windows on Day Care*. New York: National Council of Jewish Women.

Kirkpatrick, Jeanne J. 1974. *Political Woman*. New York: Basic Books.

Komarovsky, Mirra. 1940. *The Unemployed Man and His Family*. New York: Dryden Press.

———. 1953. *Women in the Modern World*. Boston: Little, Brown.

Kreps, Juanita. 1971. *Sex in the Marketplace: American Women at Work*. Baltimore: Johns Hopkins Press.

Lansing, Marjorie. 1974. "The American Woman: Voter and Activist." In *Women in Politics*. Edited by Jane Jaquette. New York: Wiley, pp. 5–24.

Lee, Nancy Howell. 1969. *The Search for an Abortionist*. Chicago: University of Chicago Press.

Lein, Laura, Maureen Durham, Michael Pratt, Michael Schudson, Ronald Thomas, and Heather Weiss. 1974. *Work and Family Life*. Cambridge, Massachusetts: Center for the Study of Public Policy. Unpublished report.

Lekachman, Robert. 1975. "On Economic Equality." *Signs: Journal of Women in Culture and Society* **1** (Autumn): 93–102.

Lemons, J. Stanley. 1973. *The Woman Citizen: Social Feminism in the 1920's*. Urbana: University of Illinois Press.

Lerner, Gerda. 1969. "The Lady and the Mill Girl: Changes in the Status of Women in the Age of Jackson." Reprinted from *American Studies Journal* **10** (Spring): 5–15. Bobbs-Merrill American History Series H-43.

Leuchtenberg, William E. 1963. *Franklin D. Roosevelt and the New Deal: 1932–1940*. New York: Harper and Row.

Levitt, Morris. 1967. "The Political Role of American Women." *Journal of Human Relations* **15**: 23–35.

Lightfoot, Sarah Lawrence. 1975. "Sociology of Education: Perspectives on Women." In *Another Voice*. Edited by Marcia Millman and Rosabeth Kanter. New York: Anchor Books, pp. 106–143.

Loeser, Herta. 1974. *Women, Work, and Volunteering*. Boston: Beacon Press.

Lynd, Robert S., and Helen Merrell Lynd. 1929, 1956. *Middletown: A Study in Modern American Culture*. New York: Harvest Books.

Maccoby, Eleanor E., and Carol N. Jacklin. 1974. *The Psychology of Sex Differences*. Stanford: Stanford University Press.

Masters, William, and Virginia Johnson. 1966. *Human Sexual Response*. Boston: Little, Brown.

Mead, Margaret, and Frances Balgley Kaplan, Editors. 1965. *American Women: The Report of the President's Commission on the Status of Women and Other Publications of the Commission (1963)*. New York: Charles Scribners.

Miller, Jean Baker, Editor. 1973. *Psychoanalysis and Women*. New York: Penguin Books.

Mincer, Jacob. 1962. "Labor Force Participation of Married Women." In *Aspects of Labor Economics*. National Bureau of Economic Research. Princeton: Princeton University Press.

———, and Solomon Polachek. 1974. "Family Investments in Human Capital: Earnings of Women." *Journal of Political Economy* **82** (March–April): S76–S108.

Moers, Ellen. 1976. *Literary Women: The Great Writers*. Garden City, New York: Doubleday.

Money, John, and Anke A. Ehrhardt. 1972. *Man and Woman; Boy and Girl*. Baltimore: Johns Hopkins Press.

Morgan, Edmund S. 1944, 1966. *The Puritan Family*. New York: Harper Torchbook.

Morgan, James N., Katherine Dickinson, Jonathan Dickinson, Jacob Benus, and Greg Duncan. 1974. *Five Thousand American Families: Patterns of Economic Progress*. Vol. I. *An Analysis of the First Five Years of the Panel Study of Income Dynamics*. Ann Arbor: Institute for Social Research, University of Michigan.

National Women's Education Fund. 1975. "Facts: Women and Public Life." Washington, D.C.: 1532 16th Street, N.W.

Nochlin, Linda. 1973. "Why Have There Been No Great Woman Artists?" In *Art and Sexual Politics*. Edited by Thomas B. Hess and Elizabeth C. Baker. New York: Collier Books.

Nye, F. Ivan, and Lois Wladis Hoffman. 1963. *The Employed Mother in America*. Chicago: Rand McNally.

Nye, Russell Blaine. 1960. *The Cultural Life of the New Nation, 1776–1830*. New York: Harper Torchbooks.

Ogburn, William F., and Clark Tibbits. 1933. "The Family and Its Functions." *Recent Social Trends* I. President's Research Committee on Social Trends. New York: McGraw-Hill, pp. 661–708.

O'Neill, William. 1969. *Everyone Was Brave: A History of Feminism in America*. Chicago: Quadrangle Books.

Oppenheimer, Valerie Kincade. 1970. *The Female Labor Force in the United States: Demographic and Economic Factors Concerning Its Growth and Changing Composition*. Berkeley: Population Monograph Series, No. 5, University of California.

Parsons, Talcott, and Robert F. Bales. 1955. *Family, Socialization, and Interaction Process*. Glencoe, Illinois: Free Press.

Piore, Michael. 1971. "The Dual Labor Market: Theory and Implications." In *Problems in Political Economy: An Urban Perspective*. Edited by David Gordon. Lexington, Massachusetts: D. C. Heath, pp. 90–94.

Poloma, Margaret M., and T. Neal Garland. 1971. "Jobs or Careers? The Case of the Professionally Employed Married Woman." In *Family Issues of Employed Women in Europe and America*. Edited by Andrée Michel. Leiden: E. J. Brill.

Potter, J. 1965. "The Growth of Population in America, 1700–1860." In *Population in History: Essays in Historical Demography*. Edited by D. G. Glass and D. E. C. Eversley. Chicago: Aldine, pp. 631–688.

Purcell, Susan Kaufman. 1974. "Ideology and the Law: Sexism and the Supreme Court Decisions." In *Women in Politics*. Edited by Jane Jaquette. New York: Wiley, pp. 131–153.

Reed, James W. 1974. "Margaret Sanger." Paper presented to the Berkshire Conference on the History of Women. Radcliffe College, October 25–26.

Resource Center on Sex Roles. 1974. *Today's Changing Roles: An Approach to non-Sexist Teaching*. Washington, D.C.: National Foundation for the Improvement of Education.

Reuther, Rosemary Radford. 1974. *Religion and Sexism: Images of Women in the Jewish and Christian Traditions*. New York: Simon and Schuster.

Roby, Pamela. 1972. "Women and American Higher Education." *Annals of American Academy of Political and Social Science* **404** (November): 118–139.

———. 1973. "Institutional Barriers to Woman Students in Higher Education." In *Academic Women on the Move*. Edited by A. Rossi and A. Calderwood. New York: Russell Sage Foundation, pp. 37–56.

Ross, Heather L., and Isabel V. Sawhill. 1975. *Time of Transition: The Growth of Families Headed By Women*. Washington, D.C.: The Urban Institute.

Rossi, Alice S. 1964. "Equality Between the Sexes: An Immodest Proposal." In *The Woman in America*. Edited by Robert J. Lifton. Boston: Beacon Press.

Rupp, Leila J. 1974. "A Reappraisal of American Women in a Men's War, 1941–1945." Mimeo.

Saario, Terry N., Carol N. Jacklin, and Carol K. Tittle. 1973. "Sex Role Stereotyping in the Public Schools." *Harvard Educational Review* **43** (August): 386–416.

Sandler, Bernice. 1973. "A Little Help from Our Government: WEAL and Contract Compliance." In *Academic Women on the Move*. Edited by A. Rossi and A. Calderwood. New York: Russell Sage Foundation, pp. 439–462.

Sawhill, Isabel, Heather L. Ross, and Anita MacIntosh. 1973. "The Family in Transition." Working Paper. Washington, D.C.: The Urban Institute.

Schoen, Robert. 1975. "California Divorce Rates by Age at First Marriage and Duration of First Marriage." *Journal of Marriage and the Family* **37** (August): 548–555.

Scott, Ann Firor. 1970. *The Southern Lady: From Pedestal to Politics, 1830–1930.* Chicago: University of Chicago Press.

————. 1972. "Making the Invisible Woman Visible: An Essay Review." *The Journal of Southern History* **38** (November): 629–638.

Seaman, Barbara. 1972. *Free and Female: The New Sexual Role of Women.* Greenwich, Conneticut: Fawcett.

Spacks, Patricia Meyer. 1971–1972. "Free Women." *Hudson Review* **24** (Winter): 559–573.

————. 1972. "A Chronicle of Women." *Hudson Review* **25** (Spring): 157–170.

Spruill, Julia C. 1938. *Women's Life and Work in the Southern Colonies.* Chapel Hill, North Carolina: University of North Carolina Press.

Sweet, James A. 1973. *Women in the Labor Force.* New York: Seminar Press.

Sydenstricker, Edgar. 1933. "The Vitality of the American People." *Recent Social Trends* I. President's Research Committee on Social Trends. New York: McGraw-Hill, pp. 602–660.

Thompson, Warren S., and P. K. Whelpton. 1933. "The Population of the Nation." *Recent Social Trends* I. President's Research Committee on Social Trends. New York: McGraw-Hill, pp. 1–58.

Tocqueville, Alexis de. 1835, 1954. *Democracy in America.* New York: Vintage Books.

Tuchman, Gaye. 1975. "Women and the Creation of Culture." In *Another Voice.* Edited by Marcia Millman and Rosabeth Kanter. New York: Anchor Books, pp. 171–202.

U.S. Bureau of the Census. 1973. Census of Population: 1970. Vol. I. *Characteristics of the Population.* Part I, United States Summary—Section 2. Washington, D.C.: U.S. Government Printing Office.

U.S. Commission on Population Growth and the American Future. 1972. *Population and the American Future.* New York: New American Library.

U.S. Department of Health, Education, and Welfare. 1972. *Digest of Educational Statistics— 1971 Edition.* Washington, D.C.: U.S. Government Printing Office.

Verba, Sidney, and Norman H. Nie. 1972. *Participation in America.* New York: Harper and Row.

Vogel, Lise. 1974. "Women of Spirit: Content, Discontent and Resistance among New England Operatives." Paper presented at Berkshire Conference on Women's History. Radcliffe College, October 25–27.

Weisskopf, Francine Blau. 1972. "Women's Place in the Labor Market." *American Economic Review* **62** (May): 161–176.

Weitzman, Lenore. 1974. "Legal Regulation of Marriage: Tradition and Change." *California Law Review* **62** (July–September): 1169–1288.

————, et al. 1972. "Sex Role Socialization in Picture Books for Preschool Children." *American Journal of Sociology* **77** (May): 1125–1150.

Wells, Robert V. 1973. "Demographic Change and the Life Cycle of American Families." In *The Family in History: Interdisciplinary Essays.* Edited by Theodore K. Rabb and Robert I. Rotberg. New York: Harper Torchbooks.

Werner, Emmy E., and Louise M. Bachtold. 1974. "Personality Characteristics of Women in American Politics." In *Women in Politics.* Edited by Jane Jaquette. New York: Wiley, pp. 75–84.

Whyte, William H. 1956. *The Organization Man.* New York: Doubleday.

Wilson, Joan Hoff. 1976. "The Illusion of Change: Women and the Revolution." In *The American Revolution: Explorations in the History of American Radicalism.* Edited by Alfred F. Young. DeKalb, Illinois: Northern Illinois University Press, pp. 365–426.

Women in 1973. 1974. Washington, D.C.: Citizen's Advisory Council on the Status of Women, May.

Women Today. 1971–. Today Publications and News Service. National Press Building. Washington, D.C.

Women's Bureau, U.S. Department of Labor. 1969. *Trends in Educational Attainment of Women.* Washington, D.C.: U.S. Government Printing Office, October.

Wooddy, Carroll. 1933. "The Growth of Governmental Functions." In *Recent Social Trends* II. President's Reaearch Committee on Social Trends. New York: McGraw-Hill, pp. 1274–1330.

Woody, Thomas. 1929. *A History of Women's Education in the United States.* 2 vols. New York: The Science Press.

Chapter Nine

POLAND: WOMEN'S EXPERIENCE
UNDER SOCIALISM

Magdalena Sokołowska

HISTORICAL AND CULTURAL HERITAGE

The national, historical, and cultural heritage plays an important role in shaping the position of women in contemporary Polish society. Therefore this study devoted to the present begins with the past.

Polish convents, liberally subsidized in the early centuries of Polish statehood, gathered within their walls mainly well-to-do women who engaged in charitable work and healed the sick. They thus contributed to raising the social importance of women, who in the Middle Ages had only two alternatives: the habit of a nun or the cap of a wife. The struggle for equal rights was first waged and won in the convents to gain equality with monks in such matters as singing in church choirs, studying Latin in the convents, and conducting schools for novices and lay girls.

As the fourteenth turned to the fifteenth century Queen Jadwiga, wife of Władysław Jagiełło, was one of Europe's most eminent women. Born and educated in Hungary in the atmosphere of European culture, she flowered under Poland's lively political and cultural activity. She owed her rapid rise to Krakow University. A bibliography has been preserved as part of her heritage, and this is the first catalog of a lay private library in Poland.

The Enlightenment and Reformation blossomed at the courts of the last Jagiellonian, moved to the palaces of the magnates, and reached the gentry and city patricians. It rapidly involved women. The reading matter of women belonging to the high nobility, wealthy gentry, and patrician classes had until this time consisted of prayer books. In the sixteenth century, however, sociopolitical writers urged women to read books of another kind and to develop their intellects. In an introduction to the Polish translation of Aristotle's *Problematics,* one professor at Jagiellonian University postulated women's right to higher education. Publication of women writers, poetesses, and scientists began to appear in the sixteenth and seventeenth centuries (Wawrzykowska-Wierciochowa, 1963).

Role of the Family. For more than 120 years, from the end of the eighteenth century until 1918, Poland did not exist on the map of Europe, and what had once been Poland fell under three different political and economic systems: Russia, Austria, and Prussia. For many years there were no independent political institutions or Polish schools, and the Polish language was banned for some time, even from the church. During this period the family remained the main national institution and the "fortress" of the national spirit. The cultural heritage, preserved in families, maintained the

Parts of this chapter are adapted from Magdalena Sokołowska's earlier study *Frauen Emanzipation und Sozialismus: Das Beispiel der Volksrepublic Polen.* Hamburg: Rowohlt Taschenbuch Verlag GmbH, 1973.

unity of the divided nation in the absence of schools and cultural institutions. Oppression and hostility toward the oppressors made for a strong
family bond. A family protected its members against the outer world and
took over some of the functions that in the free countries are performed by
other institutions. Educating youth in the native language, history, and
literature was felt to be a responsibility of the household, not only among the
noblemen, but among the working class and the peasants as well.

Such an overgrowth of the family functions was caused by the peculiar
political condition of the country (Kłoskowska, 1962). By the twentieth
century it had already become an anachronism, incompatible with the trend
of evolution in other European countries. It came to an end after World War
I, when Poland again became independent.

During the Nazi occupation the family household again started to fulfill
multiple functions, and the family was again the most important national
institution. Centers of underground political and military organizations were
located in private homes. Cultural life and the widespread unofficial educational system, including high schools, were continued in private homes as
well.

The guiding spirit of all these activities was the women. Even though their
formal scope within the patriarchal pattern was limited to the household,
their actual tasks and functions were of particular importance under the
specific conditions prevailing in Poland.

The social and political underdevelopment of the country during the era
of partition could still be felt between the two world wars. This explains why
some elements of the "estate" system have remained vital in Polish culture
until very recently and why Polish families have shown such diversity in
their patterns and customs (Kłoskowska, 1959). The peasant family constituted
the most conspicuous type, and it was the type best described by social
writers. Since the rural population was most numerous, this was the prevailing form of family life in Poland. The main feature of such a traditional
family within a backward rural economy was a subordination of its members
to the interests of the family as a whole. The economic and social functions
of a peasant family were supervised by the father, while the other members
enjoyed only a narrow scope of independence.

Urban families, both working class and intelligentsia, differed greatly from
this pattern. In a working-class family there was much more individualism
and egalitarianism. Its opportunities and aspirations, for example, as to the
future and education of children, were very much limited by the general
economic and social conditions. In comparison with the rural pattern a
working-class family was fairly emancipated from the traditional clan bond
and thus more vulnerable to change. As an economic unit it belonged to a
different type too: the husband-father was not the manager of a family

enterprise, and the household as a unit of consumption was administered by the wife-mother. The man was usually the only official source of the family's income, but as unemployment increased women frequently supported the whole household (Krahelska, 1933: 9).

The prewar intelligentsia family is known to us mainly from literary fiction. The culture of most such families resulted from an adjustment of the older patterns of the nobility to urban conditions. The new urban intelligentsia family typically depended on the father's education and profession as the basis of the family income. The number of educated women was also rapidly increasing. A woman was most emancipated in an intelligentsia family, the relationship between wife and husband came closest to being equal. The patterns of family life were conspicuously changing there. Children were less constrained and more independent in their relationships with their parents (Komorowska, 1967: 5).

Since the earliest period of Poland's independent existence, the educated class has been the leading force of the nation. There was no developed middle class in Poland. The patterns and styles of life of all the classes, strata, and environments of society were modeled after those of the intelligentsia. The economic and social changes that have occurred in Poland since World War II have accelerated the process of acceptance of the intelligentsia patterns by the whole society.

It is the urban population that now represents most of the people of the country, and thus the urban family constitutes the predominating type. Differences between the life-styles of the working class and the white-collar workers have tended to diminish. Changes have also occurred in the countryside that make the rural family more and more like its city counterpart.

Political Rights. The first constitution of the Polish state (May 3, 1791), one of the most progressive documents of the epoch, does not mention the word *woman,* even in the article devoted to the upbringing of the royal children. The Constitution speaks only of the education of sons, and their chief educator was the father. Only in the exceptional case of the father's absence, and as his substitute, does the Constitution provide for the mother assuming the role of educator. The word *queen,* who "in regencies will devote herself to the education of the royal sons" appears only once and in this context.

The definitive downfall of the Polish state came four years after the adoption of that Constitution. When Poland rose again as a state, after 120 years, the very first legal enactments established women as citizens having the full rights of the regenerated country. Within 10 days after formation of a government (November 28, 1918) a Decree of the Head of State on Elections to the *Sejm* (parliament) provided that "every citizen without distinction by sex who reached 21 years of age by election day is an elector to the Sejm" and that "every citizen of the state who has the active right to vote can be a candidate."

The active and passive electoral right "without distinction by sex" was confirmed by two constitutions adopted in 1921 and 1935. The latter, though marked by regression in the sphere of civil rights, did not abrogate equal rights for women. It stipulated that "neither social origin, religious faith, sex or nationality can be the cause of limiting the right to influence public affairs."

The recognition of women's right to influence public life almost immediately after regaining independence expressed the conviction that it constituted an inseparable component of the system of parliamentary government. Women themselves did not fight for such rights; there was no organized feminist movement in Poland. Many years of foreign domination had caused Poles, men and women alike, to fight for independence, for national distinctness and continuity, and for the right to speak their mother tongue. The tradition of civil rights in the early period of development of parliamentarianism—still a vital part of the national awareness—is among the basic cultural values of the nation, but the life under foreign rule and underground struggle did not prepare women for participation in government and for utilization of the possibilities afforded by legal rights. After 120 years of resistance, opposition to, and revolt against the occupational powers, the law—imposed by foreigners—was not considered important by Poles, and succeeding generations learned to get around it. Education for constructive citizenship was thus a fundamental problem of the Polish state (Szczepański, 1970). The formal recognition of women's rights as citizens, though an indispensable step in the process of emancipation, did not solve this problem.

Access to Education.   In Poland (as in other European countries) education has been regarded as the most important factor of social advancement. This is associated with the high esteem for intellectual and artistic creation. In the nineteenth century education was regarded as the most honorable "service to the fatherland" in Poland.

The striving for education has also been very strong among women, and it involved more than the acquisition of a profession or given qualifications. Worthy of note is the favorable attitude of eminent men toward the education of women: political and public leaders, writers, publicists, all favored women's right to an education (Hulewicz, 1939). The Commission for National Education (an early type of Ministry of Education and the first of its kind in Europe), founded at the end of the eighteenth century, had among its projects a plan for reforming the elementary schools that provided for the attendance of both boys and girls from "all estates." In 1808 a Supreme Supervisory Council, with posts all over the country filled by women, was established for the purpose of working out a program of education for girls. This was the first group of social workers of a sort recruited among enlightened, educated women. The directors of the Commission for National Education were aware of the bold innovative character of the idea; it was the first such in Europe.

Disintegration of the feudal order in the second half of the nineteenth century and the development of capitalist economic forms led to the bankruptcy of a considerable number of gentry families. Many of them moved to the cities and thus increased the ranks of the urban intelligentsia. Education of the women then became an urgent problem. Feminist circles arose to support the eminent representatives of positivism of both sexes, all of whom devoted many of their writings to the question of equal rights for women.

Defeat of the armed uprisings of the 1830s and 1860s had its political consequences: imprisonment, deportation of the men to the outskirts of the Russian empire, and the emigration of many to the West. Those who left Poland included the elite of writers, poets, and artists, among them Adam Mickiewicz, Joachim Lelewel, Julius Słowacki, Fryderyk Chopin. At that time the country began to feel a certain intellectual sterility in the male world. The men appeared pale in comparison with the female elite. "A spiritual matriarchate" ruled, in the words of the writer Tadeusz Boy-Żeleński in reference to Narcyza Żmichowska, writer and champion of women's emancipation, who demanded legal, economic, and social independence for women.

Every wave of the emancipation movement, regardless of whether it brought to the fore economic or socio-legal demands, advanced the principle of women's education. It became increasingly evident to enlightened groups in the three partitions that education was a basic factor on the road to women's independence. This postulate assumed a concrete form in the middle of the nineteenth century: extension and deepening of girls' education in the secondary schools, granting girls the right to vocational training and access to higher education, giving women the chance to work at occupations until then inaccessible to them.

Suffragettes who regarded higher education as the way to raise the social position of their sex were rare (in comparison to Western Europe) among the first generation of women who undertook higher academic studies between 1870 and 1900. More frequent among them was the type of social activist who saw in such professions as physician or teacher, for instance, realization of a social mission formed under the influence of Polish positivism. A kindred type also frequent in Poland was the socialist girl student. In entering the academic world many women were motivated by the desire for economic independence, while a considerable number had as their aim social and economic advancement.

Educational opportunities differed in the three partitions. The Prussian partition had no higher educational institutions. The Austrian had two Polish universities, in Krakow and Lvov.* The entrance of a large number of women into these schools began close to half a century later than the first journeys of women to study in Switzerland and Russia. The latter came mainly from the landed gentry of the Russian partition, while the majority of women students at Krakow and Lvov were representatives of the bourgeoisie of all three partitions. Before World War I the number of women studying at these two Polish universities was considerably greater than the number attending foreign schools.

Most of the foreign women who initiated the fight for the right for admission to higher schools in Switzerland and France were Slavic, Russian, or Polish. The first two Russian women entered Zurich University in 1864, the first Polish woman followed in 1870. At Lausanne Slavs predominated, to form the largest concentration of women at a Swiss university. The first Polish woman made her appearance at the University of Paris in 1863. Most Polish women studied at the medical school, fewer in the exact sciences. (The most eminent among the latter was the winner of two Nobel Prizes in later years, Maria Skłodowska-Curie). At the same time women began to travel to St. Petersburg, where higher courses for women were inaugurated by K. W. Bestushev in 1897. A sharp struggle was raging then in Russia for the admission of women to university faculties such as medicine. Continued failures caused by the czarist government's hostile attitude to women's education impelled the Polish gentry and Russian merchants to send their daughters to schools abroad. Polish women in the Russian partition were encouraged by the example of their Russian sisters.

Although the opposition to the admission of women to higher education was considerably weaker in Polish lands than in Western Europe, it was not easy for Polish women to practice academic professions, especially in the free professions. The professional organizations of physicians and lawyers, for instance, defended themselves against female competition for a long time. As Ludwik Krzywicki wrote in 1889:

> . . . they took to measuring, weighing and comparing the female organism . . .
> in most cases, as far as the practical social results of that quest was concerned,
> the investigators were interested in proving that women's "natural duty" was to
> be a cook and to first of all keep away from mental pursuits, while the daily sins
> of 12 hours toil in a factory were condoned (Krzywicki, 1960:273).

*Place names here follow Webster's Third Edition preferred spelling.

The principle of equal right of access to higher education gained further support after World War I in the rejuvenated Polish state. The law of 1920 admitted women to higher studies without any limitations. In the 1920–1921 academic year the proportions of women in higher educational institutions amounted to 65 percent in philosophy, 26 percent in medicine, and 11 percent in law. In the 1930s women constituted 20 percent of physicians and 2 percent of lawyers in Poland.

CONTEMPORARY POLAND: THE NEW SOCIETY

Poland was liberated in 1945 by the Soviet army and Polish divisions fighting at its side. As a result Poland transformed her political and social system to establish a communist society (Szczepański, 1970: 37).

In the first postwar years that society was composed of classes, strata, and social groups whose psyche had been molded by the interwar and war years. The changes introduced by the new government—such as socialization of industry and other economic sectors, radical agrarian reform, accelerated industrialization, wide access to education and other cultural goods—all transformed the course of daily life at a revolutionary tempo, giving the country a new image in a few brief years. The surprisingly swift transformation deeply affected the lives of the individual and the family. One such fundamental change is the mass movement of women undertaking gainful employment outside the household.

Political decisions grounded in ideological premises provided the initial impulse that set into motion deep-going changes in women's situation in socialist countries. In other words, the driving forces of these changes are found in Marxist–Leninist ideology and the political criteria based on it. One of socialism's basic principles guarantees women a position in society consonant with their human dignity (Stec, 1970: 32). In the programs of Communist and Workers parties this is expressed in the slogan "equal rights for women and men" or "equality of all citizens regardless of sex." Lenin's statement that "the proletariat cannot attain full freedom if it does not grant complete freedom for women" (Lenin, 1920) is well known. The classics of Marxism chiefly concern themselves with proletarian and peasant women, whom they regard as doubly oppressed because of class and sex, but they also point to various aspects of women's social oppression that occur irrespective of class affiliation and that are expressed in economic and legal inequality as well as inequality in social customs and habits. As August Bebel wrote in 1883: "Class domination will end once and for all and with it the domination of men over women" (Bebel, 1891).

The Marxist classics examine the role of women in two areas: the family and society. They do not limit the role of women exclusively to the biologically determined sphere of domestic life, but stress woman's role in social production. Long ago they anticipated that mass participation in the social economy would effect basic changes in women's position in the society and family. Analyses of change in this respect have taken into account many factors, but the level of a society's economic development is regarded as the principal conditioning factor. Marxism rejects the naturalistic conception of man, which predicates the immutability of human nature caused by a complex of biologically conditioned basic traits and properties. This Marxist position entails the simultaneous disavowal of widely diffused views regarding the innate incapacity of woman for anything but motherhood and family care. Marxists hold that the capitalist system shuts women off from the broader social life, thus turning them into backward and passive personalities. The socialist system, on the contrary, by freeing women from household drudgery, involving them in social production, and enabling their active participation in the broader spheres of life, creates the necessary preconditions for the full, harmonious development of each woman's personality as an equal member of the society.

The woman's position in the family also depends on her participation in social production. Engels depicts this process:

> In the old communistic household, which comprised many couples and their children, the task entrusted to the women of managing the household was as much a public, a socially necessary industry as the procuring of food by the men. With the patriarchal family and still more with the single monogamous family, a change came. Household management lost its public character. It no longer concerned society. It became a *private service;* the wife became the head servant, excluded from all participation in social production. [Engels, 1972: 137].

According to Engels, only with the development of modern, large-scale industry did women—and then only the proletarian woman at that—regain access to social production. The problem arises because when the woman fulfills her duties in the private service of her family, she remains excluded from public production and cannot earn anything; and when she wishes to take part in public industry and earn her living independently, she is not in a position to fulfill her family duties. The reason is that the modern individual family depends on the open or disguised domestic enslavement of the woman. Because the family system in contemporary society makes the man the breadwinner, at least among the propertied classes, it gives him a dominating position.

> Within the family he is the bourgeois, and the wife represents the proletariat . . . the first condition for the liberation of the wife is to bring the whole female

sex back into public industry . . . this in turn demands that the characteristic of the monogamous family as the economic unit of society be abolished [Engels, 1972: 137–138].

Lenin considered the situation of women in the Soviet Union after barely two years of existence of the Soviet government as "the ideal from the viewpoint of the most advanced states" (Lenin, 1919). But he declared at the same time that recognition of equal rights is only the beginning of the struggle for women's liberation. "Equality before the law is not yet equality in life. . . ." (Lenin, 1920). The condition for women's actual liberation, according to Lenin, is their employment in the national economy. The socialist system creates the economic basis for this, primarily by abolishing private property in land and industrial plants while initiating the technical progress that enables the employment of women in ever-wider spheres. One of the essential conditions for building the socialist society is women's participation in serving society and in political life. "Without drawing the women into public activity, into political life, it is not possible to build even democracy, let alone socialism," wrote Lenin in 1917 (Lenin, 1917). "Drawing into public activity" meant that women were to occupy directing positions in enterprises and responsible posts in all organs of the Soviet government.

Since the fundamental legal norms formulated in constitutions are based on given ideologies, one of the adopted values raised to the dignity of law in socialist countries is equal rights for women. Thus the constitution of Poland, like that of other socialist countries, treats this question fundamentally and in the most principled manner. The first Constitution of the Polish People's Republic, adopted in 1952, states: "Women in the Polish People's Republic enjoy the same rights as men in all spheres of life: state, political, economic, and cultural." The Polish Constitution of 1952 proclaims work as the right, duty, and matter of honor of every Polish citizen. Equal rights for women are guaranteed by: (1) equality with men in the right to work and remuneration according to the principle "equal pay for equal work," in the rights to rest and recreation, to social security, to education, to recognition and awards, to public office; (2) mother and child-care, aid and protection of pregnant women, vacations with full pay during and after childbirth, expansion of the network of maternity wards, lying-in hospitals, creches, and kindergartens, development of the service and catering establishments.

This legislation intended to enable women to undertake gainful employment outside the home while enjoying the privileges necessary to provide equality of opportunity to compensate for the biological burdens of the female sex as well as traditional home and family obligations. Other socialist states also elevated regulations on this question to the rank of constitutional enactments. All such provisions have in common the principle of creating the necessary conditions for the political and economic participation of women as equals to men. This is considered of particular importance for the broad program of socialist construction as well as for the implementation of the underlying principle of the socialist system: creation of conditions for the full development of every citizen.

By creating a demand for labor, industrialization has enabled the implementation of the basic constitutional guarantees of equal rights for women. Thus between 1945 and 1954 more than 6 million places of work were created in Poland, excluding agriculture (Rajkiewicz, 1965: 201–266). This made possible the elimination of both urban unemployment and rural overpopulation. The proportion of the population gainfully employed outside of agriculture rose from 40 percent in 1931 to 70.5 percent in 1970 (Maƚy Rocznik Statystyczny, 1971–1972: 26).

Immediately following World War II Polish people began to stream to the cities. Overpopulation of the villages and depopulation of the cities caused by the war and occupation accelerated the urbanization process. The vast destruction suffered by the cities did not decidedly check this process, since the planned reconstruction and expansion of the cities and industrial establishments immediately followed liberation. Trade was organized, schools were opened, and so forth. New cities arose simultaneously with the building of the more important industrial centers. Also beginning directly after the liberation was the consciously planned and directed process of transforming the country's demographic structure by shifting the surplus rural population to the cities. By 1970, 52.2 percent of Poland's population was urban (Maƚy Rocznik Statystyczny, 1971–1972: 22).

The rapid growth of the national economy, particularly of industry, created a great demand for labor. Expansion of the number of trades, occupations, and places of work, as well as their differentiation, opened up new possibilities for the better satisfaction of family needs by gainful employment outside the home. Women took advantage of this opportunity on a mass scale. During Poland's Six-Year Plan (1950–1956), which was marked by an especially rapid rate of development of industry, a great organizational and educational effort was made to induce the largest possible number of women to seek work in the socialized economy. Women were encouraged to go to work because average earnings per employee in the socialized economy were inadequate to maintain a family; a family needed an additional breadwinner (Piotrowski, 1967: 10–24).

Differences in the educational levels of men and women are being obliterated. Data from the general census of 1960 show the differences in the education of the generation of mothers (now about 50 years of age) and the generation of their daughters (young women entering adult life). The 1970 general census demonstrates a further rise in women's educational level (see Table 1). In fact, the average educational level of young women is already higher than that of their male counterparts. In the 18 to 24 age group 116 women to each 100 men have completed higher education, as compared to the 50 and over age group, which has a ratio of 34 women to 100 men. In the former age group the ratio for completed secondary education is 113 to 100, and in the latter age group 87 to 100; in the illiterate category there are 88 women to each 100 men in the 18 to 24 age group, and 231 to each 100 in the 50 and over age group (Wrochno, 1971: 24).

Before World War II a large number of working women in Poland were domestic servants. Today that number is insignificant. Women are concentrated in industrial establishments, trading enterprises, offices, and educational institutions. The rapid development of public and economic administrations, scientific institutions, health services, and various social and cultural establishments has caused a sharp rise in the number of positions available to white-collar workers. In 1931 women constituted 30 percent of white-collar workers; that percentage rose sharply in the Polish Peoples' Republic to 45 percent of both white-collar workers and of workers employed outside of agriculture. The proportion of white-collar workers is especially high among young women. Already in 1957 half of all gainfully employed women of the 21 to 30 age group were white-collar workers. This is associated with the growth in the number of white-collar jobs and the rise in women's educational level (Piotrowski, 1963: 207).

Education. The changes in education in Poland during the last 30 years consist primarily in its wide diffusion and in the development of all types of schools. Universal compulsory elementary education was introduced first to

Table 1 Educational Level of Two Generations of Polish Women (%)

	Age of Women	
Education	18–24	50 and over
Higher, including incomplete	6.8	1.5
Secondary, including incomplete	53.7	9.1
Complete elementary	36.5	36.4
Incomplete elementary	1.9	36.3
Self-taught	—	6.3
Only able to read	—	2.5
Illiterate	0.2	6.4
No data	0.9	1.5
Total	100	100

Source. National Census, December 1970.

the age of 14, in 1964 this was extended to the age of 15 and in the larger urban centers to 18. It was established that adult workers would complete their elementary education, and continued study by young workers was provided for in facilities for continued vocational training. Education in schools above the elementary level was made more universal, and the material base of these schools was enlarged (boarding schools, for instance). As a result of this policy, the proportion of young people in schools above the elementary level systematically increased. Thus 28 percent of those eligible attended in 1945–1946, 49 percent in 1958–1959, 82 percent in 1968–1969, and 86 percent in 1969–1970. There has been a marked growth in higher education. The proportion of young people in the 18 to 24 age group in schools of higher education rose from 8.1 percent in the 1958–1959 school year to 19.4 percent in 1968–1969. Adult education developed intensively both on the secondary and higher educational levels (Rocznik Statystyczny Szkolnictwa, 1968–1969: 545–547).

The functioning of the educational system, its central planning, and direction are certainly not as smooth as this cursory description might suggest. But it has undoubtedly met the test in relation to the education of girls in the Polish People's Republic. The percentage of girls in all types of schools corresponds to the general proportion of the two sexes in the population, and in some types of schools the proportion of girls is even higher. The percentage of girls is now lower than their demographic proportion only in higher education, where women constituted 43.2 percent in 1970 (34.7 percent in 1960) (Rocznik Statystyczny Szkolnictwa, 1968–1969: 545–547). That percentage, however, refers to all forms of higher education, that is, full-time studies and extramural schools for working people such as evening schools and correspondence courses.

One-fourth of girl elementary school graduates enter general secondary schools, where girls constituted 72.6 percent of pupils in the 1969–1970 school year. This numerical superiority in general secondary schools applies to other countries too and seems to indicate a certain hesitation (by the girls themselves, their families, or both) to regard an occupational career or profession as a permanent element of women's role in life. The choice of a general academic school enables one to postpone deciding the course of vocational or professional work. A girl often studies simply because social convention or prestige require the education of children. A frequently expressed concern is to assure children's personal culture and a better future, which girl students and their parents do not necessarily associate with a vocation or profession, but with successful marriage. Choice of a concrete direction of vocational or professional training expresses a more decided attitude toward the future occupation. It indicates that a woman who acquires a definite trade or profession by means of education will most probably follow it all her life. That this orientation has been growing is indicated by the considerable increase in the proportion of girls in vocational directions of education from 1959 to 1969. The number of girl graduates admitted to vocational schools increased more rapidly than the number accepted in general academic schools. The number of girls attending elementary vocational schools almost trebled, and their attendance at technical schools doubled in that period.

In the 1968–1969 school year 191,108 students attended school full-time (the most popular form of higher education); 45.2 percent of these were women, but the proportion in schools for workers was considerably lower. Women accounted for 35 percent of 72,205 students preparing for extramural degrees (prepared for at home with students coming in for examinations periodically) and 18.8 percent (of 33,144 students) in evening schools (Rocznik Statystyczny Szkolnictwa, 1968–1969: 545–547). This situation can be interpreted as follows: the living conditions of male and female full-time students are identical in Poland. Both boys and girls are generally single or married to another student. Student marriages are of the partnership type; the couples study together and share household duties as colleagues. They are often not yet independent, receiving aid from their parents in the spheres of housing, maintenance, care of children, and so forth. Those attending schools for workers are relatively older and economically independent; most have families and run their own households. It is well known that the woman carries a heavier burden in the latter system. She puts in a full day's work at her job and is usually a mother with young children. It is of course difficult to study under these conditions. And as it turns out, evening schools are most difficult, and extramural studies somewhat easier (the percentage of women is higher here), since it is presumably easier to leave the home for several days at intervals of several weeks than to be away every evening.

In present-day Poland parents in all social environments are highly motivated to educate their children of both sexes. As early as 1957 research conducted in Lodz on workers' views on the future of their children showed that even though their sentiments on the role of the wife and family were fairly traditional, they were almost uniform on the question of the education of sons and daughters (Kłoskowska, 1964). Research done between 1964 and 1968 on a national sample of urban women in the 21 to 47 age range and their families gave the same results. The findings indicated the following: (1) the majority of women desire higher education both for their sons and daughters; (2) more than half of the women who want their children to pursue a profession requiring higher education prefer the professions of physician or dentist for daughters and engineer or architect for their sons; (3) next in order of preference for sons were occupations requiring secondary technical education and for daughters, the teaching profession (Piotrowski, 1969).

In Poland, as elsewhere, opinion divides occupations into "male" and "female" domains. The medical profession is universally regarded in Poland today as a female profession. A relatively large number of women physicians already practiced in the interwar period, and in the first postwar years the highest proportion of women in higher education was in medical schools. In the following years the proportions changed, which is probably attributable to the measures applied by the authorities to check the feminization of studies in fields where it assumed great dimensions (see Table 2). Nevertheless women constituted 52.4 percent of medical and 82.9 percent of dental graduates in 1968.

As Table 2 shows, the proportion of women in the medical profession declined by 50 percent between 1951 and 1967, while their share in technical vocations doubled. This can be attributed to measures of another kind, namely, those aiming to stimulate a rise in the number of women students in fields that have relatively few women. As a result there has been a change in the structure of studies chosen by women which will most probably continue. The range of subjects chosen by women is expanding and departing more and more from those thought to be typical female preferences.

The Ministry of Education, education departments of People's Councils (of local governments), trade unions, and women's organizations have for a number of years conducted a systematic campaign to change traditional views and to shape new ones. A network of vocational consultation bureaus

Table 2   Courses of Study of Female Students in Higher Education in 1950–1951 and 1966–1967

| | Percentage of Females | |
Course of Study	1950–1951	1966–1967
Medicine	30.8	15.1
Technical	6.4	14.8
Agricultural	5.1	8.8
Mathematics and natural sciences	13.9	15.6
Law and economics	18.4	20.8
Artistic	4.6	2.3
Humanities	20.8	22.6

Source. Kobieta w Polsce (The Woman in Poland). 1968. Warsaw: The Central Statistical Office, p. xxiii.

throughout the country is conducted by departments of the People's Councils. Special regulations oblige school authorities to provide information on new occupations available to girls and to make available such information in lectures for parents and final-form elementary school pupils. Inspectors General of school districts, in agreement with employment offices, see to it that the largest possible number of girls is admitted to technical vocational schools.

Nevertheless there is no full equality of the sexes in relation to the directions of education (Wrochno, 1969a). In elementary vocational training girls concentrate chiefly in schools and courses preparing for service occupations (economic, gastronomic, trade, and health service) or for skilled work in light industries (garment, leather, food, and textile). Even in these schools, though, there has been a gradual increase in the number of girls in the chemical, precise mechanical, agricultural and forestry, and geological fields; more than 50 percent of the pupils in these fields are girls. A similar process has occurred in technical schools. Students in technical courses that prepare students for employment in service and light industries are almost 100 percent female. However the percentage of girls in chemical, geological, geodesic, communications, and building construction trades is also rising; it now stands at 40 to 50 percent. In the 1968–1969 school year, one-third of all girls beginning their studies chose "male" occupations. Further female entry into technical disciplines can be expected in post-elementary schooling.

The modern young girl in Poland has a different conception of her future than that of the early suffragettes and feminists. They were of a heroic generation that renounced husband and family. Their great granddaughters in the Polish Peoples' Republic do not want to give up anything, unless perhaps having many children. To them the question of whether to raise a family is as much an issue as what to study and what occupation to pursue. Work is something natural, both an economic necessity and a personal need. Girls are molded by the kind of social reality in which the majority of married women are gainfully employed. They are brought up with the conviction that each person must have a trade or profession, and see no future for themselves other than in the role of working woman, even though they know that their mothers, as working women, face many difficulties in combining their occupational role with that of wife and mother. According to all opinion polls, the questions of studying and raising vocational qualifications occupy a prominent place in the minds of Polish girls today. Since education is in general among the principal values in Poland's national culture, it can be assumed that in the vast majority of these girls' families education and learning enjoy high prestige. In the social model of woman's personality that has taken root in girls' consciousness, education, vocation, and work constitute inseparable elements. Although sometimes modified by life experience, this model is universally accepted.

Women and Work. An elaborate system of legal protection for working women was introduced in Poland, a devastated land, immediately following World War II. Although the benefits accorded women would be considered obvious in rich countries, in a country as poor as Poland immediately after the war, they attested to a particular concern for the protection of the working woman. The system of benefits and social services enjoyed by working women in Poland embraces health care, legal protection of jobs during pregnancy and childbirth, special care and protection during pregnancy, and paid maternity vacations as well as free leave and benefits connected with childrearing. There is also a special system for assuring the implementation of these rights and privileges. As compared with the laws in Western countries, this legislation is distinguished by regulations guaranteeing care and protection during pregnancy and, particularly, special aids for working mothers bringing up children, including child allowances, nurseries, kindergartens, and other institutions.

The jobs of working women in Poland are guaranteed during pregnancy and childbirth. This includes the prohibition of lowering wages and worsening working conditions during pregnancy. The maternity leave now lasts 16 weeks, with full pay during the entire period. A nursing mother has the right to time off that is reckoned in her working time. A mother caring for a sick child is entitled to a paid leave. Beginning in 1971 every working woman with a child four years of age or younger has been entitled to a three-year unpaid leave, not counting the maternity leave (previously that leave was for one year). During that period the working woman retains for herself and her family the right to the benefits of free health care and the family allowances generally in force. She can also return to work before the end of the three-year leave (Salwa, 1970). Laws prohibiting the holding of certain occupations by women are on the whole similar in many countries, and they evoke the same reaction. Excessive protective regulations sometimes turn against women and become not a privilege but "a factor of subtle discrimination concealed behind the slogan of 'women's biological protection,' " as several journalists called it (Wrochno, 1969a: 34; Tycner, 1965; Mir-Par, 1971). The list of occupations prohibited to women was twice brought up to date in the postwar period, which attests to the recognition by legislators of the complexity of the question.

In the postwar years the rate of growth of employment in Poland was greater for women than for men. The proportion of women in the total number of workers employed outside of agriculture rose from 32.9 percent in 1950 to 36.1 percent in 1965 and then to 39.3 percent in 1970 (Rocznik

Statystyczny, 1955: 202; 1970: 65). Thus as compared to the interwar period, the structure of women's employment changed mainly for four reasons. First was the reduction of domestic service, which before the war had absorbed the largest number of working women. This caused a general rise in the indices of other fields of employment. Second was the disappearance of women from the fields of petty trading, industrial-handicraft, and cottage industry, where they often had served as family helpers. Third was that the kind of work done by women in the different branches of the national economy changed to an even greater extent. This is expressed in the movement of women from unskilled, simple jobs as day laborers or house servants, often casual jobs of a low or indeterminate social position, to more or less skilled occupations of a steadier nature. This applies even to manual work done by women in jobs formerly performed by domestics. Such jobs are today part of the public services, the health care and trading establishments. Many women manual workers are employed in new or modernized large industrial plants where work requires given skills. This facilitates a stronger link with the vocation, steadier employment, and the continuation of work after marriage. Fourth, and even more evident, are the quantitative and qualitative changes in the employment of women white-collar workers. Before the war women in this category were concentrated in schoolteaching and cultural agencies, then in social service; these together employed 55 percent of all women white-collar workers. Now this category is more evenly divided between the different fields of white-collar work. Women white-collar workers constitute the majority of women employed in almost all economic divisions except direct production. There has been a great general shift of women from manual to white-collar occupations.

As we have seen, in 1970, 39.7 percent of workers employed in the national economy were women. Women constituted the majority of workers in the health and social care services (79 percent), in finance and insurance institutions (71.1 percent), in education and scientific establishments (67.7 percent), and in trade (66.2 percent). In the last decade the rate of growth of women's employment (61.5 percent) was greater than that of men's (22.3 percent). The most rapid rise in women's share was in industry (Jakubowicz, 1971: 15–16).

In 1931 married women constituted only 16 percent of the total number of working women. It was considered by many then that marriage and motherhood were incompatible with gainful employment. At that time married women workers came from the "lower" classes and were primarily employed in the textile industry and as rural elementary schoolteachers. In the postwar years the proportion of married women among gainfully employed women rose sharply: from 30 percent in 1956 to 55 percent in 1960 and 70 percent in 1970. The increase was especially great between

1950 and 1956, the period of intensive industrialization and enlistment of women in the labor force. The number of gainfully employed married women increased then by 130 percent, compared to the 35 percent rise in the number of unmarried women. To a great degree this phenomenon was a consequence of the check in the rise of real wages and the widening of women's employment opportunities. The mass extension of gainful occupation among married women was accompanied by a great educational campaign "for the participation of married women in social production." This undoubtedly contributed to changing the habits, attitudes, and beliefs of the women and society toward gainful employment by married women. This effected a simultaneous change in these women's social position: they ceased to be an exceptional phenomenon (Piotrowski, 1963: 105–116). At present as many as 75 percent of working women in Poland are married, and the majority of them are mothers. After their maternity leaves 70 percent of mothers return to work. Neither the number nor the ages of children exert any great influence on women's vocational activity. Thus 64 percent of mothers with children aged 3 or younger are working, as compared to 71 percent with the youngest children between 4 and 7, 74 percent with children of 14 to 18 years of age; 77 percent of mothers with one child work, as do 63 percent of those with three children (Piotrowski, 1969a).

The vocational activization of women between 1958 and 1968 included two main groups: older women without any skills, compelled to work outside the home by changes in the family situation, and young women who finished college or vocational secondary school. The second group plays an ever-greater role. Thus in 1968, 66 percent of newly employed women were graduates of vocational schools of various types. It is estimated that between 1971 and 1975 more than 77 percent of young people going to work for the first time in nonagricultural occupations will have an elementary, secondary, or higher vocational school education. Every second graduate of such a school will be a woman (Wrochno, 1971: 39–40).

Education is a decisive factor in the level of a woman's vocational activity. Unlike men, all of whom work irrespective of their education, women have a choice, and vocational activity rises with the educational level. Moreover the employment by women is different than that of men with comparable education. The majority of such women work in educational institutions and in the health service. Close to 70 percent of women with higher education and 60 percent with secondary vocational training are concentrated in those fields, whereas not quite 11 percent of women with higher education and 16 percent with secondary vocational education are employed in industry. In contrast, among men of all educational groups the largest proportion works in industry (Wrochno, 1971: 39–40).

The majority of women with higher education are concentrated in three occupations regarded as "traditionally female": physicians, dentists, and pharmacists. In 1968, 80.9 percent of dentists, 80.3 percent of pharmacists, and 47.9 percent of medical doctors were women. The teaching profession and some of the humanities have attracted mainly women in almost all countries, but the female dominance of the academic medical professions is a phenomenon specific to Eastern European countries. In addition to such factors as equal rights for women, development of an egalitarian educational system, and a need for personnel with higher education that exceeds the number of graduates, a large role is undoubtedly played here by cultural and occupational tradition. In Poland dentists were predominantly women in the interwar period, while the percentage of women physicians was higher than in most European countries.

As is known, women primarily enter occupations in which there is less competition. After 1945 many men in Poland chose technical rather than medical professions. The profession of engineer was considered more important than that of physician on the grounds that the former is productive while the latter is a service profession. Moreover the newly developing, attractive technical professions have been better paying than the medical profession (Dzięcielska-Machnikowska, 1968). It is therefore all the more interesting that the profession of medical doctor continues to occupy a very high position in the publicly acknowledged hierarchy of occupations (second place after university professor), higher than that of the engineering profession, where earnings are on the whole higher and women considerably fewer. The reason for this may be that the activity and professional knowledge of the doctor-healer, who makes people well and often saves their lives, enjoys a particularly high prestige. These factors are probably weightier than that healer's sex, especially in a country where the woman doctor ceased to be a rarity long ago.

Women have not yet achieved equal status in employment (Waluk, 1966: 172–203; Waluk, 1965: 250). Women's average wages are about 30 percent lower than men's. Since equal pay for equal work on a similar job is being observed, inequality in pay must be attributed to inequality of positions occupied. This is confirmed by daily observation and by many investigations. Men occupy higher positions in the occupational hierarchy even in such feminine fields as the textile industry. Few women occupy directing positions in industry, either in production or in administration.

Differences in earnings are to a great extent associated with the employment structures of men and women in the national economy. The majority of working women (60 percent) are grouped in such fields as wholesale or retail trade, education, science and culture, health service, and the textile and clothing industries, where pay rates are relatively lower. The higher-paying jobs, such as technical vocations, are occupied mainly by men.

Women of the same educational level work mainly in the services where the pay is lower. A man with a secondary vocational training is most often a technician; his female counterpart is a nurse, schoolteacher, or employee in trade or administration. Feminine occupations are on the whole lower paying everywhere.

However the lower earnings of women cannot be fully explained by differences in their employment, because differences in favor of men also exist in the same vocations and on similar jobs. For instance, research on engineers employed in Warsaw designing offices shows that women engineers are graded lower when they start work, are more rarely promoted, and earn less on the same post (Łobodzińska, 1967: 33–39; Łobodzińska, 1970: 167).

The integration of women's professional and family roles is proceeding rapidly in Poland. Vocational and professional activity is one of the functions of married women and forms an essential element of their roles as wives and mothers. These roles are increasingly acquiring the universal sanction of custom. Society's attitude toward married women is being transformed under the influence of the growth in their gainful employment. Such conceptions, like the whole superstructure, are derivatives of the socioeconomic processes that cause women's entry into the working world that sooner or later lead to a change in actual relations (Kaltenberg-Kwiatkowska, 1963: 365).

New customs as a rule take shape long after their material foundation and develop unconsciously in the course of socioeconomic processes. Hence woman's professional and domestic roles are not yet properly adjusted to each other, while the corresponding attitudes and social facilities are not adapted to them. The traditional conceptions, opinions, and attitudes have been undermined, but no new ones have yet emerged in their place to unambiguously designate the role of woman at work and at home. In the image of women's social role—unlike that of men—the professional and family-household functions are not linked into one whole. Nor do the women themselves do so. Many of them regard the home and gainful employment as two separate and independent systems of experience and activity. They are not sufficiently aware of the interdependence of the two systems and of the need to harmonize them in their own self-image. Scientific publications occupy themselves too much with women's so-called conflicting roles (Kobieta-Praca-Dom, 1967: 10–25).

Family and Household. Family law in the socialist countries—as contained in constitutions, family codes, special decrees—is based on the following principles: lay marriage, monogamy, support of the family, stability, equal rights for women, and protection of children born out of wedlock. The constitutions of all socialist countries contain an almost identical article on the state care of the family. In the Polish Constitution of 1952 this article reads:

Marriage and the family are under the care and protection of the Polish Peoples' Republic. Large families are surrounded by special state care. Birth out of wedlock does not limit the rights of the child.

Constitutional provisions are expanded and made concrete in family codes. In Poland such a code was drafted in 1960 and submitted to public discussion in the press, among lawyers, in the scientific community, in trade unions, and in women's organizations. This discussion and debate in the Sejm resulted in the adoption of the Family and Guardianship Code which took effect in 1964. This was the third legal enactment in the Polish Peoples' Republic that codified the basic principles of socialist family law. These are as follow: (1) liberation of family relations from the domination of extraneous property factors; (2) acknowledgment of the equal rights of partners in matrimony and of all children; (3) recognition of the child's welfare as the decisive premise in most questions of family relations.

Women's exercise of fully equal rights in matrimony is unequivocally enacted in legislation, as the following article attests:

Married couples have equal rights and duties in matrimony. They are obligated to live together, to mutual aid and loyalty and to cooperate for the good of the family which they have founded by their union [Article 23].

And further:

. . . both partners in matrimony are obligated, each according to his/her power and earning possibility, to contribute to the satisfaction of the needs of the family which they founded with their union. This obligation may also be met in whole or in part by personal efforts to bring up the children and by work in the common household.

To assess the woman's position in the family it is essential to establish who is entitled to exercise parental authority under the obligatory legal system. The family codes of socialist countries have adopted the principle that authority is exercised by both parents. The Polish Code states that parents should exercise their rights and duties as required by the welfare of the child and by the interests of society. Parents bring up the children, who are subject to and are guided by parental authority. They are obligated to care for the child's physical and spiritual development and to prepare the child to work according to capacity for the good of society. Parents are obliged to educate their children. Both parents are empowered and have the obligation to represent the persons, rights, and interests of minors in legal matters. Since the child is under the authority of both parents, each parent may act independently to maintain the children and to pay child support until they are independent. The amount of child support depends on the parents' earnings and assets, and the obligation to maintain the children may be fulfilled in whole or in part by personal efforts to bring them up.

A married woman is fully competent legally. She may resort to a court of law and take legal action without her husband's consent. Marriage has no influence on a woman's right to choose an occupation and to vocational activity (Czachórski, 1971).

A striking disproportion exists between the enormous changes in the roles of men and women outside of their homes and their roles within the family and household. The revolution has transformed the relationship between social classes, but it has by no means automatically changed the relations between family members. The patterns of family life change at a much slower pace. Although employment of married women has become an obvious thing, a rational division of labor at home is not at all accepted. Many husbands, and wives too, still adhere to the traditional image of the relationships between the spouses and between children and parents, as well as to the patriarchal model of power in the family and the ensuing division of responsibilities and duties. But the social and economic background, which once sufficiently justified those images and models, has changed radically. The new situation of a family in which a woman earns her income necessitates a redefinition of the roles of the husband-father and of the wife-mother.

The contribution to family income by women has radically changed the definition of the "head of the family." The 1970 National Census Instruction for Census Interviewers stipulated:

> A head of a family should be considered as the person who provides all or the bulk of the family household's means of subsistence. If two persons contribute these means in equal degree, the head of the household should be considered the person who mainly disposes of them.

The employment of the wife-mother has not influenced very much the distribution of domestic chores. Although the contribution of the husband and of the other household members is twice as high in the families of women who work it remains rather meager. However in the houses of working women the domestic chores tend to be generally reduced. Education of both spouses remarkably influences the process of change: in better-educated and culturally more advanced families the adjustment to the new role of women seems to be more successful (Łobodzińska, 1970: Chap. V).

The problem of child-care requires a separate discussion. In the first place, there are no important differences between the employment of women who have or do not have children, as well as between the employment of mothers of children under and above seven years of age. In all these groups the percentage of working women is 70 percent. Care and rearing of children is mainly the mothers' task, but in families in which the woman works the contribution of men is greater. No comparative studies have been made of adult performance or behavior of those whose mothers have never worked as opposed to those whose mothers worked during their entire childhood. We do not know if the factor "mother works" differentiates the children at all. In a national survey working women were asked whether they considered their work desirable or undesirable for their children. The proportion of "undesirable" to "desirable" answers was 43–57 among married mothers and 30–70 among unmarried mothers. More than 70 percent of the respondents declared that they would continue to work if and when another baby was born (Piotrowski, 1969: 99–101).

A woman's economic independence relieves a man of the enormous burden of responsibility for the family's survival and welfare. Thus the new position of women liberates a man from the conscious or unconscious stress that is inseparable from the role of being the only source of the family's maintenance. The new role of the husband-father is underway.

Changes in ideas of the roles of husband and wife are most rapid in urban families, among women with relatively high levels of education and men with relatively the same educational level. New patterns of life have traditionally been modeled by the educated class in Poland. The way of life and the cultural patterns of the "enlightened" have for centuries provided progressive models of value systems. Thus it may be expected that the new patterns of family relationships now being shaped by the educated and professionally active will be accepted and adopted by the rest of society. These patterns arise as a result of rationalization and individualization of social behavior of individual people and families. Underlying them are far-reaching changes in the systems of values cherished by men as husbands and fathers and by women as wives and mothers.

Examples of such processes of change are provided by a study of a group of married couples, living and working in Warsaw, in which both husbands and wives are engineers (Łobodzińska, 1970: Chap. V). An actual partnership of the spouses is found there, expressed, for example, in more equal division of the domestic duties, common child-care, and common holidays and pastimes. In the marriages of young engineers an important place is occupied by professional discussions and by mutual help in those matters that concern them as a couple. None of the women engineers seriously considers the possibility of quitting her work for good, and since they see their professional activity as an indispensable element in a woman's life, all like having a family as well.

Young couples who are scientific workers constitute a similar group. This category of the intelligentsia, enjoying high social prestige, was well represented among the respondents of another 1967 questionnaire (Chylińska, 1967). Remarkable in the responses was the lack of sex differentiation in the descriptions of the tiresome and time-consuming everyday chores. Sunday washing and cleaning, shopping after work hours, lunches prepared for the next day, standing in lines for consumer goods, washing diapers, walking the children to school or kindergarten, and dozens of other musts were done in haste and tension by wives and by husbands alike. All this leads us to the fairly optimistic prognosis that the stiff division of household labor between wives and husbands is likely to shift from the now-prevailing all-or-none basis and that the female's absolute sovereignty in the diapers-and-dishes empire will become obsolete.

Fertility and Family Planning.   Access to modern medical facilities in the postwar period has been accompanied by a lower rate of population growth. The rate of population increase went from 19.5 per thousand in 1955 to 8.5 in 1971 (Rocznik Statystyczny Ochrony Zdrowia, 1971: XV). There has been a dramatic decline in the birthrate, chiefly because of the decision to have smaller families; there has been an insignificant reduction in the number of first births but a considerable one in the number of second and third children. In 1968, of the total number of women with children 16 years old or younger, 36 percent had one child, 32.8 percent had two children, 18.1 percent had three, and 13.1 percent had four or more (Kurzynowski, 1971: 3–15).

The decline in the birthrate in Poland came as a surprise to some policymakers in a country traditionally characterized by high fertility rates and the strong influence of the Roman Catholic Church. The smaller size of Polish families does not seem directly related to the availability of more efficient means of contraception. The diaphragm, the contraceptive pill, and intrauterine devices became available in Poland only in the 1960s and still do not play any important role. Although the contraceptives are not very expensive and are publicized in the mass media, the idea of employing contraceptives is relatively slow in gaining acceptance. For example, only 1 percent of women in the prime childbearing period, from 15 through 49, presently use pills. Overall it has been estimated that about half of all married women have adopted some method of contraception, and among this group about half depend on coitus interruptus or the rhythm method (Sokołowska and Łobodzińska, 1973).

The dramatic decline in the rate of population growth has worried policymakers in Poland and reawakened efforts to repeal the 1956 abortion law. The Catholic Church, both a powerful and conservative institution in Poland, has consistently opposed the availability of abortions and continues to campaign against it. Despite the recent debates in the Polish Sejm it seems doubtful that the law will be rescinded. The statistical data on the frequency of abortion are far from complete and may not include all, particularly those performed in outpatient clinics rather than in the hospital. However according to the official statistics, in 1967 there was 1 abortion for every 1.9 live births (Rocznik Statystyczny Ochrony Zdrowia, 1971: 361).

The decline in the Polish birthrate reflects trends throughout Europe. However the pattern in Western Europe, where a direct relationship can be seen between more education for women and their reluctance to have a large family, does not hold in Poland. Recent surveys indicate that in Poland the wish for more children tends to grow with the educational level. Moreover the gainful employment of women is not the decisive curb on the size of family that it so often is elsewhere. Differences in the fecundity of working and nonworking women are insignificant.

Two factors contribute to the emergence of contemporary Polish demographic patterns. First, all surveys seem to indicate that two is now regarded as the ideal number of children for a family in both rural and urban environments. Thus there has been a kind of modernization in the definition of the proper size of the family. Second, the unavailability of adequate housing discourages large families. Most young couples must live with one set of parents for some time while they wait for placement in their own apartment, and the apartments themselves are usually small and cramped (Sokołowska, 1973).

To the extent that there is an official position in Poland, the leadership would certainly prefer an increase in the rate of population growth. Present employment patterns, however, preclude the discouraging of female employment as a direct means of encouraging more births. Consequently present policy aims at increasing fertility through the maintaining of special maternity benefits for women workers, expanding the system of day-care, nurseries, and kindergartens and investing in the construction of more housing.

Management and Politics.   Polish statistics reflect the general phenomenon of women occupying lower rungs on the ladder of important positions, even in the most feminine vocations. As in other countries the percentage of women filling leadership positions does not correspond to their educational level or approach the proportion of men in such positions. If the percentage of women in government, in executive boards of the governing political party, in industrial management, in union directorships, and in university professorships is assumed to be an indicator of the equal rights for women, this goal has not yet been attained in Poland. In 1968 more than half of the men with higher education occupied managerial posts in Polish industry while only 16 percent of the women with the same education held such posts. Table 3 shows the percentage of women in higher posts in Polish industry. In that year 25 percent of men and less than 10 percent of women with secondary vocational training filled supervisory posts in industry. Even in such a feminized field as schoolteaching barely 5.7 percent of women were appointed to the post of school principal, compared to 20 percent of men with higher education engaged in the teaching profession (Preiss-Zajdowa, 1967: 123).

Data on the participation of women in the ruling bodies of the Polish United Worker's Party (Communist Party) and government reveal a correspondingly low rate. Women comprise less than one-fourth of the membership in the party. There are no women in the Politburo of the Polish United Worker's Party and, as indicated in Table 4, only one woman belongs to the State Council. The proportion of women in the Sejm has been somewhat higher but since 1956 has not exceeded 16 percent of the total number of deputies (Rocznik Statystyczny, 1974: 56). Women have done somewhat better in the trade union movement, where the percentage of women members and leaders has been more symmetrical; in 1972 women comprised 39.6 percent of the general membership and 30.3 percent of the officials on the steering boards (Związki Zawodowe w liczbach, 1972). Even

Table 3   Percentage of Women in Higher Posts in Polish Industry, 1964 and 1968

	Percentage of women occupants	
Post	1964	1968
Director	1.9	1.5
Chief engineer, assistant technical director	2.2	2.3
Assistant manager	3.6	4.6
Chief mechanic, chief power engineer, chief technologist	2.7	4.2
Technical production section foreman	8.2	7.1
Technologist, mechanic, section power engineer	9.7	13.9
Senior craftsman	1.7	4.0
Foreman	3.9	5.0
Chief accountant	38.2	30.6
Director of economic department	17.5	23.6
Senior area specialist on economic matters	37.6	58.2
Economic research worker	50.8	76.9

Source.   K. Wrochno, Problemy pracy kobiet, 1971, p. 102.

Table 4 Women's Participation in Government Administration

	Number of Women
Council of State	1
Council of Ministers	0
Ministers/Secretaries of State	0
Vice-Ministers	2
Foreign Service: Ambassadors	0

in the localities, as shown in Table 5, women account for less than one-fourth of the councilors on the county, borough, and village people's councils.

In light of women's educational achievements and the high rate of labor force participation in Poland, as in the other Eastern European countries, and the strong ideological commitment to attaining equality for women, it is somewhat surprising that women have not made greater strides toward assuming more high-level decision-making positions. This disparity between women's socioeconomic and political roles, of course, reflects worldwide trends. Moreover it is only several decades since women crossed the threshold of colleges and universities, and only 30 years since women began entering the labor force in large numbers. Political leaders of the Eastern European socialist countries are aware of women's limited status. Gustav Husak, first Secretary of the Czechoslovakian Communist Party has gone on record to say that,

> The participation of women in management of the society, state and economy is unacceptably low, even in comparison with the period from 1945 to 1948 and earlier years . . . because of our relation to women and because of political reasons the present state cannot be tolerated by us [Litwin, 1971].

There are definite barriers, both philosophical and practical, to women

Table 5 Number of Women Councilors in the People's Councils and State Administration

Year	Total	Voivodship (province)	County	Town	Rural District
1958	5.8	12.2	7.6	10.0	4.7
1961	13.6	20.9	17.4	16.8	12.0
1965	15.4	22.5	19.2	18.8	13.7
1969	18.9	25.7	21.8	22.1	17.0
1973	23.1	27.5	25.3	28.1	21.2

Source. National Women's Council, 1974.

holding decision-making positions. The one most frequently mentioned is the inability to cope with simultaneous family responsibilities and the demands of a managerial post. Everyday observation proves that a regular job can be somehow fitted into the pattern of life, and that job and family duties can be reconciled without turning all the aspects of life upside down. However managerial positions cannot be held by women without radical changes of the occupational structures which now are better suited to the needs of men than women. For most women top positions are unattainable simply because there is no equality in family responsibilities and duties. Gainful employment of women does not bring about basic changes in the traditional organization of the household. Therefore although there are many female doctors in Poland, only a few are chief doctors, chairpersons of a clinic or hospital department, medical directors, or professors.

Another problem is the prejudice that continues to exist with regard to the ability of women to perform managerial functions. A survey conducted in 1964 asked a sample of women to identify the source of the most serious problems for women managers; the most frequent answers pointed to the attitudes of men, both superiors and subordinates. Another survey, of women holding managerial posts in industrial enterprises in Lodz, a major center of the textile industry, showed that an important impediment to assigning women to managerial posts was the pattern of social relations predominating there, a kind of "combat zone" system of leadership, which was considered inappropriate for women (Dzięcielska-Machnikowska and Kulpińska, 1966). Only the most capable, the most persistent, and the most ambitious women can surmount the barriers imposed by prejudice and the burden of family responsibilities.

CONCLUSIONS

It is this author's opinion that the conditions existing in Poland are more favorable to the full realization of the principle "equal rights for women" than are those in developed capitalist countries. The most decisive differentiating factor is the mass employment of qualified women in all branches of the economy as well as in cultural and academic institutions. Because the occupational structures in Poland are "infiltrated" by women, it is more probable that they will gradually change in a direction better fitting women's needs. The range of occupations and professions that women pursue is wider, and the traditional divisions between "masculine" and "feminine" occupations are less accentuated. A great majority of working women, like men, continue to be employed throughout their whole lifetime. This is a basic necessity in avoiding a marginal role at the place of work and in becoming a necessary member of the staff, with opportunities for advancement. There are high percentages of women in the professions. Obviously the work of a physician, for instance, is responsible at any level. Still, women professionals are by no means exceptional: a woman as a physician, dentist, lawyer, or engineer is a common thing in Poland today.

The influence of Freudian theories, as well as of several other conservative orientations, is much weaker than in the United States. Young professional women in the United States still must fight guilt if they leave their child, even if his care is assured. In Poland such an attitude is unknown. Gainful employment of women is accepted by all sociocultural strata and groups. The integration of women's occupational and family roles is proceeding rapidly in Poland. Occupational activity is one of the functions of married women and an essential element of their roles as wives and mothers. These roles are increasingly acquiring the universal sanction of custom. Gainful employment has become a component of women's social role. Poland and other European socialist countries have shown to what extent the position of women can be altered by changing the macrostructure of society. The possible maximization along these lines was attained through the appropriate systems of law, education, and employment. Further changes depend on transformations in social microstructures: in human and family relationships and in the traditional sex roles. Human consciousness changes less rapidly than do economic or political institutions.

Traditional forms of sex differentiation limited to formal situations the opportunities for women to meet men: in the church, at balls, in someone's home as guests. Women did not go to school with men and were absent from the male world of work and public activity. Today women and men have incomparably greater opportunities to get acquainted through coeducation and a common working milieu. They spend many hours together, day after day, in school and at work and see each other in situations from which they had once been excluded by the traditional forms of sex differentiation. They therefore see and evaluate each other differently in private life. This inevitably must lead to a stormy process of sex remodeling, culminating in the crumbling into dust of the traditional models of sex expression based on male social and economic dominance.

BIBLIOGRAPHY

Bebel, A. 1891. *Die Frau und der Sozialismus*. Stuttgart: I.H.W. Dietz.

Chylińska, K. 1964. "Zmierzch mola" (Twilight of a Bookworm). *Życie Warszawy*, March 11.

———. 1967. "Szukanie mostów" (Looking for Bridges). *Życie Warszawy*, May 16.

Czachórski, W. 1971. "Droit de famille." In *Introduction aux Droits Socialistes*. Budapest: Akademiai Kiado, pp. 515–575.

Dzięcielska-Machnikowska, S. 1968. "Problemy feminizacji zatrudnienia, zawodów i stanowisk w Polsce" (Problems of Feminization of Employment, Professions, and Occupations in Poland). Studia Socjologiczne 1: 149–161.

————, and J. Kulpińska. 1966. Awans kobiety (Women in Managerial Posts in Lodz Industry). Lodz: Wydawnictwo Łódzkie.

Engels, Frederick. 1972. The Origin of the Family, Private Property and the State. New York: International Publishers.

Gałdzicki, Z. 1967. Pracownice przedsiębiorstwa elektronicznego (The female employees of the electronic enterprise). Wroclaw: Ossolineum.

Hodoly, A. 1971. Gospodarstwo domowe i jego rola społeczno-ekonomiczna (The Household and Its Socioeconomic Role). Warsaw: Książka i Wiedza.

Hulewicz, J. 1939. Sprawa wyższego wykształcenia kobiet w Polsce w wieku XIX (Higher Education of Women in Poland during the Nineteenth Century). Krakow: Polska Akademia Umiejętności.

Izdebska, H. 1970. "Rodzice w oczach dzieci" (The Family as Seen by Children). Zagadnienia wychowawcze w aspekcie zdrowia psychicznego 4: 93–97.

Jakubczak, F. 1960. "Badanie postaw wobec pracy kobiet w środowisku warszawskich metalowców" (Attitudes toward Women's Work among Warsaw Workers in the Metal Industry). Przegląd Socjologiczny 1: 124–129.

Jakubowicz, M. 1971. "Racjonalne zatrudnienie a praca kobiet" (The Rational Economy and Women's Work). Praca i Zabezpieczenie Społeczne 4: 14–26.

Kaltenberg-Kwiatkowska, E. 1963. "Praca zawodowa kobiet w rodzinach robotniczych i inteligenckich" (Women's Work in Families of Workers and among the Intelligentsia). In Biuletyn No. 39, Edited by W. Mrozek. Katowice: Śląski Instytut Naukowy, pp. 44–66.

Kłoskowska, A. 1959. "Modele społeczne i kultura masowa" (Social Models and Mass Culture). Przegląd Socjologiczny 2: 116–124.

————. 1960. "Badanie modelu rodziny w łódzkim środowisku robotniczym" (The Study of the Model Family in the Lodz Working Class). Przegląd Socjologiczny 2: 116–124.

————. 1964. "Attitudes à l'égard des rôles respectifs et de l'égalité des deux sexes à l'égard des enfants en Pologne". In Image de la femme dans la société. International research under the direction of Paul-Henri Chombart de Lauwe. Paris: Les Editions Ouvrières, p. 109.

————. 1965. "Rodzina w Polsce" (The Family in the Polish People's Republic). In Przemiany społeczne w Polsce Ludowej. Edited by A. Sarapata. Warsaw: Państwowe Wydawnictwo Naukowe, pp. 505–551.

Kobieta w Polsce (The Woman in Poland). 1968. Warsaw: The Central Statistical Office.

Kobieta-Praca-Dom (Materials of the conference "Woman-Work-Household"). 1967. Warsaw: Wydawnictwo Związkowe.

Komorowska, J. 1966. "Rola telewizji w aktualnych przeobrażeniach stosunków rodzinnych" (The Role of TV in the Current Transformations of Family Relations). Studia Socjologiczne 1: 247–256.

————. 1967. "Rodzina warszawska w świetle badań i statystyki" (Warsaw's Family in the Light of Research and Statistics). Problemy Rodziny 5: 7–14.

————. 1969. "Rodzina wielkomiejska" (Family of the Metropolis). In Socjologiczne problemy stolicy i aglomeracji. Edited by S. Nowakowski. Warsaw: Państwowe Wydawnictwe Naukowe, pp. 159–179.

Krahelska, H. 1933. "Przeobrażenia w rodzinie współczesnej i roli kobiety" (Transformations of the Contemporary Family and of the Woman's Role). In *Życie gospodarcze a ekonomika społeczna*. Edited by L. Caro. Lvov: Dom Książki Polskiej, pp. 233–250.

Krzywicki, L. 1889. "Sprawa kobieca" (Women's Question). In *Dzieła IV*. Warsaw, 1960: Państwowe Wydawnictwe Naukowe, pp. 259–276.

Kurzynowski, A. 1967. *Ciągłość pracy a macierzyństwo*. (The Continuity of Work and Motherhood). Warsaw: Państwowe Wydawnictwo Ekonomiczne.

———. 1971. "Polska rodzina miejska" (The Polish Urban Family). *Problemy Rodziny* **3:** 3–11.

Lenin, W. I. 1917. "O proletarskoj milicji" (On the Proletarian Militia). In *Połnoje sobranie*, Vol. 31. Moscow, 1962: Gosizdat, pp. 35–47.

———. 1919. "O zadaczach żenskowo raboczewo dwiżenia w sowieckoj respublikie" (On Tasks of the Working Women's Movement in the Soviet Republic). In *Połnoje sobranie*, Vol. 39. Moscow, 1963: Gosizdat, pp. 198–205.

———. 1920. "K żenszczinam rabotnicam" (To female workers). In *Połnoje sobranie*, Vol. 40. Moscow, 1963: Gosizdat, pp. 197–205.

Łobodzińska, B. 1967. "Inzynier-kobieta" (Woman Engineer). *Problemy Rodziny* **5:** 33–39.

———. 1970. *Małżeństwo w mieście* (Urban Marriage). Warsaw: Państwowe Wydawnictwo Naukowe.

Lutyński, J. 1950. "Badania nad młodymi małżeństwami" (A Study of Young Couples). *Przegląd Socjologiczny* **1:** 105–123.

Mały Rocznik Statystyczny (Small Statistical Yearbook). 1971–1972. Warsaw: Główny Urząd Statystyczny.

Mir-Par. 1971. "Trochę polemiki" (Some Polemics). *Życie Warszawy*, June 30.

Mrozek, W. 1963. "Model społeczny współczesnej rodziny górniczej na Górnym Śląsku" (The Social Model of the Contemporary Mining Family in Upper Silesia). In *Biuletyn 39*. Edited by W. Mrozek. Katowice: Śląski Instytut Naukowy, pp. 89–112.

National Women's Council. 1974. Warsaw.

Nowakowski, S. 1965. "Procesy urbanizacyjne w powojennej Polsce" (The Processes of Urbanization in Postwar Poland). In *Przemiany społeczne w Polsce Ludowej*. Edited by A. Sarapata. Warsaw: Państwowe Wydawnictwo Naukowe, pp. 133–172.

Piotrowski, J. 1963a. *Praca zawodowa kobiety a rodzina* (Woman's Work and Family). Warsaw: Książka i Wiedza.

———. 1963b. "Zawód a struktura rodziny" (Occupation and Family Structure). In *Biuletyn 39*. Edited by W. Mrozek. Katowice: Śląski Instytut Naukowy, pp. 19–32.

———. 1964. "Attitudes à l'égard du travail des femmes." In *Image de la femme dans la société*. International research under the direction of Paul-Henri Chombart de Lauwe. Paris: Les Editions Ouvrières.

———. 1967. "Badania nad pozycją społeczną kobiet w Polsce Ludowej i wynikające stąd potrzeby społeczne" (Studies on the Social Position of Women in the Polish People's Republic and Resulting Social Needs). In *Kobieta-Praca-Dom*. Warsaw: Wydawnictwo Związkowe, pp. 10–25.

———. 1969a. "Aktywność zawodowa kobiet zamężnych i wynikające z niej potrzeby rodziny" (Family Needs Resulting from an Increased Employment of Married Women). Warsaw: Report of research carried out by the chair of Sociology of Work of the Institute of Social Economy, p. 122 (conclusions).

———. 1969b. "Obowiązki kobiety pracującej zawodowo w zakresie opieki nad dziećmi i w gospodarstwie domowym" (Family and Household Responsibilities of the Working Woman). *Praca i zabezpieczenie społeczne* **7:** 27–35.

———. 1970. "Rodzina wielopokoleniowa w Polsce" (The Multigeneration Family in Poland). *Problemy Rodziny* **5:** 1–9.

Preise-Zajdowa, A. 1966. "Preferencje zawodowe kobiet w Polsce" (Occupational Preferences of Women in Poland). In *Kobieta Współczesna*. Edited by M. Sokołowska. Warsaw: Książka i Wiedza, pp. 147–171.

———. 1967. *Zawód a praca kobiet* (Occupation and Women's Work). Warsaw: Wydawnictwo Związkowe.

Rajkiewicz, A. 1965. "Proces aktywizacji zawodowej ludności" (The Process of Activization of the Labor Force). In *Przemiany społeczne w Polsce Ludowej*. Edited by A. Sarapata. Warsaw: Państwowe Wydawnictwo Naukowe, pp. 201–206.

Rocznik Statystyczny (Statistical Yearbook). 1955, 1968–1969, 1970, 1974. Warsaw: Główny Urząd Statystyczny.

Rocznik Statystyczny Ochrony Zdrowia (Statistical Yearbook of Health Protection). 1971. Warsaw: Główny Urząd Statystyczny.

Rocznik Statystyczny Szkolnictwa (Statistical Yearbook of Education). 1968–1969. Warsaw: Główny Urząd Statystyczny.

Rosset, E. 1963. "Wiek nowożeńców w Polsce" (Age of the Newly-wed in Poland). *Studia Demograficzne* **3:** 3–37.

Salwa, Z. 1970. *Uprawnienia pracujących kobiet* (Rights of Working Women). Warsaw: Wydawnictwo Związkowe.

Sarapata, A. 1966. "Stratification and Social Mobility in Poland." In *Empirical Sociology in Poland*. Edited by J. Szczepański. Warsaw: Państwowe Wydawnictwo Naukowe, pp. 37–52.

Sobczak, L. 1967. "Problem zatrudnienia kobiet nie mających kwalifikacji zawodowych" (Employment of Women without Professional Qualifications). In *Kobieta-Praca-Dom*. Warsaw: Wydawnictwo Związkowe, pp. 135–150.

Sokołowska, M. 1962. "Wpływ sytuacji rodzinnej na stan zdrowia i możliwości pracy zarobkowej kobiet" (The Impact of Family Situation on the Health of Women and Their Capacities to Work). *Zdrowie Publiczne* **2–3:** 131–139.

———. 1963. *Kobieta pracująca—socjomedyczna charakterystyka kobiet* (Working Woman—The Sociomedical Characteristics of Woman's Work). Warsaw: Wiedza Powszechna.

———. 1973. "Family Patterns." *Polish Perspectives* **4:** 16–24.

———, and B. Łobodzińska. 1973. "Srodki antykoncepcyjne i przerywanie ciąży" (Contraceptives and Pregnancy Termination). *Problemy Rodziny* **1:** 50–55.

Stec, R. 1970. *Społeczna rola kobiety w ujęciu W. I. Lenina* (W. I. Lenin on the Social Role of Woman). Krakow: Polska Akademia Nauk.

Szabady, E. 1971. "Wpływ czynników społecznych na korzystanie z przedłużonego urlopu macierzyńskiego na Węgrzech" (The Impact of Social Factors on the Utilization of Prolonged Maternity Leave in Hungary). *Praca i Zabezpieczenie Społeczne* **3:** 9–15.

Szczepański, J. 1970. *The Polish Society*. New York: Random House.

Tycner, W. 1965. "O utajonych możliwósciach" (On Hidden Potentials). *Trybuna Ludu*, January 12.

Waluk, J. 1965. *Placa i praca kobiet w Polsce* (Women's Wages and Work in Poland). Warsaw: Książka i Wiedza.

————. 1966. "O płacy kobiet w Polsce" (On Wages of Women in Poland). In *Kobieta Współczesna*. Edited by M. Sokołowska. Warsaw: Książka i Wiedza, pp. 172–203.

Wawrzykowska-Wierciochowa, D. 1963. *Od prządki do astronautki* (From the Woman Weaver to the Woman Astronaut). Warsaw: Wydawnictwo Związkowe.

Wejroch, J. 1970. "Na marginesie ojcowskiej ankiety" (On the Survey of Fathers). *Więź* 6 (no pages marked).

Wnuk-Lipiński, E. 1969. *Wstępne wyniki badania budżetu czasu* (Preliminary Results of the Investigation on Time-budget). Warsaw: Główny Urząd Statystyczny.

Wrochno, K. 1965. "W zwykłej przeciętnej rodzinie" (In an Average Family). *Kobieta i Życie* **38.**

————. 1969a. "Przywileje czy dyskryminacja" (Benefits or Discrimination). *Kobieta i Życie* **34.**

————. 1969b. *Kobieta w Polsce* (Woman in Poland). Warsaw: Interpress.

————. 1970a. "Zanim wejdą w konflikt ról" (Before They Enter Role Conflicts). *Problemy Rodziny* **4:** 19–24.

————. 1970b. "Dziewczęta o przyszłej rodzinie" (Teenage Girls on Their Future Family). *Zagadnienia wychowawcze w aspekcie zdrowia psychicznego* **4:**45–54.

————. 1971. *Problemy pracy kobiet* (Problems of Women's Work). Warsaw: Wydawnictwo Związkowe.

Związki Zawodowe w liczbach (Trade Unions in Numbers). 1972. Warsaw: Wydawnictwo Związkowe.

Chapter Ten

CONCLUSION: DETERMINANTS OF WOMEN'S ROLES AND STATUS

Audrey Chapman Smock

The roles and status of women in the eight societies discussed in this volume—Egypt, Bangladesh, Mexico, Ghana, Japan, France, the United States, and Poland—vary considerably. Both in the past and today, significant differences have been present in women's position in the social structure: the expectations regarding women's appropriate patterns of behavior, privileges, and responsibilities; and the value ascribed to women's contributions. The roles of women in these societies diverge in their scope, in the degree to which they are differentiated by sex, and in the manner in which they relate to men's roles. In some of the countries, notably Bangladesh and Egypt, most women are confined to the home and are limited to serving as wives and mothers. In others, such as Ghana and the United States, few women experience such restrictions, and women participate more widely in economic and social life. Role allocations reflect sexual divisions more closely in Bangladesh and Mexico than they do in Poland or France. The social separation of the sexes and the distinction between male and female roles in Ghana provide women with a great deal of freedom and autonomy, whereas in Egypt, Bangladesh, and Mexico it results in female subordination. Similarly the social rank to which women can aspire and the power they can command range along a continuum from powerful to powerless, from the empresses of prehistorical Japan, the queens who jointly ruled with the pharaohs of ancient Egypt, and the queen-mothers of the Akans of Ghana, to the women of Bangladesh, whose voices are muted in the decision-making in both the domestic and the public domain.

This variety and diversity in the roles and status of women testify to the influence of culture and structure in fashioning the social order and argue against a simple biological determinism. Biological capacity merely limits the part each person can play in human reproduction. Society, through its interpretation of what it means to be female or male, and through its establishment of patterns of appropriate behavior for women and men, transforms biological potential into social actuality. The individual as a social actor has a defined position in the social structure that rests on rules and norms defining her or his constituent tasks, goals, expectations, rights, and responsibilities. These constancies of behavior of various kinds, or role systems, provide the institutionalized modes of action, relationships, and groupings that link the individual to society (Nadel, 1957: 20–21). Thus the culture and social structure of a society determine the implications of sexual distinctions for each of its generations, and the manner in which one society resolves this fundamental question may bear little relationship to the determination by another society. If this were not the case, it would be difficult to explain why women's roles have varied so significantly through time and across cultural boundaries. Unless one posits that women's biological makeup varies from era to era and from society to society, it must be conceded that variables other than physical potential shape the options available to women and men.

The eight case studies presented in this volume afford a unique opportunity to understand better the interaction of culture and structure in defining women's roles and status. The eight countries represent a wide range of cultures, levels of development, historical experience, and geographic locations. By following the same outline and systematically considering the major sectors of society affecting women's lives, they provide comparative data on a variety of subjects.

This chapter uses the empirical data of the country studies to illuminate some of the major factors determining women's roles and status. In contrast with the Introduction's intention of providing a paradigm that would generate hypotheses against which each chapter could be compared, this Conclusion focuses on the themes inherent in the data. The model in the Introduction seeks to integrate the major segments of society for the purpose of analyzing how they relate to each other in various types of societies. This chapter seeks to cut across the eight countries in order to identify the salient dimensions of culture and social structure that define women's roles and status. A second issue addressed here is the circumstances under which it is possible to effect a deliberate and rapid change in women's roles.

CULTURAL FACTORS SHAPING WOMEN'S ROLES

The values, norms, attitudes, ideals, and symbols infusing each society translate the physical underpinnings of sexual distinctions into the socially relevant categories of feminine and masculine. Being born female or male endows an individual with an unalterable biological makeup, but the definition of what it means to be female or male is given by the culture. In some cultures femininity has been deemed compatible with a wide range of economic, social, and political roles whereas in others femininity is associated almost entirely with domestic functions.

Several aspects of the culture are particularly important in determining the nature and scope of the roles that women assume: the image of women, the differences perceived between men and women, the definition of the kinds of relationships possible and desirable between men and women, the degree of concern with female sexual purity, and norms regarding the division of labor. The image of women has many relevant dimensions, among them the spiritual, sexual, intellectual, and managerial. The boundaries of male–female relations depend in large part on the perceived differences between men and women and the question of whether a true community of interest transcending sexual considerations is possible. The emphasis placed on female sexual virtue relates to the conception of female sexuality and to the degree to which the sexual conduct of the women reflects on the honor of the entire social group. Norms infusing the division of labor affect the extent to which sex figures as an important consideration in assigning sex roles and in sex-typing various economic functions.

Humankind's perpetual search for the meaning and purpose of life and for personal immortality has made religion a paramount force in most societies. The omnipresence of religion—as the expression of the highest truths, as the source of many laws and customs regulating society, as the inspiration for expressions of art and beauty, and for its association with rituals that mark important occasions in the life of the individual and the group—has made the conception of women's spiritual potential a significant determinant of the manner in which the society regards them. The spiritual image of women has many components. In religious systems with a tradition of world denial and a preoccupation with salvation, such as the pre-Islamic Buddhism and Hinduism of Bangladesh, the Buddhism of Japan, and the Medieval Christianity of Poland and France, the spiritual worth of women has depended on their faculty for achieving personal redemption or transcendence. In religions where communal observations and worship have been a central element, such as the form of Islam practiced in Bangladesh and Egypt, and the traditional Ghanaian religious systems, the considered appropriateness of women's participation in the congregation has evinced whether they are accepted as religious equals. For those world religions, such as Christianity and Islam, whose creeds and laws have become embodied in or interpreted through a religious hierarchy, the adjudged capacity of women to serve as members of these bodies provides another indicator. The nature of religious symbolism, particularly whether the ultimate being is portrayed in neutral, masculine, or feminine imagery, constitutes another element.

When measured by the foregoing criteria, most of the religious systems in the societies discussed in this book have clearly been an instrumental force in depreciating the value of women by denying them full spiritual equality. With the exception of Tantric Buddhism, once predominant in the area of Bangladesh, religions with a tradition of world denial have questioned the spiritual purity of women and have discouraged them from pursuing a life devoted to religion. Even where women have been accepted into religious orders, as in Buddhism and Christianity, the highest truths were reserved for men. Furthermore the exaltation of celibacy and monasticism and the abnegation of material pleasures have usually gone hand in hand with the portrayal of women as temptresses or sensual seducers of the flesh who must be overcome in the pilgrimage toward spiritual salvation. The early Muslim reformism which sought to remove many of women's disabilities and incorporate them as full members of the religious community soon gave way to the exclusion of women from communal worship. Neither Christian nor Muslim sects have considered women to be suitable interpreters of religious philosophy or laws or to be appropriate leaders of congregational worship, and have therefore perpetuated all-male religious hierarchies. The Christian portrayal of God as the Father and the Son and the central role of Mohammed as the prophet of Allah have cast both Christianity and Islam in the male image and have socialized countless generations to assume that masculinity is closer to spirituality.

The major exceptions to the defining of women as spiritually inferior came in the pagan religions of prehistoric Japan, pharaonic Egypt, and precolonial Ghana. These religious systems, to the extent that we know about them, were life affirming rather than world denying; accepted the importance of sexual relations, in fact, may have had elements of fertility worship; and did not distinguish between the spiritual worth of men and women. Women were not systematically excluded from communal worship and often held significant religious offices. It is not surprising then that along with this substantial religious equality women also were considered competent to fill a variety of economic, social, and political roles. Of all the societies considered here, women ascended to the most significant leadership roles and political offices in prehistoric Japan, pharaonic Egypt, and among the Akan and Ga in Ghana.

In other societies women's opportunities for greater social and political participation have had to await secularization and the decline in the importance attached to the religious valuation of women. However even when religion loses its power as the definer of goals and as the arbiter of values, traditional religious considerations often continue to affect the definition of femininity. As shown by the American experience, women suffer disabilities attributable to the belief that they have an inferior spiritual worth long after the demise of religion as a meaningful force in the life of the society. Apparently, religious symbolism retains considerable potency in shaping evaluations of women's nature even after these images have otherwise ceased to embody compelling truths.

Other researchers have also seen a relationship between elements of the religious system and women's roles in society. One study of 58 countries in Asia and Africa found a high correlation between the nature of the traditional religious institutionalization, the individuation of women's roles in the traditional society, and women's participation in the modern sector of the economy. Women who come from societies that have a high degree of religious localism were shown to be more likely to have property, marital, and inheritance rights; freedom of mobility in the traditional environment; and greater access to education and opportunity for nonagricultural employment in the modern sector (Boulding, 1972). However this correlation seems to be based on the least significant element in the religious equation. Religions in Africa and Asia that were local in character by definition had not experienced mass conversions to the world religious systems that devalued women's spiritual worth. These traditional religions accorded women significant rights and freedom, not because they lacked religious hierarchies integrated into large-scale religious networks, but because they espoused an affirmation of women's worthiness. The association between religious localism and women's roles was accidental and incidental; the link between their vision of women's abilities and her commensurate roles and status was central.

Images of women's sexual makeup and inclinations have ranged from the Muslim belief that women are driven by uncontrollable sexual impulses to the denial of women's sexuality in Victorian America and among the middle and upper classes in contemporary Mexico. In most cultures sexual fulfillment has been considered to be the prerogative of the male, irrespective of the presumed interest of the female. The recognition in Ghana, as in most other parts of sub-Saharan Africa, that the sexual dimension is but one component among many in women's nature and the Ghanaian acceptance of women's sexual needs as natural and legitimate stand in marked contrast with the attitudes of most other countries. Until very recently it has generally been assumed that sexuality and spirituality were two diametrically opposed elements for women—but not for men. Therefore the idealization of women as virtuous and spiritually pure, as in medieval France or in Mexico, could come only through negating women's physical character and desires. From the opposite perspective, the acknowledgment of women's sexual needs by some cultures, such as Muslim Egypt and Bangladesh, has come at the expense of deeming women incapable of possessing social and spiritual concerns.

The interpretation of women's sexuality assumes particular importance in cultures that also stress the need for feminine chastity. The matter-of-fact acceptance of women's sexual needs as natural among the traditional Ghanaian societies was related to a lack of concern with the implications of women's search for sexual fulfillment; since their cultures did not highly value virginity before marriage and tolerated infidelity for both sexes, the legitimization of female sexual desires did not pose a threat. As part and parcel of this willingness to accord to women the same sexual freedom as men in the precontraceptive age, most of the Ghanaian ethnic groups provided for the incorporation of a child conceived out of wedlock into the lineage of the mother, the father, or the mother's legal husband without any taint of illegitimacy.

The recognition of female sexuality by a society that has a high valuation of female sexual virtue leads to quite a different configuration, especially when female sexual conduct is thought to reflect on the honor of male-dominated social groups. The Muslim image of women as subject to uncontrollable physical drives has had quite different implications than in Ghana. In Muslim societies this recognition of women's sexual needs has invested women with the capacity to undermine one of the most cherished male values, the honor of the family. It has left men perpetually vulnerable to suffering shame inflicted on them for the transgressions of the female members of their kinship group. To protect their reputations, through the course of centuries men have established institutional safeguards and have perpetuated social norms designed to countervail women's sexual unreliability. Muslim societies have fashioned one of the most thorough systems of male supervision and control by confining women to domestic roles that can be performed in the home under the supervision of male members of the kinship group, by secluding women from contact with men outside their families, and by strictly regulating many aspects of feminine behavior. Despite their supposed inclinations to the contrary, Muslim women are socialized to act with extreme modesty, demureness, and restraint. The penalties for violating these strictures have been quite severe and have often amounted to social stigmatization.

Thus the interplay between the assumed uncontrollable female drive for sexual fulfillment and the male obsession with honor has had definite repercussions for female roles. By severely restricting the boundaries of permissible activity, Muslim cultures have virtually eliminated any role options other than those of wife and mother. The definition of femininity in these cultures has become synonymous with domesticity, while masculinity is associated with mobility and opportunity in the supradomestic sphere. As the chapters on Egypt and Bangladesh pointed out, female rates of economic participation in the Muslim world are far lower than elsewhere. The patterns of female seclusion within the home and their exclusion from the public sphere have barred women from many occupational sectors historically associated with female employment on the grounds that such employment might necessitate interaction with male strangers. Until very recently in Egypt, and even today in Bangladesh, education has been considered irrelevant for girls and potentially disruptive because it might make them less compliant and willing to accept the dictates of the male head of the family. On the whole, women in these cultures have had less freedom to shape their lives than those in any other of the societies.

Many societies show a relationship between the degree of sexual freedom for women and the scope of their roles. This is understandable because women's pursuit of roles in the public sphere involves contacts with men outside of the family group. The existence of structural and ideational controls designed to ensure the fidelity of women cannot help but inhibit women's opportunities for education, employment, and participation in social and political activities. Consequently, culturally prescribed variances in appropriate sexual behavior for women and men have usually been central to the conception of femininity and masculinity and to the legitimation of men's greater opportunities. Sexual freedom for women necessitates control over their own bodies and the accommodation by the social system for both supporting and accepting without stigma children conceived out of wedlock. It seems unlikely that other societies will institutionalize the kinds of mechanisms that enabled the traditional Ghanaian groups to cope with the consequences of women's sexual freedom, but the revolution in contraceptive technology and the new attitudes toward abortion prevalent in many societies allow a similar outcome. The discovery of more effective contraceptive techniques may constitute a major watershed in the evolution of women's roles by providing the impetus for an irreversible trend toward greater sexual freedom in those economically developed societies that choose to utilize the new technology. It is no accident of history that the mass production and adoption of the "pill" and "loop" in the United States was followed by the emergence of a movement concerned with increasing the opportunities for women's "liberation."

Intellectual ability is another element in the composite image cultures develop of women. Many cultures perceive women as basically more emotional than and therefore intellectually inferior to men. The presumed inability of women to cope with decision-making has been employed as a major justification for extreme paternalism and for the legal treatment of women as minors throughout their entire lives, subject to the jurisdiction of first their father, then their husband, and eventually perhaps their son. Many societies have used women's presumed lack of aptitude for exacting scholarship as a rationale for excluding them from male educational institutions and for the establishment of special educational tracks preparing women for domestic roles. Until very recently women were caught in a vicious cycle. By denying girls access to education, societies ensured that there would be no female scholars. Then the male leadership, through the benefit of their self-fulfilling prophecy, could justify the continued exclusion of women from educational opportunities.

Even in modern societies today, when it has become unfashionable to denigrate women's intellectual capacities, vestiges of the former depreciation of women's intellectual abilities remain. The common assumption that women and men have very different intellectual aptitudes finds expression in an intellectual division of labor, with many of the more prestigious and demanding disciplines reserved for men. However the subjects considered appropriate for women or men often differ considerably from one society to another. For example, medical and dentistry student bodies are predominantly male in the United States, predominantly female in Poland, and more equally divided in Mexico and Egypt. Of the countries analyzed in this book, only one of them, Poland, has attempted to overcome these cultural stereotypes and to make a serious effort to attract girls to the once exclusively male technical, vocational, and scientific fields.

More than any other dimension of culture discussed thus far, the belief in man's special aptitude for governing has come close to being a universal trait. Leadership involves the exercise of power, and hitherto virtually all societies have regarded power as a male prerogative. Irrespective of other elements in their role definition, women have been socialized to consider themselves unsuitable for leadership or have been taught that it is not feminine to desire power (Safilios-Rothschild, 1974: 141). The case studies show that the major exceptions to this tendency to associate leadership with masculinity occurred in ancient Japan, pharaonic Egypt, and among some of the groups in Ghana. However even in contemporary Ghana, where vestiges of the traditional institutional order remain, political leadership in the modern political system has been given over exclusively to men. Historically the belief that women are unsuited for leadership positions generally reflected a composite image of women as inferior in many respects: in spiritual worth, in emotional stability, and in intellectual powers. Such a line of reasoning is embodied in the commentary on the Quran made by a leading Muslim scholar who sought to explain the reservation of key secular and religious leadership roles for men by, "Allah has preferred the one sex over the other in the matter of mental ability, and good counsel, and in their power for the performance of duties and for the carrying out of divine commands" (quoted in Levy, 1965: 99). Although Baydain, the ulema quoted above, lived seven centuries ago, most Muslim men still endorse this notion that they have a divinely ordained right to rule.

In modern, secular societies the resort to divine will as a rationale for social patterns is no longer stylish, and the perceived disparities between men and women have diminished in many spheres. In the face of prospects that women may attempt to penetrate the bastions of male supremacy, some men have sought to legitimate their continued leadership roles by arguing that male dominance is rooted in biological heredity. One such case for the "inevitability of patriarchy" claims that differences in male and female hormones enable men to be superior in logical thinking and abstract thought and also cause men to be more aggressive. According to the author of this theory, these sex-linked genetic factors account for the historical and contemporary prevalence of men in leadership roles (Goldberg, 1973). This jump from hormones to destiny is simplistic, however, because it fails to appreciate the extent to which human beings, in contrast with animals, determine their own fate through the cultural notions they perpetuate and the institutions they create.

The most exhaustive review conducted to date of the research and the literature on psychological sex differences concludes that "there is nothing inevitable about male achievement of all available leadership positions" (Maccoby and Jacklin, 1974: 370). The development of sex differences in all societies has depended on the interaction of three groups of factors: genetics, shaping of sex-appropriate behavior by parents and other socializing agents, and the child's spontaneous learning of behavior designated as suitable for her or his sex through imitation (Maccoby and Jacklin, 1974: 360). Thus the greater male predisposition toward aggression, far from being an inevitable fact of life, may either be accentuated or diminished by the social learning process, and societal restraints can counterbalance male tendencies to express aggression. Moreover aggression is not the method by which leadership is exercised over groups of mature human beings. Skills in articulating demands, negotiating compromises, formulating a consensus, and inspiring confidence all play a far more important part. It may well be that the cultural syndromes that have made women more compliant than men and thus easier to exploit have had more to do with the disproportionate tendency for men to govern than has any inherent male aptitude (Maccoby and Jacklin, 1974: 368–371).

The extension of suffrage to women has failed to inaugurate a new era in women's active political participation because it has not yet been accompanied by a fundamental revision in the cultural strictures defining femininity. Irrespective of whether the enfranchisement of women occurred in response to pressures by women themselves, as in the United States, or through the imposition of a new political order, as in Japan, cultural definitions of femininity have usually sanctioned little beyond casting a ballot in an election. Consequently even the presence of higher voting rates among women than men, as among the younger women in Japan, has not propelled women toward seeking political office since this is still perceived as inappropriate for women. Some cultures endorse female volunteerism in a range of social causes, but many countries lack such a tradition. The major exception in industrialized societies to the discouragement of female office-holding has been in local community affairs where the major issues relate to subjects like education and social welfare that are more likely to be associated with the feminine sphere.

Further evidence that culture determines the perceived aptitude of a sex for political leadership lies in the fact that as some societies have altered their images of the appropriateness of women participating in politics, male and female differences have diminished. In the United States women and men have similar voting records because the culture endorses this activity for both sexes, but in Egypt and Bangladesh, where many men still consider it unfeminine to cast a ballot, women's voting participation is quite low. The greater acceptance of female political activism in the United States may be having significant repercussions on the socialization of children. A recent retesting of American school children that employed a questionnaire from a survey conducted some 10 years earlier did not find the significant divergences between boys and girls shown in the earlier testing. One possible explanation for this decrease in childhood differences in political orientations is that it reflects the new political role expectations for women. Changes are occurring in the real and symbolic models available for children to imitate, and young girls are perceiving political activism as being consistent with other feminine role requirements (Orum, Cohen, Grasmuck, and Orum, 1974).

As well as defining the dimensions of femininity and masculinity, and in the process influencing the development of sex differences in the society, cultural concepts have played a large role in determining the implications of these divergences. The eight societies studied here have one of three general types of interpretation. Some cultures, such as the traditional Ghanaian, emphasize the differences between women and men without placing the sexes in a hierarchical ordering. A second kind of culture places values on sex differences that lead to an estimation of clear male superiority and female inferiority, as in prewar Japan and in Bangladesh. A third type might be designated as modified male superiority. In France, the United States, and particularly Poland sex differences are now considered to be less clear-cut, and at least in some spheres men and women are viewed as being relatively equal. Although it remains a theoretical possibility, none of these societies, nor any known to the author, have considered women and men to be so equal that sex differences have been thought to be irrelevant.

The cultural interpretation of the kinds of relationships possible and desirable between women and men depends very much on which of the three models of male–female sex differences have inhered. Cultures that emphasize differences between men and women without ranking them often have social separation and complementary roles. Men and women go their separate ways with neither being subordinated to the other. In these societies the most deeply felt affective tie is between mother and child, not between man and wife. Men and women are seen as drawn together by mutual sexual needs and by the desire to have children, but it is not deemed possible that a true community of interest transcending sexual considerations will develop.

Cultures that stress male–female differences and endorse the notion of male superiority also preclude the emergence of a shared relationship. The more extreme expression of this dichotomy tends to sharply differentiate between the female and male spheres and to exclude joint activities or socializing. Occasionally, as in the medieval European codes of chivalry or in the expressions of gallantry in upper-class, nineteenth century South American society, the wide gulf between the female and male world could be bridged by romantic love, but even then the women was more likely to be the object of a romantic attachment than the participant in a two-sided love relationship. Moreover in a relationship of unequals the temptation always remains to treat women as subordinates born to the task of attending to the needs of men.

The potential for a reciprocal relationship based on communication and sharing comes only when the culture begins to minimize the significance of sexual differences. The empathy required of such a relationship cannot develop until there is a blurring of the boundaries between the female and male roles and a greater similarity in their spheres of consciousness. Although some couples in all societies have probably gone beyond traditional prescriptions to develop a mutuality, the cultural sanctioning of a participatory role for women greatly enhances the possibilities for the emergence of a balanced relationship.

Cultural interpretations of masculinity and femininity underlie the designation of some roles as appropriate for women and others as suitable for men. Thus the division of labor between the sexes in any society derives more from cultural conditioning than from economic determination. Each society tends to hold the sexual division of labor inhering in its distribution of roles as inviolate and to believe that it reflects the most fundamental nature of woman and man. However the wide disparity in role assignments from one culture to another testifies to the malleability of both sexes. Even roles that are often assumed to have a basis in biological differences, like childrearing, have been dealt with in a variety of ways. With changes in technology, particularly those externally introduced, new role possibilities arise that necessitate a retyping of sex roles. The historical experience of the eight countries demonstrates how arbitrary this process of sex-typing can be, how much the sexual division of labor can be a product of historical accidents, and how the placement of cultural considerations before economic rationality can inhibit productivity and development.

Two dimensions of the division of labor have had particular import for the roles of women in society: the degree to which sex figures as a major criterion in role assignments, and the extent to which it is believed possible for women to combine domestic roles with outside activities. Although some sex role-typing is observable in all the societies considered here, the relative importance of sex in comparison to age, social class, or merit as a basic ordering category varies. Societies also differ in how rigidly they adhere to systematic sex-typing.

Deeply perceived distinctions in the aptitudes and inclinations of women and men do not necessarily find expression in the division of labor. Among the traditional Ghanaian groups, for instance, the social separation of women and men inspired the evolution of many sex-specific institutions but did not find expression in a clear-cut designation of economic tasks on the basis of sex. Men sometimes specialized in clearing the fields, warfare, and fishing, but overall there was a great deal of similarity in the farming and trading undertaken by men and women. The more thorough differentiation of roles characteristic of Egypt and Bangladesh has originated more in response to the strictures of seclusion and the obsession with protecting the honor and reputation of the family than from a desire for economic specialization. These societies have historically reserved all economic functions that cannot be performed at home to men. However the modernization of the economy and the establishment of educational institutions for women have raised the possibility for a new mode of organization: two parallel but separate role systems, each catering to the needs of one sex and avoiding contact with the other. In this model, as in the Ghanaian, the social segregation of the sexes matters more than the delineation of particular occupations as the prerogative of one sex.

The extent to which it is believed possible for women to combine domestic roles with outside activities very much influences the scope of their roles. The opposition between domestic and public roles has been cited by one theorist as the source of the universal asymmetry in the evaluation of the sexes (Rosaldo, 1974). Although women in all societies have spent a good part of their adult lives concerned with the birth and rearing of children, the extent to which women's maternal roles have been perceived as incompatible with extradomestic or public activity has varied considerably. Until the advent of the industrial era, child-care and housekeeping were rarely considered to be full-time occupations. Even in the more restrictive cultures, such as in the Muslim world, women in the confines of the home traditionally performed a variety of economic tasks related to farming, food processing, or handicraft production. In Ghana women's responsibility for providing for part of the family's sustenance has constituted an integral dimension of self-definition. And today in the more industrialized countries there is a discernible trend toward reintegrating married women into the labor force and a decline in the social disapproval of combining marriage and childbearing with continued employment. This process of reinterpreting the demands of family life on women has progressed farthest in Poland, where the desire to remain at home has been labeled as parasitic behavior.

It should be noted that a perceived incompatibility between domestic and extrafamilial roles for women may derive from quite dissimilar considerations. In some societies, particularly those within the Muslim sphere, cultural strictures enjoin women from working because such economic roles would weaken familial control and expose women to potentially compromising situations. In contrast, for women in France, particularly those from the bourgeoisie, the motivation for devoting themselves to the family has stemmed from the ideology of the *femme au foyer*. This ideology of motherhood has offered positive incentives for remaining at home by elevating the functions of motherhood and childrearing. Woman's role in the socialization and education of their children has become linked with the perpetuation of French civilization; the ideology of the *femme au foyer* identifies the mother as the most important, irreplaceable agent in inculcating modes of life, manners, taste, cultural heritage, and morals in a culture that highly values its civilization. Thus marriage and motherhood have become an attractive alternative to a career outside of the home.

Even when women are not confined to domestic roles, though, and even within a cultural milieu that does not consider mothering incompatible with a career outside the home, women are socialized to place a different value than men on their work experience. The identification of the female with the domestic sphere and the male with the public domain continues to characterize, although not with the same rigidity, such countries as the United States and France, where many women have roles outside of the family and men frequently play an important part in family life and decision-making. Within all of the cultures discussed here, with the exception perhaps of Poland, it has been the norm for women to accord primacy to their family responsibilities, and it is this ordering of priorities that has been the decisive factor. The secondary role of nondomestic work in women's lives has placed considerable restrictions on the type of jobs women have sought and their possibilities for career advancement. Thus compelling domestic requirements have had a systematic impact on women's performance in the public domain. Women's attitudes toward work also seem to be related to status considerations. That is, the degree to which women's status depends on their familial connections encourages or discourages women from attributing importance to their nondomestic activities. In cultures where women have the possibility of at least a partially nonderived lifetime status, particularly Ghana, Poland, and the United States, their motivation for working and their willingness to subordinate their domestic lives appear much greater.

STRUCTURAL VARIABLES INFLUENCING WOMEN'S ROLES AND STATUS

Ideals, values, norms, and attitudes play a significant part in shaping the institutional order of a society, and the structure in turn helps to define the form in which the cultural potential is realized. Interaction between culture and structure makes impossible a rigorous analysis of either of these determinants of women's roles and status in isolation from the other. Therefore this section discusses the other major element in the equation. Some of the major structural variables that influence the lives of women in the eight societies are the following: the manner in which female and male roles relate to each other; the effectiveness of institutions competing with the family; the access of girls to education on equal terms and from the same curriculum as boys; the type of economic system, particularly the degree of public as against private control and the nature of the economic opportunities it offers to women; and the existence of significant class, regional, or ethnic divisions.

As alluded to previously, the eight societies discussed in this volume have opted for one of three types of female–male role relationships: complementary, hierarchical, or modified hierarchical. The nature of this relationship has had considerable import for the roles allocated to women and their channels for acquiring status.

The complementary role relationship characteristic of the traditional Ghanaian societies led to the establishment of parallel female–male roles in the family, the economy, and the sociopolitical institutions. It was not uncommon for wife and husband to live apart and pursue separate lives. Although Ghanaian women could not envision a life devoid of children and childbearing responsibilities, they would have had equal difficulty in perceiving themselves within an exclusively domestic environment. Women had key responsibilities in farming, trading, and handicraft production, and the economic survival of the family depended on their fulfilling these functions. The independence of the female and the male role spheres also made the regulation and control of women essentially a female prerogative. For this reason most of the groups provided for the representation of the feminine viewpoint within kinship and community councils. Among some of the groups the male chief also had a female counterpart invested with the power to oversee female affairs. Furthermore women's participation in a wide range of nonfamilial functions gave women definite corporate interests and a direct stake in matters outside of the domestic domain. Although it is somewhat difficult at this point in time to make judgments about the status systems inhering in these societies, it does not seem likely that women's status was completely derivative. Kinship connections defined eligibility for some offices, but there seem to have been opportunities for individual achievement by both male and female.

The hierarchical system provides women with quite a different situation—the distinction between the female and male spheres reflects the pervasive element of male supremacy. Women's confinement to essentially domestic roles under the supervision of male kinsmen gives men a monopoly over the public domain. Irrespective of whether women contribute to the economic well-being of the household, the fulfillment of their responsibilities is reckoned through their marriage and motherhood roles. Even when women commonly work outside of the home before marriage, as was the case in prewar Japan, their social placement depends entirely on their marital status. A woman's social position in these societies is defined entirely through the men in their lives: as her father's daughter, as her husband's wife, and as her son's mother. Security and social approval come through satisfying these men and particularly through producing male heirs for the husband's family. An independent woman has no legal or social place within society. The completely derived nature of women's status means that the woman who aspires to an independent role above and beyond her familial functions risks her social placement and well-being. By choosing to compete with men she loses the respect and consideration that go with the acceptance of traditional female roles, while at the same time the sharp distinction between the female and male role definitions precludes her achieving status through participation in the male domain.

The modified hierarchical systems characteristic of the industrialized countries described in this book encompass a wide diversity of relationships ranging from considerable male dominance to substantial equality. The modified hierarchical system differs from the hierarchical in the less clear-cut distinction between female and male roles, the more flexible relationships between the sexes, and the smaller degree of social segregation. Women's primary status is still derived, but there are some opportunities for self-fulfillment and recognition outside the home. The primacy of domestic responsibilities, however, deprives most women of the option of foregoing marriage and motherhood while also requiring women pursuing an independent career to fulfill simultaneously two sets of demands, from their home and from their employment. By making available to women potential resources outside the family through education, through work, and through networks of social contacts, the modified hierarchical systems also provide women with greater possibilities for influencing decision-making within the family. Thus the distribution of power both within and outside of the family becomes more situational, more open to adjustments and manipulation, and more dependent on the qualities of the individuals involved. Nevertheless most women remain in a subordinate position with fewer options and less opportunity than men to determine their own lives.

The centrality of the family in the social organization constitutes another key structural variable influencing women's roles and status. When the welfare of the family reigns supreme, whether it is a nuclear or an extended family, the needs of women are often subordinated to the interests of the family group, and the wife is restrained from acting individually or independently. Underlying this system is the assumption that the family comprises a unit under the unique leadership of the husband. Because a woman is considered to be an integral part of a family unit and usually lacks an autonomous legal existence, this also limits the extent of her civil rights and her ability to act as an independent agent outside the family. By qualifying and offsetting the demands of the family, competing institutions can confer greater freedom and enhance the possibilities for a woman's self-determination.

The societies considered here vary significantly in the centrality of the family. In France during the early Middle Ages and in precolonial Ghana the individual was also a member of other societal groups, and ties within the nuclear or conjugal family were often weak. Among the Ghanaian groups, particularly matrilineal ones, women could employ the conflicting claims and obligations of their kinsmen and husbands to their own advantage and neutralize the control of either. The relatively equal authority of the husband and brother counterbalanced each other, thus conferring considerable autonomy on the woman. Among the Akan in Ghana, as in other matrilineal societies in which neither the husband nor the brother is dominant, the total male authority over women was less and the independence of women greater than in most patrilineal systems (Schlegel, 1972: 7). Among all of Ghana's constituent communities, irrespective of whether they followed matrilineal or patrilineal descent patterns, women's considerable autonomy also derived from their membership in women's groups that protected and represented their corporate interests. During the early Middle Ages women in France retained substantial equality because they had recourse to agencies other than the family; the family was not a major center of loyalties or of transmission of property, and wife and husband could act as two independent economic agents. Blood ties played a lesser role as a basis of social organization than did other types of human associations such as the guild and the village community.

At the other end of the spectrum the dominance of the family over the lives of its members has been strongest in Muslim cultures where woman's status and identity are derived entirely from her placement in a kinship unit. Changes in medieval France that strengthened blood ties also gradually undermined the status and position of woman in the household, and by the time of the Renaissance the French married woman had been stripped of her legal rights. Within the three-generation household common in Japan before the war, as in the other family-oriented societies, the young wife had the lowest status of all family members and was expected to devote herself to their needs. In Egypt, in Bangladesh, in France, and in Japan, until the promulgation of fairly recent legal reforms the social subordination of women also had definite ramifications in the limitation of their civil rights both within and outside of the family.

Even within societies in which the influence of the family has been quite strong, the existence of competitive institutions may diminish the control of the family over the lives of its women. The situation in many Latin American countries provides one such illustration of the qualification of familism. Despite the prevalence of cultural norms that vest the honor of the family in the sexual virtue of its female members, women in Latin America have not been as constrained and subordinated to the dictates of the family as those in Muslim societies. Their opportunities for education and their rates of labor force participation have been far higher. Part of the discrepancy between male ideals of feminine confinement and female behavioral patterns results from the inability of Latin American men to impose their authority as completely and as successfully as their male counterparts in the Middle East. Much of the explanation relates to the historical role of the Catholic Church. The decision by the clergy in the nineteenth century to cultivate women as a lay apostolate in an effort to strengthen and perpetuate the prominence of the Church led to the development of the clergy as a competitive agency vis-à-vis the family unit. Church-established schools and social organizations came to furnish an institutional infrastructure that middle- and upper-class women could use to balance the demands of the family. By playing off the two authorities one against the other, women have gained flexibility and have enhanced their prospects for self-determination (Youssef, 1973: 336–346).

In a somewhat similar fashion, the evolution of the advanced industrial nations has gradually stripped the family of many of its functions and weakened its control over the lives of its members. The family long ago ceased to be an economic unit. Much of the key process of socialization now occurs in and through the schools rather than within the domain of the family. National and local legislation impinge on the sanctity of the family and regulate many aspects of family life. The provision of social services reduces the dependence of individuals on the family for economic support. Even women who assume traditional roles as wives and mothers find that their lives are inextricably woven into the fabric of the larger society.

The availability of equal educational opportunities for women, more than any other structural variable, has led to women's assumption of a range of social roles. The case studies in this book show that progressively greater exposure of women to education has generally resulted in an increased sharing of authority within the family, more continuous employment in professional and technical occupations, lower fertility patterns, and greater participation in social and political activities. There are some exceptions to these trends, and the impact of education on particular social roles varies from society to society, but the data from the various countries attest to the efficacy of education as a major force in redefining women's roles. Education for women has both microscopic and macroscopic implications; that is, education may transform the attitudes and the self-image of the individual woman, while on a societal level it often alters the balance in male–female roles and widens the sphere of permissible feminine activities.

In societies that until now have required that women's lives be governed by the structure and precepts of the family, the acquisition of the principles of conduct and norms provided by the schools may constitute an even greater element of discontinuity for girls than for boys. The significant sex differences in the traditional processes of socialization have generally shielded females far more than males from exposure to social and cultural changes. It is, therefore, possible that the cumulative impact of formal education is greater for girls than for boys or that it is more difficult for girls to reconcile with traditional role behavior. Informal learning and traditional socialization practices tend to be particularistic, foster traditionalism, and fuse the emotional and intellectual domains. By contrast, formal education in a school environment places the emphasis on the content rather than on the instructor, depends on verbal formulations, and inculcates independence, achievement, universalism, and specificity (Scribner and Cole, 1973; Dreeben, 1968). Orientations transmitted through traditional socialization reflect the needs and priorities of the family, whereas formal education brings with it the intellectual and cognitive perspective of the modern world.

Access to higher education can expand the boundaries of women's social roles by endowing them with greater skills and resources as well as by transforming their attitudes and self-image. The results of a considerable amount of survey research suggest that the status and influence of women within the home depend to a significant extent on their opportunities and control over resources outside of the home. The greater the personal resources a woman brings into a marital relationship in the form of her education, employment experience, and range of social contacts—the closer her resource base approximates that of her husband—the greater is the chance that she will be able to influence family decision-making (Rodman, 1972). Even in societies where women have traditionally exerted considerable authority within the home, an imbalance in the education attained by the husband and wife can severely reduce that prerogative. Modernization brings with it new issues, changed relationships within the family, and involvement of the family with outside social institutions. Education is indispensable for understanding and coping with these changes. Therefore more equal educational opportunities for boys and girls enhance the prospect for relative equality within the home.

Higher education can also provide women with credentials for more rewarding and prestigious forms of employment. One of the most important variables used to adjudge the roles of women within a society is the proportion of working women engaged in a professional and technical capacity. Since women comprise only a small fraction of the top administrators and managers in all eight societies, including Poland, this professional category seems to offer the greatest possibility for female occupational mobility; it represents the most realistic goal for women to aspire to in a modified hierarchical society. Professional employment obviously depends on the access of women to higher education. Hence in many of the countries a correlation exists between the percentage of students in institutions of higher education who are women and the percentage of professionals and technicals who are women. Furthermore in many of the countries for which information is available—France, Poland, Egypt, Bangladesh, and Japan—women with higher education are more likely to pursue a career after marriage and childbearing. This probably reflects that sufficient satisfaction and status are offered by the type of employment available to women with higher education to motivate them to combine motherhood with a career.

A recent study by the United Nations of the interrelationship of the status of women and family planning concludes that, "The educational level of women appears to be one of the most important factors influencing family size and birth rates" (Report of the Special Rapporteur, 1973: 52). For many of the eight countries there was an association between women's educational level and their fertility. In Egypt, Ghana, Bangladesh, the United States, and France (among the *classes moyennes* but not the bourgeoisie), women with higher education tend to have considerably smaller families. Poland, where national fertility rates are already very low and higher education often brings with it access to better housing, constitutes a major exception to this inverse relationship between education and fertility. Another exception occurs in the case of Mexico, where the literature does not substantiate consistent trends.

Formal education affects women's fertility in a variety of ways. Education can reduce the desired family size by causing a woman to aspire to a standard of living for herself and for her children that is incompatible with a large family. By doing so, education changes the attitude toward children as parents calculate that additional babies will entail the major expenses of schooling, clothes, and so forth, rather than being assets and contributing to the economic productivity of the family. Higher education frequently provides women with channels other than childbearing for raising their status. Moreover, by enabling women to earn an income and support themselves if need be, education makes women less dependent on children for support when divorced or widowed. Higher education often postpones marriage and childbearing by extending the period of time that women devote to their studies. In some societies higher education may inhibit marriage entirely by reducing women's marital prospects. Furthermore with greater exposure to education women are more likely to be exposed to information about birth control, to be more favorably inclined toward employing contraception, and to be better able to use contraceptive devices successfully (Report of the Special Rapporteur, 1973: 52–55).

Because of the potential of education for modifying women's roles, structural factors that accelerate its impact have considerable importance. The efficacy of education as a force in redefining women's roles depends to a considerable extent both on the level of female enrollments, particularly in higher education, and on the nature of the education available to women. Contrary to what might be expected, there is not a direct correlation between the stage of economic devleopment or industrialization attained by a society and the relative availability of higher education to women. Educational opportunities for women seem to be more a product of historical accident, cultural attitudes toward women, governmental decisions, and national priorities. Economic development brings with it greater resources and thus provides for more flexibility in making societal investments in a variety of social welfare enterprises, but whether revenues are heavily invested in education and the extent to which women benefit from this expansion vary among societies.

The availability of education for women in the eight countries demonstrates the lack of correlation between economic development and women's relative educational access. The ranking of the countries from lowest per capita income to highest is Bangladesh, Egypt, Ghana, Mexico, Poland, Japan, France, and the United States (Statistical Office, 1974: 590–592). All of the countries, except for Egypt and Bangladesh, have nearly equal numbers of the two sexes entering primary school, although the female dropout rate is somewhat higher during primary school for the less developed states. At the secondary school level the overall proportion of female enrollment in the countries is listed from lowest to highest as Bangladesh, Ghana, Egypt, Japan, the United States, France, and Poland (UNESCO, 1974: 164, 170, 176, 180, 182). The variation with regard to university education is even greater. Women in Egypt, one of the least developed of the countries, have nearly the same access as women in Japan, a country whose per capita income is some 10 times that of Egypt. The United States, by far the wealthiest economy, does not provide as much educational opportunity for women as Poland. The records of the eight systems in furnishing women with higher education indicate that Bangladesh does least well, followed by Ghana, Mexico, Egypt and Japan, the United States and France, and Poland (UNESCO, 1974: 274–281).

Some of these disparities in women's educational access result from government policies. For example, although the extensive investment in primary and middle school education in Ghana opened more places to girls, the government did not proportionately increase girls' opportunities at the secondary and university levels. In contrast, Egypt has provided for greater female educational opportunities at the higher levels. Japan has not seen the need to expend public funds to redress the sexual imbalance in university education, whereas Poland has assigned this considerable priority.

With regard to the structure and curriculum of the educational system, the critical variable is not whether schools are single-sex or coeducational institutions, but rather whether girls are exposed to the same curricula, standards, and options as boys. A centralized system of education in which progression from one stage to another and placement in particular schools depends primarily on examination results often improves women's access to secondary and university education. The degree to which the curriculum explicitly attempts to reinforce traditional sex role stereotypes plays a part as well. The cost of education at various levels and the availability of scholarships also tend to have a greater effect on girls' schooling than on that of boys, because parents are generally more reluctant to invest in the education of their daughters.

Despite the considerable amount of rhetoric on the subject, coeducation does not seem to matter as much as encouragement for girls to follow the same course of studies available to boys. The French experience shows that sex-separate education need not be inferior in quality or restrict women from educational advancement. Moreover in several of the predominantly coeducational systems—Mexico, Japan, and the United States—girls continue to elect very different programs than boys, leading to inferior education with less vocational relevance. In Mexico women tend to choose separate educational tracks beginning at the secondary school level to prepare them for teacher training institutions. In Japan women seek admission to junior colleges rather than to the better universities despite the lower tuition requirements of the higher status national universities. In the United States, no less than in Mexico and Japan, higher education for women is still valued more for its enhancement of marital prospects rather than for preparation for a career. When coeducational schooling is combined with an intent to break down traditional intellectual stereotypes regarding the kind of education appropriate for women, as it has been in Poland, the results can be quite different. Then coeducation can provide for greater flexibility in locating facilities and allocating personnel. Nevertheless the critical factor in the Polish experience has been the resolve of the government to move toward true equality of educational opportunity rather than coeducation.

There does not appear to be a correlation between the level of economic development or the degree of industrialization and women's economic participation. The relationship between economic development and women's employment seems to be as random as it was with regard to women's relative access to education. Within particular systems, as in the case of France, industrialization and rapid economic development do not necessarily affect the overall rates of female participation; despite a very different economic structure, women comprised nearly the same proportion of the labor force in 1962, 32.4 percent, as they had in 1866, 30.8 percent. Among the various societies represented in this volume, the countries with the greatest industrialization and the highest per capita incomes do not offer noticeably better economic opportunities to women. In the United States women comprise a smaller proportion of the total work force than in many of the less affluent countries, whereas Ghana, probably the second least industrialized economy among the eight, has a very high female activity rate. Other cross-cultural examinations of women's economic options and employment patterns have similarly concluded that there is no linear relationship between a country's level of development and women's options (Safilios-Rothschild, 1970; Boulding, 1972).

Women's economic opportunities appear to be related to a variety of factors. Two of these, cultural values relating to the sexual division of labor and educational opportunities for women, have already been discussed. Other attributes of the economic system that seem significant include the degree of public versus private control and the extent to which the jobs available to women have been compatible with their domestic responsibilities.

The thesis that private ownership and control of the means of production inhibit women's economic roles and act to depress women's economic status does not, of course, originate here. One does not, however, have to subscribe in toto to Frederick Engels's radical critique of the origins of private property and its association with the subjection of women within the family to accept such a relationship. As Evelyne Sullerot has commented,

> The distance dividing men from women is much less in a collectivist system than under capitalism. In all capitalist economies, there is a difference in power, wages, incomes, civic responsibilities, to the disadvantage of women, who are turned into a female lumpenproletariat occupying the lowest rung of the social ladder [Sullerot, 1971: 34].

Studies comparing samples from many countries have found correlations between the economic participation of women and the type of economic system; one such investigation employed official data from 82 countries and concluded that women in "Western" (i.e., predominantly capitalist) countries had lower activity rates than women in countries with "neutral" or "communist" politics (Sawyer, 1967).

In the eight countries analyzed here the most symmetrical economic relationships are found among the traditional Ghanaian communities and in Poland, both of which are collectivist economies. Similarly women's economic roles and status were far more equal in France during the early Middle Ages than afterwards, when private property became the prevalent mode of ownership. In many countries—such as France, Ghana, and Egypt—the expansion of women's prospects in the modern economy has come through job opportunities for women in the public sector. Therefore the trend observable in all countries and across all types of economic systems toward greater public ownership and/or control augurs well for women.

It should be noted that the benefits for women of a collectivist economic system or of public regulation of the economy vary depending on the level of development. In subsistence agricultural economies, such as Ghana, the communal ownership of land provided women with access to plots for farming. This availability of land enabled women to cultivate crops independently of their husbands' control and, thus, to keep the profits they made. The introduction of cocoa into Ghana at the end of the nineteenth century, however, among its other consequences began the process of breaking up large communal holdings into private parcels. The exclusion of women from the land-buying collectives and the male inheritance patterns have been major factors in limiting women's participation in cocoa production. In industrialized societies public ownership or regulation has usually involved an element of concern with equity, justice, and restoration of a balance between the privileged and the underprivileged. The acceptance of national responsibility toward a fairer distribution of opportunities and rewards cannot be anything but to the advantage of women. The communist systems, inspired by ideological commitments toward sexual equality and by manpower needs, have gone the farthest toward eradicating the economic domination of men over women that inheres in classical capitalism, but virtually all advanced industrialized nations have moved toward governmental management of the economy and have adopted measures to mitigate economic discrimination on the basis of sex.

Another dimension of the economic system that affects women is the extent to which it affords women employment prospects that can be reconciled with domestic responsibilities. All societies, some more and some less, sex-type occupational sectors, and the greatest opportunities for female employment usually come in those categories designated as appropriate for women. Thus whether traditionally or potentially female sectors of the economy are expanding has more import for female economic participation than does the overall level or rate of economic development. Women often fare well in predominantly agricultural societies because it is often considered acceptable for them to farm either independently or as part of a family unit. Industrialization has usually been profoundly disruptive to the balance in women's and men's economic roles because men tend to monopolize most production jobs in the modern sector with the result that men become increasingly independent of the economic contributions of women while at the same time women and children become more economically dependent on men (Boserup, 1970; Blake, 1974). High rates of female economic participation during the process of industrialization, as in the case of France during the nineteenth and early twentieth centuries, sometimes reflect the continued importance of the rural sector and the availability of jobs for women in agricultural and small-scale industrial enterprises located in the rural areas. The frequently observed improved economic status of women in the advanced stages of industrialization results from a confluence of factors, one of the most important of which is a rapid growth in the service sector of the economy. This enhances women's job prospects because this sector generally has many positions labeled as suitable for women.

Women's rates of economic participation also depend on their ability to reconcile the types of employment available for women with their domestic responsibilities. In predominantly agricultural systems women often have less of a problem reconciling roles because of the flexibility in the work schedule. The two most common economic activities of Ghanaian women, for example, farming and trading, involve little role conflict since they can be performed with children present and at a variety of places and times. Industrialization brings new problems since the rigidity in factory employment makes it less easily combined with motherhood and family life; as a consequence women have had little choice but to retire to the home. Along with the expansion of the service sector of the economy, the improved employment prospects for women in the highly industrialized countries are related to a lessening of the conflict between work and familial roles. The demographic transition to smaller families means that fewer years of an adult woman's life are devoted to bearing and raising children. The introduction of labor-saving devices in the home, the lengthening of compulsory education, and the establishment of child-care facilities also contribute to the decreased burdens of domesticity. Changes in labor legislation and attitudes of employers sometimes offer alternatives in time schedules and work patterns.

Another major structural variable determining the roles and status of women is the existence of significant class, regional, or ethnic divisions. In the societies characterized by such schisms the roles and status of women reflect their placement as members of their major social group as well as their biological community. Women partake of the advantages or disadvantages conferred by their class, regional, or ethnic origins but still face the special problems intrinsic to being female. As a consequence within the societies beset by deep social cleavages the roles and status of women usually vary significantly from group to group. The life-style and opportunities of the upper-class woman in one country may bear a greater resemblance to a woman of similar background elsewhere than it does to a fellow countrywoman from a lower class.

Many of the societies included in this volume have such deep social divisions, and they have been fundamental in defining women's roles and status. Class divisions in Mexico, France, Bangladesh, and Egypt very much influence women's access to education, their options to work, their participation in family decision-making, and their inclinations to limit the size of their families. Ethnic distinctions in Mexico, in Ghana, and to some extent in the United States invest women with very divergent opportunities and life-styles that depend on their backgrounds. The rural-urban dichotomy affects women's mobility and freedom in virtually all of the countries discussed in this book.

Traditionally women from upper-class backgrounds have had greater protection and security and the prestige attending it. Families of humbler origin could not afford the luxury of secluding their women and excluding them from the labor force. Women from lower-class families, therefore, frequently had greater freedom, but this freedom cost them much of the respect and deference accorded to women who conformed to the norms defining appropriate feminine behavior. Some of this traditionalism still remains, particularly in Bangladesh, Mexico, and France. For the privileged social classes in Mexico, the idleness of the wife comprises an essential part of the life-style. Similarly the bourgeoisie in France continue to subscribe to the ideology of the *femme au foyer* to a greater extent than the other social classes; they thus exert more pressure on the woman to devote herself to her family. The prevalence of the *purdah* mentality in Bangladesh means that upward mobility depends on stricter adherence to strictures of female seclusion. In all three of these countries poor women, by virtue of economic necessity, contribute a greater portion of the family's livelihood and are not subjected to the confinement imposed on upper-class women. Their prospects for upward mobility and respect, however, suffer commensurately.

In a dynamic situation in which women's roles are being expanded, middle- and upper-class women frequently have more opportunities to take advantage of these new options. This relates in part to the fact that women and men of higher social status are always allowed a wider range of alternatives and can escape censure for behavior that would be considered deviant for the majority of the population. Middle- and upper-class families can accord greater freedom to their women because it entails fewer risks. In class societies privileged women also have greater access to the higher education which can provide the channel for escape from traditional confinements. The general lack of competition between women and men at the upper levels of the employment status hierarchy also works to the benefit of these women; once they enter the labor force they are absorbed or assimilated as representatives of their social class, and they often avoid the forms of discrimination women usually confront. Because of the salience of class identity, though, these elite women seldom feel a sense of affinity or community with women in general. Since they do not suffer the same disabilities as other members of their sex, women with the greatest resources and skills, the highest social status, and the other potential attributes of leadership are not encouraged to invest their energies in attempting to improve the conditions of life for other women.

The disparities in the life-styles among women in the same society raise some fundamental questions. In characterizing the roles and status of women in a particular society, for instance, is it more relevant to cite the limits to which an elite woman can aspire or the conditions that the common woman must endure? Does one mark progress for women by the percentage of women who have been co-opted to high level management and/or political leadership roles or by the quality of life available to the common woman? There is no doubt that upper- and middle-class women play a critical role as pioneers to break down barriers, as role models for young girls to emulate, and as the nucleus of a potential leadership representing the corporate interests of women. Nevertheless it does not seem representative of the overall situation within a society to concentrate exclusively on the problems and the achievements of elite women as they struggle to gain greater equality with men. The process of reformulating the image of women and modifying codes of behavior has another dimension, the need to reduce inequalities among women so that all women can benefit from new opportunities (Castillo, 1974). Otherwise efforts to improve the status of women will ameliorate the conditions of only a small group and perhaps even depress the lot of most others. This has already happened in some of the societies considered here, for example, in Mexico, where the benefits of modernization have accrued disproportionately to the elite at the expense of the masses.

TOWARD A CHANGE IN WOMEN'S ROLES AND STATUS

As the eight case studies show, there is nothing final or fixed about the roles that women assume or the status accorded to them in a particular society. In all the countries discussed, women's roles underwent changes, usually gradually but occasionally abruptly, often (in the past) in the direction of the narrowing of options, and sometimes (more often in the present) toward an expansion in opportunities. Much of this role remodeling has occurred indirectly or unintentionally as the by-product of other events, movements, and shifts. It has come through the adoption of new value systems, through religious conversion or the acceptance of different ideologies, through improvements in technology, through political revolution, through legislative reforms, through expansion of educational systems, and through demographic transitions.

The sensitivity to and concern with the problems of women now being exhibited by many societies, as well as the increased public awareness and momentum for reform being generated by the designation by the United Nations of 1975 as International Women's Year, invest the historical experiences of these nations with contemporary relevance. By establishing the potential impact of certain types of developments on the roles and status of women, the case studies in this book help to illuminate the possibilities and limitations of calculated efforts to improve women's position in society. Women's roles and status are always being transformed through ideational and structural changes in the society. Even if women's roles remained constant, exposure to modernization and to international currents would virtually ensure that society's perception and valuation of these roles would be subject to modification. At issue are the circumstances under which it is possible to effect a deliberate remodeling at a faster pace. If a society adopted as its goal equal access for women to societal resources and social benefits, if it sought to expand women's role options to create a greater symmetry between the opportunities available to men and women, if it purported to invest the roles and contributions of women with more value, what could it learn from the history of our eight cases? In the discussion that follows we investigate the past impact of the following factors on the roles and status of women as a guide toward future efforts at role remodeling: changes in value systems, adoption of new technologies, rapid expansion of higher education for women, and legislative reform.

The centrality of religious thought, symbols, and values in many cultures and the impact religions have had in defining the spiritual image and worth of women raise the question of what contribution conversion to a different religion or transformation of an existing religion might make to improving women's position in society. The conversion to Buddhism in Japan, to Islam in Egypt and Bangladesh, and to Christianity in Ghana demonstrate how very slowly one religious system displaces another. Religious conversion initially affects primarily the elite, and often for the masses culminates in a syncretism of beliefs and customs. Particularly when the new value system involves a fundamental reinterpretation of sex roles, as occurred in several of the cases, it often has taken many centuries to realign norms and practices. The increasing trend toward secularization in many parts of the world also reduces the efficacy of religion as a social force. Nevertheless with time the removal of women's disabilities within the major world religions would help to expunge the spiritual inferiority of women from the collective consciousness. A recasting of the deity or the ultimate spiritual reality in neutral rather than masculine imagery, the admission of women to the clergy with full rights to officiate over the sacraments and to interpret religious doctrine, and the rewriting of religious history to show that women as well as men have played a significant part in the search for truth and meaning of life, all would advance the cause of making women equal members of the religious community.

The adoption of new ideologies, however radical their intent or however explicit their commitment to equality, have rarely benefited women to the same extent as men. The liberty, equality, and fraternity proclaimed by the French Revolution and the Nasserite socialism inaugurated through the deposition of the Egyptian monarchy provide two such examples. In the past radical ideologies and the men who have professed them have often had a conservative bent with regard to their relevance for women. For this reason, despite the solidarity between women and men in the fight to overthrow the *ancien régime*, the French Revolution of 1789 did not substantially alter the position and rights of women. The refusal of the male revolutionaries to introduce a declaration of women's rights or to invest the new titles of *citoyen* and *citoyenne* with true civil equality heralded the pattern that most social revolutions have followed. Women who have fought in the ranks with men and who have been accepted as integral members of a cause have usually discovered that once the battle is over and the cause is won, the proposed benefits apply only to men. Or alternatively, as with Nasser in Egypt, the new leadership does not accord the plight of women sufficient importance to take the risk of incorporating women into the new order and extending the reforms to them.

Unlike many other movements Marxist–Leninism in Poland and liberal democracy in Japan have given rise to extensive changes that have ameliorated the condition of women. They constitute two major examples of situations in which subscribing to a new ideology has had significant import for women's roles and status. Partly because both of these ideologies were embodied in reforms to uplift women that simultaneously improved women's access to education, elevated their position within the family, made them equal citizens, and also provided for greater protection in work situations, their precepts have had direct application to many spheres of life. That these legislative reforms were so extensive and systematic probably has more to do, however, with the historical circumstances that placed each country under the supervision of a victorious nation after World War II than it does with the ideology itself. Both the United States and the Soviet Union believed that they had a direct stake in a thorough effort to remodel the state under its jurisdiction in its own image; they consequently inspired and, to some extent, directly or indirectly oversaw the changes. In the case of Japan the principles of democratic philosophy were carried to their logical conclusion and made to apply directly to women, far more so than in the United States of that era.

The efficacy of the ideologies also relates to the new opportunities opened for women that enabled them to give their equal rights concrete meaning. In these two war-ravaged states the desperate need for manpower—first to rebuild the economy and then to sustain the continued economic growth—meant that women were recruited into the labor force and encouraged to redefine their obligations to their families. Other critical elements in the new equation were the reform and expansion of the educational systems so that girls were accorded equal access to primary and secondary education and placed in the same educational track as the boys. It is unlikely that the new ideologies would have had such a permanent and significant impact if their adoption had not been accompanied by these economic and educational changes.

Japan and Poland also provide some interesting models of the limitations of ideological incentives in redefining women's roles and status. In both cases the systems have had better records in the economic and educational spheres than in transforming family relations or in opening up the citadels of power to women. Much of the traditional social separation of the sexes still inheres in the family relations in contemporary Japan. Women have not gone beyond merely voting to the point of office-holding in the national political system. The refusal of men in Poland to accept any substantial household responsibilities has increased the burdens placed on Polish women since they must now fulfill the demands of both their jobs and household. Moreover Poland, no less than any other political system, exhibits the universal phenomenon of women occupying lower rungs on the employment ladder. Even in the most feminine occupations the percentage of women filling leadership positions does not approach the proportion of men. In light of the strong ideological commitment to attaining equality for women, the educational achievement of women there, and the high rate of labor force participation by women in Poland, it is particularly disappointing that women have not yet eliminated the disparities between their socioeconomic and political roles. Whether this will come in time is impossible to predict.

Changes in technology have had varying effects on the roles and status of women. The modernization of agriculture often displaces women and reduces their roles. In many countries the introduction of new crops and the transition from subsistence to cash cropping has given men disproportionate opportunities.

Male plantation owners and male agricultural extension services have generally dealt only with men, even if women were the major agriculturalists, and effectively accorded to men a monopoly over the new crops, techniques, seed, fertilizer, and pest-control sprays that have been instrumental in improving production, raising yields and increasing income. Mechanization, particularly when it affects food processing, as is being planned in Bangladesh, more often deprives women of the chance to make an economic contribution than it does men. As we have seen, both in the past and today, in many of the less developed countries women who migrate to industrial centers with their husbands cannot find jobs for which they are qualified and which can be combined with household responsibilities. Industrialization, therefore, usually changes the balance in women's and men's economic roles and places women in the home, dependent on male productivity, while at the same time sending men to the factory and making them independent of the economic contributions of their wives. The major exceptions to these trends have come in countries, like Ghana, where urbanization brought new opportunities for women in the trade and service sectors of the economy, or where, like in France, the rural sector retained its importance and small-scale cottage type industry was not eliminated. In contrast with the modernization of agriculture or the movement from an agricultural to an industrial economy, transition from one stage of industrialization to a more advanced one often increases the options for women. The extent to which women are brought back into the labor force depends on their previous economic roles, the need for manpower, their training and educational qualifications, and whether traditionally female sectors of the economy are expanding.

In the past the impact of technology on women's roles has occurred in large part because no system attempted to plan for and thus determine the social effects of changes in modes of economic production. There is nothing inevitable about women being displaced by the modernization of agriculture or by industrialization. Men have benefited from modernization of agriculture and from industrialization in large part because there has been an active intervention on their behalf with no countervailing support for women. If extension services had directed their efforts at women rather than men, the imbalance in the modern agricultural sector would have been in another direction. Similarly if factories had established adequate child-care facilities or had been given financial incentives for employing part-time laborers, women might have found it easier to escape from being moved from the field into home during the early stages of industrialization. Just imagine how different employment patterns might now be in all societies if there had been a universal consensus that schooling was more commensurate with female intellectual processes than with male, and if national educational systems had catered predominantly to women rather than to men.

All of the foregoing is to demonstrate that while further technological evolution is probably inevitable, the consequences of these economic changes for sex roles is subject to human determination. By directing a concerted effort to address women agriculturists through extension services, by giving women the same opportunities as men to train and prepare for industrial and vocational openings, by eradicating the sex-typing that conveniently reserves the management positions in professional and vocational fields for men, and by providing child-care facilities that would reduce the burdens of domesticity, it would be possible to alter drastically the liabilities women have suffered. In the past governments have only found it in their interests to attempt to actively redress the imbalance in economic roles when confronted with a national crisis or a severe manpower shortage, such as in a war economy or in a period of reconstruction, when it became too costly to give vent to traditional prejudices. It is to be hoped that the future will offer positive incentives to move toward greater social equality.

Education has been shown to be a critical determinant of women's roles and status. A rapid expansion of women's educational opportunities, particularly their access to higher education, could very likely have a considerable impact in many systems. It would change the self-image of the women involved, impart new skills, and affect the socialization of the next generation. The prestige and value associated with higher education would elevate the social standing and raise the status of the women so trained. By providing the wherewithal for women to enter the labor force in professional and management positions, higher education for women could redress somewhat the economic imbalance in the sex roles and provide new role models for young girls. As mentioned previously, it is very possible that increasing exposure to education would lead women to play a greater part in decision-making in the family, make a greater commitment to permanent employment, and feel less desire for large families.

The impact of improved access for women to higher education would, of course, vary from system to system. In countries, such as Ghana and Bangladesh, where women are seriously underrepresented in the enrollments at the secondary and university levels, merely opening up more places for women and encouraging greater sexual parity at all levels of the educational system through positive incentives for female attendance might have a dramatic effect. Particularly where, as in the case of Ghana, disparities in educational opportunity for women and men have been a major barrier to women's advancement in the modern sector of the economy, an investment in female higher education could significantly improve women's prospects for employment in responsible positions. Still unanswered are such critical questions as whether this investment will come before women's relatively high traditional status is eroded and whether the asymmetrical educational and employment patterns will become frozen. It seems possible that time is running out for many Asian and African countries to redress societal imbalances introduced during the colonial era. Soon historical accidents that occurred in the development of the modern educational system and the resultant division of labor in the modern sector will be perceived as reflecting fundamental differences in women's and men's aptitudes.

Availability of education for girls does not, of course, ensure that parents will allow their daughters to take advantage of the new opportunities, but structural and financial incentives could encourage enrollment. In many countries female attendance would increase substantially if more sex-segregated schools with women teachers were provided so that education would not contravene strictures calling for female seclusion. A reduction in school fees for girls through scholarship aid, greater government financing of female education, and perhaps even a tax advantage for families with young girls in school would go a long way toward encouraging parents to send their daughters to school. Governmental efforts to publicize the importance of education for girls by stressing the benefits to the family as well as to the nation also might promote more regular female attendance.

In many, although not all, industrialized countries the expansion in educational systems has brought about near parity of enrollments for girls and boys through the secondary school level and greater access for women to higher education, but has failed to guarantee true equality of educational opportunity. The history of France, the United States, and, to a somewhat lesser extent, Poland shows that the opening up of more places for women does not assure equivalence in the educational experiences offered to girls and boys. In these countries women still have not surmounted substantial cultural and structural barriers to their educational advancement. A 1973 report by the Carnegie Commission on Higher Education, for instance, concludes that despite women's nearly equal enrollments at the undergraduate level, American women, both today and in the past, have been disadvantaged in higher education, with the result that men are given comparatively more opportunities to use their mental capabilities. According to the report, discrimination against women exists in admission to prestigious colleges, in acceptance into graduate schools, in acceptance into and promotion within faculties, and in salaries. Cultural circumstances, particularly the roles presented to females in early life, the greater absence of relevant role models for women at the higher stages of academic life, and prejudice, deter women from making full use of their intellectual talent (Carnegie Commission on Higher Education, 1973: 1–3). This is then reflected in the decline in the percentage of women and even more so in their low representation in faculty and administrative positions at successive key points on the academic ladder.

Thus the realization of true equality of educational opportunity depends both on the removal of barriers to the advancement of women, in the form of inadequate facilities and discrimination in admission, and on the transformation of attitudes and expectations for girls. Active intervention by the state can more easily redress the former. The government can open more places in schools for girls, lessen the financial burdens of education for women, reform curricula and counseling to encourage girls to formulate nontraditional career goals, and centralize the educational system to ensure greater equivalence of educational experiences for girls and boys. However sexual disparities in educational opportunity spring as well from deep-rooted cultural notions relating to differences between the sexes. In all cultures girls are socialized from birth to have quite different goals than men and are systematically taught to subordinate all other considerations to making a good marriage and raising children. The socialization process also inculcates patterns of behavior, norms, values, and orientations that often inhibit the educational advancement of girls. Until and unless these fundamental cultural determinants of inequality are changed, true equality of educational opportunity cannot be realized.

Several of the countries discussed in this book have attempted to improve the condition of women or to protect their interests through the aegis of legislative reform. Hence the experiences of these countries highlight some of the possibilities and limitations of relying on legal remedies to achieve greater equality for women. The measures undertaken have ranged from single laws prohibiting discrimination of a specific type to sweeping efforts to lay down a new legal and structural basis for equal rights for women. In some cases governments have sought through a series of legislative acts to engage in a form of social engineering that would transform social relationships fundamentally by conferring on women greater opportunities for self-direction. In others legal reforms have followed upon and reflected prior social change. As might be expected, the effectiveness of the legislation has depended on a variety of factors, among them the intent of the administration and the vigor with which it enforced the law, the degree of support for the reform in the society, and the extent to which the proposed reforms have contravened fundamental cultural norms. Overall, systems have been more successful when resorting to legislative reform to remove legal and structural disabilities than when attempting to remold social relationships or to transform fundamental values.

A formal pledge of equality for women, constitutional guarantees, and the ratification of the United Nations' pledges to end discrimination in and of themselves mean nothing unless the government involved has the will and the way to make these resolutions stick. It has become a mark of modernity and enlightened rule in the second half of the twentieth century to issue such commitments in favor of equality for women, just as political systems strove to keep in fashion by proving themselves democratic in the first half. However the intent of governments to give these formal undertakings concrete meaning and to enforce prohibitions against discrimination has varied immensely. Because measures designed to ameliorate the condition of women usually threaten male prerogatives and monopolies, only the most vigorous and determined implementation can counteract efforts to sabotage such reforms. The resolve of the Polish government stands in marked contrast to the commitment of the Japanese regimes, and both of these in marked contrast to the Bangali administrations, in enacting and enforcing legislation for women. In general, governments have been far more resolute when either, as in the case of Poland, they have perceived such equality as directly in the national interest, or, as more recently in the United States, they have been subjected to considerable political pressure.

The degree of support for a proposed reform influences the timing of its enactment and the attitude of governments toward its enforcement. Obviously support for a measure and its legislation by an influential segment of the population tends to embolden an administration to act, thus facilitating enforcement. Nevertheless an issue such as women's rights will almost always engender controversy and will have strong opponents. To move ahead, therefore, a government must be willing to mold public opinion rather than merely reflect the accepted wisdom of past generations. The success of the Polish regime derives to a considerable extent from its activist role in educating its people to accept new patterns of behavior and different role expectations for women. The seven other political systems discussed here have been reluctant to undertake such blatant social engineering and for this reason have been far more conservative.

Law as an instrument of social reform can remove legal liabilities far more easily than it can create new relationships and values. For this reason the eight countries have been more successful in altering women's legal status than in bringing into existence new life-styles. It is possible to eliminate legal and political disqualifications by fiat, but the attainment of true equality in any sphere involves fundamental changes in the conception of femininity and the weakening of male control. Hence systems have vested women with greater civil rights but have not had the will or the way to ensure women's use of them to seize power. As might be expected, nowhere have men been willing to relinquish this prerogative since they consider it to be an essential attribute of masculinity. Similarly in the economic sphere governments have had better records in assuring equal treatment to women and men employed in the same position than they have in endowing women with identical opportunities for occupational mobility and promotions. The response to economic inequities has usually been to pass protective measures that prohibit women's employment in certain occupations and under certain conditions rather than to open traditionally male occupations or positions to women. Male regimes have accorded to women special maternity benefits, benefits it might be added that frequently deter female employment by making women more expensive to hire. However the same governments have been very reluctant to enact and enforce affirmative action–type legislation that would require employers to redress the sexual imbalance in their management staffs.

The central position of the family in the life of the individual woman and the society as a whole means that a change in women's position in society cannot be accomplished without basic modifications in the character of the family. However the nature of the family and the pattern of relationships within it touch on many of the most fundamental values and beliefs within any culture. Consequently the reform of personal or family law always meets with intense opposition, and its enforcement has been very difficult since it requires the state to impinge on the sanctity of the individual family. Unfortunately it is precisely in those societies where male dominance within the family severely restricts women's opportunities in all spheres of society that women have been the least able to take advantage of fundamental reforms of family and marriage laws. As shown by the failure of legal reform in Bangladesh, the greater the male control over the family, the easier it is for men to thwart the enactment of reforms by discouraging women from taking advantage of their new rights. For this reason the French approach— first introducing modifications of the legal status of women outside of the family and then eliminating the principle of subordination of the wife to the husband in the family's interest—has some merit. In the French case the delays in eliminating women's legal disabilities were unfortunate and even absurd in light of women's educational and occupational accomplishments. Nevertheless French women, by virtue of their economic and educational preparation, can better enforce their legal equality with their husbands.

Through legislative reform and incentives for affirmative action, governments can ensure substantially greater equality of opportunity for women within the educational and economic sectors. Such measures promise far fewer results in the political and family spheres, both because politicians and administrators have been reluctant to act on such matters and because law is less effective as an instrument for change in the face of strong countervailing cultural values. Equality for women, however, requires a fundamental redistribution of the burdens of domesticity and access to the levers of power. Only through men's sharing the time-consuming and encumbering demands of housekeeping and childrearing can women be freed to take full advantage of new opportunities they receive for self-realization and mobility. Otherwise women's efforts to pursue a career and activities outside of the family will come at the expense of increasing their work load and inevitably depressing the quality of their lives. Moreover women will remain at a substantial disadvantage in the competition for responsible positions that require overtime and flexibility in the work schedule. Just as equality for women entails a reorganization of family responsibilities, the sign that women have achieved such an improvement in their status will come through their seizing substantial political power. True equality between the sexes, if and when it ever comes, will entail a political revolution. The revolution will probably be peaceful and it may be accomplished gradually and imperceptibly over the course of generations, but it will bring with it one of the most fundamental redistributions of power accomplished in human history.

BIBLIOGRAPHY

Blake, Judith. 1974. "The Changing Status of Women in Developed Countries." *Scientific American* **231** (September): 136–147.

Boserup, Ester. 1970. *Woman's Role in Economic Development.* New York: St. Martin's Press.

Boulding, Elise. 1972. "Women as Role Models in Industrializing Societies." In *Cross National Family Research.* Edited by M. Sussman and B. Cogswell. Leiden: Brill, pp. 11–34.

Carnegie Commission on Higher Education. 1973. *Opportunities for Women in Higher Education: Their Current Participation, Prospects for the Future, and A Recommendation for Action.* New York: McGraw-Hill Book Co.

Castillo, Gelia T. 1974. "On 'Liberating' Filipino Women: Which Women." Paper presented at the Seminar on Prospects for Growth in Rural Societies: With or Without the Active Participation of Women. Princeton University, December.

Dreeben, Robert. 1968. *On What Is Learned in School.* Reading, Massachusetts: Addison-Wesley Publishing Co.

Goldberg, Steven. 1973. *The Inevitability of Patriarchy.* New York: Morrow.

Levy, Reuben. 1965. *The Social Structure of Islam.* Cambridge: The University Press.

Maccoby, Eleanor Emmons, and Carol Nagy Jacklin. 1974. *The Psychology of Sex Differences.* Stanford: Stanford University Press.

Nadel, S. F. 1957. *The Theory of Social Structure.* London: Cohen and West Ltd.

Orum, Anthony M., Roberta S. Cohen, Sherri Grasmuck, and Amy W. Orum. 1974. "Sex, Socialization and Politics." *American Sociological Review* **39** (April): 197–209.

Parrinder, Geoffrey. 1969. *Religion in Africa.* Middlesex: Penguin Books.

Report of the Special Rapporteur. 1973. *Study on the Interrelationship of the Status of Women and Family Planning, Addendum.* New York: United Nations Economic and Social Council, December.

Rodman, Hyman. 1972. "Marital Power and the Theory of Resources in Cultural Context." *Journal of Comparative Family Studies* **III** (Spring): 50–69.

Rosaldo, Michelle Zimbalist. 1974. "Woman, Culture, and Society: A Theoretical Overview." In *Woman, Culture, and Society.* Edited by Michelle Zimbalist Rosaldo and Louise Lamphere. Stanford: Stanford University Press, pp. 17–42.

Safilios-Rothschild, Constantina. 1970. "A Cross-Cultural Examination of Women's Marital, Educational and Occupational Options." *Acta Sociologica* **14:** 95–113.

———. 1974. *Women and Social Policy.* Englewood Cliffs, New Jersey: Prentice-Hall.

Sawyer, Jack. 1967. "Dimensions of Nations: Size, Wealth, and Politics." *American Journal of Sociology* **73** (July): 145–172.

Schlegel, Alice. 1972. *Male Dominance and Female Autonomy: Domestic Authority in Matrilineal Societies.* New Haven, Connecticut: Human Relations Area Files Press.

Scribner, Sylvia, and Michael Coie. 1973. "Cognitive Consequences of Formal and Informal Education." *Science* **182** (November): 553–559.

Statistical Office. 1974. *Statistical Yearbook, 1973.* New York: United Nations.

Sullerot, Evelyne. 1971. *Woman, Society and Change.* Translated by Margaret Scotford Archer. New York: McGraw-Hill Book Co.

UNESCO. 1974. *Statistical Yearbook. 1973.* Paris: UNESCO Press.

Women's Bureau. 1969. "Trends in Educational Attainment of Women." Washington, D.C.: U.S. Department of Labor, Wage and Labor Standards Administration.

Youssef, Nadia. 1973. "Cultural Ideals, Feminine Behavior and Kinship Control." *Comparative Studies in Society and History* **15** (June): 326–347.

AUTHOR INDEX

SUBJECT INDEX